A Lifetime of Achievement

OUR COLLECTION OF PRESTIGIOUS LISTEES

A LIFETIME OF ACHIEVEMENT

VOLUME II

MARQUIS Who'sWho®

Marquis Who's Who Ventures LLC
© 2021 Marquis Who's Who Ventures LLC
ISBN: 978-0-8379-7806-2
ISSN: 2769-1306

SERIES 2
All rights reserved. No part of this publication may be reproduced, stored in a retrieval system or transmitted in any form or by any means — including, but not limited to, electronic, photocopying, recording or otherwise — or used for any commercial purpose whatsoever without the prior written permission of the publisher and, if the publisher deems necessary, execution of a formal license agreement with the publisher.

For information, contact:
Marquis Who's Who
350 RXR Plaza
Uniondale, NY 11556

Manufactured in the United States of America.

MARQUIS Who's Who®

MANAGEMENT TEAM

Erica Lee CHIEF EXECUTIVE OFFICER
Deborah Morrissey EXECUTIVE VP OF HUMAN RESOURCES
Renée Dutcher-Pryer DIRECTOR OF EDITORIAL SERVICES
John Sartoris DIRECTOR OF DIGITAL AND PRINT PUBLICATIONS
Iris Cannetti DIRECTOR OF CUSTOMER SERVICE AND COMPLIANCE

PRODUCTION STAFF

SENIOR EDITOR

Shaina Indovino

STAFF WRITERS

Betsy Abraham	Ryan Lazarus
Thomas Gurinskas	Jason Ripple
Kenneth Hanley	Sage Viscovi
Marlo Jappen	Kitty Williams

GRAPHIC DESIGNER

Henry Monge

BRANDING SERVICES

Nikki Masih SENIOR DIRECTOR

BRANDING SPECIALISTS

Mindy Black	Sheryl Pernick
Awilda Cruz	Jen Prudenti
Roe Grossman	Tina Ruggiero
Ilene Horowitz	Sue Tyson
Meaghan LaPorte	Elizabeth Venditto
Renée Molino	Heather Villani
Maria Nania	

Table of Contents

Featured Members

ARCHITECTURE / CONSTRUCTION / DESIGN

David Wells Beer, FAIA 1
Ralph Decker Bennett Jr. 3
William Pancsovai Graff 5
Donna Swansen 8

ARTS

Kristi A. Baker, DMA 10
Vincent Di Fate 12
Zinovy Goro 14
Francis Joseph Greb, BFA, MS 16
Lance J. Hermus 18
X.J. Kennedy 21
Aaron Burton Krosnick 23
Richard Lytle 25
Jane Matthews 27
John McKay, DMA 29
Alyce Mae Nielson 32
J. Frank Sampson 34
Chyrl Lenore Savoy 36
Donna Jean Register Smoot 39

BUSINESS SERVICES

Ernest W. Baker Jr. 41
Angela Anderson Brady 43
Stephen B. Friedheim 45
Jack Papageorgis 47
Sanghyun Park 49
Alan M. Siegel 51

COMMUNITY / SOCIAL WORK / NONPROFIT

Stephen Robert Cohen 55
Steven L. Martinson, MSW 57
Carole Lynne Morrison 61
Ruth D. Sanchez-Way, PhD, MSW 63
James E. Smith, MSW, MPA, PhD, LSCSW 66

EDUCATION

Margaret Ishler Bosse, EdD 69

Nancy G. Boyer, PhD ... 71
D. Heyward Brock, PhD ... 73
Betty Jane Brown ... 75
April Graham Buonamici ... 77
Judith Shulamith Langer-Surnamer Caplan ... 79
Judith Ann Caskey, EdD ... 81
Kim L. Creasy, PhD ... 83
Philip E. Devine, PhD ... 86
Joy A. Dyer-Raffler ... 88
Carol A. Eppright ... 90
John Karl Fisher, EdD ... 92
Robert V. Haynes, PhD ... 95
Leonard Guy Heldreth ... 97
Patricia Ann Helms, PhD ... 99
Valerie J. Hoffman, PhD ... 101
Vera Rebecca Johnson, BS, MS ... 103
Theodore Jojola, PhD ... 105
Zema L. Jordan, PhD ... 108
Harold Stanley Kachel, EdD ... 110
Louise Lamphere, PhD ... 112
Mary Hoyle Mahan, EdD ... 115
Linda Ellen Miller ... 118
Alfred Frantz Myers ... 120
Patricia Herbert Raynor ... 122
Paul J. Reiss, PhD ... 124
Victor M. Renteria ... 126
Ruth Freddie Carleson Robinson ... 130
Joseph Salvatore Salemi, PhD ... 132
Walter R. Schumm, PhD ... 134
Jane Sheets ... 136
Lillian June Shuldes ... 138
Biljana B. Sljivic-Simsic, PhD ... 140
Donald K. Sorsabal, EdD ... 142
Charleszetta Stalling, EdD ... 144
John "Jack" Dickerson Todd III ... 146
Lloyd Ultan ... 148
Donna R. Vocate, PhD ... 151
Rebecca Ann Wilson ... 153

ENGINEERING

Sil Louis Arata Sr. ... 157
John W. Barrier ... 160
Richard C. Chou ... 163
Simon A. Ginzburg, PhD ... 165

Table of Contents

Francis T. Jones, PhD 167
Richard G. Merrell 169
Leticia Rustia Miranda 171
John R. Pate, BCCC, BE 173
Jack Andrew Wagner Jr. 175
Kurt V. Wipior 177

FINANCE / FINANCIAL SERVICES

Michael Braude 179
Alfonso G. Finocchiaro, PhD 181
Alicia Johnson Foster, CPA 184
Alan I W Frank 187
Robert Truman Handy 189
James Joseph Odorizzi 192
Hobart Robinson 194
William D. Rutherford 196
Marc A. Schoen 199
Alan Roger Shaw 201
Robert Charles Tengdin 203
Tony Vecchiotti 205

GOVERNMENT / PUBLIC SERVICE

Thomas Patrick Costin Jr. 207
L. Karen Darner 210
William H. Garrigan III 212
John W. Jaacks 214
Marie A. Langan 216
Myles James McTernan 218
Diana "Dee" Miskill 220
Edward George Schwier 222
Thomas Michael Thompson 225
Karon Lynette Uzzell-Baggett, OTD 227
Robert D. Walz 229

INFORMATION SCIENCE

Melanie L. Freese, MLS 231
Miriam C. Giebel 233
Virginia Lee Kinney 235
Barbara Pickthorn 237

A Lifetime of Achievement

LAW / LEGAL SERVICES

Janet L. Bassitt	240
Robert W. "Joe" Bishop, Esq.	244
David Sinclair Bouschor	246
Shelley A. Bower, Esq.	248
Arnie Rolf Braafladt	250
Darwin Bünger, JD	253
James C. Carpenter	255
William N. Clark	257
Edward Xavier Clinton Sr.	259
H. Fred Cook	261
June Resnick German, Esq.	263
Douglas M. Halsey	266
David R. Hayes Sr., Esq.	268
Roberta Karmel	270
Louis Mangano	272
Allan Mantel	274
Harry L. Munsinger	276
James Francis O'Rorke Jr.	278
Benjamin K. Phipps	280
John W. Pope	282
C. E. Schmidt	284
Hon. Jon J. Shindurling	286
Alvin L. Snowiss	288
James Kevin Toohey	291

MEDIA / ENTERTAINMENT

Thomas Bruce Birkenhead	294
Richard A. Carvell	296
Ron Daley	298
Leslie Grainger-Haynes	300
Richard Stewart Mason	302
Molleen Matsumura	304
Lucy Rosenthal	306
H. Donald Winkler	308

MEDICINE & HEALTH CARE

Marilyn K. Bither	311
B. Thomas Brown, MD, MBA	313
Theodora M. Capezio	315
Edward Sawyer Cooper, MD	317
Richard L. Coulson, PhD	321

Table of Contents

Richard J. Duma, MD, PhD 324
Glen R. Elliott, PhD, MD 327
Daniel L. Flugstad, MD 329
David William Furnas, MD 331
Robert J. Gerety, MD, PhD 334
Robert E. Hammer, PhD 337
Marjorie I. Hartog-Vander Aarde 340
William Orris Houston, DDS 343
Nikzad S. Javid, DMD, MSc, MEd, FICD 345
Federico R. Justiniani, MD, MACP 348
Alma Louise Young Kicklighter 351
Mary Ann Chudy Levy, MD 353
Deepak K. Malhotra, MD, PhD 355
Jacqueline C. Mashin 357
Sandra T. McBride, RN, MSN 359
Don Lewis McCord, MD 361
James Minard, PhD 363
Georg Noren, MD, PhD 365
Charles S. O'Mara, MD, MBA 367
Stephen M. Pastores, MD 369
Stuart P. Pegg, MD 371
Suzanne Zein-Eldin Powell, MD 373
Carol J. Schneider, PhD 376
Martin William Schwarze, DO 378
Estherina Shems, MD 381
Stanley S. Siegelman, MD 383
Helene Tanous, MD 385
Robert Lee Warren, DDS, MAGD 387
Devora Whiting, RN 389
Lou Ann Wieand, PhD 391

RELIGION / SPIRITUAL SERVICES

Rev. Rayann Burnham Cummings 393
Michael Ralph Ladra 395

RESEARCH & SCIENCE

Joseph A. Adamo, PhD 397
James A. Amick, PhD 399
Amiya Kumar Banerjee, PhD, DSc 401
James L. Blankenship Jr., PhD 403
Fairfid Monsalvatge Caudle, PhD 405
Michael Chase Davis, ScD 407
Janet E. Del Bene, PhD 409

A Lifetime of Achievement

Stevens Heckscher, PhD 411
Gertrude Wilma Hinsch, PhD 413
Barbara F. Howell, PhD 415
David Arthur Lienhart 417
Gerard Rushton, PhD 420
Charles Ozwin Rutledge, PhD 422
John M. Snyder, PhD 425
Moon K. Song, PhD 428
Larry E. Stevens 431
Paul J. Voss Jr. 434
Holland D. Warren, PhD 436
Oliver Wendell Welch 438
Fritz G. Will, PhD 440
Laszlo Zaborszky, MD, PhD 444

TECHNOLOGY

Gloria Christine Blair 446
Wes Coates, MBA 448
Ronald Jack Crymes 450
Gus A. Galatianos, PhD 453
Roy B. Woolsey, PhD 455

A Lifetime of Achievement

OUR COLLECTION OF PRESTIGIOUS LISTEES

A LIFETIME OF ACHIEVEMENT

VOLUME II

MARQUIS Who'sWho®

A Lifetime of Achievement in **Architecture / Construction / Design**

David Wells Beer, FAIA

Founding Partner & Architect (Retired)
Brennan Beer Gorman Monk Interiors

NEW YORK, NY UNITED STATES

A fter graduating from Phillips Exeter Academy in 1952, David Wells Beer, FAIA, prepared himself for his profession through the pursuit of a formal education at a number of esteemed academic institutions. He first earned a Bachelor of Architecture, magna cum laude, from Harvard College in 1956. He went on to earn a Master of Architecture from the Harvard Graduate School of Design, graduating in 1959 and earning an Alpha Rho Chi Medal. Subsequently, he became a registered architect in New York, New Jersey, Georgia, Florida, Connecticut, Virginia and Washington, D.C. Mr. Beer is a founding partner of Brennan Beer Gorman Architects, and he worked with Brennan Beer Gorman Monk Interiors from 1985 until his retirement in 2015.

Now celebrating a career that has spanned more than five decades, Mr. Beer initially worked as a designer for Pedersen and Tilney in New York City from 1960 to 1962, going on to serve as associate designer for Hoberman and Wasserman in New York City from 1962 to 1965. He then worked as design director for Welton Becket and Associates from 1965 to 1974 before advancing to senior vice president of design from 1974 to 1984. A knowledgeable member of his field, Mr. Beer has given architectural seminars at Harvard University, Columbia University, Cornell University and New York University about hotel architecture.

Drawing upon a lifelong affinity for putting things together, Mr. Beer has contributed his skills to numerous projects in his industry, notably working in such diverse locations as the Congo, St. Petersburg, Shanghai and Hong Kong and finding multicultural inspiration for his designs. His main accomplishments include the St. Regis Hotel restoration in New York, the Mellon Bank World Headquarters, the Barclays Bank World Headquarters, the Mandarin Oriental Hotel in New York and the Peninsula Hotel in Shanghai and Bangkok. Mr. Beer was the recipient of the Office Building of the Year Award in 1986, 1987, 1988, 1993 and 1995, and he was honored with the Platinum Circle Award in 1996. He also received first prize in the FDR Memorial Competition in 1962.

Interested in maintaining industry connections, Mr. Beer is a fellow of the American Institute of Architects. He also belongs to The Century Association, The Metropolitan Opera Club, The Knickerbocker Club and The Delphic Club. He has worked with the Preservation League of New York State, the Friends of the Upper East Side, Save Venice Inc., Friends of the Shanghai Museum, and The Metropolitan Museum of Art, among other prominent civic organizations. Due to his accomplishments, he has previously been selected for inclusion in such honors publications as the 30th edition of Who's Who in Finance and Industry. He was also listed in six editions of Who's Who in America, one edition of Who's Who in Science and Engineering, two editions of Who's Who in the East and three editions of Who's Who in the World.

Mr. Beer was born on June 29, 1934, in New York City to mother Florence Louise Fay Beer and father Walter Eugene Beer Jr. He is the proud father of two children named Elizabeth Amory Beer and Andrew David Beer. Moreover, he has five grandchildren named Tea, Nuala, India, Orla and Ona. In his free time, he enjoys participating in such activities as traveling internationally, fundraising, and attending the opera and theater.

A Lifetime of Achievement in **Architecture / Construction / Design**

Ralph Decker Bennett Jr.

Founding Principal (Retired)
Bennett Frank McCarthy Architects, Inc.

SILVER SPRING, MD UNITED STATES

With more than 50 years of experience to his credit, Ralph Decker Bennett Jr. has emerged as one of the East Coast's leading architects. He served as the founding principal of Bennett Frank McCarthy Architects, Inc., a leading architectural firm based out of Silver Spring, Maryland, that specializes in residential, commercial and urban multifamily projects. He thrived in this role from 1989 to 2019. Prior to this position, Mr. Bennett served as the principal of Ralph Bennett Architects from 1986 to 1989 and the principal of MassDesign Architects, operating out of Cambridge, Massachusetts, and Silver Spring, Maryland, from 1972 to 1986. The early days of his career were spent as an architect at Sert Jackson and Associates, in Cambridge, from 1968 to 1970, and at Kallman and McKinnell, in Boston, from 1966 to 1968 and again from 1970 to 1972.

Respected as a leader in his field, Mr. Bennett is also an experienced educator. He found success as an assistant professor at Harvard University in Cambridge from 1972 to 1977, and then at the University of Maryland, College Park, where he served a variety of positions, including an associate professor of architecture, a professor, the acting dean, and the chairman of the university senate. Since 2008, Mr. Bennett has held the position of a professor emeritus at the university.

A registered architect in Maryland, Massachusetts, Virginia, Delaware and Washington, D.C., Mr. Bennett has had the privilege of working on several landmark projects during the course of his illustrious career.

Among them are the North End Skating Rink in Boston, Massachusetts, the Kirkwood House in Baltimore, Maryland, the Brandermill Apartments in Midlothian, Virginia, and Massanutten Manor in Strasburg, Virginia. For his many achievements, he has been recognized by the Federal Republic of Germany, as the winner of the Fremont Civic Center Competition and named recipient of the Progressive Architecture Design Award in 1976. The American Institute of Architects named Mr. Bennett a fellow in 2015, and he earned LEED AP BD+C certification in 2010 for his commitment to environmentally friendly construction practices and buildings.

Outside of his professional responsibilities, Mr. Bennett has lent his leadership and expertise as the president of Purple Line NOW since 2011. Having joined the Purple Line NOW board in 2008, in his role as president, Mr. Bennett leads an alliance of businesses, residents, and community organizations working with officials on various levels of government to build a light rail line connecting suburbs in the Washington, D.C., metropolitan area. He has also contributed as the vice chair and the co-chair of the affordable housing conference of Montgomery County, in addition to serving as the president of the Northwood-Four Corners Civic Association from 1980 to 1984. Mr. Bennett also maintains affiliation with Omicron Delta Kappa, a national leadership honor society.

Prior to beginning his prolific professional career, Mr. Bennett gained a valuable education at Princeton University, where he earned a Bachelor of Arts in architecture in 1961 and a Master of Fine Arts in architecture in 1966. During this time, he also served as a lieutenant in the U.S. Army Reserve from 1962 to 1964. Born on January 10, 1940, in Boston, Massachusetts, Mr. Bennett has been married to Caroline Elise Kerr since February 27, 1966. Together, they have two children, Ralph Decker III and Katherine Elise. In his free time, Mr. Bennett enjoys motorcycle touring.

A Lifetime of Achievement in **Architecture / Construction / Design**

In Memoriam

William Pancsovai Graff

Architect

SARASOTA, FL UNITED STATES

With more than four decades of architectural practice, William Pancsovai Graff has been recognized as an outstanding practitioner in that profession. Born in Budapest, Hungary, to Vilmos Pancsovai Graff II and Klara Pejtsik in 1925, Mr. Graff's career spanned many countries. Educated in his early years in Italy, he grew up among some of the most famous structures of the world. Back in Hungary, he obtained his Master of Architecture at the Budapest Technical University, one of the four such institutions in Europe at that time.

Due to political considerations, Mr. Graff escaped from Hungary in 1949 and worked in Rome until his emigration to Canada in 1951. Once there, he worked at Marani and Morris and John B. Parkin in Toronto on both the Crown Life and the Confederation Life buildings.

In 1954, he was fortunate to gain entry into the United States, working first with Maguolo and Quick in Baltimore, Maryland. In 1956, he joined Hugh Stubbins and Associates in Cambridge, Massachusetts, where he participated in the design of Boston's first condominium at 330 Beacon St., as well as plans for the Berlin Kongress Halle, a gift in 1956 from the United States to that beleaguered city.

When Walter Gropius' The Architects Collaborative was awarded the design of Baghdad University by King Feisal of Iraq, Mr. Graff moved as one of its members to Rome in 1960 to participate in this challenging 11,000-student project, which included housing not only for the students but also for the faculty and all their families, with religious, medical and educational accommodations. During the 2002 Iraqi war, the campus incredibly was not damaged.

In 1962, Mr. Graff joined the Società Generale Immobiliare in Rome to lead the Studio Gábor Ács, which was entrusted with several international projects, the most important of these being The Watergate Project in Washington, D.C., whose primary designer was Luigi Moretti of Rome. Other major projects were the Tour de La Bourse with Pier Luigi Nervi and the Port Royal residencies in Montreal, the Hotel Mirabeau in Monte Carlo and the 82 Champs d'Elysées in Paris. Then, in 1964, Mr. Graff was selected as the project architect for The Watergate and moved back to the United States with his family.

By 1967, Mr. Graff and Henry C. Holle formed the Holle and Graff Partnership. Several large condominium projects for IDI in the Capital City area followed, starting with the Watergate at Landmark, the Rotonda, the Montebello, the Porto Vecchio and the Belvedere, as well as office buildings such as the International Club at 1800 and the office complex at 1801 K St. NW, and the Wink and Westin City Center Hotels. Following these projects, the partnership designed the twin office buildings at 8200 Greensboro Drive, McLean, Virginia, for IDI, and the Bush Hill and Hoffman Office Centers in Alexandria, Virginia, as well as the One Central Plaza on Rockville Pike, the National Central Research, the Plaza 270 and the headquarters of the National Cash Register Co. buildings in Rockville, Maryland. Before leaving Holle and Graff, his partnership developed the area's first Leisure World in Aspen Hill, Maryland.

In 1982, Mr. Graff joined Ralph Parsons for the planning of Yanbu City on the Red Sea, during which time he was also entrusted with the design of an island vacation palace for the Saudi Royal Family.

The invitation by the U.S. Department of State Foreign Buildings Office arrived in 1983, to participate in the intergovernmental negotiations concerning 15 real estate properties in Budapest, some of which had been expropriated after 1945 by the government of Hungary. Mr. Graff wished to express his gratitude and to honor both his native and adoptive countries by accepting this unique and very challenging assignment.

Ambassador Nicolas M. Salgo, of conglomerate fame, led the talks for almost two years, assisted by Mr. Graff's professional and language skills. Part of the successful settlement was the building of an American International School in the Buda Hills, the renovation of all American diplomatic residences and the construction of additional housing for the growing American diplomatic staff.

His most exciting personal project was the design of the first two solar houses in Washington, D.C., one being his own residence on Arizona Terrace NW.

Since 1972, Mr. Graff was a member of the Hungarian Association of the Sovereign Military Order of Malta. He joined the American Institute of Architects in 1967, and was registered with NCARB and in several states. Due to his outstanding achievements, he was honored in numerous editions of Who's Who in America, including the 73rd edition. His partnership also received awards from builders' groups since the condominium projects were bestsellers throughout the United States.

In 1959, the year he became an American citizen, Mr. Graff married Clara Lenke Marot, daughter of the formerly Hungarian General Staff Major Béla N. Marót and his wife, Lenke Legendai Radwány, in Stamford, Connecticut. They went on to become the proud parents of four children: Marcella, Carlo, Guido and Mattias, as well as six grandchildren: Chiara, Fabiola, Fiona, Lily, William and Henry. Mr. Graff died in 2019, after a long and fulfilling life.

Donna Swansen

Landscape Designer & Owner (Retired)
Donna Swansen Design
GWYNEDD, PA UNITED STATES

Donna Swansen is a retired landscape designer, consultant, owner and operator of Donna Swansen Design in Ambler, Pennsylvania. Serving the surrounding areas of Montgomery County, Pennsylvania, just north of Philadelphia, for more than 25 years, she established her business in 1983, concluding her very successful career in 2008. She formerly served as partner at Swansen & Borie in Ambler between 1977 and 1982 and Corson, Borie & Swansen in Ambler in 1976. Prior to entering the field, Ms. Swansen was a bridal consultant and an assistant buyer for the retail field.

During her career, Ms. Swansen has lent her expertise on numerous committees at her alma mater, Temple University, including the search committee for the chair of the department of landscape architecture and horticulture. She co-founded the Friends of the Rising Sun in Ambler, was the first president of Plant Ambler, and judged several competitions, including the Association of Professional Landscape Designers competition and the Bucks County Beautiful Flower Show, among other roles.

Furthermore, Ms. Swansen served as the editor of the "International Directory of Landscape Designers" in 1993. She is also a longtime member, co-founder, former board of directors member and former first president of the Landscape Design Network of Philadelphia and the Association of Professional Landscape Designers (APLD), which she co-founded with Margaret S. Connors, FAPLD, of Boston in 1989.

During her years with the organization, she received a Distinction Award in 1996 and served as a judge for their International Design Competition in 2002, 2003 and 2006.

Locally, Ms. Swansen was the vice president of Energy Islands International Inc. in East Troy, Wisconsin, between 1963 and 1994. She was the recipient of the Key to the Borough by the borough of Ambler in 1972, the winner of the Urban Beautification Project by the Roadside Council of America in 1975 and the recipient of an Athena Award from the Wissahickon Valley Chamber of Commerce in 1996. She received an Honor Award from Temple University in 2006, and was named to the Alumni Gallery of Success at Ambler College of Temple University in 2004.

Before entering the landscape design profession, Ms. Swansen sought to expand her knowledge through the pursuit of a formal education at a number of prestigious academic institutions. She first attended the University of Wisconsin and earned an associate degree in integrated liberal studies in 1956. She continued her studies at Temple University in Philadelphia, Pennsylvania. She graduated from the school in 1982, achieving an associate degree in landscape design. Subsequently, she became a fellow of the Association of Professional Landscape Designers.

Ms. Swansen was born on July 8, 1931, in Green Bay, Wisconsin, to mother Ella Marie Rose Warner Maloney and father Arthur Anthony Maloney. She later married Samuel Theodore Swansen on June 27, 1959. Together, they are the proud parents to three children named Jessica Swansen Bonelli, Theodor Arthur Swansen and Christopher Currie Swansen. Moreover, they have 14 grandchildren and two great-grandchildren. In her free time, she enjoys encouraging women, travelling and gardening.

In recognition of her contributions to the field, Ms. Swansen has previously been selected for inclusion in a number of honors publications, including eight editions of Who's Who in America, one edition of Who's Who in Science and Engineering, and two editions of Who's Who in the East. She has also been listed in three editions of Who's Who in the World and nine editions of Who's Who of American Women.

Kristi A. Baker, DMA

Pianist & Composer

TOPEKA, KS UNITED STATES

A brilliant pianist, composer, musician and educator of many years, Kristi A. Baker, DMA, spent her entire career working and teaching in Kansas. She also found much success as a freelance recitalist and a master clinician. Teaching music and serving as the choral director at the elementary, middle and high school levels for many years, Dr. Baker provided her skills and expertise to such academic entities as Wakefield Public Schools, Ware Elementary School, Junction City Middle School, Abilene High School, and Osawatomie High School and Middle School between 1981 and 2010.

In addition to her full-time career, Dr. Baker began teaching as an adjunct instructor of applied piano at Ottawa University in Kansas in 2006. She has also been a member of the commission on music and liturgy for the Episcopal Diocese of Kansas since 2001, a church organist and choirmaster at several area churches in Manhattan, Junction City and Abilene, Kansas, since 1988 and a private piano and voice instructor in Junction City, Abilene and Osawatomie, Kansas, since 1981. A performing artist at the Piano Texas International Festival in 2014, 2015, 2017 and 2018 and at the World Piano Conference in Novi Sad, Serbia, in 2015, 2016, 2017 and 2019, Dr. Baker notably composed "A Song for Advent" in 1998, "The Magic of Your Dreams" in 2000 and "Saint John's Mass" in 2006 and performed on six European tours with the St. David's Psalm Project.

Over the years, Dr. Baker has been affiliated with several professional organizations, including the Music Educators National

Conference, the Music Teachers National Association, the American Choral Directors Association and the Order of the Eastern Star. She is a past president of the Kansas Music Teachers Association and a member and the former chairman of the north central district and middle level honor choir programs of the Kansas Music Educators Association. Moreover, Dr. Baker has been active as a member of the Job's Daughters of Kansas, where she served in several capacities.

Prior to establishing herself as a trusted voice in the field, Dr. Baker sought to expand her knowledge through the pursuit of a formal education. She first attended Kansas State University, where she earned a Bachelor of Science in 1979. She continued her studies at the same esteemed academic institution and obtained a Master of Music in 1984. Ultimately, she achieved a Doctor of Musical Arts from the University of Kansas in 2012. Subsequently, she became certified as a K-12 music teacher in Kansas in 1979 and a nationally certified teacher of music in 2008.

In light of her many achievements, Dr. Baker has gained recognition in the form of various awards and accolades. Notably, she was the recipient of "Superior Plus" ratings by the National Guild of Piano Teachers several times between 1968 and 1975. She was also recognized as the winner of the Youth Talent Auditions by the Topeka Symphony Orchestra in 1974. She has been featured in several editions of Who's Who of American Women and Who's Who in American Education, as well as the 73rd edition of Who's Who in America.

Dr. Baker was born on December 10, 1957, in Topeka, Kansas, to mother Lila Ann Kern Williams and father J. Roland Williams. She later married Charles Burton Baker, who has since passed away. Together, they were the parents of two children named Elizabeth Baker Emery and Barbara Baker McCall. She currently has six grandchildren. In her free time, she enjoys participating in such activities as needlepoint, sewing and water sports.

A Lifetime of Achievement in **Arts**

Vincent Di Fate

Illustrator
WAPPINGERS FALLS, NY UNITED STATES

Vincent Di Fate is a talented freelance illustrator of 50 years who also worked in various other areas of the arts and entertainment business throughout his career. After graduating from higher education, he earned a freelance position with a science fiction magazine that led to a very successful tenure in the paperback market. Briefly working as an assistant animator for Krantz Films in 1967, Mr. Di Fate also became involved in education, teaching art at the Saints John and Paul School in Larchmont, New York, from 1968 to 1969 and various courses at the Fashion Institute of Technology in New York City, where he has been on the faculty since the mid-1980s and has been a professor since 2001.

Throughout his career, Mr. Di Fate provided his expertise as a consultant for MCA Inc. and MGM/UA Entertainment Company in Los Angeles. He further found success as a columnist for the "Science Fiction Chronicle" in Brooklyn, New York. Moreover, he authored and illustrated two of his own books, "Di Fate's Catalog of Science Fiction Hardware" in 1980 and "The Science Fiction Art of Vincent Di Fate" in 2001. Mr. Di Fate additionally authored and edited "Infinite Worlds: The Fantastic Visions of Science Fiction Art" in 1997.

A lifetime member and the past president of the Society of Illustrators, Mr. Di Fate is an active member and the former chair of permanent collections of the Museum of American Illustration as well as a member, the former chair of the grievance committee and the past president of the Association of Science Fiction and Fantasy Artists. He is also a longtime member of the Science Fiction and Fantasy Writers of America and the Graphic Artist Guild. In his free time, Mr. Di Fate is a prolific collector of artwork and films.

The recipient of the Distinguished Educator in the Arts Award from the Society of Illustrators, Mr. Di Fate has been inducted into the Science Fiction Hall of Fame in 2011 and the Illustrators Hall of Fame in 2019. He was notably presented with the Lensman Award in 1990, the Skylark Award in 1987, the Frank R. Paul Award from the Nashville Science Fiction Association in 1978, and the Science Fiction Achievement Award as the Best Professional Artist from the World Science Fiction Association in 1978, among other accolades. Likewise, Mr. Di Fate has been cited in the first edition of Who's Who of Emerging Leaders in America and the 21st edition of Who's Who in the East.

Originally intrigued by science fiction films as a child, Mr. Di Fate discovered a great artistic ability by the time he had entered high school. Earning a full scholarship to attend art school, he later received a Master of Arts in illustration from Syracuse University in 2003. Mr. Di Fate was certified in illustration by the New York Phoenix School of Design in 1967.

Born in Yonkers, New York, Mr. Di Fate was married to his late wife, Roseanne, for many years, who passed away six years ago in 2014. He has since remarried his second wife Joanne, who has given him a renewed sense of excitement about life. Lucky to have had two wonderful women in his corner, he was also inspired by his mother, Carmina. He credits all three of these beautiful women for his ability to create great artwork and become so successful in his career.

Zinovy Goro

Clarinetist

Arranger & Composer

SANTA CLARITA, CA UNITED STATES

With more than 60 years of experience to his credit, esteemed clarinetist Zinovy Goro has found success in a variety of roles. A native of Ukraine, he discovered his musical prowess at a young age. Mr. Goro began playing the violin at 5 years of age and later graduated from a violin school. A gifted musician, he then focused his attention on the clarinet. He attended the Tchaikovsky State Conservatory in Kiev, Ukraine, receiving a Masters of Fine Arts in performing and composition in 1970. He subsequently found success as a principal clarinetist in state-honored radio and TV orchestras from 1970 to 1979, including contributing as the music director of the Ukrainian Union's jazz orchestra.

After immigrating to the United States in 1979, Mr. Goro became a private music instructor in Los Angeles, California, a position he continues to thrive in. He then excelled as a solo clarinetist for "Ghetto," a play about the Vilna ghetto in Poland during World War II that was performed at the Mark Taper Forum in 1986. Following this success, he lent his talents to recordings for Warner Bros. and Universal Studios in Los Angeles. Also, from 1993 until 2016, he was working in the Universal Studios Music Library in Hollywood doing music copying and music preparation. Over the course of his career, he has composed music for eight full-length documentaries.

In addition to his primary professional endeavors, Mr. Goro has served as a principal clarinetist and a frequent soloist for the Los

Angeles Jewish Symphony since 1994. He is also the founder and the musical director of the award-winning ensemble, the Golden State Klezmers, which plays music attached to the Ashkenazi Jews of Eastern Europe. Klezmer music was forbidden in Ukraine while Mr. Goro was living there, and upon immigrating to America and seeing its popularity, he was inspired to form a group that would allow him to not only enjoy the music, but also share it with others. The group has met with tremendous success since its founding in 1980, performing more than 500 concerts, recording three albums and participating in recordings for albums, movies and commercials.

Mr. Goro received additional training from the Trebas Institute of Recording Arts in Los Angeles in 1991. Well-regarded as an expert in his industry, he has composed and written multiple pieces, including "Clarinet Concerto" in 2015 and a collection of "Pieces for Ensemble of Clarinets." In recognition of his tremendous achievements and contributions to the music industry, Mr. Goro has been recognized with the Blue Sphere Alliance Award for Best Original Music and was also named in the first edition of Who's Who in Entertainment. He is further the recipient of the Albert Nelson Marquis Lifetime Achievement Award, presented to individuals who have demonstrated extraordinary leadership and made notable advances in their field.

Mr. Goro was born to Veniamin Goro and Reva Kotliarker Goro in Kiev, Ukraine, then known as the USSR, on December 23, 1946. He is married to Tanya Grimberg and is the proud father of Alexey and David Ray. Mr. Goro is also the doting grandfather of Madison. In his free time, he enjoys fishing. Looking toward the future, he hopes to continue playing music, as well as expand his teaching and composing efforts.

Francis Joseph Greb, BFA, MS

Designer & Artist

DEERFIELD, IL UNITED STATES

After securing a Bachelor of Fine Arts in industrial design from Carnegie Mellon University in Pittsburgh, Pennsylvania, in 1953, Francis Joseph Greb, BFA, MS, began his career as a designer with Bert J. Long Advertising in Pittsburgh. His design career was interrupted by a call to military service, where he served in the U.S. Army's Occupation Forces in Esslingen, Germany, from 1953 to 1955. He continued his career as an apprentice designer with Richard I. Felver Design in Pittsburgh between 1955 and 1956, as well as a junior designer for the product and packaging design department with Montgomery Ward, now Montgomery Ward Company Complex, in Chicago, Illinois, from 1957 to 1959.

Mr. Greb further progressed with Montgomery Ward, accepting the position of a senior designer from 1959 until his departure in 1963. Subsequently, he began his 26-year tenure with Mel Boldt and Associates, holding the posts of senior designer from 1963 to 1966, associate from 1968 to 1978, and senior associate from 1978 to 1984 before concluding his time with the company as the vice president from 1984 to 1989. From 1989 until his retirement in 2000, he served as the project manager for Zenith Electronics Corporation in Chicago. Throughout his career, he was responsible for designing major appliance lines, an award-winning bath fixture line, the Zenith radios, VCRs, DVDs, headsets, cable box products and all packaging, the Presto Hot Topper, and Bausch & Lomb fashion eyewear, as well as the Bally Life-cycle redesign and numerous corporate identity programs including Moen's iconic overlapping water drop symbol.

Civically, Mr. Greb was involved with the Boy Scouts of America in Chicago from 1966 to 1983. In addition, he served as an election judge for Lake County between 2000 and 2018. A member of the Engineers' Society of Western Pennsylvania, he also maintains affiliation with the Industrial Designers Society of America, the Chicago Artists Guild (CAG), the Wagner Society and The American Legion. Furthermore, Mr. Greb holds seven U.S. patents and was presented with a CAG honorable mention for the Mel Boldt Christmas card promotion piece.

A successful artist, Mr. Greb had oil paintings exhibited in the Miami International Exhibition in 1949, and the European All Army Art Competition in 1954, winning a second-place prize. He also participated in the Annual Exhibition with the Associated Artists of Pittsburgh in 1952. Around this time, Mr. Greb completed architecture coursework at Carnegie Mellon University and obtained a Master of Science in product design at the Illinois Institute of Technology in 1957. He has previously been selected for inclusion in such honors publications as the 22nd edition of Who's Who in the Midwest, which was published in 1989. Reflecting on his career, he is grateful for the mentorship he received from Richard I. Felver, George Mendenhall and Mel Boldt.

Mr. Greb was born on November 16, 1931, in Pittsburgh, Pennsylvania, to mother Cecilia C. Fritz and father Frank Xavier. He married Ruth Greb in June 1959. After she passed away, he remarried Elaine Sukman Hirsch on January 2, 1987. He is the proud father to three children named Stephen Francis, Eric William and Gordon Christopher. Moreover, he has four grandchildren named Jennifer, Christopher, Sophia and Sharif. In his free time, he enjoys participating in such activities as painting, listening to classical music, camping and traveling. Impressively, he has run in 19 marathons and numerous additional shorter races.

A Lifetime of Achievement in **Arts**

Lance J. Hermus

Art Appraiser

NEW YORK, NY UNITED STATES

Driven by a love for sharing his passions with others, Lance J. Hermus has enjoyed an illustrious career as an art appraiser and a sports coordinator. He has found success as the director of sports programming for the Big Apple Program for New York City since 2019. Simultaneously, he has been active as the sports coordinator for the Public Schools Athletic League, a division of the New York City Department of Education, since 2003. In addition to these positions, Mr. Hermus provided invaluable guidance as the director of the summer breakfast and lunch program for New York City from 2003 to 2018. Previously, he was employed by the New York City Department of Finance, where he thrived as the deputy register for the Manhattan and Brooklyn Offices of the City Register Office, for five years.

In addition to his passion for sports, Mr. Hermus has flourished in creative roles. Possessing myriad talents, he found success early on in his career as a freelance photographer and an artist in Staten Island, thriving in this role for 20 years. Mr. Hermus was further associated as a video production art director for Master Productions in Staten Island from 1988 to 1990. Well-regarded for his skills, he was also a valuable addition to the Snug Harbor Cultural Center & Botanical Garden, where he excelled as an artist and as a member of the photo restoration department from 1990 to 1993. Possessing a love for sharing information and teaching, Mr. Hermus also enjoyed a position as an assistant lecturer in the education department of the Metropolitan Museum of Art. Since 2018, he has remained active as an assistant to the Central Iowa Art Association.

Having obtained a Bachelor of Arts in art with highest honors from the College of Staten Island — part of the City University of New York system — in 1992, Mr. Hermus is further equipped with a certification in art appraising from New York University and has been qualified as a registered art appraiser from the Appraiser Association of America. After this role, he continued his professional journey as a conservator, a curator and an appraiser for Santo Bruno Fine Art in Staten Island from 1992 to 1996, while simultaneously involved with the William Meyers Collection in New York City as a conservator and a curator from 1993 to 1994. Subsequently, he held the positions of an appraiser and an art consultant with Hermus Fine Arts in Staten Island, and currently, he is active as an appraiser with the Noble Maritime Collection, a cultural center in Staten Island that contains the works of marine artist John A. Noble.

To stay up to date on changes in his field and expand his understanding of the art world, Mr. Hermus is affiliated with a number of notable organizations. He is an associate of the Appraisers Association of America, as well as a member of the American Institute for the Conservation of Historical and Artistic Works. Beyond his primary professional endeavors, Mr. Hermus has been active as a member of the Democratic County Committee and has served his community as a poll watcher.

With myriad accomplishments of which to be proud, Mr. Hermus attributes his success to great mentors, including noted jewelry historian Penny Proddow and professors Nanette Solomon and Elaine Stainton. Additionally, he credits Santo Bruno for teaching him everything he knows about art restoration, and inspiring him to become an art appraiser. In light of his many achievements, Mr. Hermus has been the recipient of a number of notable awards. He has been listed in several honors publications, including Who's Who in America, Who's Who in the East and Who's Who in the World. As a further testament to his success, he is the recipient of the prestigious Albert Nelson Marquis Lifetime Achievement Award, presented to individuals who have demonstrated exceptional leadership and made a notable difference in their field.

Mr. Hermus is the proud father of three children, Jennifer Barbara Hermus-Washburn, Christopher William Hermus and Benjamin

Hermus, and the doting grandfather of one granddaughter, Addison-Rose. Looking toward the future, he hopes to continue researching art and visiting museums, as well as assisting art institutions and individuals as an art appraiser and a consultant. Beyond his art endeavors, Mr. Hermus enjoys writing, reading and coaching basketball in his free time.

X.J. Kennedy

Writer & Poet

LEXINGTON, MA UNITED STATES

With more than 55 years of experience to his credit, X.J. Kennedy is currently the co-editor of "The Bedford Reader," a collegiate literature textbook also utilized for teaching the AP English Language and Composition test. He began his career teaching English at a number of universities between 1963 and 1978, including the University of Michigan, the University of North Carolina at Greensboro, and Tufts University. In addition, he worked as a visiting professor at Wellesley College, the University of California, Irvine, and the University of Leeds. In the early 1970s, Mr. Kennedy co-edited the influential journal, Counter/Measures, and served as poetry editor for "The Paris Review."

Notably, Mr. Kennedy's poetry has been published in The New Yorker, Poetry, and The Hudson Review. In his youth, he began writing under the name "Joe Kennedy." A science fiction fan, he published well-regarded fanzines such as Vampire from 1945 to 1947 and The Vampire Annuals. Around this time, Mr. Kennedy began writing science fiction for pulp magazines, became a member of various amateur press associations and co-founded the Spectator Amateur Press Association.

In 1961, Mr. Kennedy wrote his first adult novel, "Nude Descending a Staircase: Poems, Songs, a Ballad," followed by his first student textbook, An Introduction to Poetry, in 1966. Co-editing the textbook Mark Twain's Frontier: A Textbook of Primary Source Materials Research and Writing with James Camp in 1963, he would later author his first children's book, "One Winter Night in August and Other Nonsense Jingles," in 1975. In 1978, Mr. Kennedy officially became a full-time freelancer.

Prior to embarking on his professional path, Mr. Kennedy pursued a formal education at Seton Hall University in South Orange, New Jersey, earning a Bachelor of Science in 1950. He then enrolled at Columbia University in New York, where he obtained a Master of Arts in 1951. Following his graduation, he completed four years of service as an enlisted journalist in the U.S. Navy Atlantic Fleet before studying at the Sorbonne in Paris from 1955 to 1956. For the next six years, Mr. Kennedy was a doctorate candidate at the University of Michigan.

Subsequently, Mr. Kennedy received an honorary Doctor of Humane Letters from Lawrence University in 1988, a Doctor of Fine Arts from Adelphi University, and a Doctor of Letters from Westfield State University in 2002. Notably, he has authored nearly 40 books, co-authored three books, and edited seven books. Additionally, Mr. Kennedy was a translator for "French Leave: Translations" in 1983 and compiler for "Talking Like the Rain: A First Book of Poems" in 1992.

Widely recognized for his light verse, Mr. Kennedy was the subject of the Bernard E. Morris biography, "Taking Measure: The Poetry and Prose of X.J. Kennedy," published by Susquehanna University Press in 2003. He was the first recipient of the Michael Braude Award for Light Verse from the American Academy of Arts and Letters in 1989, with future recipients consisting of Robert Conquest, Thomas M. Disch, Christopher Reid and Roger Angell, among others. A fellow of the John Simon Guggenheim Memorial Foundation and the National Council on the Arts, Mr. Kennedy was presented with the Lamont Poetry Prize by the Academy of American Poets in 1961, a grant from the National Endowment for the Arts and the Bess Hokin Prize by Poetry Magazine.

Likewise, Mr. Kennedy accepted the Shelley Memorial Award between 1969 and 1970, the Los Angeles Times Book Award in 1985, and the Golden Rose of the New England Poetry Club. In the 2000s, he was recognized with the National Council of Teachers of English Award in 2000, the Poets' Prize in 2004, and the Robert Frost Medal by the Poetry Society of America in 2009. More recently, Poets & Writers honored him with the Jackson Poetry Prize in 2015. He was notably published in the 73rd edition of Who's Who in America.

Mr. Kennedy was born on August 21, 1929, in Dover, New Jersey, to mother Agnes Kennedy and father Joseph Kennedy. He later married Dorothy Kennedy, who passed away in 2018. Currently, he is the proud father to five children. Moreover, he has six grandchildren named Emily, Iris, Noah, Daniel, Caleb and Sarah.

Aaron Burton Krosnick

Musician & Music Educator (Retired)

JACKSONVILLE, FL UNITED STATES

With more than 35 years of experience to his credit, Aaron Burton Krosnick is currently retired, having excelled as a professor at Jacksonville University from 1978 to 1998. Prior to this appointment, he held the position of an associate professor at Jacksonville University from 1972 to 1978. Previously, he served as an assistant professor of music at Jacksonville University in 1967. Mr. Krosnick began his career at Wittenberg University in Springfield, Ohio, as an instructor of music from 1962 to 1967.

Before embarking on his professional path, Mr. Krosnick pursued an education at Yale University, earning a Bachelor of Arts in French in 1959. Following these accomplishments, he furthered his musical efforts at the Meadowmount School, studying violin for one summer under Ivan Galamian. He continued his musical efforts at The Juilliard School, graduating with a Master of Science in violin in 1961. Subsequently, Mr. Krosnick concluded his studies at the Royal Conservatory of Brussels in Belgium, completing a Fulbright scholarship under the tutelage of Arthur Grumiaux between 1961 and 1962.

Beyond his responsibilities within the field, Mr. Krosnick has participated in numerous endeavors outside of his professional circles. He has contributed to the faculty of Syracuse University in 1964, the Kneisel Hall Chamber Music School and Festival in Blue Hill, Maine, from 1965 to 1968, and the Sewanee Summer Music Center in Tennessee on a number of occasions between 1969 and 1983. Furthermore, he held the role of concertmaster for the Springfield Symphony Orchestra in

Ohio from 1962 to 1967 and the Jacksonville Symphony Orchestra from 1970 to 1980. Featured on the recording of the Music of Fredrick Delius for the Musical Heritage Society, Mr. Krosnick found much success with his creative works, flourishing as an artist-in-residence since 1980 and a featured artist at the Rome Festival in 1977, 1985 and 1986.

Additionally, Mr. Krosnick remains affiliated with various organizations in relation to his areas of expertise. He has maintained his involvement with the American Federation of Musicians and the American String Teachers Association. He was also active with the Music Teachers National Association and the National Federation of Music Clubs. Moreover, Mr. Krosnick is a member of the Florida State Music Teachers Association.

In light of his exceptional undertakings, Mr. Krosnick has accrued several accolades throughout his impressive career. In 1961, he was recognized as a semifinalist in the Young Artist Auditions for the National Federation of Music Clubs. In 1970, he was selected as a semifinalist in the Nicolo Paganini International Violin Competition in Genoa, Italy. Likewise, Mr. Krosnick has been celebrated in multiple editions of Who's Who in Entertainment.

Inspired by his father, a pediatrician who played chamber music and devoted 25 years to the first violin section of the New Haven Symphony, and his mother, the first graduate of the Yale School of Music to receive a scholarship to Juilliard, Mr. Krosnick was mentored by Howard Boatwright, a concertmaster of the New Haven Symphony, and Joseph Fuchs, with whom he studied for eight years. Separated from his artistic peers due to his loyal association to Jacksonville for over 50 years, during which time he has left a mark on the community, he has encountered countless highlights throughout his career, having performed as a soloist with orchestra, becoming a recorded artist, and performing a sonata duet with his wife, Mary Lou, to name a few. Looking toward the future, Mr. Krosnick hopes to continue enjoying his retirement alongside his family while cementing his legacy as a musician and educator.

A Lifetime of Achievement in **Arts**

Richard Lytle

Painter

Professor Emeritus
Yale University School of Art
WOODBRIDGE, CT UNITED STATES

With years of experience to his credit, Richard Lytle has set himself apart as a leader in the art and academic worlds. A renowned painter, he taught for many years and served as the acting dean at the Yale University School of Art. Hired as an instructor in 1960, he remained in this role for three years before accepting a position as the dean at the Silvermine College of Art. In 1966, he returned to Yale University, where he spent the remainder of his career, ultimately retiring in 2002.

Included in the famous "Sixteen Americans" exhibition at the Museum of Modern Art in 1959, Mr. Lytle has since become a well-known master of color with works that have included both watercolor and charcoal. Particularly fond of painting botanical landscapes, he spent the first part of his career as an assistant to Josef Albers, a German-born American artist and educator, before entering academia. Mr. Lytle was also selected to travel to Ukraine in 1990, where he spent two weeks curating art to bring back to the United States.

Mr. Lytle's exhibitions were recently on display in a one-man show at the Giampietro Gallery in New Haven, Connecticut. On display at Fairfield University just prior to the Giampietro Gallery, he has also held numerous one-man shows at other locations, and has been exhibited in group shows at the Museum of Modern Art, the Whitney Museum of American Art, the World's Fair in Seattle, Washington, the

Pennsylvania Academy of the Fine Arts, and the Bruce Museum. In addition, he has works in permanent collections at the Yale University Art Gallery, the Museum of Modern Art, the Minneapolis Institute of Art, and the National Gallery of Art in Washington, D.C. Mr. Lytle's proudest achievement was being included at the Festival of the Arts on the Green in New Haven, where his work was chosen as number one by Judge Dorothy Miller, a curator at the Museum of Modern Art, which purchased the painting. He was also excited when two of his abstract paintings were purchased by Governor Rockefeller, one of which was for display in the governor's mansion and the other for his home, which serves as the center of his collection.

A consultant for several years with the Rockefeller Fund in New York during the 1960s, Mr. Lytle also served as the director of the Yale Summer School in 1976 and 1977. Furthermore, he was an artist-in-residence at Dartmouth College in 1986. He served on the Region 5 Board of Education in Woodbridge, Connecticut, for more than 15 years and was the chair for nearly 10 years, in addition to contributing as a member of the board of finance for the city of Oxford, Connecticut, from 1964 to 1966.

Graduating number one in his class at the Cooper Union in New York City in 1955, Mr. Lytle went on to pursue both a Bachelor of Fine Arts in 1957 and a Master of Fine Arts in 1960 at Yale University. A Fulbright fellow from 1958 to 1959, he was honored by the Cooper Union in 1985 with a St. Gaudens Award. He has been showcased in Who's Who in American Education and Who's Who in the East, in addition to being recognized with the Albert Nelson Marquis Lifetime Achievement Award. Married to Berit Ore Lytle since 1959, Mr. Lytle has three children, Mara, Claudia and Dorian, and four grandchildren, Claire, Sophie, Malin and Scarlett. Currently a professor emeritus of painting at the Yale University School of Art, he enjoys gardening in his free time.

Jane Matthews
Artist & Writer

LULING, TX UNITED STATES

A well-respected artist and writer, Jane Matthews has enjoyed a long career pursuing creative endeavors while simultaneously helping her community. With nearly 60 years of professional experience to her credit, she continues to excel as a freelance writer and artist. In addition to her primary responsibilities, she inspired readers with a weekly poetry column for the Victoria Advocate from 2010 to 2012. A prolific writer, she was also a contributor to the New Texas Handbook from 1998 to 2010 and the Victoria Oral History Collection from 1999 to 2000, in addition to submitting articles on Texas history for Texas State Stripes Magazine from 1993 to 2010. Ms. Matthews has also served as a research writer for Everett, Munson, McClanahan Magazine and the Victoria County Genealogical Magazine from 1990 to 2012.

Beyond her talents on the page, Ms. Matthews has thrived in numerous artistic endeavors. In addition to her work as a painter, a storyteller and a designer, she found success as a producer and an artist for the Art Project Play from 1992 to 1995. As a member of the National Endowment of the Arts from 1990 to 1991, Ms. Matthews was involved with a traveling art show that performed throughout the U.S. and raised funds for homeless people in a number of cities. Additionally, she held the role of the director of the One Seguin Art Center from 1982 to 1985 as well as the producer of the musical "Godspell" at the Texas Theater from 1981 to 1982. Earlier in her career, Ms. Matthews was a teacher with Project Y at the Children's Pavilion of the HemisFair '68 from 1968 to 1969.

A Lifetime of Achievement | Jane Matthews

Ms. Matthews began her career as a student at Southwestern University in Georgetown, Texas, completing coursework from 1955 to 1966. She continued her education at the University of the Incarnate Word in San Antonio, Texas, from 1967 to 1968, as well as at Trinity University in San Antonio from 1969 to 1971. She subsequently studied at San Antonio College, earning an Associate of Arts in graphic arts and communications in 1971. Ms. Mathews is an elected vestry member of the Episcopal Church of the Annunciation and pursued additional coursework at the Seminary of the Southwest in Austin, Texas, from 1977 to 1979.

Ms. Matthews' interest in art was sparked at home, inspired by her mother, Alice Bradshaw Rogers, who demonstrated her creativity through her work in advertising. Though her husband's job required her family to move around the country, she found familiarity in art. When she moved to San Antonio, Texas, Ms. Matthews discovered an invaluable artists' community that challenged her creatively. A respected voice in her industry, she is a member of the Daughters of the American Revolution, DRT, Zeta Tau Alpha, the Victoria Genealogical Society, the Clergy Wives Association and the Diocese of West Texas. The president of the Seguin Study Club, Ms. Matthews has further excelled as a board member of the Regional Art Luling Oil Museum.

Notably, Ms. Matthews has received several grants for her creative efforts, including from the Texas Commission on the Arts, the Victoria Cultural Commission on the Arts, the Nave Museum, and the National Education Association. In recognition of outstanding contributions to her profession and her community, she has also been presented with the Albert Nelson Marquis Lifetime Achievement Award. Ms. Matthews is currently working on a genealogy project for her family, as well as continuing her writing endeavors. Despite her many accomplishments, she is most proud of her three children, who are all creatively inclined.

John McKay, DMA

Concert Pianist

Professor (Retired)
Gustavus Adolphus College
ST. PETER, MN UNITED STATES

With several decades of professional experience to his name, John McKay, DMA, has enjoyed a successful career as a concert pianist and a professor in higher education. He dedicated the majority of his work to holding the title of professor of music at Gustavus Adolphus College in St. Peter, Minnesota, from 1976 to 2004. Previously, he excelled as an assistant professor at Dalhousie University in Halifax, Canada, from 1972 to 1974. His first appointment was as a teacher of piano at the University of Toronto and at the Royal Conservatory of Music from 1969 to 1972.

Outside his primary endeavors, Dr. McKay founded the Minnesota Valley Sommarfest, a summer chamber music festival that ran from 1990 to 2006. Reflecting on his work, he is grateful for the mentorship of Lubka Kolessa and John Newmark in Montreal, Bruno Seidlhofer in Vienna, and Eugene List in Rochester, New York. He has also enjoyed work as a teacher, whether in the classroom or in the studio, teaching piano. He often made points by telling amusing anecdotes from his own experience. On one occasion, the woman turning pages for him was sick, and wheezed at the end of every phrase in the piece he was performing.

While still a student, Dr. McKay participated in a contest organized by the Canadian Broadcasting Corporation. He played the first movement of Brahms' Piano Concerto No. 2 with the CBC Orchestra conducted by Sir Ernest McMillan, an astonishing feat for such a young musician.

Dr. McKay's professional training began at the Provincial Conservatory of Music in Montreal. In 1962, he won the "Prix d'Europe" (the "European Prize"), in a contest sponsored by the province of Quebec, which allowed him to study for two years in Vienna, Austria, and Cologne, Germany. Subsequent grants from the Canada Council allowed him further study in Brussels, Belgium. He began his professional career as a concert pianist with tours of the major capitals of Europe in 1967 and 1969. For these programs, he received many glowing reviews.

While teaching in Toronto, he performed the complete works for solo piano by Johannes Brahms in a series of four recitals in the 1971-72 season to commemorate the 75th anniversary of Brahms' death.

In the mid-80s, at Gustavus Adolphus College, he performed Beethoven's 32 piano sonatas in eight recitals. In 2002, Dr. McKay completed his survey of Beethoven's music for solo piano with a performance of the Diabelli Variations, Op. 120, Beethoven's crowning achievement for piano. Dr. McKay considers these experiences to be some of the highlights of his career as a performer.

Prior to establishing himself as a trusted voice in the field, Dr. McKay sought to expand his knowledge through the pursuit of a formal education at a number of esteemed academic institutions. He first attended McGill University in Montreal, and earned a Bachelor of Music in 1961. He continued his studies at the Eastman School of Music, where he obtained a Master of Music in 1975, and a Doctor of Musical Arts in 1978.

Long before his academic pursuits, Dr. McKay developed a passion for classical music. Both his parents were sympathetic to classical music, and his father would often play the piano, mostly music that was popular in the early part of the 20th century, especially the songs of Irving Berlin. His father had him begin taking piano lessons just before his eighth birthday. At the time, many of his friends were taking piano lessons also. He credits this environment with sparking his desire to pursue music professionally.

In his retirement, Dr. McKay has become increasingly involved with the Presbyterian Church, and served as moderator of the Presbytery of Minnesota Valleys in 2014, and moderator of the Synod of

Lakes and Prairies in 2020. In 2019, Dr. McKay and his wife Sara, a choral conductor, were inducted into the Minnesota Music Hall of Fame. Unfortunately, the induction ceremony occurred only a few days after Sara died, resulting in her being inducted posthumously.

Dr. McKay was born on November 11, 1938, in Montreal, Quebec, Canada. He married his late wife, Sara Hayden McKay, on September 9, 1964, and they were the proud parents of three children named Johanna, Murray and Elizabeth. They immigrated to the United States in 1976, and Dr. McKay became an American citizen in 1985. In his free time, he enjoys reading, completing crossword puzzles, Shakespearean scholarship and Christian studies.

A Lifetime of Achievement in **Arts**

Alyce Mae Nielson

Poet

SAUGERTIES, NY UNITED STATES

O ver the past five decades, Alyce Mae Nielson has established a career of helping others, whether it was through motivating them to pursue healthy lives or inspiring them through the written word. Prior to embarking upon her professional path, she earned an Associate of Science in food from the State University of New York at Cobleskill in 1963. She launched her career as a school lunch manager at Brooklyn Public School 61 from 1963 to 1964. Afterward, Ms. Nielson pursued a position as a clerk in the stock and bond dividend department at the First National City Bank in New York City from 1966 to 1969. Subsequently, she thrived at Weight Watchers in Brooklyn and Staten Island, serving as a lecturer, a trainee, a group leader and a center manager over nearly two decades. At Weight Watchers, she helped educate members on healthy eating and safe ways to lose weight, providing support and guidance to help individuals reach their goals.

After excelling for many years at Weight Watchers, Ms. Nielson retired and began pursuing her love of writing. Today, she has found success as a poet, providing her exemplary written works such as "Melting Glaciers" and "Words are Treasure" to various anthologies, in addition to self-publishing a number of texts, including "Blessings" and "Poems, Prayers and Inspiration." An active church member, Ms. Nielson draws her inspiration from the Bible, eager to share the good in it with others through poetry. Her writing is marked by its observational style, with Ms. Nielson drawing from what she is familiar with and from past experiences. To continually sharpen her craft and maintain her connections with others in the field, Ms. Nielson remains active as a member of the International Society of Poets.

In addition to her professional endeavors, Ms. Nielson is an active community volunteer. During her spare time, she knits and crochets for the needy, selflessly contributing to such organizations as Warm Up America in Kingston, New York. Further, she has volunteered at Bizzy Bee's in Kingston, New York, since 2003. Ms. Nielson has been a nurturer and creative force since childhood. She was a member of 4-H from the time she was 9 years old until she was in college, an experience that allowed her to make her own dresses, care for animals, and garden. A talented chef, Ms. Nielson has always maintained a passion for cooking as well, a hobby that later inspired her to pursue her career path.

Although she has experienced many highlights over the years, Ms. Nielson is especially proud of helping other people throughout the entirety of her career. She has been recognized for her efforts several times, earning Editor's Choice Awards between 1995 and 2003. Ms. Nielson also had the distinct honor of being named to the International Poetry Hall of Fame in 1996. In recognition of her achievements, leadership qualities and success, Ms. Nielson has also been presented the Albert Nelson Marquis Lifetime Achievement Award.

Born on February 27, 1943, in Saugerties, New York, Ms. Nielson is the daughter of George John Wodischeck and Martha Elizabeth Casler. She married David Bruce Nielson on October 5, 1963, and together, they have two children, Kenneth David and Nancy Lynn Nielson Nowicki, as well as five grandchildren. She is a second-degree black belt in taekwondo, and enjoys tai chi and listening to music, and is now enjoying yoga. Looking toward the future, Ms. Nielson intends to experience the continued success of her writing.

J. Frank Sampson

Artist

Professor Emeritus of Fine Arts
University of Colorado Denver

BOULDER, CO UNITED STATES

J. Frank Sampson is an American artist and a professor emeritus of fine arts at the University of Colorado Denver, where he taught on campus for 29 years. Hired in 1961 as an assistant professor, he later served as an associate professor from 1968 to 1972 before becoming a full professor. He attained emeritus status in 1990. Outside of his primary endeavors, he has been the focus of one-man shows at the Walker Art Center in Minneapolis in 1954 and the Denver Art Museum in 1975. He has also shown creative work at the Arvada Center for the Arts and Humanities in Colorado in 2003 and the Boulder Museum of Contemporary Arts in 2018.

Impressively, Mr. Sampson's work is represented in permanent collections at the Colorado Springs Fine Arts Center, the Des Moines Art Center, the Dulin Gallery of Art in Knoxville, the Joslyn Art Museum in Omaha, the Library of Congress, the Littleton Museum and the Minnesota Museum of American Art in St. Paul. He is further represented in permanent collections at the Mulvane Art Museum, Washburn University in Topeka, the Sheldon Museum of Art, the University of Nebraska-Lincoln and the Springfield Art Museum in Missouri. In addition, permanent collections at the Walker Art Center in Minneapolis, the Boston Public Library and the Nelson-Atkins Museum of Art in Kansas City, Missouri, all feature his work.

Mr. Sampson summarizes his work as art that is a way of life and almost a religion. His art has helped him to reach a spiritual level and a higher feeling of life, creation and spirit, like meditation. Moreover, he found great joy in teaching because it helped him to learn and grow himself. Reflecting on his career, he is grateful for the mentorship of Cyrus Running, a teacher at Concordia College; Mauricio Lasansky, an artist from Belgium; Madam Strebell, who owned the studio he rented in Belgium; and Michel de Ghelderode, a writer from Belgium who liked Mr. Sampson's work and wrote an article about it for a magazine. He was greatly inspired by his mother, a former teacher, to go into art because, when he was little, she would make up incredible fantasy stories that included many animals.

Prior to establishing himself as a trusted voice in the field, Mr. Sampson sought to expand his knowledge through the pursuit of a formal education at a number of esteemed academic institutions. He first attended Concordia College in Moorhead, Minnesota, where he earned a Bachelor of Arts in 1950. He continued his studies at the University of Iowa, where he obtained a Master of Fine Arts in 1952. From there, he served in the U.S. Army for two years from 1954 to 1956. Ultimately, he returned to the University of Iowa to complete postgraduate coursework from 1956 to 1959.

In light of his many accomplishments over the years, Mr. Sampson has gained recognition in the form of various awards and accolades. Notably, he was a Fulbright fellow from 1959 to 1961. He has previously been selected for inclusion in numerous honors publications, including the 23rd through 25th editions of Who's Who in the West and the 73rd edition of Who's Who in America. Mr. Sampson was born on March 24, 1928, in Edmore, North Dakota, to mother Mabel Elizabeth Trimble Sampson and father Silas Abner Sampson. In his free time, he enjoys exercising and listening to classical music. The advice he can offer to the next generation or others aspiring to work in his profession is to be true to yourself, don't get discouraged, conjure up a strong desire to pursue, and work hard.

Chyrl Lenore Savoy

Artist

Art Professor
University of Louisiana at Lafayette
YOUNGSVILLE, LA UNITED STATES

Following 40 years of excellence in her field, Chyrl Lenore Savoy retired after many years working as an art professor at the University of Louisiana at Lafayette in 2015. Hired by the university in 1973 as an assistant professor of fine arts, she accepted the post of a full professor in 1978, in which she excelled for the duration of her teaching career. Prior to her tenure in Louisiana, she worked as a teacher of art at Saint Martin de Porres High School in Detroit from 1969 to 1970.

Prior to embarking on her professional path, Ms. Savoy earned a Bachelor of Arts at Louisiana State University in 1966 and a Master of Fine Arts at Wayne State University in 1970. While studying for her master's degree, she contributed as a graduate assistant at Wayne State University in 1970. She additionally spent a year of study in Florence, Italy, studying sculpture and drawing at the Academy of Fine Arts and language at the University of Florence, where she received a diploma.

Upon completing her graduate degree, Ms. Savoy entered a piece of her artwork in a biannual exhibition in New Orleans for the very first time. She won an award and was recommended for purchase, which gave her the confidence she needed to continue producing and showing her work. She has since participated in numerous solo exhibitions at such locations as the New Orleans Museum of Art, the Artists Alliance in Lafayette and the Contemporary Art Gallery on the campus of Southeastern Louisiana University. Ms. Savoy also participated in exhibitions on an international level at the University of the Americas in Puebla, Mexico. She has also been featured in group shows many times and has been on display at permanent collections for the Hilliard University Art Museum, the New Orleans Museum of Art and the Alexandria Museum, among other locations.

Throughout her career, Ms. Savoy has worked in collaboration with a number of other artists. She did the majority of her collaborative work with Sunny Savoy, including "Colors I, II," a collaboration between dancer and painter, and "Molluscan Myriad," a collaboration between choreographer and sculptor. She also composed the electronic music for the latter piece. "Molluscan Myriad" has been performed in the United States and Mexico and was also presented at Danse a Paris Concours International de Choreographie at Cirque d'Hiver in Paris.

Other collaborative works include "Intersectar," a sculpture installation incorporated into an interdisciplinary performance and later reconstructed and redesigned for the stage, which has been performed all over Mexico. In "Dialogo," she did the original music and text collage. "Dialogo" has been performed all over Mexico and was selected as one of the four finalists at the Octavo Premio Nacional de Danza de Mexico in 1987 at the Palacios de Bellas Artes in Mexico City.

A member of the drawing committee at the University of Louisiana at Lafayette during 1985, Ms. Savoy has been active on several other committees, including the sculpture committee and studio position search committee. She has co-chaired the sculpture position search committee, directed the school of art and architecture search committee and been a member of the visual arts department curriculum committee. Locally, Ms. Savoy was affiliated with the R.S. Barnwell Memorial Garden and Art Center as both a member and the chairman of the art committee.

Involved with multiple organizations relative to her work, Ms. Savoy is a former adviser for the Art and Architecture Student Association. She is also associated with Artists Alliance Inc. and Phi Beta. Recognized as Teacher of the Year by the Beacon Club at the University of Louisiana at Lafayette in 2000, she further accrued a grant from the Board of Regents Support Fund in 2004 and an instruction and improvement grant in both 1985 and 1986. Likewise, Ms. Savoy has previously been selected for inclusion in such honors publications as the seventh edition of Who's Who in American Education, the 24th and 25th editions of Who's Who in the South and Southwest, the 25th edition of Who's Who of American Women and the 73rd edition of Who's Who in America.

Ms. Savoy was born on May 23, 1944, in New Orleans, to mother Bobby Adrienne Rawls and father Frank Peter Savoy Jr. She is the oldest of five siblings, including a sister named Sunny Savoy Perez. Now, she is the proud mother of one daughter named Bobby Frances Savoy. In her free time, she enjoys participating in such activities as listening to music and reading poetry.

Donna Jean Register Smoot

Music Educator (Retired)

LARAMIE, WY UNITED STATES

With more than 50 years of professional experience to her credit, Donna Jean Register Smoot has passed on her love of music through education to countless students. Prior to her retirement in 2008, she thrived as the director of bands for the Unified School District 443 in Dodge City, Kansas, since 2002, for which she additionally held the post of instrumental music teacher since 1993. Prior to these roles, Mrs. Smoot served as an instrumental and vocal teacher with the Mexico Central School District from 1990 to 1992 and with the Unified School District 443 from 1980 to 1990. She further excelled as an instrumental teacher with the Laramie County School District in Wyoming from 1971 to 1974 and as a music teacher with Poudre R-1 School District in northern Colorado from 1968 to 1971. Earlier in her career, Mrs. Smoot launched her career as a music teacher with the West Burlington School District in Iowa from 1966 to 1968.

Mrs. Smoot's professional journey began with a scholarship to Iowa Wesleyan College, located in Mount Pleasant, where she studied piano. She soon realized her passion lay in teaching and encouraged by her mentor, Dr. Kraus, she obtained a Bachelor of Music in music education in 1966. Following this accomplishment, she concluded her studies at Wichita State University in Kansas, earning a Master of Arts in music education in 1986. Moreover, Mrs. Smoot is certified as a teacher by the Kansas State Department of Education.

A leading voice in her community, Mrs. Smoot has been affiliated with a number of organizations in her field. She is a life member of the National Education Association and the National Association for Music Education. Mrs. Smoot is further an associate of Phi Beta Mu and the Kansas Bandmasters Association, which promotes programs, educational opportunities and awards for musicians, students and band directors throughout Kansas.

Known by her peers as a fair and caring educator, Mrs. Smoot's career has been marked by a commitment to her students' success. She is passionate about music education in schools and firmly believes in the power of instrumental music in the development of the brain. Mrs. Smoot has been recognized throughout her career for her accomplishments with various awards and accolades, including induction into the Blue Key Honor Society at Iowa Wesleyan College and being named an Outstanding Instrumental High School Band Director for southwest Kansas. Furthermore, Mrs. Smoot has been featured in numerous publications, including multiple editions of Who's Who of American Women. She has also been named the recipient of the prestigious Albert Nelson Marquis Lifetime Achievement Award, presented to individuals who have demonstrated exceptional leadership and made notable contributions to their field.

Mrs. Smoot was born on January 27, 1944, in Mount Pleasant, Iowa, to Carl Jay and Mae Lucille Simkin Register. She married the late Robert Earl Smoot on December 30, 1962, and together the two are the proud parents of two daughters, Kristen Kay and Tina Renee Ballard. Mrs. Smoot is also the doting grandmother of one grandson. In her free time, she enjoys knitting and cross-stitching, using her talents to make blankets for babies being christened at the St. Paul Newman Center. Mrs. Smoot continues to play the piano, a hobby she considers to be therapeutic. She continues to share her musical knowledge with the next generation by occasionally giving private lessons to select students.

A Lifetime of Achievement in **Business Services**

Ernest W. Baker Jr.

Advertising Executive (Retired)

OAKLAND TOWNSHIP, MI UNITED STATES

With more than 50 years of experience to his credit, Ernest W. Baker Jr. is currently retired, having excelled as the executive vice president of BBDO in Detroit, Michigan, from 1993 to 2000. Prior to this appointment, he worked as the chairman for DDB Worldwide in Troy, Michigan, from 1990 to 1993. Mr. Baker previously thrived as the chairman and chief executive officer of Baker, Abbs, Cunningham & Kleppinger in Birmingham, Michigan, from 1964 to 1990.

Mr. Baker additionally flourished as an account executive with Denman & Baker Inc. in Detroit from 1951 to 1963. He began his career as a copywriter for the Zimmer-Keller Advertising Agency from 1948 to 1951. Furthermore, Mr. Baker was active as the owner and operator of Baker's Apple Orchard for more than 25 years.

Before embarking on his professional path, Mr. Baker completed service in the U.S. Army, serving with the 96th Infantry Division in the South Pacific as a part of the Pacific theater of operations in World War II between 1944 and 1945. During his time in the service, he received nine medals, including the Bronze Star Medal. Subsequently, he pursued an education at the University of Missouri, earning a Bachelor of Journalism in 1948. He received an honorary doctoral degree in business sciences from Cleary University in 1972.

Beyond his primary responsibilities in the field, Mr. Baker has participated in numerous endeavors outside his professional circles. Since 1987, he has contributed to the board of visitors for the School of Nursing at Oakland University in Rochester Hills, Michigan. Moreover, Mr. Baker was a distinguished clown in America's Thanksgiving Day Parade for 15 years.

Mr. Baker has found additional success with his written works, authoring his autobiography, "A 50-Year Adventure in the Advertising Business," for Wayne State University Press in 1999. The book received glowing reviews, including high praise from such respected figures in advertising as Jeffrey Caponigro of Caponigro Public Relations, Dan Ewald of the Detroit Tigers, Dick Johnson of BBDO Detroit and Tom Clark of BBDO Worldwide. He has also penned the novel "My Brother Danny," which was published by iUniverse in 2006. Both of Mr. Baker's books are available for purchase on Amazon.com.

In light of his exceptional undertakings, Mr. Baker has accrued various accolades throughout his impressive career. He was inducted into the Adcraft Club of Detroit's Hall of Fame, and was further recognized as the National Volunteer of the Year by the National Association of County Park and Recreation Officials in 2001. Likewise, Mr. Baker was included in multiple editions of Who's Who in Finance and Industry, Who's Who in America, Who's Who in the Midwest and Who's Who in the World.

During his formative years in the advertising business, Mr. Baker was greatly influenced by Keith Reinhard, an icon in the field, who he cites as a great mentor. He was initially drawn to advertising by his family, which had ties to the copywriting and advertising business and supported his advancement through a number of major companies. Mr. Baker is particularly proud of his grandson, Reid Baker, who has had a clothing line in Portugal named in his honor, obtained a scholarship for his soccer skills at California State University, Fullerton, and played soccer professionally for several years. Looking toward the future, Mr. Baker hopes to continue enjoying his well-deserved retirement while cementing his personal and professional legacy.

A Lifetime of Achievement in **Business Services**

Angela Anderson Brady

Human Resources Recruiting Coordinator
PruittHealth
LAWRENCEVILLE, GA UNITED STATES

With 30 years of experience to her credit, Angela Anderson Brady has worked as a human resources recruiting coordinator for PruittHealth, a Southeast regional leader in long-term health care, since 2000. In this post, she is responsible for job postings, assisting in-house recruiters, pre-screening candidates, administrating the applicant tracking system, and entering new hire information to state and federal government systems. She additionally investigates complaints, handles employee relations, performs compliance audits, maintains personnel files, and supervises new hire orientation. Furthermore, Ms. Brady troubleshoots PruittHealth's issues with applications, networks, hardware and information technology.

Prior to this appointment, Ms. Brady held the position of a network administrator for the Oconee Regional Medical Center from 1998 to 1999. Maintaining network infrastructure for this establishment, she participated on the Y2K committee during this time as well. Moreover, Ms. Brady has installed software for medical equipment and servers while providing backups for all hardware and software in this role.

Previously, Ms. Brady served Tenneco in Hartwell, Georgia, as a network analyst from 1995 to 1998. Certified as a Novell engineer, she upgraded the network infrastructure for the aforementioned company while installing application software and administrating the server. Likewise, Ms. Brady garnered valuable expertise in human resources in this position, as she managed personnel in the IT department and worked with the accounting department on payroll.

A Lifetime of Achievement | **Angela Anderson Brady**

Ms. Brady began her career as a computer programmer for Michelin in Greenville, South Carolina, between 1989 and 1995. Over the course of her tenure with Michelin, she developed real-time applications that controlled production specifications, worked on the sizing of databases of applications and application issues, and approved the specifications of hardware needs for employees. Training employees on applications as well, Ms. Brady contributed to the installation and troubleshooting of the WAN application.

Before embarking on her professional path, Ms. Brady pursued an education at Spartanburg Community College in 1986, from which she graduated with an Associate of Arts and Sciences in information technology, with honors, in 1989. She concluded her studies at Columbia Southern University, completing coursework in business administration, management and human resources while seeking a bachelor's degree in human resources from 2012 to 2018. Beyond these accomplishments, she remains affiliated with various organizations in relation to her areas of expertise, including the National Women's Leadership Association and the International Women's Leadership Association. Ms. Brady is also a member of Alpha Phi Omega, a national co-ed service fraternity that provides myriad opportunities for college students in such areas as community service, leadership development and social endeavors.

Recognized among the Top Female Executives, Professionals & Entrepreneurs by Worldwide Branding and featured in Pro-Files Magazine in 2016, Ms. Brady is proud of her achievement in building the first Citrix server for PruittHealth, allowing better communication within the different divisions of the company and the information technology department. An expert communicator who can speak with people at all levels, she has also noted that she was often the only woman in the room while working in the field of information technology, allowing her to compete in a more challenging environment that allowed her to become more well-rounded as a professional. Looking toward the future, Ms. Brady plans to continue to grow within PruittHealth while learning as much as she can about the process of recruiting and going above and beyond to help others.

A Lifetime of Achievement in **Business Services**

Stephen B. Friedheim

Educational Consultant

Founder
Education Systems & Solutions, Inc.

DALLAS, TX UNITED STATES

Stephen B. Friedheim celebrates an eclectic career that has spanned more than 60 years, taking him from radio broadcasting in the late 1950s to educational consulting in the present day. Inspired by his father, an executive vice president of ZIV Television, he pursued his Bachelor of Arts in both theater and radio production from the University of Arkansas. Upon graduating in 1956, Mr. Friedheim aligned with station KBRS in Springfield, Arkansas, as a radio announcer. He transitioned to news broadcasting the following year, working in Joplin, Missouri, for station KZRG, formerly known as station KFSB, until he enlisted in the U.S. Army. Mr. Friedheim left the armed forces after four years of service, whereupon he accepted a position as the director of public relations for the American Counseling Association from 1961 to 1966.

Leveraging his certification as an association executive, Mr. Friedheim went on to occupy leadership roles for much of his career, garnering a laudable reputation as the vice president of the American Society of Medical Technology from 1966 to 1976, the president of the Association of Independent Colleges and Schools from 1976 to 1984, and as the senior vice president of Campbell Communications, a position he held concurrently with a similar role for King Education Services. At this time, he was also the president of the ESS College of Business in Dallas, Texas, from 1984 to 2001. Upon concluding his appointment there, he found success as the vice president of public relations for the College of American Services, Inc., from 2001 to 2011. During this time, Mr. Friedheim founded and remains active with Education Systems & Solutions, Inc., a consultation company that provides institutions of higher learning with curriculum development and accreditation services.

Highly sought after in his field, Mr. Friedheim has lent his expertise to companies such as South-Western Publishing Co., Richard D. Irwin, Inc., Johnson & Wales University, the KD Studio Actors Conservatory, and Vatterott College. He has also contributed his time and efforts to various organizations, serving on the board of directors of St. Aidan's School in Virginia from 1979 to 1982 and the Trinity River Arts Center from 2002 to 2006, as well as maintaining involvement as a highly placed member of the Workforce Development Board of Dallas County from 1996 to 2001 and acting as the vice chairman for Workforce Leadership Texas from 2000 to 2001. Mr. Friedheim further served as a trustee for Dollars for Scholars from 1982 to 1984, a vestryman for Ascension Episcopal Church in Houston, Texas, and in various leadership positions for the Texas Discovery Gardens. Over the years, he has also been a member and served on the boards of numerous pertinent societies, including the American Vocational Association, the Career College Association, the National Alliance of Business, the Work Force Commission Creative Service and the Career Training Foundation. Well-regarded as an expert in his industry, Mr. Friedheim found additional success as an editor for The Lead Generation and the Texas Times.

For Mr. Friedheim's earlier service in the armed forces and as a radio broadcaster, he was the two-time recipient of an award from the Freedoms Foundation, and a broadcasting award from the American Legion Auxiliary in 1963. His accomplishments and leadership have earned him inclusion in numerous editions of Who's Who in America, including the 73rd edition, Who's Who in American Education, Who's Who in the South and Southwest, and Who's Who in the World. Mr. Friedheim has also been honored with the Albert Nelson Marquis Lifetime Achievement Award, presented to individuals who have made extraordinary achievements in their industry. He is happily married to his wife of 35 years, Jan, with whom he has three children. Together, they have welcomed three grandchildren into their family.

A Lifetime of Achievement in **Business Services**

Jack Papageorgis

Small Business Owner
PATERSON, NJ UNITED STATES

Jack Papageorgis has overcome numerous challenges to build a successful career as a small business owner, establishing himself as a dedicated and hardworking leader in his industry.

Originally a native of Greece, he relocated to the United States in 1951 with little money and an incomplete high school education. That same year, Mr. Papageorgis accepted the position of a general helper at Libby's Lunch, a diner located in Paterson, New Jersey, that is beloved for its hot dogs, burgers and American cuisine. As he progressed within the company, he found success in the posts of a cook, a counterman, and a manager until his departure in 1963. Mr. Papageorgis later excelled as the co-owner, the secretary, and the treasurer of the Libby's A Corporation in Paterson, further advancing to the position of the president between 1963 and 1985.

Subsequently, Mr. Papageorgis worked as an officer for the Passaic County Sheriff's Department in Paterson, New Jersey, from 1985 to 1988. After a two-year break, he was hired by the Division of Youth and Family Services in Newton-Pompton Lakes, New Jersey, contributing as a family service specialist between 1990 and 1992. Moreover, Mr. Papageorgis has found success as a food service associate with Sodexho-Marriott at William Paterson University in Wayne, New Jersey, since 1993. For his achievements with the aforementioned company, he was the recipient of an award.

In the midst of his career, Mr. Papageorgis earned a Bachelor of Science from Seton Hall University in South Orange, New Jersey, in 1974 — an accomplishment made even more notable by the fact that he had arrived in the United States without finishing his high school diploma or mastering the English language. Soon thereafter, he graduated from Fairleigh Dickinson University in Teaneck, New Jersey, with a Master of Business Administration in 1978. After receiving a certification in international business from Seton Hall University in 1983, Mr. Papageorgis concluded his academic pursuits with a Master of Business Administration from the aforementioned institution in 1987. As he looks back on a lifetime of success, he credits his achievements to the quality education he received, specifically his time at Seton Hall University. Guiding Mr. Papageorgis along his professional journey was Denis Kapas, a coworker who encouraged him to finish his schooling and assisted him in mastering the English language.

Civically, Mr. Papageorgis has remained active in several organizations that keep him in touch with his Greek heritage. A member of the American Hellenic Educational Progressive Association, he received the organization's 25th anniversary award in 1992. Mr. Papageorgis has also contributed his leadership abilities and talents as the secretary and the vice president of the Pan-Zakynthian Brotherhood. Additionally, he has been an active member of Saint Nicholas Greek Orthodox Church since 1970. An exceptionally distinguished Marquis listee, Mr. Papageorgis has been selected for numerous editions of Who's Who in America and Who's Who in the World. He has further been designated as a recipient of the prestigious Albert Nelson Marquis Lifetime Achievement Award, presented to individuals who have demonstrated extraordinary dedication to their field.

Mr. Papageorgis was born in Gaitani on the island of Zakynthos in Greece on February 19, 1933, to Anastasios and Eftihia Papageorgis. He is the proud father of Marie and doting grandfather of Katie and Jack. In his free time, Mr. Papageorgis enjoys jogging, reading and investing.

A Lifetime of Achievement in **Business Services**

Sanghyun Park

Management Consultant
Seoul Credit Guarantee Foundation

SEOUL, SOUTH KOREA

Supported by 30 years of professional excellence, Sanghyun Park currently works as a management consultant with the Seoul Credit Guarantee Foundation, a professional role he has remained in since 2011. At the start of his career, he accrued valuable expertise with Korea Marvel Co., Ltd., now Hansol Technics Co., Ltd., from 1987 to 1990, Samsung Kloeckner Co., Ltd., Samsung Heavy Industries Co., Ltd., from 1990 to 2001, and JMI Co., Ltd. (Jeongmoon Information Co., Ltd., JMI SK s.r.o., Pishionsys Co., Ltd.) from 2003 to 2010.

Over the years, Mr. Park provided consulting services for such organizations as the Ministry of SMEs and Startups, the Small Enterprise and Market Service, the Korean Institute for Advancement of Technology, the Korea Foundation for Cooperation of Large and Small Business, Rural Affairs, and the Korea Institute of Marine Science & Technology Promotion. He has also dedicated his time and consulting knowledge to serving the Institute for Information and Communications Technology Promotion, the Foundation of Agri. Tech. Commercialization & Transfer, and the Korea Creative Content Agency.

In addition, Mr. Park has been a consultant for the Korea Technology & Information Promotion Agency for SMEs in 2009, the Disabled Enterprise Business Center in 2010, the Korea Institute of Start-up and Entrepreneurship Development in 2010 and the Korea Agro-Fisheries & Food Trade Corporation in 2010 and 2012. In 2015, he lent his expertise as a strategic trade consulting expert with the Korea Strategic Trade Institute. Notably, his first professional role was as a member of the Korea Management and Technology Consultant Association, a position he held for one year in 2007.

Before establishing himself as a trusted voice in the field, Mr. Park prepared for his professional path through the pursuit of a formal education at various esteemed academic institutions in Seoul, the Republic of Korea. He first attended Kookmin University and earned a bachelor's degree in Korean history in 1987, having previously graduated from Kyungdong High School in 1980. He continued his studies at the National Institute for Lifelong Education, where he obtained a bachelor's degree in accounting in 2009. He remained at the same school and ultimately achieved a Bachelor of Business Administration in 2010. Prior to his academic career, he served in the Korean Army, Capital Mechanized Infantry Division, from 1982 to 1984.

The highlight of his career thus far has been creating nearly 3,000 management-consulting reports for self-employed businesses as well as small and medium-sized businesses in the Seoul Credit Guarantee Foundation. Additionally, Mr. Park holds a plethora of certifications as a management consultant registered in the Ministry of SMEs and Startups, including a certificate in management consulting and technology consulting in 2007, a certificate in treasury management in 2010, and a certificate in ERP training in 2010. He further earned certification as a small and medium-sized enterprises financial adviser through the Korea Banking Institute in 2014 and an industry security expert through the Korea Association of Industrial Technology Security in 2011.

Mr. Park was born on February 1, 1961, in the Republic of Korea to mother Hyunkyoun Oh and father Kwansoo Park. He later married Hyejung Kim on March 7, 1994, and together, they are the proud parents of three children, one son named Namjoon Park and twin daughters named Seonwoo Park and Seonmin Park. In his free time, he enjoys participating in such activities as reading and watching movies. Looking toward the future, Mr. Park intends to experience the continued growth and success of his career with the Seoul Credit Guarantee Foundation.

A Lifetime of Achievement in **Business Services**

Alan M. Siegel

President & Chief Executive Officer
Siegelvision
NEW YORK, NY UNITED STATES

Alan M. Siegel is the founder, president and chief executive officer of Siegelvision, a New York City-based, award-winning brand identity and communications consultancy established in 2011. Siegelvision strives to solve tough branding and communications problems for purpose-driven organizations. Some of the brand identity and voice programs his firm have created include NPR, National Geographic, the Lupus Foundation, City University of New York, Cornell College of Engineering, John Jay College of Criminal Justice, the IRS, Fannie Mae, AeroVironment, Inc., Fidelity & Guaranty Life Insurance, The College Board, the Tony Awards and K2 Intelligence.

As a longtime marketing, communications and design consultant, and a leader in his field, Mr. Siegel founded Siegel+Gale Inc., where he served as chairman and chief executive officer from 1969 to 2011. Having popularized the concept of a brand voice back in the 1980s, he later championed the internet as a powerful tool for this concept in the 1990s. Some of the companies he has designed for over the years include Xerox, American Express, Caterpillar, 3M, the Girl Scouts, the NBA, MLB, the Rockefeller Group, Mastercard, Prudential, UnitedHealth, Harley-Davidson, The College Board, Mount Sinai Medical Center, AARP, the U.S. Air Force, and Carnegie Mellon University in Pittsburgh, among hundreds of other recognizable brands.

Mr. Siegel helped pioneer the plain English movement in business and government in the early 1970s, was an adjunct associate professor at Fordham University School of Law in New York City, where he taught a groundbreaking course on writing contracts in plain English, and an adjunct associate professor and co-director of the Communications Design Center at Carnegie Mellon University, where he taught a graduate program focusing on simplifying complex legal, technical, business and medical communications. He has also served on the executive committee for the Document Design Project at the National Institute of Education and was chairman of the advisory board of the College of Architecture, Arts and Planning at Cornell University. Prior to founding Siegel+Gale, Mr. Siegel worked as an account executive for Sandgren and Murtha, Inc., a corporate identity firm; Ruder Finn Inc., a public relations firm; and as an account executive and secretary for the new products development group at Batten, Barton, Durstine & Osborn, a leading advertising agency, between 1964 and 1969.

Mr. Siegel co-authored several books, including "Simple: Conquering the Crisis of Complexity" in 2013, "Writing Contracts in Plain English" in 1981, "The Wall Street Journal Guide to Money and Markets" in 1989, "The Wall Street Journal Guide to Personal Finance" in 1992, "The Wall Street Journal Guide to Understanding Money and Investments" in 1993, "The Wall Street Journal Guide to Understanding Taxes" in 1994 and contributed articles to many professional journals. His new book, "Voice Lessons," will be released in 2019. In addition to his writings, Mr. Siegel's TED Talk on simplification has been viewed by over 1 million people.

Mr. Siegel is a member of the Authors Guild, the University Club of New York, NationSwell, and The Paley Center for Media. He has served on numerous boards including the International Center of Photography, the Museum of Modern Art's photography department, the John Jay College of Criminal Justice, the American Theatre Wing's Tony Awards, and the Nathaniel Wharton Fund for Research and Education in Brain, Body and Behavior, as well as Common Good. While serving on the board of directors with The Legal Aid Society, he developed a brand identity program for them.

Honored numerous times throughout his career, Mr. Siegel recently received Transform Awards in both 2016 and 2018. He also received Design Value Awards from the Design Management Institute in 2012, 2015 and 2018. He was recognized by the city of New York for contributions to the city in 2013. Other awards include the Rebrand 100 Award in 2009, the GCS Education Award in 2011, the Lupus Foundation

Visionary Award in 2015, The Legal Aid Society Award in 2009, Museum of Arts & Design Visionary Award in 2008, and the Girl Scouts Leadership Award in 2014. He has notably been cited in several editions of Who's Who in America and Who's Who in the World.

First acquiring a Bachelor of Science from the School of Industrial and Labor Relations at Cornell University in 1960, where he was a member of the ROTC from 1956 to 1960, Mr. Siegel then attended New York University School of Law in 1961. After serving as a first lieutenant in the U.S. Army in an 8" Howitzer Battalion stationed in Germany, between 1961 and 1962, he continued his education at Alexey Brodovitch's Design Laboratory and in an advanced photography program at The New School for Social Research.

Mr. Siegel attributes his success to a combination of a passion for simplifying complexities, a problem-solving mentality, a challenging conventional wisdom, and a deep-seated commitment to learning and growing. Reflecting on his career, he recognizes that he took on the most challenging assignments and was committed to bold and memorable solutions. Moreover, he always recruited a true interdisciplinary team of writers, strategists, graphic designers, advertising and digital media professionals. Together, they constantly break new ground and challenge conventional patterns of behavior. He is proud of conquering the crisis of complexity that plagues communications. His mantra: Clarity Above All.

An expert in the field, Mr. Siegel considers himself to be accomplished at defining what is unique, relevant and compelling for corporations, products and services. He is also skilled at simplifying complexities in business, government and academic communications. Over the course of his career, he has learned many skills that have benefitted his professional growth, including how to assemble effective teams of professionals, how to evaluate the impact of solutions, and how to constantly grow and improve. He is grateful for the mentorship of the famous Russian design director Alexey Brodovitch.

Einstein expressed his guiding philosophy when he said, "Try not to become a man of success, but rather try to become a man of value." This reflects how Mr. Siegel hopes to be remembered by his peers. Born in New York City, he married Gloria Fern Mendel in 1965 and recently celebrated their 54th wedding anniversary. He is the proud father of one child, Stacey Siegel, and grandfather of two, Leo Bloom and Ruby Bloom.

Among his many interests, Mr. Siegel enjoys reading, playing tennis, rowing, swimming, attending the theater, classical music concerts and modern dance. He is a distinguished collector of photography. He curated his collection for a show at the Johnson Museum of Art at Cornell University that was developed into the book, "One Man's Eye," published by Abrams. He also curated a photography show at the International Center of Photography highlighting the circus photography of Edward J. Kelty that was also developed into a book, "Step Right This Way," published by Barnes & Noble.

A Lifetime of Achievement in **Community / Social Work / Nonprofit**

In Memoriam

Stephen Robert Cohen

Founder & President (Retired)
Jewish Foundation for Group Homes
CHEVY CHASE, MD UNITED STATES

Prior to his passing in 2020, Stephen Robert Cohen enjoyed a prolific career, with achievements in both the professional and civic world. In 1990, he served as the founder and owner of Cosons, following a successful tenure at the Stewart Petroleum Corporation as a senior sales representative in Washington, D.C. Earlier in his career, Mr. Cohen thrived as the sales manager at Amerada Hess, located in Landover, Maryland, from 1962 to 1979, and as a secretary at a Washington, D.C., fuel company from 1949 to 1962.

Among Mr. Cohen's greatest accomplishments was founding the Jewish Foundation for Group Homes in 1982. He also lent his leadership expertise to the nonprofit as its second president. The organization presently supports more than 200 individuals in over 80 sites throughout the Washington, D.C., metropolitan area who suffer from intellectual disabilities, mobility impairments, deafness or hearing loss, visual deficiencies, chronic mental illness, communication disorders or other developmental disabilities. The headquarters, located in Rockville, Maryland, is currently located in a building named after Cohen and his wife, and he is further commemorated by the S. Robert Cohen Award, presented annually at the organization's gala.

Outside of his professional endeavors, Mr. Cohen volunteered his time and efforts to numerous civic organizations. In 1982, he served on the board of directors of the Jewish Social Service Agency, an organization providing hospice care, senior services, and counseling throughout Montgomery County, Maryland, and as the president of the Jewish Foundation for Group Homes from 1982 to 1984. Mr. Cohen has been further affiliated with the Bender JCC of Greater Washington from 1980 to 1982 and the Hebrew Home of Greater Washington. He also served as a co-honoree of the housing opportunities commission of Montgomery County, Maryland, in 1986.

Mr. Cohen has been recognized on numerous occasions for his many achievements and contributions. He was named to the Housing Honor Roll by the Housing Opportunity Commission in Montgomery County, Maryland, in 1985, and the recipient of an award from the Hebrew Home for the Aged in 1986, the distinguished service award by the National Governments Association in Traverse City, Michigan, the Joseph Ottenstein Award from the Jewish Social Service Agency in 1988, and a humanitarian award from Jewish service organization B'nai B'rith. Mr. Cohen was further named the Washingtonian of the Year by Washingtonian Magazine in 1986, presented to residents making a difference, as well as recognized as the recipient of a JCC Award and the Jewish Community Relations Council Award. His achievements have also earned him inclusion in the 22nd edition of Who's Who in the East, published in 1988.

Prior to embarking on his professional career, Mr. Cohen earned a Bachelor of Science in economics at the prestigious Wharton School of the University of Pennsylvania, located in Philadelphia, in 1949. He was born on April 2, 1927, in Washington, D.C., to Aaron N. and Bessie Gensberg Cohen. Prior to his passing, Mr. Cohen and his wife, Joy A. Weiss, had been happily married for more than 60 years and enjoyed living in Maryland. Together, they were the proud parents of five children: Barry (Kamal), Alan, Brian (Madeleine), Douglas (Sheri) and Daniel. They were also the doting grandparents of one grandson, Samuel Alexander Cohen, and one granddaughter, Sunitha Cohen Barron (Joshua). Well-regarded for his kind and approachable nature, Mr. Cohen's nickname was "the doughnut man," a moniker he earned because of his affinity for delivering donuts to his friends.

A Lifetime of Achievement in **Community / Social Work / Nonprofit**

Steven L. Martinson, MSW

Health Services Administrator (Retired)

ROCKLIN, CA UNITED STATES

A dept in the areas of substance abuse, social services and health services administration, Steven L. Martinson, MSW, began his professional career as an assistant at Florida State University in 1972, remaining in this position for two years before joining the Kern View Community Mental Health Center and Hospital in Bakersfield, California. He worked for the center as a social worker and mental health counselor from 1974 to 1975, and from 1975 to 1976, he served the Kern County Department of Mental Health as a mental health planning analyst. Achieving great success with the department, Mr. Martinson rose to the position of the manager of the drug division, where he was responsible for the administration of nearly $1 million in program funds for Kern County's drug abuse programs until 1989. From 1989 to 1994, he continued to serve the Kern County Department of Mental Health as the mental health division manager and the Kern County alcohol and drug administrator, where he was responsible for more than $7 million in program funds, as well as developing and presenting the county budget for substance abuse services in coordination with the chief financial officer.

Mr. Martinson pioneered a new trend in media-based substance abuse prevention, or life skills marketing. The project was predicated upon the belief that advertising can be effective in prevention of substance abuse, but, if it is going to compete in the marketing world, we had to play by the rules of corporate advertising. Prevention commercials had to be fun, exciting and enticing, creating the desire in the youth to "buy" a lifestyle that was free from alcohol and drugs. Kern County used both local and national talent in achievement of that goal.

MC Hammer granted the county video rights to his No. 1 hit song, "U Can't Touch This," and the Baker Boys, a local rap group, wrote a rap that was in the top five most requested songs on KKXX, a local radio station, for several weeks in a row. Kern County's radio and TV productions encompassed any number of subjects ranging from roller-blading, mountain biking and dancing to school projects and academic subjects, choosing partners who are alcohol and drug free, water sports and enjoying family, and child care free from substance abuse. One "commercial" appeared during a Super Bowl, and the program won numerous advertising awards locally and nationally for quality in advertising, including the "Grand Pizazz," several Addys, a Telly Award from National Independent Advertisers, and an Emmy.

One component of the Kern County Life Skills Development Project designed by Mr. Martinson included teaching youth between the ages of 9 and 18 how to feel good about what they do and who they are. The goal of this part of the program was to teach the youth to change their attitudes on how they saw themselves. However, rather than attempting to change their self-esteem, the program taught them how to act, dress, talk and, eventually, think like a success. In the first year pilot, this part of the program was implemented in a local continuation high school and resulted in a decline in the dropout rate from 40% to 10% with an average of 1 point increase in grade point average. As a result of this success, the program was adopted by all high schools in Kern County.

Following his departure from the Kern County Department of Mental Health, Mr. Martinson transitioned to Placer County Health and Human Services, leveraging his experience and expertise as a social service practitioner in the division of alcohol, drugs and tobacco for two years. In 1996, he accepted the post of a client services program supervisor and program evaluator for the Children's System of Care, where he was responsible for designing and implementing comprehensive evaluation, data collection and analysis systems. Over the course of nearly 20 years, he worked to integrate the department's substance abuse, child welfare and probation services. In 2015, he retired from his full-time professional endeavors.

Inspired by the poem "Invictus," by William Ernest Henley, Mr. Martinson was particularly influenced by the line "Out of the night that covers me, black as the pit from pole to pole, I thank whatever gods may be for my unconquerable soul." He places great importance on self-confidence, and believes in the importance of persistence and dedication to one's values. Prior to the start of his career, Mr. Martinson pursued his formal education at the University of Minnesota, earning a Bachelor of Arts in 1971. He then matriculated at Florida State University in Tallahassee, where he earned a Master of Social Work in 1974. Since his graduation, Mr. Martinson has leveraged his expertise in his written work, contributing myriad articles to professional journals.

Outside of his primary trade, Mr. Martinson maintains involvement with a number of organizations related to his field, including holding a lifetime membership to Optimists International. Previously, he was also affiliated with the Association of California Drug Abuse Program Coordinators and the National Association of Social Workers. In light of Mr. Martinson's exceptional undertakings, Kern County was awarded a $1.4 million federal building grant for construction of a new Mental Health Services building in 1975, and, as noted above, has received an Emmy Award in 1993 for his substance abuse prevention commercials. He created the fourth largest drug court in the United States, as well as the Together We Can community mobilization project, a community based planning and development process. Furthermore, Mr. Martinson was selected for inclusion in the first edition of Who's Who of Emerging Leaders in America, the 20th edition of Who's Who in the West and was a recipient of the Albert Nelson Marquis Lifetime Achievement Award in 2017.

Now enjoying his retirement, Mr. Martinson is married to his loving wife of 50 years, Kathleen Ann Peterson Martinson, with whom he participated in his proudest accomplishment, raising four wonderful children. His oldest son, Eric Beowulf, holds a doctorate in engineering and computer science; his second son, Matthew Tor, holds a Bachelor of Arts in digital art and animation; and his daughter, Kira, holds an Associate of Arts in fashion design and a Bachelor of Arts in business administration and marketing, and currently works in analytics and statistics. Mr. Martinson is additionally the father of one late son, Michael Odin, who passed away due to complications from autism. In his leisure time, he plays the guitar, takes photographs and spends time with his friends.

Mr. Martinson advises others who are looking to enter his field to follow their own dreams, take every opportunity that they see and always question what they hear. He attributes his success to his respect for others, and believes in participatory management. There is always more than one way to get a job done, and he knows that even though he may have one idea, his proposed method may not always be the most effective. Mr. Martinson has always been known for his quick wit and keen sense of humor.

A Lifetime of Achievement in **Community / Social Work / Nonprofit**

Carole Lynne Morrison

Community Volunteer

ROSE HILL, KS UNITED STATES

With more than 30 years of experience to her credit, Carole Lynne Morrison is currently retired, having excelled as a paraprofessional at Rose Hill High School from 1991 to 2007. Prior to this appointment, she held the position of a volunteer at Rose Hill High School and Elementary School from 1988 to 1991. She further worked as a volunteer and an aide for the Burlington Elementary School in Longmont, Colorado, between 1980 and 1987. Ms. Morrison additionally excelled as a bookkeeper for Dan's Nautilus and the Citizen Newspaper in 1980 and 1978, respectively.

Previously, Ms. Morrison served at the Mountain States Children's Home as a secretary and a bookkeeper from 1969 to 1976. Moreover, she was active as a switchboard operator for Zellner Hall at Abilene Christian University from 1967 to 1969. She began her career as a food server for Catchings Cafeteria at the aforementioned university from 1964 to 1967. During this time, Ms. Morrison pursued an education at Abilene Christian University, earning a Bachelor of Science in education in 1969.

Beyond her responsibilities within the field, Ms. Morrison has participated in numerous endeavors outside of her professional circles. From 2009 to 2015, she contributed as a ladies Bible class teacher in Andover, Kansas. A parent volunteer for the school improvement leadership team at Rose Hill High School from 1993 to 2000, she flourished as a volunteer for the clothing giveaway program from 2015 to 2019. Ms. Morrison found success as a speaker and lecturer as well, providing her wealth of knowledge at retreats and lectureships for the Akron Church of Christ in 1994, the Winfield Church of Christ in 1995, the Andover Church of Christ in 1995, and the Rose Hill Public Library board of directors from 2009 to 2015.

In addition to her primary vocation, Ms. Morrison remains affiliated with various organizations in relation to her areas of expertise. Since 1987, she has maintained her involvement as a Bible class teacher with the Andover Church of Christ. She was also associated with the Longmont Church of Christ from 1974 to 1987 in the same capacity. Furthermore, Ms. Morrison was a volunteer for the Rose Hill Stoll Media Center in 1987 and the Rose Hill Community Library from 2004 to 2009, for which she was the vice president from 2005 to 2009.

In light of her exceptional undertakings, Ms. Morrison has accrued several accolades throughout her impressive career. In 1983, she was recognized as an Outstanding Young Woman in America. Likewise, Ms. Morrison was selected for inclusion in the 22nd edition of Who's Who of American Women and multiple editions of the Who's Who in the Midwest.

Inspired to become an educator by her mother, Calvena Hastings, who wanted her to seek a higher education despite not having the resources to do so, Ms. Morrison recalls her experiences in the classroom, including staying after school, cleaning the chalkboard, and grading papers, to have cemented the direction of her career. Enjoying helping people, she was motivated by a number of mentors, including her father, Joseph Hastings, her sister, Anne Reid, Janie Barnard and Blanche Boggs. She is especially proud of her two wonderful children, Brett and Brian, who have become active, productive citizens. Looking toward the future, Ms. Morrison hopes to continue enjoying her retirement while spending time with her growing family.

A Lifetime of Achievement in **Community / Social Work / Nonprofit**

Ruth D. Sanchez-Way, PhD, MSW

Public Health Administrator

SHADY SIDE, MD UNITED STATES

With nearly 40 years of professional experience to her credit, Ruth D. Sanchez-Way, PhD, MSW, most recently found success as a grant reviewer for the U.S. Department of Health and Human Services and the vice president of training and community development at Management Sciences for Development, a consulting firm, from 2003 to 2010. Prior to obtaining these roles, she was the associate director of the Center for Faith-Based and Community Initiatives at the HHS from 2002 to 2003 and the director of the Center for Substance Abuse Prevention with the Substance Abuse and Mental Health Services Administration of the HHS from 2000 to 2002, a position she considers to be a career highlight. Previously, she was the acting director of the Center for Substance Abuse Prevention from 1997 to 1998, having been the acting deputy director in 1997.

From 1991 to 1997, Dr. Sanchez-Way thrived as the division director of state and community development at the Center for Substance Abuse Prevention, and from 1993 to 1996, she also served in a dual capacity as the associate administrator of minority health concerns at the Substance Abuse and Mental Health Services Administration. Previously serving as the deputy director of adolescent pregnancy programs at the HHS from 1985 to 1991, she was the associate deputy administrator of equal employment opportunity with the Office of the Assistant Secretary of Health, HHS, from 1979 to 1985. Earlier in her career, Dr. Sanchez-Way contributed as a special assistant to the director and as a public health adviser with the National Institute on Alcohol Abuse and Alcoholism at the HHS from 1971 to 1979.

Dr. Sanchez-Way began her career as a student at St. John's University in New York City, where she obtained a Bachelor of Science in chemistry in 1962. Motivated by a desire to help others, she decided to follow in the footsteps of her mother, a social worker. After she took a position at Catholic Charities of New York, the organization encouraged her to pursue a Master of Social Work, which she obtained at Fordham University in New York in 1965 prior to earning a Doctor of Philosophy in public administration from New York University in 1978.

Dr. Sanchez-Way was selected to participate in the highly competitive first HHS Senior Executive Service Candidate Development Program in 1981 to 1983. She later received certificates in management development from Emory University in Atlanta in 1981, from the Interagency Institute for Federal Health Care Executives at The George Washington University in Washington, D.C., in 1993, and from the Public Health Service Primary Care Fellowship in 1996. She has also been licensed as a certified social worker in the states of New York and Maryland, and a certified prevention professional by the Maryland Association of Prevention Professionals and Advocates, and by the Academy of Certified Social Workers, National Association of Social Workers. Furthermore, Dr. Sanchez-Way was awarded an honorary Doctor of Humane Letters from Fordham University in 2006, the first social worker to receive this recognition.

To stay up to date with changes in the field, Dr. Sanchez-Way maintains membership with the National Association of Social Workers. Outside of her professional responsibilities, she has lent her expertise to many related organizations. She has served on numerous nonprofit boards and advisory committees such as the Lions Quest Program Advisory Committee for the Lions Clubs International Foundation in Oak Brook, Illinois; the National Health Council and the National Organization on Adolescent Pregnancy, Parenting and Prevention in Washington, D.C.; the National Council on Alcoholism and Drug Dependence in New York City; and the Catholic Charities of the Archdiocese of Washington.

Dr. Sanchez-Way currently serves on the Friends of Pax Lodge Committee of the World Foundation for Girl Guides and Girl Scouts, as a national volunteer partner for the Girl Scouts of the USA, and on the executive committee of the Chesapeake Yacht Club Ladies' Auxiliary.

Previously, she has also been active as a disaster volunteer with the American Red Cross of Central Maryland and on the pastoral council and Women's Guild as treasurer for Our Lady of Sorrows Church in West River, Maryland.

For her many accomplishments in the field, Dr. Sanchez-Way has been recognized with the Excellence in Government Service Award from the Mexican American Legal Defense and Educational Fund, the Presidential Meritorious Executive Rank Award and the Secretary's Award for Distinguished Service from the Department of Health and Human Services. Her professional leadership and excellence have also earned her inclusion in numerous honors publications, including multiple editions of Who's Who in America, Who's Who in Medicine and Healthcare, Who's Who in Science and Engineering, Who's Who in the East, Who's Who in the World and Who's Who of American Women. She is also a recipient of the prestigious Albert Nelson Marquis Lifetime Achievement Award. A New York City native, Dr. Ruth Sanchez-Way currently resides in Maryland and Arizona with her husband, David V. Way. In her free time, she enjoys traveling around the world, sailing, skiing, Jazzercise and reading mystery books.

A Lifetime of Achievement in **Community / Social Work / Nonprofit**

James E. Smith, MSW, MPA, PhD, LSCSW

Professor
Washburn University
TOPEKA, KS UNITED STATES

James E. Smith, MSW, MPA, PhD, LSCSW, has dedicated his career to helping others, as well as equipping students with the tools and knowledge they need to do the same. Supported by 25 years of educational experience, he currently works as a tenured professor at Washburn University, where he teaches graduate classes in the clinical practice of social work, advises students regarding classes and scheduling, and maintains a scholarship and a research program. At the beginning of his teaching career in the early 1990s, Dr. Smith was an adjunct professor at Kansas State University in the department of sociology, anthropology and social work. Over the years, he found success through his work in academia as an adjunct professor with the University of Alaska Fairbanks and as a full-time tenured associate professor of social work at the University of Wyoming.

Dr. Smith served with distinction in the Medical Service Corps of the U.S. Army as an active duty social work officer from 1978 until his honorable discharge from active service in 1993. Serving with the 1st Infantry Division, also known as "The Big Red One," with division mental health, he was deployed to Saudi Arabia and Kuwait for Operations Desert Shield and Desert Storm between December 19, 1990, and May 13, 1991. He served an additional 10 years in two combat stress control detachments for the U.S. Army Reserve until his retirement from the military in 2003. In his 25 years of military service, he rose in rank from commissioned first lieutenant, through Army ROTC, to lieutenant colonel at the time of his retirement. Dr. Smith has provided his considerable knowledge to the U.S. Army in executive positions regarding community mental health, human resources, family support and social work services.

Post military retirement, he has additionally excelled in private social work practice, first as an adult psychotherapist with Pawnee Mental Health Services in Junction City, Kansas, and as a marriage and family therapist with the Psychology Clinic LLC and the Alliance for Growth: Counseling & Consulting LLC, both in Laramie, Wyoming. In preparation for his career, Dr. Smith earned a Bachelor of Arts from Hampton University, a Master of Social Work from Virginia Commonwealth University, a Master of Public Administration from the University of La Verne, and a Doctor of Philosophy in family life education and consultation from Kansas State University.

A renowned expert in his field, Dr. Smith has given presentations around the world, speaking on the relationship between physical illness and emotions in Canada, multicultural competence in social work practice in Australia, and emotional intelligence and professional learning through the use of narrative journaling with social work students for interpersonal and intrapersonal professional academic and practice competence in Oregon and Spain. Throughout his career, he has also authored and co-authored articles such as "Social Work Standards Competence: A Model for Global Community Engagement," "Development of Emotional Intelligence in First-Year Undergraduate Students in a Frontier State" and "The Change Agency of Emotional Connectedness: The Link Between Emotions, Emotional Intelligence and Spirituality." In addition, Dr. Smith has been featured in a number of publications, including the Journal of Social Work Values and Ethics and the International Journal of the Humanities.

Outside of his professional work, Dr. Smith has served on the finance subcommittee of the Kansas Medical Education Foundation board of directors since 2009 and is a valued member of the Man's School Mentorship Program. In the past, he has also contributed to several of Washburn University's committees. He has been an active member of the board of directors of Valeo Behavioral Health Care, a community mental health organization in Topeka, Kansas, since 2012. In order to remain aware of changes in the industry, he maintains his affiliation with the Academy of Certified Social Workers, the National

Council of African American Men, the Society of Spirituality in Social Work and the National Association of Social Workers. Looking toward the future, Dr. Smith intends to retire, but still teach in a limited capacity at Washburn University.

Due to his outstanding work in academia, Dr. Smith was inducted into the honor societies of Kappa Omicron Nu, the National Honor Society for the Human Sciences; the Phi Alpha Honor Society for Social Work; the Phi Beta Delta Honor Society for International Scholars; and the National Society of Scabbard and Blade, a military honor society. Additionally, he was selected for inclusion in Madison Who's Who of Executives and Professionals, Who's Who Among American Teachers and Educators, Who's Who of Emerging Leaders in America and Who's Who Among Human Services Professionals. Notably profiled in the 73rd edition of Who's Who in America, Dr. Smith has amassed a number of military awards in his 25 years of service: a Combat Medical Badge, an Expert Field Medical Badge, two Meritorious Service Medals, three Army Commendations Medals, two Army Achievement Medals, two Army Reserve Component Achievement Medals, a Southwest Asia Service Medal, a National Defense Service Medal, an Armed Forces Reserve Ribbon, an Army Service Ribbon, a Liberation of Kuwait Medal from the Kingdom of Saudi Arabia, and a Kuwait Liberation Medal from the government of Kuwait.

A Lifetime of Achievement in **Education**

Margaret Ishler Bosse, EdD

Professor Emeritus
University of Northern Iowa
SURPRISE, AZ UNITED STATES

With more than 40 years of industry experience to her credit, Margaret Ishler Bosse, EdD, has been recognized as a professor emeritus of the University of Northern Iowa in Cedar Falls since 2000. She began her teaching career as an English teacher at Bald Eagle Area High School in Pennsylvania in 1956, remaining in this position for one year before transferring to the Marion Central School District in New York from 1957 to 1959 and York Suburban High School in Pennsylvania from 1959 to 1960. Dr. Bosse served as an adjunct instructor of English at the York campus of The Pennsylvania State University from 1962 to 1964 prior to instructing at York College for one year in York, Pennsylvania. Then moving to Toledo, Ohio, she taught English in the Community and Technical College at the University of Toledo from 1966 to 1968 as an adjunct instructor. She entered the doctoral program in the College of Education at the University of Toledo and served as a graduate assistant from 1969 to 1971.

In 1972, Dr. Bosse completed her doctoral work and joined the faculty at Bowling Green State University in Ohio, moving up the ranks from an assistant professor to a professor between 1972 and 1990 and directing its field experiences and standards compliance section for five years. Continuing on her professional path, she joined the University of Northern Iowa in 1990, teaching and heading the department of curriculum and instruction for six years. Teaching curriculum and development from 1997 to 2000, she also served as the acting director of teacher education from 1998 to 1999. In addition to this tenure, Dr.

A Lifetime of Achievement | **Margaret Ishler Bosse**

Bosse served on the board of examiners for the National Council for Accreditation of Teacher Education from 1983 to 2003.

Prior to the start of her professional career, Dr. Bosse pursued a formal education at The Pennsylvania State University, earning a Bachelor of Arts in English education in 1956 and a Master of Arts in English in 1960. Following these accomplishments, she attended the University of Toledo, where she obtained a Doctor of Education in 1972. Always knowing that she wanted to be a teacher, Dr. Bosse was inspired by her mother, Margaret Fisher Hess, who was a business teacher, and her grandmother, who was an elementary school teacher.

Active in her local community, Dr. Bosse served on the board of directors at Wittenberg University in Ohio from 1984 to 1986, the Lutheran Campus Ministry in Columbus, Ohio, from 1986 to 1987, and the Lutheran Student Chapel advisory board in Bowling Green, Ohio, from 1988 to 1990. In Iowa, she was on the Christian Community Development Board in Waterloo, Iowa, from 1992 to 1996. She also chaired the task force to develop state standards for the induction of new teachers and licensure for the Iowa Department of Education. She was elected to the board of the Association of Teacher Educators in 1994 and became the national president for 1996 to 1997. A prolific writer, Dr. Bosse has co-authored four books, "Creating the Open Classroom" in 1974, "Teaching in a Competency-Based Program" in 1977, "Dynamics of Effective Teaching" and "Dynamics of Effective Secondary Teaching," totaling six editions from 1998 through 2008. Likewise, she has contributed myriad articles to professional journals in her field.

During Dr. Bosse's years as director of field experiences at Bowling Green State University — 1985 to 1990 — the college was awarded a Christa McAuliffe Showcase for Excellence Award in 1990 for its collaborative programs with area schools to enhance teacher training. Furthermore, she has been selected for inclusion in the seventh edition of Who's Who in American Education and the 26th edition of Who's Who in the Midwest, as well as in numerous editions of Who's Who in America, Who's Who in the World and Who's Who of American Women. Her accomplishments have also been commemorated with the Albert Nelson Marquis Lifetime Achievement Award. Now in retirement, Dr. Bosse resides in Arizona with her loving husband, Richard C. Bosse, and is the proud mother of two wonderful sons, Frederick and Theodore. In her free time, she enjoys traveling, playing golf and writing poetry.

A Lifetime of Achievement in **Education**

Nancy G. Boyer, PhD

Department Chair
Golden West College
FOUNTAIN VALLEY, CA UNITED STATES

Supported by more than 45 years of professional excellence in language education, Nancy G. Boyer, PhD, has worked as department chair for Golden West College in Huntington Beach, California, since 2000. She began working at this school as an English as a second language instructor in 1991. Over the years, she has served in the same role with a plethora of institutions, including the Church College of Western Samoa from 1977 to 1978, Brigham Young University-Hawaii from 1979 to 1980, Brigham Young University in Utah from 1980 to 1983, and Arkansas State University from 1983 to 1984. She later taught English as a second language at Kuwait University from 1984 to 1990 and Pasadena City College in California from 1990 to 1991.

Dr. Boyer has always wanted to be a teacher. As a child, she looked up to her aunt who was a teacher. From that time on, the only thing she had to decide was what she wanted to teach. Carrying this passion into adulthood, she sought to expand her knowledge through the pursuit of a formal education at a number of esteemed academic institutions. She first attended Oregon State University in Corvallis, Oregon. Deciding she wanted to become a Spanish teacher, she earned a Bachelor of Arts in Spanish in 1972. Upon graduating, she found that there were very few Spanish teaching jobs in Oregon.

Subsequently, Dr. Boyer decided to go to Madrid, Spain, with a friend. During her time there, she found a job teaching English as a second language. She taught at the Briam Institute/American Cultural Center from 1972 to 1973. She then returned to the United States and decided to pursue a master's degree. She continued her studies at Brigham Young University in Provo, Utah. There, she completed coursework and obtained a Master of Arts in teaching English as a second language in 1976. Ultimately, she achieved a Doctor of Philosophy in international education from the University of Southern California in 1998.

An active presence in the field, Dr. Boyer has maintained memberships with numerous prestigious organizations, including the Teachers of English to Speakers of Other Languages, now the TESOL International Association. She is further associated with the California Teachers of English to Speakers of Other Languages (CATESOL). In addition, she dedicates her time to serving her community as well. Notably, she is a member of the Huntington Beach Community Emergency Response Team.

In light of her professional successes, Dr. Boyer has gained recognition in the form of various awards and accolades. Impressively, she has previously been selected for inclusion in such honors publications as the 25th and 26th editions of Who's Who in the West. Though these acknowledgements are impressive, she considers the highlight of her career to be the work she did with her students. She is especially proud of making a positive impact on the lives of her students. She loves being in the classroom and is considering going back to volunteer at the college to spend more time in the classroom with students.

Dr. Boyer was born on July 15, 1950, in Martinez, California, to mother Esther Mabey Boyer and father John Marcus Boyer. In her free time, she enjoys participating in such activities as investing, gardening, quilting and traveling.

A Lifetime of Achievement in **Education**

D. Heyward Brock, PhD

Professor
University of Delaware
NEWARK, DE UNITED STATES

With more than 55 years of experience to his credit, D. Heyward Brock, PhD, has worked as an instructor and a professor for the University of Delaware in Newark, Delaware, since 1968, teaching classes on such subjects as literature, the culture of biomedicine, and the ethical aspects of health care, among others. During his time with the University of Delaware, he also excelled as a senior associate dean of arts and sciences from 1987 to 2001, an associate chair of the English department from 1985 to 1987, the director for the Center of Science and Culture from 1977 to 1979, and an assistant dean of arts and sciences in 1969. Moreover, he served as a professor in the department of literature at the University of Essex in Colchester, England, from 1981 to 1982. Dr. Brock began his career as an assistant instructor at the University of Kansas from 1963 to 1968.

Before embarking on his professional path, Dr. Brock pursued an education at Newberry College, earning a Bachelor of Arts in English literature in 1963. He continued his studies at the University of Kansas, obtaining a Master of Arts in English literature in 1965. Following these accomplishments, Dr. Brock concluded his academic efforts at the University of Kansas in 1969, graduating with a Doctor of Philosophy in English literature.

A Renaissance literature scholar, Dr. Brock remains affiliated with various organizations in relation to his areas of expertise. Since 2019, he has maintained his involvement with PLFB Enterprises, LLC, in the post of general manager. A member of the animal welfare committees for the DuPont Company from 1990 to 1995 and TSD Bioservices from 1991 to 2010, he was also active as the vice president of the Waves Council of Owners, Inc., from 1990 to 2005 and a member of the professional consultation committee for the Medical Center in Stanton, Delaware, from 1989 to 1994. From 1979 to 1984, Dr. Brock was a member of the National Board of Consultants and the National Endowment of the Humanities.

Beyond his responsibilities within the field, Dr. Brock has participated in numerous endeavors outside of his professional circles. He additionally contributed to the University of Delaware as the co-director of study abroad programs in Australia, New Zealand, Ireland and England, as well as the founder of the Master of Arts in liberal studies program and several undergraduate programs. Married to Patricia Lee Farmer since 1963, Dr. Brock is the proud father of three children, and has welcomed eight grandchildren and two great-grandchildren into his immediate family.

Dr. Brock found success with his creative works as well, having authored "A Ben Jonson Companion" in 1983 and both "Sign of Jonah" in 2010 and "Elsburg, USA" in 2013 under the pseudonym Jon Benon. The co-author of Ben Jonson: A Quadricentennial Bibliography, 1947-1972, in 1974 and The Ben Jonson Encyclopedia in 2016, he has edited numerous books on science and culture, penned myriad articles for professional journals, assembled a collection of short stories, and provided his skills as a consulting editor for Literature and Medicine. Currently, Dr. Brock is dedicated to writing an epistolary novel and a book on doctor and healer as well as a film on 16th and 17th century playwright Ben Jonson.

In light of his exceptional undertakings, Dr. Brock has accrued several accolades throughout his impressive career. In 1980, he accepted grants from the National Science Foundation and the National Endowment of the Humanities. A fellow of the Institute for Humanistic Computation with the National Science Foundation in 1979, he was further presented with grants from the American Philosophical Society from 1981 to 1982. Likewise, Dr. Brock was selected for inclusion in the 26th edition of Who's Who in the East and the 73rd edition of Who's Who in America.

Betty Jane Brown

President
Tehama County Board of Education

Educator (Retired)

CORNING, CA UNITED STATES

With nearly 50 years of classroom leadership to her credit, Betty Jane Brown has set herself apart as a celebrated figure in academics. The first woman in her family to earn a college degree, she was inspired to pursue a career in education after being mentored by her two aunts, one of whom was a teacher. Ms. Brown excelled during her studies, earning 150 units above her degree requirements. She graduated from California State University, Chico, with a Bachelor of Arts in education in 1956. Ms. Brown then embarked upon a fulfilling career as a teacher in the Gridley and Richfield School Districts in California. In addition to her primary responsibilities, she also served on the board of directors of the School Site Council and as a member of the County Language Arts Committee and the Learning Council.

Throughout her career, Ms. Brown has been proud of the lasting relationships she has cultivated with her students. She often reconnects with former students in adulthood who have achieved success after taking her classes. She has been grateful to provide a safe and secure learning environment for all of her students, crediting her ability to bring humor and understanding into difficult circumstances as key to her success. Her selfless contributions to education have been recognized with numerous honors. She was the recipient of the prestigious Milken Family Foundation National Educator Award in 1994 and has twice been recognized by the Tehama County Reading Council for her literacy efforts. For her leadership, professional triumphs and accomplishments, Ms. Brown was also bestowed with the Albert Nelson Marquis Lifetime Achievement Award and featured in the 73rd edition of Who's Who in America.

In her retirement, Ms. Brown continues to influence the future of education as the president of the Tehama County Board of Education. Along with her fellow board members, she plays an integral role in providing service, support and leadership to 14 local districts and schools, in addition to supervising an adult education program. As an area director of Delta Kappa Gamma, an international society for women educators, Ms. Brown also inspires academic professionals and promotes their personal growth. A lifelong learner dedicated to continual advancement, she has maintained her affiliation with the American Association of University Women and the California Retired Teachers Association.

In addition to her professional activities, Ms. Brown has been a dedicated member of her community, contributing her time and talents to the Tehama County Concert Series, the Tehama County Reading Council, the Corning Chamber of Commerce, the Tehama County Shrine Club Wives, the Maywood Women's Club and the Tehama County Red Hat Society, as well as volunteering as a Girl Scout troop leader. For the past five years, she has also served as the president of the Kelly-Griggs House Museum, an 18th century home that teaches visitors about the Victorian age, Native Americans and Tehama County. In her free time, Ms. Brown enjoys reading, biking, skiing and traveling, in addition to spending time with her family and friends.

A California native, Ms. Brown was born on April 19, 1934, to Hugh Jerry Moran and Leana Belle Dobkins Moran in Red Bluff. She and her late husband Richard Owen Brown had three daughters, Karen, Gretchen and Heidi, whom she credits as being extremely supportive and helpful over the years. Ms. Brown also has three grandchildren, Michael, Brittany and Rachelle, as well as two great-grandchildren, Madison and Grayson.

April Graham Buonamici

Elementary School and Music Educator (Retired)

BOZEMAN, MT UNITED STATES

With more than three decades of diligent service to her credit, April Graham Buonamici has influenced the lives of countless students as an educator. She is a former elementary school and music teacher who retired in 2005 after many years of finding success in the Ohio public school system. Inspired to pursue teaching by her high school English teacher, Ms. Buonamici received an education at Bowling Green State University in Ohio, earning a Bachelor of Arts in music in 1972 and a Master of Education in 1973. She is a certified music and elementary school teacher in the state of Ohio.

Ms. Buonamici began her career in 1972 as a teacher for the Toledo City Schools. She then excelled in academic positions for the Euclid City School and Lyndhurst City Schools. Taking a brief hiatus between 1976 and 1978, Ms. Buonamici traveled to Venezuela, where she taught at the Colegio Internacional Caracas, an international school that educates nursery level through grade 12 students. Upon returning to the United States, she accepted a position as a teacher at Solon City Schools in Ohio, where she thrived from 1978 until her retirement in 2005.

Certain that education is the key to everything in life, Ms. Buonamici believes in the power of lifelong learning. Throughout her career, she worked tirelessly to give her students every learning opportunity possible and to bring out the best in children. Involved in numerous extracurricular activities, she is a long-standing member of the Solon Education Association, where she notably served as the organization's president, the vice president, the grievance chairman and a trustee between 1979 and 2005. Outside of her professional endeavors, Ms. Buonamici contributed as the composer of the 1969 percussion ensemble, "Boredom." She is also the author of the 2011 book, "The Truth Behind Running for Office in America," which recounts her experience running for the Montana State House of Representatives and the lessons she learned along the way. Continually looking to give back, Ms. Buonamici is also the treasurer of the board for Liberty Place, the premiere home in Montana for people with a traumatic brain injury. Locally, she has been very active with the First Church of Christ in Painesville and Chagrin Falls, Ohio, having served as the president and on the board of directors. Likewise, Ms. Buonamici has also volunteered with the Bozeman Boy Scouts of America.

Among Ms. Buonamici's most significant accomplishments was establishing a nonprofit 501(c)(3) organization for the Montana Committee on Publication for Christian Science. For her exceptional leadership and numerous contributions to her community, she has been included in several honors publications, including multiple editions of Who's Who in America, Who's Who in American Education, Who's Who in the World and Who's Who of American Women. A prominent educator, Ms. Buonamici was also the recipient of the Albert Nelson Marquis Lifetime Achievement Award, presented to individuals who have accrued noteworthy successes in their industry.

Ms. Buonamici was born on April 16, 1950, in Maumee, Ohio, to John and Claudine Graham. Currently a Montana resident, she and her husband, James, have been married for more than 40 years and are the proud parents of three sons: Domenick, Brett and Byron. She is also the doting grandmother of one grandchild. In her free time, she loves to practice playing the piano and to go skiing.

A Lifetime of Achievement in **Education**

Judith Shulamith Langer-Surnamer Caplan

Genealogist
Up, Roots! Genealogy Services

Educator (Retired)

LONG BEACH, NY UNITED STATES

J udith Shulamith Langer-Surnamer Caplan has left her mark not only as a beloved educator, but as a noted genealogist. Prior to embarking on her professional path, she earned a Bachelor of Arts in English from Brooklyn College in June 1966. Subsequently, Ms. Caplan enrolled at Syracuse University in New York, where she obtained a master's degree in communications and television in 1968. She formally began her career as an English teacher at Andries Hudde Junior High School in Brooklyn, New York, from 1966 to 1967, later accepting the same role at George W. Wingate High School from 1969 to 1972. It was at this esteemed academic institution that Ms. Caplan met English department chairman Samuel Kostman, a mentor who helped her build and hone her teaching skills.

The aforementioned positions provided valuable experience that served Ms. Caplan well in her next post as a Hebrew teacher at the Congregation Beth Jacob in Atlanta, where she excelled from 1975 to 1977 before subsequently serving in the same post with the Congregation Shearith Israel in Atlanta between 1978 and 1979. Upon returning to New York, she continued her career as a Hebrew teacher for the Merrick Jewish Center and Temple Israel on Long Island, New York, as well as an English teacher at Far Rockaway High School in New York. Ms. Caplan concluded her professional teaching career at Springfield Gardens High School in New York, where she taught English from 1985 to 2001.

Since 1995, Ms. Caplan has thrived as a genealogist with Up, Roots! Genealogy Services in Long Beach, New York, where she offers assistance to clients all over the world who are seeking additional information on their family history. She also created The Rabbi Samuel Langer Database, a searchable online record of almost 6,000 entries detailing the people with which her father interacted and the life events he oversaw during his rabbinic career. To remain aware of changes in this field, Ms. Caplan is affiliated with the Jewish Genealogy Society of Long Island, the Jewish Genealogy Society of New York and the Association of Professional Genealogists.

Ms. Caplan has been designated as an editor emerita for the LitvakSIG Online Journal since 2009. An expert in her specialty, she has contributed her knowledge of genealogy and Jewish history via numerous published articles, including "My Hashava Experience," "1946 Medingen Mystery — and Miracle," "Another Surnamer Surfaces," "Following the Weber Trail: Of Genealogical Haystacks and Cakes," "How to Read a Hebrew Tombstone" and "What Does a Litvak Look Like?" Ms. Caplan has also offered her talents to more creative works, penning poems for several poetry publications.

Throughout her storied career, Ms. Caplan has been recognized with numerous accolades. Notably, she was presented with an award that highlighted her outstanding contributions to student editing and writing in 1988 and 1989, an award from Poet's House for excellence in teaching of poetry in 1992 and an award from JewishGen for her contributions to the success of the family tree of the Jewish people in 1999. Ms. Caplan's professional excellence and commitment to others have also been memorialized in the 57th, 58th and 73rd editions of Who's Who in America. In addition, she is the recipient of the prestigious Albert Nelson Marquis Lifetime Achievement Award.

Ms. Caplan was born on February 3, 1945, in Brooklyn, New York, to Rabbi Samuel Langer and Gladys Surnamer Langer. She is married to Neil Howard Caplan, MD, with whom she has had two children, Hillel and Baruch. The proud grandmother of nine grandchildren, Ms. Caplan credits her father for imparting in her a love for writing, and her mother for instilling in her a love of gardening and sewing as creative outlets.

A Lifetime of Achievement in **Education**

Judith Ann Caskey, EdD

Educational Director
MOUNT VERNON, TX UNITED STATES

With many years of practiced experience under her belt, Judith Ann Caskey, EdD, excels as a professional service provider for schools that are deemed academically unacceptable. At the start of her career, she joined the Waco Independent School District in Texas as a teacher. From there, she worked for Texas A&M University in College Station as a teaching assistant. Over the years, Dr. Caskey gained valuable expertise as an educator with Talents Unlimited, the Region VIII Education Service Center in Mount Pleasant, as well as with the Daingerfield, Johnson City, Bellville and College Station Independent School Districts.

Prior to establishing herself as a trusted voice in the field, Dr. Caskey sought to expand her knowledge through the pursuit of a formal education. She first attended Baylor University in Waco, where she earned a Bachelor of Science in 1969. She continued her studies at the same esteemed academic institution and obtained a Master of Science in 1970. From there, she completed postgraduate coursework at Texas A&M University from 1971 to 1976. In 2018, she enrolled as a student at Texas A&M University-Commerce, achieving a Doctor of Education in 2020. Outside of these degrees, she is certified as a supervisor and counselor, as well as in secondary education, secondary English, history, Latin and journalism in the state of Texas. She is also certified as a curriculum auditor through Curriculum Management Systems Inc.

An active presence in the field, Dr. Caskey has maintained memberships with several prestigious organizations, including the Association for Supervision and Curriculum Development, the Texas Association for Supervision and Curriculum Development, the National Council of Teachers of English, Phi Delta Kappa International and the International Legal Honor Society of Phi Delta Phi. With the Delta Kappa Gamma Society International, she served as president of the Nu chapter from 1985 to 1988 and president of the Delta and Eta chapters from 1992 to 1994 and again from 2000 to 2002. The organization honored her with an Achievement Award in 1988.

Whenever she wasn't working, Dr. Caskey gave back to those less fortunate through the Literacy Council of Daingerfield and Mount Pleasant and the Blanco County Fair & Rodeo Association. Due to her outstanding work in the field, she has previously been selected for inclusion in such honors publications as the 22nd edition of Who's Who of American Women, which was published in 2000, the 21st edition of Who's Who in the World, which was published in 2003, and the 26th edition of Who's Who in the South and Southwest, which was published in 1998. She was also featured in the 54th through 57th and 59th editions of Who's Who in America.

Dr. Caskey was born on December 3, 1947, in San Antonio, Texas, to a mother who worked as a nurse and a father who served in the Air Force. She grew up alongside one brother who is now a computer specialist. She later married Robert D. Caskey, on January 1, 1977. He was a teacher, athletic director and principal. Together, they are the proud parents of one child named Kyle, who now works as a football coach and is married to an occupational therapist. Moreover, they have two grandchildren named Olsen and Kolten. In her free time, she enjoys participating in such activities as reading, cooking, walking, researching and traveling. Looking toward the future, Dr. Caskey intends to experience continued success in her career.

A Lifetime of Achievement in **Education**

Kim L. Creasy, PhD

Associate Professor
University of Northern Colorado
GREELEY, CO UNITED STATES

Kim L. Creasy, PhD, has enjoyed a successful career in academia, currently serving as an associate professor at the University of Northern Colorado, located in Greeley, Colorado. He has thrived in this role since 2013, previously serving in the same position at Slippery Rock University in Butler County, Pennsylvania. Dr. Creasy launched his professional experience as a classroom teacher for the Slippery Rock School District, sharing his expertise with countless elementary school students from 1977 to 2003. His tenure as a teacher led him to his future roles in academia, as many Slippery Rock University student teachers gained firsthand experience in his classroom.

Dr. Creasy credits his mother as a huge influence in his decision to pursue a career in education. To prepare himself for the field, he attended Ashland University, then known as Ashland College, in Ohio, where he earned his Bachelor of Science in education in 1977. He subsequently went on to Westminster College in New Wilmington, Pennsylvania, where he obtained his Master of Education in 1978, later completing coursework to successfully earn his Doctor of Philosophy in curriculum and instruction at the University of Akron in 2005. Mentoring him along the way were Dr. Ray Klingensmith, who taught religion classes in his undergraduate program at Ashland College and helped shape his values and perspectives, in addition to Carole and Isadore Newman, his dissertation professors at the

University of Akron, who modeled how a university professor should support their students.

In addition to Dr. Creasy's primary responsibilities in the classroom, he has played a major role in the University of Northern Colorado's College of Education and Behavioral Sciences. He is the creator and the director of the National Field Experience Conference, which draws educators from across the country to learn more about practices, policies and research concerning the experience of teacher candidates in schools. Dr. Creasy is notably also the founder and editor of The Field Experience Journal, a biannual compilation of research manuscripts submitted by top educators. An expert in his field, he has contributed numerous articles and reviews to professional journals, such as the Journal for Curriculum and Teaching, the Excellence in Education Journal, and Current Issues in Education. He has further shared his knowledge by presenting at national and international conferences.

Well-recognized by his peers in education, Dr. Creasy has been elected by his fellow faculty members to chair multiple university-wide committees and was selected by the president of Slippery Rock University to be a fellow to the Institute for Education Leadership in Washington, D.C., and to the Educational Policy and Leadership Center in Harrisburg, Pennsylvania. He was also named the Pennsylvania fellow in the Association of Teacher Educators Clinical Fellows Program. Outside of his professional endeavors, Dr. Creasy is a committed civic member, serving as the president of the Colorado Association of Teacher Educators, a Scout leader, and on the board of directors of the western Pennsylvania chapter of the Cystic Fibrosis Foundation.

To stay up to date on changes in education and academia, Dr. Creasy has maintained affiliations with the National Network for the Study of Educator Dispositions, the College and University Faculty Assembly, the National Council for the Social Studies, and the Association of Teacher Educators. His exceptional contributions to the field have been recognized on numerous occasions, including with the Kappa Delta Pi Educators Make The Difference Award in 2006, the Walt Disney Company's American Teacher Award nomination, the American Family Institute's Gift of Time Tribute, and the Slippery Rock Area School District Top Ten Recognition from the Slippery Rock School District School board of directors. Dr. Creasy has further been honored by the Boy Scouts of America and the Cystic Fibrosis Foundation of Western Pennsylvania.

Dr. Creasy was born on July 5, 1955, to Rae Marlin Creasy and June Loretta Creasy. He is married to Betty Creasy, and is the father of five children, Parker, Jordan, Abigail, Victoria, and the late Rae. Dr. Creasy is also the proud grandfather of one grandchild. In his free time, he enjoys golfing, fishing and traveling.

A Lifetime of Achievement in **Education**

Philip E. Devine, PhD

Professor Emeritus of Philosophy
Providence College
PROVIDENCE, RI UNITED STATES

P hilip E. Devine, PhD, celebrates many years of experience in philosophy, and has set himself apart for his achievements, leadership qualities, and credentials in the field. He is a professor emeritus of philosophy who challenged the minds of his students at Providence College in Rhode Island between 1990 and 2016. An expert in religious, social and political philosophy, Dr. Devine also taught continuing education courses at Emerson College in Boston, in addition to instructing classes at several other institutions in Massachusetts, including Tufts University in Medford, Lesley University in Cambridge, and Stonehill College in North Easton. Prior to these positions, he served as an assistant professor at St. Cloud State University in Minnesota and the University of Scranton in Pennsylvania. Dr. Devine began his career in academia as a lecturer at the University of Wisconsin.

Dr. Devine fell in love with philosophy after taking just one course in college, where Professor Richard Bernstein inspired his desire to pursue a similar career path. After earning a Bachelor of Arts at Yale University in Connecticut in 1966, he attended the University of California Berkeley. While Dr. Devine was a student, the campus was in the national spotlight for student protests and political activism centered on civil rights, free speech and the Vietnam War. Being in the midst of such social and cultural change further stirred his interest in philosophy, having graduated in 1971 with his Doctor of Philosophy.

Dr. Devine's passion for the subject was further cultivated while he was a liberal arts fellow at Harvard Law School in Harvard College from 1980 to 1981.

Over the course of his career, Dr. Devine has authored several books, including "The Ethics of Homicide" in 1978 and 1990, "Relativism, Nihilism, and God" in 1989, "Human Diversity and The Culture Wars" in 1996 and "Natural Law Ethics" in 2000. He also recently contributed his expertise to the essay, "Abortion: A Communitarian Pro-Life Perspective," which was published in a larger text analyzing the moral, ethical and philosophical issues surrounding abortion. Furthermore, Dr. Devine has written numerous articles for scholarly journals and served on the editorial board for the Legal Studies Forum from 1984 to 1988. In addition to his writings, he has made several presentations on such topics as marriage and the crisis of liberalism, the concept of Europe, the proper use of science fiction examples in moral reasoning, and the principles and paradoxes of international law. He is currently working on a critique of liberalism, inspired by the work of Alasdair MacIntyre.

Although he is retired, Dr. Devine maintains affiliation with the American Catholic Philosophical Association, the Society of Christian Philosophers and the Rhode Island Humanities Forum in order to remain aware of developments in his field. He is also a former member of the American Philosophical Association, the American section of the International Association for Philosophy of Law and Social Philosophy, the National Association of Scholars and the Rhode Island Association of Scholars. For his achievements, Dr. Devine has previously been cited in the 26th edition of Who's Who in the East. In recognition of his outstanding contributions to his profession, he has also been presented with the Albert Nelson Marquis Lifetime Achievement Award.

Dr. Devine was born on December 18, 1944, in Evanston, Illinois, to James Francis and Eleanore Edwards. He is married to Celia Curtis Wolf, a fellow teacher and philosopher. In his free time, Dr. Devine enjoys music, hiking and reading about Civil War history.

A Lifetime of Achievement in **Education**

Joy A. Dyer-Raffler

Special Education Diagnostician & Art Teacher (Retired)
Tucson Unified School District
TUCSON, AZ UNITED STATES

Marquis Who's Who, the world's premier publisher of biographical profiles, is proud to present Joy A. Dyer-Raffler with the Albert Nelson Marquis Lifetime Achievement Award. An accomplished listee, Ms. Dyer-Raffler celebrates many years' experience in her professional network, and has been noted for achievements, leadership qualities, and the credentials and successes she has accrued in her field. As in all Marquis Who's Who biographical volumes, individuals profiled are selected on the basis of current reference value. Factors such as position, noteworthy accomplishments, visibility, and prominence in a field are all taken into account during the selection process.

Retiring as a special education diagnostician and art teacher in 2005, Ms. Dyer-Raffler taught in the field for 35 wonderful years in the Tucson Unified School District. Hired in 1970, she is certified in special education, learning disabilities and art education. In 1969, she earned a Bachelor of Arts from The University of North Carolina at Chapel Hill. Ms. Dyer-Raffler would go on to earn a Master of Education in secondary education in 1974 and a Master of Education in special education in 1976 at The University of Arizona.

Inspired to pursue a career in education by her father who was also a schoolteacher, Ms. Dyer-Raffler reflects back on her career with admiration. Notably, she has maintained membership with the Arizona Education Association as well as the Cub Scouts of America, for which she served as den mother from 1968 to 1969. The recipient of a grant by the Tucson Unified School District in 1977, Ms. Dyer-Raffler has been included in approximately 40 editions of Who's Who in America, Who's Who in American Education, Who's Who of American Women and Who's Who in the World. She was notably profiled in the 73rd edition of Who's Who in America.

Enjoying painting, weightlifting, skiing, tennis and running in retirement, Ms. Dyer-Raffler is a former competitive tennis player of 10 years, where she focused on singles and mixed doubles and was a member of a high-ranking girls team. Marrying her second husband John William Raffler Sr. in 1993, who has since passed away, Ms. Dyer-Raffler is the proud mother of one son.

In recognition of outstanding contributions to her profession and the Marquis Who's Who community, Joy A. Dyer-Raffler has been featured on the Albert Nelson Marquis Lifetime Achievement website. Please visit www.wwlifetimeachievement.com for more information about this honor.

A Lifetime of Achievement in **Education**

Carol A. Eppright

Professor Emeritus
Weatherford College
RICHMOND, TX UNITED STATES

With 35 years of experience to her credit, Carol A. Eppright has been designated as a professor emeritus of Weatherford College in Weatherford, Texas, since 2015. Prior to this appointment, she excelled as a college instructor at Weatherford College from 1974 to 2015, during which time she taught the principles of economics, American history, leadership, Western civilization, and sociology, among other subjects. Previously, Ms. Eppright began her career as a college instructor at Platte Technical Community College in Columbus, Nebraska, from 1970 to 1974.

Before embarking on her professional path, Ms. Eppright pursued an education at Texas Woman's University in Denton, Texas, earning a Bachelor of Science in 1971. She concluded her academic efforts at Texas Woman's University later in that same year, graduating with a Master of Arts. In addition to these accomplishments, she has been inspired and motivated by a number of mentors, including Monte Guyer, her first grade teacher, Lela Maye Erwin, her fourth grade teacher, Professor Mozelle Hines, Professor Glenda Simmons, Professor Dr. Mona S. Hersh and Brad Tibbitts.

Beyond her responsibilities within the field, Ms. Eppright has participated in numerous endeavors outside of her professional circles. She has notably contributed to such charitable and philanthropic entities as The Salvation Army, the American Cancer Society, and multiple food banks. She formerly found success as the deacon and the elder for the Grace First Presbyterian Church of Weatherford, Texas. Furthermore, Ms. Eppright was affiliated with various organizations in relation to her areas of expertise, including the Texas Community College Teachers Association, for which she has attended conventions, and Phi Theta Kappa.

In light of her exceptional undertakings, Ms. Eppright has accrued several accolades throughout her impressive career. In 2004, she was presented with the Continued Excellence Award from Phi Theta Kappa, which subsequently honored her as the Advisor of the Year. Likewise, she was selected for inclusion in the 64th edition of Who's Who in America, published in 2009. In 2013, Ms. Eppright established an eponymous scholarship at Weatherford College, which is bestowed to students with aspirations of becoming an educator to this day.

The daughter of George David and Alice Victoria Eppright, Ms. Eppright cites attaining her emeritus status in 2015 as the highlight of her career. Influenced by her teachers at an early age to seek a career in education as opposed to medicine, she discovered working with her students to be the most rewarding aspect of her occupation. In her spare time, Ms. Eppright enjoys reading, cross-stitching, knitting, and traveling throughout the United States and internationally, especially in Ireland.

Moreover, Ms. Eppright is incredibly proud of the rapport she had with her fellow teachers and colleagues, as they had a good relationship with one another and had a genuine interest in one another's lives. Always displaying a concern and interest for her students and their lives both inside and outside of the classroom, she attributes her success to her ability to listen to her students, who would show an interest in her lessons in return and would become more likely to respond and react to her questions if they needed help. Looking toward the future, Ms. Eppright hopes to continue making the most of her retirement while cementing her legacy as a dedicated and exemplary teacher who cared and was cared about by her peers.

A Lifetime of Achievement in **Education**

John Karl Fisher, EdD

Academic Administrator (Retired)

RIDGEFIELD, CT UNITED STATES

With more than 60 years of experience to his credit, John Karl Fisher, EdD, has been retired since 2017, having worked as a consultant for Saint Basil's College from 2008 to 2010. Previously, he served as the president of Saint Vincent's College from 2004 to 2008. Furthermore, he held a number of positions at Norwalk Community College, including as the dean of academic affairs from 1995 to 2004, the dean of health, science and technology from 1994 to 1995, the dean of technology education from 1992 to 1994 and the president of Norwalk State Technical College from 1986 to 1992. Dr. Fisher was additionally active as the vice president for academic affairs at Alfred State College, a part of the State University of New York system, from 1983 to 1986.

Prior to this appointment, Dr. Fisher excelled in multiple capacities with Edinboro University, such as the executive assistant to the president from 1980 to 1983, the assistant vice president and associate vice president for academic affairs between 1969 to 1980, and the professor of psychology from 1967 to 1969. From 1966 to 1967, he contributed to The Pennsylvania State University as an associate professor. He further held the post of an assistant professor for The George Washington University from 1965 to 1966. Dr. Fisher began his career as the assistant director of the Interprofessional Research Commission on Pupil Services at the University of Maryland in College Park from 1963 to 1966.

Before embarking on his professional path, Dr. Fisher pursued an education at Alfred University, earning a Bachelor of Arts in 1952. He continued his academic efforts with a Master of Science in 1953, also at Alfred University. Following these accomplishments, he accepted a National Science Foundation fellowship at The Pennsylvania State University in 1958 and 1959. Dr. Fisher concluded his studies at the University of Maryland in 1964, graduating with a Doctor of Education.

Beyond his responsibilities within the field, Dr. Fisher has participated in numerous endeavors outside of his professional circles. Notably, he completed his service as a sergeant in the U.S. Army Chemical Corps from 1953 to 1955 and the U.S. Army Reserve from 1955 to 1961. He was the president of Fisher and Farabaugh Consulting from 1980 to 1983. He held roles in Edinboro, Pennsylvania, including as a volunteer for the United Cerebral Palsy Drive from 1974. An author of myriad monographs and articles, Dr. Fisher found success on the long range planning commission for northwestern Pennsylvania from 1981 to 1983, and as a consultant in Harrisburg, Pennsylvania, from 1977 to 1983.

In addition to his primary vocation, Dr. Fisher remains affiliated with various organizations in relation to his areas of expertise. He currently maintains his involvement with the Ridgefield Men's Club, The American Legion and the Ridgefield Owls Club, for which he has held the title of the president since 2016. He was also associated with Rotary International, the Knights of Columbus and Lions Clubs International. Moreover, Dr. Fisher was a member of the American Personnel and Guidance Association.

In light of his exceptional undertakings, Dr. Fisher has accrued several accolades throughout his impressive career. In 1995, he was recognized as a Distinguished Alumnus of the University of Maryland.

He was additionally presented with Distinguished Service Awards from the Gamma Sigma Sigma Sorority at Edinboro University in 1982 and Alfred State College in 1986. Likewise, Dr. Fisher was celebrated with both the Distinguished Alumnus Award from Alfred University in 1977 and the Distinguished Administrator Award from the Edinboro University Alumni Association in 1983.

Hailing from a family of educators and academic administrators, Dr. Fisher was greatly inspired by Walter Waetjen, a scholar and professional football player who served as his mentor. Married to his wife, Beulah Marie Fisher, for 60 years as a result of patience, understanding and compromise, he attributes his success to his diligence, attention to details, hard work and his superb work ethic. Looking toward the future, Dr. Fisher hopes to remain engaged in his community service while cementing his legacy as a dependable educator defined by his integrity.

A Lifetime of Achievement in **Education**

Robert V. Haynes, PhD

Professor Emeritus
Western Kentucky University
BOWLING GREEN, KY UNITED STATES

After accruing more than 50 years in the field, Robert V. Haynes, PhD, retired from his work as professor emeritus with Western Kentucky University in 2010. He first joined the university in 1984 as the vice president of academic affairs and also served as a professor from 1996 until 2009. A dedicated and hardworking professional, he began in education with the University of Houston as a faculty member in the mid-1950s. Over the next three decades, he also worked as a history professor, the acting director of African American studies, the interim director of libraries, the director of libraries, associate provost and deputy provost. Although his career has been filled with highlights, he is especially proud of getting involved in the civil rights movement. A Mississippi native, Dr. Haynes was asked to teach the first class about African American history at the University of Houston.

From 1950 until 1951, Dr. Haynes served in the U.S. Air Force before obtaining a Bachelor of Arts from Millsaps College in Jackson, Mississippi, in 1952. He went on to earn a Master of Arts from the George Peabody College for Teachers in Nashville, Tennessee, in 1953 and a Doctor of Philosophy from Rice University in Houston, Texas, in 1959. In order to stay abreast of changes in the industry, he maintained professional alignment with the Mississippi Historical Society, the Organization of American Historians, the Southern Historical Association, the Texas Association of College Teachers and the Omohundro Institute of Early

American History and Culture. Additionally, Dr. Haynes dedicated himself to his community by way of the Houston Committee on the Humanities, the Presbyterian Church (USA) and the United Campus Ministry of Greater Houston.

An expert in his field, Dr. Haynes authored many works, including "The Mississippi Territory and the Southwest Frontier, 1795-1817," "The Natchez District and the American Revolution" and "A Night of Violence: The Houston Riot of 1917." He has been awarded for excellence in historical education throughout his career, earning a Carnegie fellowship in 1952, a National Endowment for the Humanities fellowship in 1973, the McLemore Prize in 2010, and the Richard Wright and Natchez Literature Awards in 2015. Industry publications such as Who's Who in America, Who's Who in American Education, and Who's Who in the South and Southwest have also recognized Dr. Haynes for outstanding work. He was notably profiled in the 73rd edition of Who's Who in America.

A Lifetime of Achievement in **Education**

Leonard Guy Heldreth

Professor Emeritus
Northern Michigan University
MARQUETTE, MI UNITED STATES

Leonard Guy Heldreth, a former educator and administrator, retired in 2005 as the associate provost of academic affairs at Northern Michigan University in Marquette, Michigan, after five years in his role. Beginning his career on campus in 1970 as an instructor in the English department, he later moved into the roles of assistant professor, associate professor and full professor by 1981. Dr. Heldreth twice served as head of the English department between 1988 and 1991 and again from 1992 to 1998. He also served as interim dean of the College of Arts and Sciences, associate dean and assistant vice president of academic administration. Prior to his academic career, Dr. Heldreth was an abstractor and editor for the National Council of Teachers of English ERIC Clearing House in Urbana, Illinois, from 1968 to 1970.

Throughout his career, Dr. Heldreth was active as an advisory board member of the Journal of Popular Film and TV and was a member of the Northern Michigan University Press editorial board. He has continued to serve on the university's development board since 1997. Dr. Heldreth is also a member and former secretary of the International Association for the Fantastic in the Arts, member and former treasurer and secretary of the Michigan Association of Departments of English, and former member of the board of directors with the Michigan Humanities Council.

Prior to establishing himself as a trusted voice in the field, Dr. Heldreth sought to expand his knowledge through the pursuit of a formal education. He first attended West Virginia University and earned a Bachelor of Science in physics in 1962. He continued his studies at the same esteemed academic institution, obtaining a Master of Arts in English two years later. Ultimately, he achieved a Doctor of Philosophy in English from the University of Illinois in 1973.

Active with a number of professional organizations, Dr. Heldreth is currently chairing the area of fantasy and science fiction for the Popular Culture Association. He is a longtime member of the Science Fiction Research Association, the University Club of Northern Michigan University, Rotary International and the Rotary Club of Marquette. Locally, Dr. Heldreth served as past president of the Urbana-Champaign Community Theater from 1968 to 1969.

Outside of his primary endeavors, Dr. Heldreth has contributed many articles to scholarly journals over the years. He also served as the editor for "The Blood is the Life: Vampires in Literature" in 1999. He has dedicated time as a reviewer of movies for radio station WNMU-FM in Marquette from 1983 to 1989 and as a reviewer of movies for the Marquette Monthly newspaper since 1988.

In light of his notable accomplishments, Dr. Heldreth has gained recognition in the form of various awards and accolades. Honored with several research grants from Northern Michigan University between 1983 and 1987, he also received a Distinguished Faculty Award from the university in 1987. He has previously been selected for inclusion in numerous honors publications, including seven editions of Who's Who in America, one edition of Who's Who in American Education, and six editions of Who's Who in the Midwest.

Dr. Heldreth was born on April 8, 1939, in Shinnston, West Virginia, to mother Grace Louise Myers Heldreth and father Orie Guy Heldreth. He later married Lillian Ruth Marks on June 18, 1964, and together, they have two children named Randall Thomas and Terrence Lon. Moreover, they have five grandchildren named Rio, Aria, Grace, Elizabeth and Solon.

A Lifetime of Achievement in **Education**

Patricia Ann Helms, PhD
Professor Emeritus of Textile Marketing
University of Rhode Island
WAKEFIELD, RI UNITED STATES

With more than 40 years of professional experience, Patricia Ann Helms, PhD, has been recognized as professor emeritus of textile marketing at the University of Rhode Island in Kingstown, Rhode Island, since 1999, having been an associate professor since 1989 and an assistant professor since 1971. During her tenure at the university, she developed two new bachelor's degrees — one in textile marketing and one in consumer affairs. She also designed four new courses for the department. She considers this work of hers to be one of the highlights of her career. Prior to obtaining these roles, she was a cooperative extension agent with Dade County, Florida, from 1963 to 1968, and an educator with the Palmetto Middle School in Miami, Florida, from 1962 to 1963. Earlier in her career, Dr. Helms was an educator with the Limestone Community High School in Bartonville, Illinois, from 1958 to 1962.

Outside of her primary endeavors, Dr. Helms has contributed many articles to professional journals. She has also authored various technical publications in the field. She spent time as a consultant for Alexander J. Patton in 1981, a visiting scholar at the Rhode Island School of Design from 1988 to 1991 and a distinguished visiting professor at the school from 1987 to 1988. Notably, she is a technical expert and speaker in the field and spent time as a director of a textile trading company. Resulting from her publication in 1994, "What Consumers Know About

Flammable Fabrics," she became a nationally known expert witness in legal cases resulting from garment fires.

Dr. Helms became involved in her profession because she had a home economics teacher in high school and she wanted to be just like her. Following this passion into adulthood, she prepared for her professional path through the pursuit of a formal education. She began her career as a student at Bradley University in Peoria, Illinois, where she obtained a Bachelor of Arts in vocational home economics in 1958. She continued her studies at Florida State University in Tallahassee, and she completed a Master of Science in textile and clothing in 1970. Remaining at the same esteemed academic institution, she ultimately graduated in 1971 with a Doctor of Philosophy in textiles.

A respected voice in her areas of expertise, Dr. Helms has been an active leader in her community as well. She is a member of the American Society for Quality Control, where she serves on the editorial review board. In addition, she is on the standards review committee D13 with ASTM International. She is further associated with the American Association of Textile Chemists and Colorists and the American Association of College Professors of Textiles and Clothing. With the American Apparel Manufacturers Association, she is on the consumer affairs committee and is involved with various offices. Using her published research on consumer knowledge of fabric flammability, she served as an expert witness for the plaintiff in many cases of personal injury.

Throughout her career, Dr. Helms has been recognized for her contributions. Notably, she was a grantee of the University of Rhode Island Foundation in 1984 and 1988 and Burlington Industries in 1986, among others. In light of all her accomplishments, Dr. Helms has previously been featured in numerous honors publications, including multiple editions of Who's Who of American Women. Dr. Helms was born on October 31, 1936, in Peoria, Illinois, to mother Nettie Pauline Smith Helms and father Alonzo Franklin Helms. In her free time, she enjoys designing and building houses. Always giving to others, she has put a young man through college in Kenya. Additionally, she adopted two gorillas in Rwanda at the Dian Fossey Gorilla Fund.

A Lifetime of Achievement in **Education**

Valerie J. Hoffman, PhD

Professor
University of Illinois Urbana-Champaign
URBANA, IL UNITED STATES

With more than 35 years of professional excellence in academia and religious studies, Valerie J. Hoffman, PhD, has been serving as a professor at the University of Illinois Urbana-Champaign since 2011, where she also worked as a visiting lecturer from 1983 to 1986, assistant professor from 1986 to 1994, associate professor from 1994 to 2011, and head of the department of religion from 2015 to 2019. Her initial interest in this work was sparked when she was a child because she would make frequent visits to the Metropolitan Museum of Art with her parents. She recognizes learning about other cultures to be a deeply enriching experience.

From 2011 to 2015, Dr. Hoffman also worked as the director of the Center for South Asian and Middle Eastern Studies at the University of Illinois Urbana-Champaign. In that role, she secured grants for the center that funded new faculty positions, courses, scholarships, workshops and lectures. Even though she has experienced many highlights throughout her career, she is especially proud of the textual and anthropological style research that led to the publication of her book titled "Sufism, Mystics, and Saints in Modern Egypt," which was published in 1995.

An expert in her field, Dr. Hoffman holds a Bachelor of Arts in anthropology from the University of Pennsylvania and a Master of Arts and Doctor of Philosophy in Islamic studies from The University of Chicago, where she was inspired by Fazlur Rahman. Between her undergraduate and graduate degrees, she pursued postgraduate studies at the American University in Cairo as well. Utilizing her extensive knowledge of Middle Eastern studies, she contributed 70 articles to journals, books and encyclopedias. Moreover, she authored "The Essentials of Ibadi Islam" in 2012 and contributed to the documentary "Celebrating the Prophet in the Remembrance of God, Sufi Dhikr in Egypt" in 1997. Recently, she served as an editor of "Making the New Middle East: Politics, Culture, and Human Rights" in 2019.

Dr. Hoffman has furthered her expertise through her affiliation with the Association for Middle East Women's Studies, the American Research Center in Egypt on their fellowships committee, and the Institute for the Study of Islamic Thought in Africa on their advisory committee. Likewise, she is active with the International Journal of Middle East Studies, the Journal of the American Academy of Religion, the American Academy of Religion and the Middle East Studies Association.

In light of her professional accomplishments, Dr. Hoffman won the Arnold O. Beckman Award in 2000 and the William and Flora Hewlett Award in 1996, and an Alumni Discretionary Award from the University of Illinois Urbana-Champaign in 2008. She accepted fellowships through the National Endowment for the Humanities between 1991 and 1992 and the American Research Center in Egypt from 1980 to 1981. In addition, she was a Fulbright research fellow in Oman and Yemen between 2000 and 2001 and received the University Scholar Award from the University of Illinois Urbana-Champaign in 1996. Between 1976 and 1979, she was also a National Defense Education Act Title VI fellow through The University of Chicago.

Dr. Hoffman was born on April 27, 1954, in Rockville Centre, New York, to mother Dolores Muriel Ogren Hoffman and father Edward Hoffman. She later married Kirk Oliver Hauser on January 10, 1998. She is the proud mother of three children named Rachel Ladd, Michael Ladd and Deborah Ladd. In her free time, she enjoys hiking, singing, playing guitar, gardening, cooking, sewing and traveling. She is currently writing a book on evolvology and how the evolvees think about themselves. Looking toward the future, she plans to return to Oman for her research on Islam.

A Lifetime of Achievement in **Education**

Vera Rebecca Johnson, BS, MS

Teacher & Administrator (Retired)

STONY BROOK, NY UNITED STATES

Vera Rebecca Johnson, BS, MS, is a retired teacher and administrator who spent more than 40 years in the field. During her tenure, she taught pre-K through sixth grade with the public school systems in Buffalo and Roosevelt, New York, and Springfield, Massachusetts, between 1966 and 1997. She was also an executive director for the Day Care Coordinator Council in Newark, New Jersey, from 1970 to 1972 and a training coordinator for the Economic Opportunity Commission of Nassau County in Hempstead, New York, from 1979 to 1982. Once Ms. Johnson retired from the classroom, she spent another 10 years as a curriculum specialist for the Washington-Rose Elementary School in Roosevelt between 1998 and 2008.

Early in her career, Ms. Johnson served as the director of programs for the public schools in Buffalo, Roosevelt and Springfield during 1970. She also taught as an adjunct professor at Bloomfield College in New Jersey between 1977 and 1978 and was a teacher and mentor at the Leadership Training Institute in Hempstead for five years between 1995 and 2000. Many years later, Ms. Johnson served as a part-time coordinator of the adult education program in the Roosevelt Public Schools between 2003 and 2006. Outside of her primary endeavors, she is a regular contributor to magazines.

Early in her career, while teaching the third grade, Ms. Johnson was tasked with tutoring several sixth grade students on the side. Very upset that these students could not read, she began working with them intently to get them up to speed. While doing so, she was observed by the reading inspector who then told her that she should consider specializing as a reading teacher because she was so good. Soon after, Ms. Johnson was offered a position doing just that, and she accepted. She was very proud of teaching students how to read.

By the time Ms. Johnson was in the first grade, she had already decided that she wanted to someday become a teacher. She has notably held a Bachelor of Science and a Master of Science in elementary education from the University at Buffalo in New York since 1971 and is a certified school administrator, supervisor and school district administrator through the New York State Education Department. Looking back on her early schooling, she is grateful for the many teachers from her childhood that have inspired and influenced her, including Karine Williams, her third grade teacher, and Ann Harris, her reading teacher.

A longtime member of the New York State United Teachers, Ms. Johnson was the recipient of a grant from the Corporation for Public Broadcasting and Levar Burton of "Reading Rainbow" in 1996 and has since been highlighted in the 26th and 27th editions of Who's Who of American Women. Reflecting on her career, she considers the highlight to be any time she made a change in a child's life. She always feels good when she sees her students and they tell her all of the wonderful things they are doing now.

Ms. Johnson is the daughter of Mary and Mark Lloyd. She later married Stanley L. Johnson on November 24, 1983, and together, they had two children named David Simms and John Michael Johnson. Stanley passed away on May 9, 1994. Currently, Ms. Johnson is the proud grandmother to three grandchildren named Amahli, Ajahni and Ayahni. In her free time, she enjoys reading and line dancing. She also likes to do trivia, crossword puzzles and tai chi.

A Lifetime of Achievement in **Education**

Theodore Jojola, PhD

Professor
The University of New Mexico
ALBUQUERQUE, NM UNITED STATES

H aving worked in the industry since the 1970s, Theodore Jojola, PhD, currently serves as a professor for the master's program in community and regional planning at The University of New Mexico in Albuquerque. He began his teaching career as an intern planner with the National Capital Planning Commission in Washington, D.C., in 1973, later becoming a legal historical researcher at the Institute for the Development of Indian Law in 1976. A visiting research associate at the Institute for Philippine Culture at Ateneo de Manila University for one year, he coordinated UNM's ethnic minority director's coalition from 1983 to 1985. Dr. Jojola then served the University of California, Los Angeles, as a postdoctoral fellow of American Indian studies and visiting professor of urban planning in 1984.

Continuing on his professional path, Dr. Jojola served as an associate faculty member of the National Resource Center at The University of New Mexico in 1987 and a Martin Luther King Jr. — Cesar Chavez — Rosa Parks visiting professor at Northern Michigan University in 1988. He then directed NMU's Native American studies section from 1980 to 1996. Many years later, he went on to become a visiting distinguished professor in the School of Geographical Sciences and Urban Planning at Arizona State University from 2008 to 2011.

In addition to this tenure, Dr. Jojola has participated in many regional and nationwide scholarly exhibitions, including "Come the

Redmen, Hear Them Marching: The Legacy of the Albuquerque Indian School" at the Albuquerque Museum in 2002 and "Just Like Us," part of the New Mexico Bataan Experience by the Urban Enhancement Trust Fund in 2004. Later on, he was a cultural consultant for the Studio Ma architects at the Native American Cultural Center of Northern Arizona University in 2009 and the co-curator of an additional exhibit on the Albuquerque Indian School at the Indian Pueblo Cultural Center in 2014. Dr. Jojola has also served as a member on the board of directors for the Indigenous Digital Archive in 2017 and as a consulting scholar for an exhibit at the New Mexico Museum of Indian Arts & Culture since 2016, among other roles.

Prior to the start of his professional career, Dr. Jojola pursued a formal education at The University of New Mexico, earning a Bachelor of Fine Arts in architecture, with a double minor in mathematics and music, in 1973. Continuing his studies, he obtained a Master of Science in city planning from the Massachusetts Institute of Technology in 1975 and a Doctor of Philosophy in political science from the University of Hawai'i at Mānoa in 1982. In 1984, Dr. Jojola completed postdoctoral coursework in planning and American Indian studies at the University of California, Los Angeles, also receiving a certificate in international human rights law from the University of Strasbourg in France that same year.

Active in his local community, Dr. Jojola served on the advisory boards for Zetac, the Zuni Public School District and the College of Education at The University of New Mexico from 2013 to 2017. Additionally, he has served on the board of directors of the Bataan-Corregidor Memorial Foundation of New Mexico from 2001 to 2017, the Chamiza Foundation since 2001 and the Tricklock Company since 2003. A prolific writer, Dr. Jojola notably co-authored the book "How It Is: The Native American Philosophy of V.F. Cordova" in 2007. He also co-edited the book "Reclaiming Indigenous Planning" in 2013 and has contributed numerous articles to professional journals such as Indigenous Planning, Native American Studies and Community Development.

Outside of his primary trade, Dr. Jojola keeps abreast of trends in his field through affiliations with numerous related organizations. He has maintained involvement with the American Planning Association, the Association of Collegiate Schools of Planning, the Planners Network and the 21 Club at The University of New Mexico. Furthermore, he is a tribal member of the Pueblo of Isleta.

In light of his exceptional undertakings, Dr. Jojola has received myriad accolades throughout his impressive career. A visiting fellow of the division of humanities at Curtin University in Perth, Western Australia, in 2002, he received the Faculty Acknowledgement Award from American Indian Student Services at The University of New Mexico in 2005 and the Richard W. Etulain honorary lectureship in 2011, among other honors. In 2014, Dr. Jojola was honored with the Creative Bravos Award at the 29th annual ceremony of Creative Albuquerque, the Award of Merit for planning publications by the Canadian Institute of Planners and two accolades from the New Mexico chapter of the American Planning Association, the Innovation in Planning: Education and Outreach Award and the Planning Award for the Taos Pueblo Comprehensive Indigenous Community and Land Use Plan.

A Lifetime of Achievement in **Education**

Zema L. Jordan, PhD

Curriculum Consultant

DETROIT, MI UNITED STATES

Over the course of a 30-year career, Zema L. Jordan, PhD, has amassed a reputation as a leader in the field of education and academia. Since 1980, she has thrived as a curriculum consultant in the professional growth center for Detroit Public Schools and Wayne State University. She has also been an administrative unit head at Von Steuben Middle School in Detroit, Michigan, since 1977 and a part-time instructor of English at Wayne County Community College since 1969. Likewise, Dr. Jordan contributed as an administrative unit head at Richard Middle School from 1976 to 1977, the head of the English department at Farwell Junior High School from 1968 to 1975 and as an English instructor at Southwestern High School from 1964 to 1968.

In Florence, South Carolina, Dr. Jordan served as an English instructor and part-time guidance counselor at Wilson Junior High School from 1954 to 1964. Prior to that post, she was an English instructor at Liberty High School in Liberty, Mississippi, from 1953 to 1954. She also spent time as an English instructor at Hutchins Junior High School and as head of the social studies department at Cooley High School in Detroit. Since 1983, Dr. Jordan has been a volunteer leader of the Junior Great Books Discussion Group. She was also involved with the Adult Great Books Discussion Group in Detroit from 1965 to 1981. A well-respected educator, Dr. Jordan continually challenged her students to do the greatest good for the greatest number of people and to consider how they could use their profession to assist others.

Inspired by her elementary school teachers, Dr. Jordan has been fascinated with English, writing and language since childhood. She began her academic pursuits at Tennessee State University, formerly known as Tennessee Agricultural and Industrial State University, where she earned a Bachelor of Arts in 1953. Dr. Jordan then continued her academics at Wayne State University in Detroit, Michigan, where she obtained a Master of Education in 1963. In 2010, she began her Doctor of Philosophy work, also at Wayne State University.

As an established professional, Dr. Jordan has earned membership in such prestigious organizations as the National Association for the Advancement of Colored People, the TESOL International Association, the International Platform Association, the Metropolitan Detroit Reading Council and the Michigan Council of Teachers of English. She also holds membership in the National Council of Teachers of English, the National Association of State Boards of Education, the Metropolitan Detroit Alliance of Black School Educators, the Organization of School Administrators and Supervisors, and Pi Lambda Theta. Other organizations of which she is a member include Delta Sigma Theta Sorority, Inc., and Top Ladies of Distinction, Inc. Dr. Jordan also excelled as an adviser for Top Teens of America from 1988 to 2001, and has contributed many articles to professional journals.

For all of these accomplishments, Dr. Jordan was listed in Poetic Voices of America in 1994, International Who's Who in Education in 1987, the World's Who's Who of Women and the International Who's Who of Intellectuals. She has also been listed in the third volume of Men and Women of Distinction and the Dictionary of International Biography. Dr. Jordan has previously been featured in Who's Who in the Midwest and Who's Who of American Women. For her extraordinary contributions and leadership to her field, she has also been presented with the Albert Nelson Marquis Lifetime Achievement Award.

While she has a long list of awards and achievements, Dr. Jordan considers her greatest reward to be seeing her students succeed in the classroom. As the youngest of eight children, she credits her parents for instilling in her a drive to do her best at all times. In her free time, Dr. Jordan enjoys reading, exercising and playing the piano, a skill she began to learn in 2013.

A Lifetime of Achievement in **Education**

Harold Stanley Kachel, EdD

Professor & Academic Administrator (Retired)

BEAVER, OK UNITED STATES

Harold Stanley Kachel, EdD, commenced his career in the U.S. Army Air Forces, where he served in World War II with the Air Transport Command and the Headquarters Squadron at Tokyo International Airport in Japan. On active duty from 1946 to 1948, he subsequently attended college through the GI Bill at Oklahoma Panhandle State University, where he received a Bachelor of Science in industrial arts in 1952. Continuing his education, he earned a Master of Science in secondary administration and curriculum from Oklahoma State University in 1955. After completing postgraduate coursework at Oregon State University in 1956, he attended the University of Northern Colorado and obtained a Doctor of Education in industrial arts and curriculum in 1967. Ultimately, he completed postdoctoral coursework at the University of New Mexico in Albuquerque in 1995.

Embarking on his professional career after receiving his bachelor's degree, Dr. Kachel was a teacher and principal in the Yarbrough School District in Eva, Oklahoma, between 1952 and 1957, before progressing from instructor to professor at Oklahoma Panhandle State University over the course of the following 32 years. During this time, he was also active as the chair of the divisions of applied arts and business, the department head of applied arts, the department head of industrial education and technology, and the registrar. From 1989 to 1990, he notably served as vice president of academy administration at the university. Retiring from his career in 1992, his final role was as registrar for the No Man's Land Historical Museum in Goodwell, Oklahoma, a position he had held since 1968.

During his tenure in education and museums, Dr. Kachel sat on the accrediting committee of the Oklahoma State Department of Education. In addition, he is a prolific author, having co-authored two books, "Images of America: Beaver County" and "Images of America: Texas County" in 2011 and 2013, respectively. To remain current with developments in the field, he maintained affiliation with multiple organizations, including the American Industrial Arts Association, the International Technology and Engineering Educators Association, the American Association of University Professors, the National Education Association, the Oklahoma Education Association and the Oklahoma Anthropological Society. He is further associated with the No Man's Land Historical Society, the Oklahoma Historical Society, the Santa Fe Trail Association, Lions Clubs International, Kappa Delta Pi and Phi Kappa Phi.

As a testament to his longevity in the industry, Dr. Kachel garnered numerous accolades and honors. The recipient of an Appreciation Award from the Rotary Club of Guymon in Oklahoma in 1989, he also earned the Palette Award from Artists' Studio Northwest in 1982 and was recognized for distinguished service by the Area Artists' Studio in Amarillo, Texas, in 1976. However, when asked of his career highlights, Dr. Kachel cites being cleared by the FBI for top-secret material while in the Air Force as a crowning achievement.

Dr. Kachel was born on January 25, 1928, in Elmwood, Oklahoma, to mother Mary Bukowski Kachel and father Samuel W. Kachel. His parents were farmers and taught him strong work ethics. He later married Barbara Joan Overton on August 9, 1955, and together, they are the proud parents of three children named Connie Lynn, Stanley Duane and Lea Ann. Moreover, he is the proud grandfather to three grandchildren. In his free time, he enjoys collecting various items, including Indian artifacts, guns, coins, barbed wire and bottles.

A Lifetime of Achievement in **Education**

Louise Lamphere, PhD

Distinguished Professor Emerita
The University of New Mexico
ALBUQUERQUE, NM UNITED STATES

Louise Lamphere, PhD, has been distinguished professor emerita at The University of New Mexico since she retired in 2009. At UNM, she was a distinguished professor of anthropology between 2001 and 2008 and appointed as a university regents' professor during the three years prior. She was president of the American Anthropological Association from 1999 to 2001 and awarded an honorary Doctor of Humane Letters from Brown University in 2015.

Professor Lamphere attended Stanford University and earned a Bachelor of Arts in 1962. She was admitted to the department of social relations at Harvard University in the fall of 1962 and earned a Master of Arts in 1966 and completed a Doctor of Philosophy in social anthropology in 1968.

Professor Lamphere began her teaching career as a one-year visiting assistant professor of anthropology at the University of Rochester, followed by becoming an assistant professor of anthropology at Brown University from 1968 to 1975. When she was denied tenure at Brown in 1974, she filed a Title VII class action sex-discrimination suit in federal court against Brown. While the suit was in process, she was selected to be an associate professor in the department of anthropology at The University of New Mexico, a position she held between 1976 and 1979. The suit, Lamphere v. Brown, was settled out of court with a consent decree in September 1977. Professor Lamphere returned to Brown as an associate professor, and she was promoted to full professor in 1985. In 1986, she returned to The University of New Mexico as a full professor and remained there until she retired.

Professor Lamphere's research interests include feminist anthropology, women and work, urban anthropology, immigration, and Navajo family and kinship. She published eight books and edited collections during her career. Her research on the Navajo reservation in 1965 and 1966 and her continued connections to Navajo families are dealt with in her books "To Run After Them: The Social and Cultural Bases of Cooperation in a Navajo Community," published by The University of Arizona Press in 1977, and "Weaving Women's Lives: Three Generations in a Navajo Family," published by The University of New Mexico Press in 2007, as well as a special issue on Navajo ethnology for the Journal of Anthropological Research in 1990.

She co-edited "Woman, Culture and Society" with Michelle Zimbalist Rosaldo, which was published by Stanford University Press in 1974. This book was one of the two most important collections of articles on feminist anthropology in the mid-1970s. She also co-edited a collection of feminist articles for the classroom, with Helena Ragoné and Patricia Zavella, titled "Situated Lives: Gender and Culture in Everyday Life," which was published through Routledge Press in 1997.

Her research on working women in Rhode Island and New Mexico can be found in "From Working Daughters to Working Mothers: Immigrant Women in a New England Industrial Community," published through Cornell University Press in 1987, and "Sunbelt Working Mothers: Reconciling Family and Factory," co-authored with Patricia Zavella, Felipe Gonzales and Peter B. Evans through Cornell University Press in 1993. Professor Lamphere's participation in the Ford Foundation-funded project on new immigrants and established residents resulted in "Structuring Diversity: Ethnographic Perspectives on the New Immigration," with The University of Chicago Press in 1992, and "Newcomers in the Workplace," co-edited with Guillermo Grenier through Temple University Press in 1983.

Her research has been funded through a fellowship and grant from the National Institute of Mental Health and through grants from the National Science Foundation, the Ford Foundation and the Russell Sage Foundation. She has also held a number of fellowships that helped her secure leave time in order to write up and publish her research. These included a faculty research fellowship at the Radcliffe Institute for Advanced Study at Harvard University from 1975 to 1976, a faculty development fellowship with the Wellesley Center for Women in 1981, a fellowship at the Pembroke Center for Teaching and Research on Women at Brown University from 1984 to 1985, a visiting scholar position at the Russell Sage Foundation from 2001 to 2002 and a visiting fellow position at Princeton University in 2007. Finally, she has been connected as a co-principal investigator, co-director or senior anthropologist for several large institutional or research grants on behavioral health reform and Medicaid managed care in New Mexico, the development of the Alfonso Ortiz Center at UNM, and the Changing Relations Project that examined the relationships between new immigrants and established residents in five U.S. cities.

Before being president-elect, 1997 to 1999, and president, 1999 to 2001, of the American Anthropological Association, she was head of two other anthropological associations that are part of the AAA: president of the American Ethnological Association, 1987 to 1989, and chair of the Association for Feminist Anthropology, 1995 to 1997. Finally, Professor Lamphere has received a number of awards for her research and publications. These include the Conrad Arensberg Award from the Society for the Anthropology of Work for outstanding contributions to the field in 1994, the Society for the Anthropology of North America Prize for the Critical Study of North America in 1995, and the Squeaky Wheel Award given by the American Anthropological Association committee on the status of women in anthropology in 1998.

At the end of her career, she was given two awards, the Franz Boas Award for Exemplary Service to Anthropology from the AAA in 2013 and the Bronislaw Malinowski Award for Exemplary Professional Achievements in Pursuit of Solving Human Problems Using the Social Sciences from the Society for Applied Anthropology in 2017. Each is awarded every year, and both are considered the highest honor given by that professional organization. Featured in the 73rd edition of Who's Who in America, she was selected to give two important lectures at The University of New Mexico: the Snead-Wertheim lectureship in history and anthropology in 1994 and the 1997 annual research lecture, which is given each year by a UNM faculty member.

A Lifetime of Achievement in **Education**

Mary Hoyle Mahan, EdD

Professor Emeritus
Miami Dade College
FORT LAUDERDALE, FL UNITED STATES

With more than four decades of professional experience as a physical educator and athletics administrator to her credit, Mary Hoyle Mahan, EdD, has helped thousands of students enjoy healthier lives. Her passion for athletics began at a young age, as she demonstrated a keen interest in sports, exercise and dance. She began playing basketball in fifth grade, and in junior high, her physical education teacher played a life-changing role by exposing her to other sports.

With a desire to teach others about her passion for athletics, Dr. Mahan attended Bridgewater State University in Massachusetts, where she earned a Bachelor of Science in physical education in 1960. To further expand her knowledge of the field, she completed the necessary coursework to obtain a Master of Science in physical education at the University of North Carolina in 1963. Dr. Mahan concluded her studies at Nova Southeastern University in Broward County, Florida, where she earned a Doctor of Education in 1975.

Dr. Mahan's professional career began as a teacher of physical education and as a coach at Stoughton Junior High School in Massachusetts from 1960 to 1962. She then accepted a position at the Locust Valley Middle and High School in New York, where she served as a physical education teacher and as a coach from 1963 to 1965. Dr. Mahan continued her career as a professor of physical education and as a coach at Central Connecticut State University in New Britain from 1965 to 1971. With a wealth of experience behind her, Dr. Mahan then joined Miami Dade College's north campus, where she held a variety of positions, including associate athletics director, department chair, professor and coach, from 1971 to 2001. Currently, she holds the title of professor emeritus at that institution of higher education.

Outside of her teaching endeavors, Dr. Mahan is the CEO and president of The Teaching Well in Fort Lauderdale, Florida. A leader in her field, she has also lent her expertise as a member of the education foundation for Villanova University and on the board of trustees for the Bridgewater State University Foundation. She maintains her affiliation as a member of the National Association of Two-Year Colleges Athletics Administrators and Delta Psi Kappa, a national honors fraternity focused on health, physical education, health sciences and recreation. With a passion for education, Dr. Mahan has previously served as an American Red Cross instructor in first aid, CPR and water safety, as well as a trainer for water safety instructors.

For her professional accomplishments and contributions to the field, Dr. Mahan has been recognized with numerous awards and accolades. She has been presented with the Dr. Catherine Comeau Award for Professional Achievement in Physical Education from Bridgewater State University, the Delta Psi Kappa Alumna of the Year Award, the Miami Sports Society Lifetime of Giving Award, three Outstanding Faculty Awards from Miami Dade College and the National Girls and Women in Sports Pathfinder Award. She received an endowed chair from Miami Dade College for excellence in teaching. Further, Dr. Mahan has been named to five halls of fame, including Weymouth High School Alumni, the Florida Community College Activities Association, the National Association of Two-Year Colleges Athletics Administrators, the Florida College System Women's Basketball Coaches and the Bridgewater State University Athletics Hall of Fame. She has also been listed in various honors publications, including Who's Who of American Women and Who's Who in America.

Notably profiled in the 73rd edition of Who's Who in America, Dr. Mahan was born on July 19, 1939, in Boston, Massachusetts, to Frederick John Hoyle and Mary Dwyer Hoyle. She enjoyed nearly 30 years of marriage to J. Roger Mahan Jr. before his passing in 1999. Dr. Mahan enjoys a close relationship with her brother, Fred Hoyle, and sister, Dianne Hoyle Gustin, as well as three nieces and three nephews. An avid golfer, Dr. Mahan is the president of the Woodlands Women's Golf Association. In her free time, she enjoys interior decorating, traveling and entertaining.

Linda Ellen Miller

Museum Administrator & Education Expert (Retired)

HAWTHORNE, NJ UNITED STATES

With several decades of practiced professional experience to her name, Linda Ellen Miller has enjoyed a successful career as a museum administrator and education expert. Most recently, she dedicated two decades to working with the Vernon Township Historical Museum in Vernon Township, New Jersey. There, she was a curator and administrator from 1995 until her retirement in 2015. She retired to gardening and working on behalf of the First Reformed Church of Hawthorne as a disability coordinator.

Before entering her final professional position, Ms. Miller dedicated her time and knowledge to serving as a curator of education at the Clinton Historical Museum in Clinton, New Jersey, from 1993 to 1995. Previously, she excelled as an educator with the kaleidoscope kids program with the New Jersey State Museum in Trenton, New Jersey, from 1992 to 1993. Her first professional role was as an educator and later was promoted to curator of education at Old Barracks Museum in Trenton, New Jersey, for three years from 1989 to 1992.

Prior to establishing herself as a trusted voice in the field, Ms. Miller sought to expand her knowledge through the pursuit of a formal education at a number of esteemed academic institutions over the years. She first attended Upsala College, a private college located in East Orange, New Jersey. After completing her studies, she obtained a Bachelor of Arts in human resource management in 1983. She continued her studies at the Bank Street College of Education, a nonprofit educational institution located in New York City. There, she ultimately achieved a Master of Science in museum leadership and education in 1992. Subsequently, she received a certificate of accomplishment from the Rutgers Cooperative Research and Extension Master Gardener Program in October 2005.

An active presence in the field, Ms. Miller maintains memberships with several prestigious professional organizations, including the Museum Education Roundtable and the New Jersey Association of Museums. With the League of Historical Societies of New Jersey, she served in various leadership roles, including as chairman of the education committee and trustee from 1994 to 1997 as well as the vice president beginning in 1997. In addition, she found success as a member of the national education committee with the American Association of Museums, where she also holds a membership. From 1993 to 1994, she sat on the steering committee of the New Jersey Studies Academic Alliance.

In light of her many professional successes and contributions to the field, Ms. Miller has gained recognition in the form of various awards and accolades over the years. She has previously been selected for inclusion in such honors publications as the 20th edition of Who's Who of American Women, the fifth edition of Who's Who in American Education and the 73rd edition of Who's Who in America.

Ms. Miller was born on August 31, 1947, in Paterson, New Jersey, to mother Flora M. Christen Douglas and father Edward E. Douglas. She later married Philip R. Miller on September 19, 1970, and together, they are the proud parents of one child named Douglas Scott. Moreover, they have two grandchildren named Juliette and Gabrielle. In her free time, she enjoys participating in her hobbies as an artist as well as a naturalist. She has remained in New Jersey over the years and now lives in the town of Hawthorne.

Alfred Frantz Myers

State Education Official (Retired)

ENOLA, PA UNITED STATES

Supported by years of professional experience and an impressive education, Alfred Frantz Myers led a prolific career as a state education official for over 35 years. A graduate of Lehigh University in Bethlehem, Pennsylvania, he received a Bachelor of Arts in 1958 and a Master of Arts in 1966. He is grateful for the mentorship of Joseph Dowling, his history professor who sparked in him an interest in history and education. He also completed postgraduate coursework with the Peabody College of Education and Human Development at Vanderbilt University in Nashville, Tennessee, between 1971 and 1972. During this time, he served to first lieutenant in the U.S. Air Force from 1958 to 1963 before progressing to captain with the U.S. Air Force Reserve from 1963 to 1971.

Mr. Myers began his career as an instructor for the Grand River Academy in Austinburg, Ohio, in 1966, further serving the same role with Culver Academies in Culver, Indiana, from 1966 to 1968 and Kiskiminetas Springs School, now known as The Kiski School, in Saltsburg, Pennsylvania, between 1968 and 1971. Mr. Myers continued his work, holding the post of assistant professor of social studies at Indiana State University from 1972 to 1973, division trainer with Encyclopedia Britannica from 1973 to 1975 and manager of Rupp's from 1976 to 1977.

Later, Mr. Myers worked as a criminal justice system planner with the Pennsylvania Commission on Crime and Delinquency from 1977 to 1980 and research associate with the Pennsylvania Department of Education from 1980 to 1989. He also excelled as a basic education associate for the Pennsylvania Department of Education in Harrisburg, Pennsylvania, from 1986 to 1998, as well as an associate for EdVise from 1998 until his retirement in 2001.

While fulfilling his primary responsibilities, Mr. Myers volunteered as a social worker in the Dominican Republic in 1958. Additionally, he acted as a volunteer teacher for Global Volumes in Xi'an, China, in 1999. An active presence in the field, he maintains memberships with numerous prestigious organizations, including the Pennsylvania Federation of Teachers, the Pennsylvania Association for Adult Continuing Education, the Conference of Latin American Geography and the American Historical Association.

Mr. Myers is affiliated with the American Academy of Political and Social Science, the Academy of Political Science, The Pennsylvania Historical Association, the National Braille Association and the Organization of American Historians. He is further associated with Phi Beta Kappa, Phi Delta Kappa International, The American Legion, Pi Gamma Mu, the Travelers' Century Club and the Pennsylvania Association of School Retirees. With the Middle States Council for Social Studies, he served as president from 1987 to 1988.

As a testament to his accomplishments, Mr. Myers was selected for inclusion in the third edition of Who's Who Among Human Service Professionals, as well as multiple editions of Who's Who in America, Who's Who in American Education, Who's Who in the East and Who's Who in the World. However, in a career filled with highlights, he enjoyed being surrounded by people who helped each other.

Mr. Myers was born on February 19, 1936, in Crooked Creek State Park, Pennsylvania, to mother Ida Gertrude Schaeffer Myers and father Jacob Alfred Jr. He was blessed to have an inspirational partnership with Gordon David Jones from July 11, 1977, until he passed away in 2016. He was also his colleague. In his free time, Mr. Myers enjoys hiking, exploring new places and reading history.

A Lifetime of Achievement in **Education**

Patricia Herbert Raynor

Special Education Teacher
Essex Community School District

CLARINDA, IA UNITED STATES

Supported by many years of practiced experience in her field, Patricia Herbert Raynor currently excels as a special education teacher with the Essex Community School District in Iowa. Over a career spanning more than 30 years, she has taught special education, family and consumer science, keyboarding and math, among other subjects. When she is not teaching full time, Ms. Raynor continues her passion for education as a substitute teacher in the Bedford, Clarinda and Essex community school districts.

At the beginning of her career, Ms. Raynor thrived as a legal secretary for John Kosmas & John Greene, and Smith, Biggins, Bollman & Mogilner. Following these appointments, she worked in an administrative capacity for Centre City Hospital, the Waubonsie Mental Health Center and the Farmer Assistance Project before focusing her efforts on special education. Over the years, Ms. Raynor served as the co-owner and vice president of Clarinda Home Medical, and was additionally appointed as an inaugural member of the Iowa Behavioral Initiative for three years.

Ms. Raynor was just 8 years old when she decided she wanted to pursue a career in education. She earned an Associate of Arts from San Diego Mesa College in 1976, a Bachelor of Arts from San Diego State University, in addition to completing a five-year teacher education program, and a Master of Science in education from Northwest Missouri State University. While a graduate assistant at the aforementioned university, Ms. Raynor gained valuable experience teaching preschool, cognitive-oriented kindergarten, and the after-school program.

In order to remain aware of changes in the field, Ms. Raynor is affiliated with the Iowa State Education Association, the National Education Association and the American Association of University Women, as well as the Bedford Teachers Association, where she served as the grievance committee chairman for the 1997-1998 school year. Additionally, after teaching at the Essex Community School District, she also served as the president of the Essex Community School Education Association. Outside of her professional endeavors, Ms. Raynor has been an active community volunteer. She taught Sunday school to fourth through eighth graders at her local church for five years, in addition to helping lead summer vacation Bible school sessions.

Ms. Raynor is also a skilled dog trainer, with her own Shetland sheepdog winning eight titles for agility. A well-respected expert, she has shared her knowledge and skills as a co-leader of the Clover K-9's 4-H Project Club in Page County, Iowa, for many years. In this role, Ms. Raynor addressed dog training for conformation, obedience and agility. Further, she has lent her time and talents as a step aerobics instructor for the Essex Community School District's wellness program.

Although her career has been filled with highlights, Ms. Raynor is especially proud of working alongside parents to better her students' education. For her professional excellence, she was selected for inclusion in four volumes of Who's Who in America, including the 73rd edition, and one volume of Who's Who in the Midwest. Ms. Raynor is additionally a recipient of the prestigious Albert Nelson Marquis Lifetime Achievement Award. She attributes her success to hard work, perseverance and the desire to learn.

Ms. Raynor was born to Maurice Dooling and Audrey Claire in Oakland, California, on December 15, 1949. She married Gailen McArthur Raynor on June 23, 1979, and is the stepmother to David and Robin. In her free time, Ms. Raynor enjoys sewing, swimming, traveling, exploring genealogies and learning about history. Looking toward the future, she intends to experience the continued success of her career in special education. A lover of animals, she hopes to also continue volunteering at local animal shelters.

A Lifetime of Achievement in **Education**

Paul J. Reiss, PhD

President Emeritus
Saint Michael's College
LAKE PLACID, NY UNITED STATES

A renowned sociologist who is a respected voice in the academic community, Paul J. Reiss, PhD, has more than six decades of leadership on both a professional and personal level to his credit. His father, Julian, was a major influence in his decision to study sociology. When Dr. Reiss was in high school, his father was appointed to serve on a newly formed commission that would implement and guide the development of New York state legislation that barred employers from discriminating on the basis of race, creed or national origin. Seeing his father's work, and the need for such a law in the first place, he was inspired to learn how people related to one another.

Dr. Reiss pursued higher education at the College of the Holy Cross, where he attained a Bachelor of Science. Following this accomplishment, he earned a Master of Arts at Fordham University, and a Doctor of Philosophy in sociology at Harvard University in 1960. He has also received honorary degrees from Showa University in Japan, Middlebury College in Vermont and Saint Michael's College in Vermont.

Dr. Reiss began his career as an assistant professor at Marquette University in Milwaukee, Wisconsin, before being appointed to the role of the chairman of the sociology department. He continued his professional efforts at Fordham University, where he served successively as the chairman of the department of sociology and anthropology, the dean of the College at Lincoln Center, the vice president for academic affairs and as the executive vice president. Dr. Reiss concluded his career in academia as the president of Saint Michael's College in Vermont for over 10 years before retiring in 1996.

In his retirement, Dr. Reiss was actively involved in several international and community projects, including his management and support of the Julian Reiss Foundation, a nonprofit organization started by his father that provides educational summer camp programs for boys and girls from Hispanic communities in New York City. Assuming these posts in 1960, he passed on his responsibilities to his children around 2010. In 2007, Dr. Reiss was the founding president of Mercy Care for the Adirondacks, which seeks to extend love and mercy to elders and enable them to enjoy living in their own homes and communities for as long as possible.

Over the years, Dr. Reiss has been involved in various professional organizations including many years as editor of the journal, Sociology of Religion, and as an active member of the American Sociological Association and the Association of the Sociology of Religion. He has also dedicated his expertise and knowledge to numerous associations and boards as well. In addition to serving on the board and as the past president of the Lake Placid Sinfonietta, a classical music orchestra, Dr. Reiss has held the title of president for the boards of the Association of Vermont Independent Colleges and Vermont Higher Education Council. Likewise, he contributed his efforts as a member of the Vermont Business Roundtable, the National Association of Independent Colleges and Universities, and the Association of Catholic Colleges and Universities.

Dr. Reiss' noteworthy accomplishments have earned him myriad accolades. He was presented with the Liberty Bell Award by the Essex County Bar Association in 2010 and the honor of a Distinguished Citizen by the Green Mountain Council of the Boy Scouts of America in 1996. His successes and leadership have also been recognized in more than two dozen editions of Who's Who in America, Who's Who in American Education, and Who's Who in the East. Dr. Reiss has also been celebrated with the Albert Nelson Marquis Lifetime Achievement Award.

A Lifetime of Achievement in **Education**

Victor M. Renteria

Secondary School Educator

EL PASO, TX UNITED STATES

Victor M. Renteria's "first stage" (1950-1970), began with the "audio/visual/linguistic phase." It opened with Brown v. Board of Education, included the Beatles, the Rolling Stones, the entire "British Invasion," the fulfillment of President Kennedy's challenging goal "...to land and safely return a man from the moon..." and with Mr. Renteria's pursuit to obtain a degree. Each of these would frame his pursuits in the future, they so have proven. Though neither of his parents went beyond the fifth grade, both were excellent teachers. From his father, he learned how to use every hand tool and how to play football, baseball and basketball. From his mother, he learned how to dance, many social skills, and every domestic skill needed to live independently.

Mr. Renteria feels he has fulfilled the Commandment to "Honor Thy Parents" and now honors his brother and niece, Oscar and Jacqueline, as his sources of inspiration, dedication and motivation. He owes enormous "heart-print" thanks to all of his teachers from Alta Vista and Hillside Elementary through Ross Intermediate and Burges High School, all of whom he can still name by grade and subject.

Mr. Renteria's "second stage" (1970-1990), his "body/kinesthetic/interpersonal phase," was developing through uses of his growing "skills bank." This period was highlighted by disco, the phrase "wax on, wax off," and with the entry of "enablers" who would eventually advance Mr. Renteria's development in a vocation he'd never thought of entering. His biggest personal milestones were his graduation from The University of Texas at El Paso and his "intrapersonal growth" as a member of the Gamma Gamma chapter of TKE. His fraternity brothers and the fraternity experience helped him deepen his "skills bank" for teamwork, management, planning, personal responsibility and interpersonal activities.

During his undergraduate schooling, Mr. Renteria twice served as the president of the Gamma Gamma chapter of TKE and once as chapter historian. In 2018, he was notified that he is designated as a "Life Loyal Teke" for his contributions to the TKE Educational Fund. Recognized as a TKE International Honor Historian, he had memberships in the International Society for Technology in Education and the Mathematical Association of America, and is a 40-year contributor to both UTEP's Alumni Association and TKE's Alumni Association.

Mr. Renteria's "Sensei," Lynn L. Nichols, and each of his belt-level instructors: David Burrola, Sr. and Jr., James Hebert, Gregory K. Allen, Mike Grijalva, Rayme Parra, Glenn Pierce and Daryl Watts, taught him that persistent demonstration, setting rigorous sessions, requiring high expectations, and standards are, in the long term, metaphoric for the possible difficulties in life. He attained a fourth-degree black belt in karate, but that was more honorary and for persistence than physical skills. He taught Butokan Taekwondo for nearly 20 years.

Prior to entering education, Mr. Renteria worked in the field of electronics manufacturing for seven years as a production test supervisor for Rockwell International for two years and a production test technician in quality assurance for GUS Manufacturing the previous five years. He also worked as the engineering content instructor for the summer with the Texas Pre-Engineering Program (TexPrep) at UTEP from 1992 to 2008.

Mr. Renteria was a former member of the parental task force and campus improvement team, which he chaired for three years. He is both a certified teacher in the state of Texas and a Nearpod user, and began online hours with Microsoft in education. Moreover, he has over 600 CPE hours from attending continuing professional development sessions provided by the El Paso Independent School District.

The recipient of an EPISD's 25-Year Service Pin in 2018, Mr. Renteria has been named as a National Honor Roll's Outstanding Teacher every year since 2004. He has been cited in multiple editions of Who's Who in America and Who's Who in American Education.

Mr. Renteria's current stage (1990-present), his "metacognitive/logical-mathematical phase," includes the entry of "guardian angel enablers," who helped him to realize that he must continue improving his "teaching skills bank" to fulfill his part in completing life's cycle of "Paying It Forward!" Life's inclusion of these "guardian angel enablers" eased the passing of both of his beloved, unschooled, but extremely talented and generous parents. He owed this stage of his career to, firstly, Thomas A. Woods, Anne Batchelder and Norma Rodriguez, PhDs in UTEP's Alternative Certification Program, and PhDs J. Michael Gray, Sam and Marsha Self, Manuel Berriozábal and Sally Blake for his 16 summers as a TexPrep instructor. He offers his most profound thanks to the late Paul J. Strelzin, his hiring principal, who retained him after being surplused each of his first three years. The writings of Howard Gardner, Arthur L. Costa, Bena Kallick and Ruby K. Payne, PhDs, and Kathy Seufert and the recently deceased Amy Boatright in EPISD's staff development added to his "teaching skills bank." The most significant teaching event of this time was leaving an unfulfilling lab assignment of six years and returning to a "teaching classroom." He owes this rejuvenating return to his colleagues, at that time, teachers Patti True and Cecilia Lafon, and Nick Cobos, his "interim principal."

In his current stage, the most important contributors to Mr. Renteria's earning this Lifetime Achievement Award have been all of his past and present students and colleagues at Bowie High School, who've made his career challenging, meaningful, purposeful and enjoyable. To him, every day in every year presents more opportunities to learn more about each student. The challenge is in learning students' personalities, skills, deficiencies, life goals and what it will take to motivate each one to reach their potential. "Paying It Forward" became his motto upon hearing that phrase at a fraternity brother's memorial service. He thinks that phrase embodies and describes teaching the best.

Outside of his work in the classroom, Mr. Renteria has been a contributor to the Special Olympics since 1996, SPLC since 1993, the Paralyzed Veterans of America, MDA, Habitat for Humanity, and the WWII Museum. When he isn't teaching, he enjoys several avocations in his free time. Staying active by reading, exercising, weightlifting and dancing, he collects CDs and other rock 'n' roll memorabilia, as well.

All the above listed individuals in Mr. Renteria's "stages in education," in their own individual and collective way(s) through "life's contact" and personalities, are the reasons he remains in the classroom to continue to try to make a difference by "Paying It Forward" as best as he can. Finally, he would also like to pay an extra, extra special thanks to whichever former colleague or student nominated him in 2004 because without that individual, he believes this totally unexpected honor would probably never have occurred.

A Lifetime of Achievement in **Education**

Ruth Freddie Carleson Robinson

High School Teacher (Retired)
Gresham-Barlow School District
PORTLAND, OR UNITED STATES

With 30 years of professional experience to her credit, Ruth Freddie Carleson Robinson is currently retired, having excelled for the majority of her career as a high school teacher for the Gresham-Barlow School District in Oregon. Prior to attaining this position, she worked for one year with the Hillsboro School District in Oregon, beginning in 1959. In addition to her primary responsibilities, Ms. Robinson served on the site council for the Sam Barlow High School in Gresham from 1994 to 2002, also holding the post of the chair of the council from 1998 to 2002. In this role, she worked with parents, teachers, administrators and community members to create and oversee the school's improvement plan, helping to steer the public school into the future. Having influenced countless students, Ms. Robinson has found teaching teenagers to be a satisfying and uplifting profession.

Ms. Robinson demonstrated a proclivity for education at a young age, holding the post of the valedictorian of both her eighth grade and high school graduating classes. Her grandfather encouraged her to pursue a career in teaching, and prior to embarking on her professional path, she pursued an education at Oregon State University in Corvallis, where she earned a Bachelor of Science in 1959. Following this accomplishment, she completed three full years of postgraduate coursework at Oregon State University and Portland State University.

In order to remain aware of developments in her field, Ms. Robinson has maintained her affiliation with the National Education Association, the Oregon Education Association and the American Association of University Women. Well-regarded as an expert in her field, she has also lent her expertise and leadership talents to the Gresham-Barlow Education Association as the vice president from 1994 to 1995 and as the president from 1995 to 1996, the East Multnomah County UniServ as a secretary from 1989 to 1992 and a president from 1993 to 1995, and the American Association of Individual Investors as the vice president of the Portland chapter from 2004 to 2008, the president from 2009 to 2012, and the past president from 2012 to 2015. For her many accomplishments and contributions to her field, Ms. Robinson has been featured in multiple editions of Who's Who in America, including the 73rd edition, Who's Who in American Education, Who's Who of American Women and Who's Who in the World. She is also the recipient of the Albert Nelson Marquis Lifetime Achievement Award.

Outside of her professional memberships, Ms. Robinson has explored her interests through various clubs and organizations. She has been involved with the International Ivory Association in addition to the BMW Car Club of America, an organization devoted to BMW enthusiasts. An avid reader, Ms. Robinson also participates in three book clubs: Sleuth Sisters, Modern Fiction and the Barlow Book Club. She is a talented ballroom dancer as well, devoting 20 hours a week to dance and performing at national and international ballroom dancing events.

Born in Salem, Oregon, to Richard Victor and Opal Charlotte Carleson, Ms. Robinson spent many happy years married to her late husband, Kenneth Oliver Robinson. Likewise, she is the proud mother of two children, Grant Kenneth and Victoria Ruth, and grandmother to three wonderful grandsons. With a great love of opera, she was a regular contributor to the Portland Opera Association from 1982 to 2014. Enjoying collecting and traveling in her spare time as well, Ms. Robinson is associated with a number of art museums and gardens such as the Portland Japanese Garden, the Lan Su Chinese Garden, and the Asian Art Museum in San Francisco, among others.

A Lifetime of Achievement in **Education**

Joseph Salvatore Salemi, PhD

Professor of Humanities
New York University
NEW YORK, NY UNITED STATES

With a dedication to scholarship, Joseph Salvatore Salemi, PhD, has emerged as an expert in the field of English literature, as well as in Greek and Roman classics. With more than 40 years of professional experience to his credit, he has excelled as a professor of humanities for New York University since 1983. In addition to his primary role, Dr. Salemi has served as a professor of classics with Hunter College, a part of the City University of New York system, since 1989. Previously, he has found success as a professor of classics with Brooklyn College from 1993 to 2000, a professor of English with Fordham University from 1988 to 1989, and a professor of English with Nassau Community College from 1984 to 1986. Earlier in his career, Dr. Salemi worked as a professor of composition and literature with Pace University in New York from 1977 to 1984.

Dr. Salemi demonstrated an interest in reading from a young age, drawn to any subject requiring that area of focus. His interest in poetry was greatly influenced by his grandfather, Rosario Previti, a noted Sicilian poet, translator and newspaper columnist who wrote a series of satirical columns on American life. To further expand upon his skills, Dr. Salemi initially pursued an education at Fordham University, where he obtained a Bachelor of Arts in 1968. Following this accomplishment, he continued his studies at New York University, earning a Master of Arts in 1970. He concluded his academic efforts at New York University in 1986, graduating with a Doctor of Philosophy. Permanently certified as an English teacher in the state of New York, Dr. Salemi is a member of the National Association of Scholars, The American Literary Translators Association and The Renaissance Society of America.

A prolific writer, Dr. Salemi has authored six poetry collections titled "Skirmishes," "Steel Masks," "Formal Complaints," "Nonsense Couplets," "Masquerade" and "The Lilacs on Good Friday." His poems and translations have been published in more than 100 journals, and he further serves as a book reviewer, an editor, and a regular commentator for The Pennsylvania Review and Expansive Poetry Online. Dr. Salemi has written several literary criticisms, in addition to penning numerous influential exposés that have confronted the powerful in academia through his work as an investigative journalist for the monthly newsletter Measure and California-based publication Heterodoxy.

Dr. Salemi has been celebrated on numerous occasions for his contributions to the field. The recipient of a Classical and Modern Literary Journal Award, he was recognized as a Musurillo scholar by the City University of New York Graduate Center, a senior fellow of the National Endowment of the Humanities, and a Lane Cooper fellow of New York University. Dr. Salemi has been featured in numerous publications as well, including multiple editions of Who's Who in America, Who's Who in American Education and Who's Who in the World. In light of his leadership and exceptional accomplishments, he has also been named a recipient of the prestigious Albert Nelson Marquis Lifetime Achievement Award.

Dr. Salemi was born on February 1, 1948, in New York City to Salvatore Joseph, a decorated World War II combat veteran, and Liberty Luce Previti Salemi, a legal secretary who worked for a major law firm. He and his wife, Helen Louise Palma, a translator, currently live in Brooklyn, New York. In his free time, Dr. Salemi enjoys military research.

A Lifetime of Achievement in **Education**

Walter R. Schumm, PhD

Professor
Kansas State University
MANHATTAN, KS UNITED STATES

A highly esteemed educator with nearly 40 years of experience to his credit, Walter R. Schumm, PhD, currently serves as a professor at Kansas State University in Manhattan, Kansas, a post he has remained in since 1990. He joined Kansas State University in 1979 and held the title for five years before accepting a position as an associate professor from 1984 to 1990. Outside of his primary endeavors, he has dedicated his time and knowledge to the U.S. Army Research Institute in Alexandria, Virginia, as a member of the science advisory committee from 1987 to 1990.

When he was 8 years old, Dr. Schumm had a conversation with his father about what he wanted to do when he grows up, and he told him that he found psychology to be interesting. As he grew up, he developed a skill for experimental physics, but realized he lacked a talent for higher-level mathematics. Wanting to become an expert in the field, Dr. Schumm sought to expand his knowledge through the pursuit of a formal education at various esteemed academic institutions. He first attended the College of William and Mary and obtained a Bachelor of Science in physics in 1972. During this time, he challenged himself by taking calculus courses as well as social anthropology and psychology courses.

After receiving this degree, Dr. Schumm was open to studying new subjects. He decided to continue his studies at Kansas State University, and upon graduating from the esteemed school in 1976, he earned a

Master of Science in family-child development. Ultimately, he achieved a Doctor of Philosophy in family studies from Purdue University in 1979. Subsequently, he became certified as a family life educator by the National Council on Family Relations.

Outside of his teaching responsibilities, Dr. Schumm has served in the U.S. Army as a second lieutenant and commander of the 6th Brigade from 1972 to 1974. Later, he was with the U.S. Army for the mobilization during Operation Desert Shield/Storm from 1990 to 1991 and a colonel in the U.S. Army Reserve from 1994 to 2002. He was also a commander of the 6th Brigade in the 95th Division from 1999 to 2002. Notably, his brigade headquarters was selected as the best U.S. Army Reserve unit in the world in 2001. Recognized on numerous occasions for his achievements, he was the recipient of a Decorated Legion of Merit from the U.S. Armed Forces.

An active presence in the field, Dr. Schumm has contributed his knowledge and expertise to multiple creative works. In addition to writing articles for peer-reviewed journals, he has written two books. In light of his exceptional undertakings, Dr. Schumm was selected for inclusion in several honors publications, including the third edition of Who's Who Among Human Services Professionals and the 22nd edition of Who's Who in the Midwest, as well as many editions of Who's Who in America and Who's Who in American Education.

Dr. Schumm was born on January 9, 1951, in Bethesda, Maryland, to parents Brooke and Elisabeth Darling Schumm. He later married Kimberly Shawn Ring on August 4, 1979. Together, they are the proud parents of seven children named Jonathan, Joshua, Phillip, Miriam, Deborah, Martha and Daniel. Reflecting on his career, he notes that both Tony Jurich and Steve Bollman were mentors to him.

A Lifetime of Achievement in **Education**

Jane Sheets

School Librarian & Elementary School Educator (Retired)

ALBERTVILLE, AL UNITED STATES

With more than 35 years of experience to her credit, Jane Sheets is currently retired, having excelled as an elementary librarian for the Marshall County Board of Education in Guntersville, Alabama, from 1976 to 1991. Prior to this appointment, she served as a reading teacher for the Marshall County Board of Education from 1962 to 1976. Previously, Ms. Sheets began her career as a children's librarian for the Cleveland Public Library from 1956 to 1958 and an information operator for the Bell Telephone Company in 1953.

Before embarking on her professional path, Ms. Sheets pursued an education at Snead State Community College, formerly known as Snead Junior College, earning an Associate of Science in 1953. She continued her academic efforts with a Bachelor of Science at The University of Alabama in 1956 and a Master of Education at Auburn University in 1968. Following these accomplishments, she graduated from the Institute of Children's Literature in 1992 and Writer's Digest University in Cincinnati in 1996. Certified as a teacher and a school librarian in Alabama, Ms. Sheets concluded her studies with coursework at the National Radio Institute in Washington, D.C., in 1997.

Beyond her responsibilities within the field, Ms. Sheets has provided her time and resources in numerous endeavors outside of her professional circles. From 1992 to 2000, she contributed as a volunteer tax preparer in Guntersville. Furthermore, she held the role of a private reading tutor in Albertville, Alabama, since 1968. Since 1994, Ms. Sheets has found success with the Women's Health Initiative, where she participates in a number of research and studies and will do so for the rest of her life.

In addition to her primary vocation, Ms. Sheets remains affiliated with various organizations in relation to her areas of expertise. Notably, she has maintained her involvement as a lifetime member of the National Education Association. She was also active with the Alabama Education Association and the Alabama Retired Teachers Association. Moreover, Ms. Sheets is a member of both the Marshall County Retired Teachers Association and the American Association of Retired Persons.

In light of her exceptional undertakings, Ms. Sheets has accrued several accolades throughout her impressive career. In 1955, she was recognized as a scholar of the Daughters of the American Revolution. Ms. Sheets is also a graduate of the Kate Duncan Smith DAR High School.

Ms. Sheets is the proud mother of four wonderful children: Wanda Kay, Jeffrey Lee, Sue Ann Sheets and Cagle Whitmire. She has also welcomed eight grandchildren and two great-grandchildren into her growing family. Harboring a lifelong passion for reading, Ms. Sheets proudly recalls learning how to read from her mother, Floria Mae Campbell, at the age of 3, which remains the highlight of her experiences.

Separated from her peers due to her quiet demeanor, Ms. Sheets enjoys reading, storytelling, volunteering, gardening and teaching crocheting at her local senior center in her free time. She attributes her success to her love for reading as well as her guidance from the Lord. She was additionally inspired by the constant reminders of love and innocence from the children in her classrooms, as it allowed her to be more forgiving and compassionate toward them. Looking toward the future, Ms. Sheets hopes to continue enjoying her retirement while cementing her legacy among her peers as a flexible, selfless and helpful figure in the field of education.

A Lifetime of Achievement in **Education**

In Memoriam

Lillian June Shuldes

Elementary School Educator (Retired)

SOUTH BARRINGTON, IL UNITED STATES

Having spent several decades as an elementary school educator, Lillian June Shuldes dedicated her career to educating children and guiding them through their academic years. Notably, she found success as an elementary school teacher with the Chicago Board of Education for more than three decades from 1951 to 1987. Outside of her primary endeavors, she was a speaker in the field. She was most proud of the fact that no child would go through her classroom for a semester without leaving as a very loyal American. She had a very strong emphasis on patriotism and on teaching the nation's history to the children.

Even as a child, Ms. Shuldes knew she would grow up to become a teacher. Her interest was first sparked from the time she began her schooling. Carrying this passion into adulthood, she sought to expand her knowledge in the field through the pursuit of a formal education. She first attended Northwestern University in Evanston, Illinois. After completing coursework there, she earned a Bachelor of Science in education in 1951. Her professors there served as mentors who motivated and inspired her. She continued her studies at the same esteemed academic institution and ultimately achieved a Master of Arts upon graduating in 1956.

Previously, Ms. Shuldes maintained memberships with such prestigious organizations as the American Association of University Women, the Concerned Women for America and the Great Barrington Historical Society. In addition, she was affiliated with the Chicago Collie Club, the Collie Club of America and the Barrington Women's Club. She was further associated with the South Barrington Garden Club, the Christian Women's Club, the Green Thumb Garden Club, the Barrington Lyric Opera and Delta Kappa Gamma.

Ms. Shuldes was equally involved in her community through civic activities. She was the vice chair of the 13th Congressional District Representative Women Organization from 1958 to 1962. She acted as chairman of the American History Essay Contest Signal Hill chapter of the National Society Daughters of the American Revolution from 1988 to 1992, later serving as chaplain from 1994 to 1996. Notably, she was an honorary conductor for the Elgin Symphony Orchestra in 1988. She considered this to be the highlight of her career. There were 22,000 people in the audience for this once-in-a-lifetime experience of hers.

In light of the many successes she had during her life and career, Ms. Shuldes gained recognition in the form of many awards and accolades over the years. In both 1971 and 1972, she was the recipient of the George Washington Honor Medal from the Freedoms Foundation in Valley Forge, Pennsylvania. She was also honored with a Valley Forge Teachers Medal in 1972 and a pageant honor certificate in 1973. She was previously selected for inclusion in such honors publications as the sixth edition of Who's Who in American Education, which was published in 2003, and the 20th and 22nd editions of Who's Who of American Women, which were published in 1997 and 2000, respectively.

Ms. Shuldes was born in Chicago, Illinois, to mother Lillian Evans Baldwin and father Clarence Andrew Sr. She passed away on June 20, 2017, at the age of 87. Married to Robert William Shuldes on June 19, 1954, she was the proud mother of two children named Judith Yvonne Shuldes Turley and Eugene Robert. Moreover, she had four grandchildren and nine great-grandchildren. Outside of her professional endeavors, she liked to garden, travel, and raise and show collies.

Biljana B. Sljivic-Simsic, PhD

Professor Emerita
University of Illinois at Chicago
WILMETTE, IL UNITED STATES

Growing up in communist Serbia, Biljana B. Sljivic-Simsic, PhD, initially obtained an assistantship at the University of Belgrade from 1957 to 1962. From there, she decided to study linguistics, interested in a career in academia in spite of her family's pressure to pursue medicine. She achieved a diploma in 1955 and soon received a Harvard fellowship for graduate students, which helped her leave the communist environment of her earlier education. After immigrating to the United States in 1962, she continued her pursuit of a formal education at Harvard University in Cambridge, Massachusetts. She earned a Master of Arts in 1963, remained at the same esteemed academic institution, and ultimately graduated with a Doctor of Philosophy in 1966.

Demonstrating occupational persistence, Dr. Sljivic-Simsic began her career as a lecturer at the University of Clermont-Ferrand in France. After moving to the United States, she became a visiting lecturer and a visiting assistant professor at the University of California, Los Angeles. Growing in her profession, she also worked as a teacher at the University of Kentucky, the University of Pennsylvania and Princeton University before becoming an associate professor in the department of Slavic and Baltic languages and literature at the University of Illinois at Chicago in 1973. Dr. Sljivic-Simsic swiftly became professor and head of her department prior to her retirement in 2009, celebrating a lengthy academic career.

In addition to her professional accomplishments within the United States, Dr. Sljivic-Simsic spent time as an exchange professor for the

University of Amsterdam in 2000 and 2002 and for the University of London and the University of Cambridge from 1989 to 1990. She has been a senior writer for The Ohio State University and has served the U.S. Department of Education as a consultant and panelist for their Fulbright fellowship. Exhibiting remarkable knowledge in her chosen field, she authored eight volumes of Serbo-Croatian Textbooks for Individualized Studies, which were published from 1983 to 1988. She also co-wrote Serbo-Croatian, Just For You, Serbo-Croatian-English Dictionary and "Judeo-Spanish Ballads from Bosnia," utilizing her skills for the benefit of the academic community.

Dr. Sljivic-Simsic has been recognized with numerous grants for the completion of her work, and she received scholarships from Radcliffe College and Harvard University, due to her academic skill and commitment. Consistently interested in industry developments, she has acted in leadership positions for the North American Society for Serbian Studies and has been involved with the Association of Serbian Writers of Belgrade. She has been involved with the Chicago Horticultural Society and the Harvard and Radcliffe Clubs of Chicago.

Moving forward, Dr. Sljivic-Simsic plans to work on memoirs concerning her early life in Serbia for the benefit of her grandchildren. She has previously been selected for inclusion in such honors publications as the 58th through 70th editions of Who's Who in America, the seventh and eighth editions of Who's Who in American Education and the 36th through 42nd editions of Who's Who in the Midwest. She has also been listed in nine editions of Who's Who in the World and three editions of Who's Who of American Women.

Dr. Sljivic-Simsic was born on January 20, 1933, in Belgrade, Serbia, to mother Radoyka Pesic Sljivic and father Branko M. Sljivic. She was married to Branislav S. Simsic from 1953 to 1963, and together, they had one child named Violet Ljubica and one son-in-law named Tim Hancock. Moreover, she has three grandsons. In her free time, she enjoys participating in such activities as practicing photography, traveling, gardening and reading.

A Lifetime of Achievement in **Education**

Donald K. Sorsabal, EdD

Vice President of Administrative Services (Retired)
El Camino College
UPLAND, CA UNITED STATES

Donald K. Sorsabal, EdD, is a leader in the fields of education and administration, building a strong reputation as a trusted name in academia. After accruing 40 years of professional excellence, he retired from his role as the vice president of administrative services with El Camino College in Torrance, California. At the beginning of Dr. Sorsabal's career, he completed service with the U.S. Army from 1945 until his honorable discharge in 1947. Subsequently, he worked as a teacher with the San Pasqual Union School District and the Garden Grove Unified School District, where he also held the post of the principal.

Over the years, Dr. Sorsabal found success in academic administration as a consultant for the Orange County superintendent of schools and the assistant superintendent of business at the Santa Barbara Unified School District, a position he also held in the Santa Barbara City College District. He briefly left academia to assume the position of the vice president of the National Pacific Investors Corporation in Santa Barbara, but returned to the field to serve as the assistant superintendent for Chaffey College from 1981 to 1985. Dr. Sorsabal also maintains his affiliation with the Masonic Order and the Association of Chief Business Officials.

Beyond his professional endeavors within academia, Dr. Sorsabal has been an enthusiastic and committed volunteer for Shriners Hospitals for Children, a network of more than 20 nonprofit medical facilities across North America that provides specialized care to pediatric patients regardless of their ability to pay. He cites his time as the treasurer at his local chapter of Shriners International, a philanthropic fraternity that promotes camaraderie, self-improvement and men of good character, among the highlights of his career. In addition, Dr. Sorsabal has contributed to El Bekal Shrine as a potentate, where he joined other individuals to generate capital for Shriners Hospitals. To further support his community, he has been involved in his regional Kiwanis and Rotary clubs.

Prior to embarking on his professional path, Dr. Sorsabal pursued an education at Fullerton Junior College in California, initially earning an Associate of Arts in 1949. He continued his studies with a Bachelor of Arts from Whittier College in California. Following these accomplishments, he obtained a Master of Arts from San Diego State University. To better his understanding of his fields, Dr. Sorsabal concluded his academic efforts at the University of Southern California, graduating with a Doctor of Education in business and finance.

In recognition of his outstanding work, Dr. Sorsabal was featured in the 24th and 25th editions of Who's Who in Finance and Industry. His leadership and professional achievements have also been commemorated with the Albert Nelson Marquis Lifetime Achievement Award. In addition to his professional accomplishments and charitable efforts, Dr. Sorsabal is well-regarded by his peers for his sense of humor. He is an avid pilot, having learned how to fly in 1970 from a college professor, and purchased his first plane in 1986. In addition to his pilot's license, Dr. Sorsabal has accrued securities and life and disability licenses from the National Association of Securities Dealers.

Dr. Sorsabal was born on March 3, 1928, in Downey, California, to Andrew Joseph and Earma May Thompson. He was married to Daretha Clark for more than 40 years before her unfortunate passing in 2017. Dr. Sorsabal is the proud father of Deborah Sue, Rachael Michele and Lawrence Timothy. Looking toward the future, he intends to continue his charitable and philanthropic endeavors.

A Lifetime of Achievement in **Education**

Charleszetta Stalling, EdD

Educational Trainer & Consultant

ELK GROVE, CA UNITED STATES

Charleszetta Stalling, EdD, is an educational trainer and consultant with more than 40 years of distinguished service to her field. Inspired by the support of her mother and by witnessing the successes of her father, who taught himself to read, she developed a love of learning that blossomed into her vocation. She initially pursued an education at Los Angeles City College, earning an Associate of Arts in English in 1965 before graduating from California State University, Los Angeles, in 1969 with a Bachelor of Arts in language arts. Dr. Stalling later obtained a Master of Education in education and reading from Harvard University in 1972, and a Doctor of Education in human services and applied behavioral sciences from the University of Massachusetts Amherst in 1977.

From 1978 to 1979, Dr. Stalling worked as a Vocational Education Act program coordinator at the Los Angeles Trade-Technical College, where she subsequently served as the assistant dean of extended opportunity programs and services from 1979 to 1985. From 1985 to 1986, Dr. Stalling was active as the assistant dean of student services for the Los Angeles Trade-Technical College. The school's notable alumni include U.S. House of Representatives member Matthew G. Martinez, American artist David Hammons and contemporary artist Allan McCollum, as well as several prominent fashion designers. From 1990 to 1991, Dr. Stalling held the posts of a trainer and an instructional services coordinator for California State University, Sacramento, before leaving to focus on K-12 education, nonprofit grant writing and program development from 1991 to 1993.

Following these positions, Dr. Stalling excelled as associate faculty member at National University in Sacramento, California, from 1998 to 2001 and both a reading coach and a special assignment faculty member for the Sacramento City Unified School District between 1996 and 2001. She flourished as a TUPE specialist for the district from 2003 to 2004, and since 2004, she refocused her career toward private consulting as a trainer for Stalling Enterprises & Associates of Sacramento, where she has provided her wealth of knowledge to educational and enterprise clients alike.

The highlight of Dr. Stalling's career was the publication of "Bridge: A Cross-Culture Reading Program" because it was the result of the combination of three writers — herself, her late husband and Grace Holt. They were able to put all of their years of experience together. Dr. Stalling and Ms. Holt were reading specialists, and her husband was a psychologist. They compiled about 45 years of their combined experience to create the booklet, which was very popular, but also controversial. The philosophy was simple: start where the child is, and take the child where he or she needs to go while bringing their background in. They wanted to work with African American inner-city children, and if they came to school speaking nonstandard English, they used that as a foundation to bring them to standard written English without putting down their natural dialect. Dr. Stalling is also proud of enjoying life and taking in God's natural beauty and wonders.

Dr. Stalling is the author of numerous works on reading instruction and cultural factors, with a focus on the cultural history and pedagogy of reading and Black learners. She hopes to continue cementing her legacy as an esteemed and versatile figure in the field of education in the years to come. Additionally, she would like to be remembered as a kind friend, a considerate mother and a thoughtful sister.

John "Jack" Dickerson Todd III

Coach
Spartanburg High School
SPARTANBURG, SC UNITED STATES

With 40 years of experience to his credit, John "Jack" Dickerson Todd III has excelled as a dedicated and passionate coach of cross-country and track at Spartanburg High School in Spartanburg School District 7 since 2008. Prior to this appointment, he held multiple positions at the South Carolina School for the Deaf and the Blind in Spartanburg, South Carolina, including the director of residential life from 2006 to 2008, the director of media and library services from 1991 to 2006, and the director of physical education in 1991. Mr. Todd began his career at the South Carolina School for the Deaf and the Blind as a teacher and a coach of track and cross-country from 1979 to 1990, during which time he coached seven individual state champions.

Before embarking on his professional path, Mr. Todd pursued an education at Wofford College, earning a Bachelor of Arts in sociology in 1974. He continued his academic efforts at the University of South Carolina, obtaining a Master of Arts in Teaching in health and physical education in 1977. Following these accomplishments, Mr. Todd concluded his studies at the University of South Carolina in 1996, graduating with a Master of Arts in library and information science.

Beyond his responsibilities within the field, Mr. Todd has participated in numerous endeavors outside of his professional circles. Working in a number of national and international coaching posts at the United States Association of Blind Athletes since 1980, he contributed

A Lifetime of Achievement | John "Jack" Dickerson Todd III

to the founder and the president for the South Carolina Foundation for Disabled Athletes since 1990. He further held the role of the director of the Out of Sight Road Race from 1986 to 1999, the Pan American Games for the Blind in 2001, the National Goalball Championships in 2004, the World Goalball Championships in 2006, the Out of Sight Road Race in 1986 to 1999, and the Eye Opener Cross Country Meet since 1984. The chairman of the Spartanburg Sports Commission from 2002 to 2003, Mr. Todd found success on the board of directors for the YMCA of Greater Spartanburg from 1991 to 1993 and the Spartanburg Area Chamber of Commerce from 2002 to 2005.

In addition to his primary vocation, Mr. Todd remains affiliated with various organizations in relation to his areas of expertise. From 2006 to 2009, he had maintained his involvement on the Sports Technical Committees for the International Paralympic Committee. He is also a member of the South Carolina Association of Blind Athletes, for which he was active on the board of directors from 1980 to 1996 and as the president in 1984. A graduate of Leadership Spartanburg in 2003, Mr. Todd proudly recalls his organization, staging and the direction of the World Goalball Championships in 2006 as the highlight of his career.

In light of his exceptional undertakings, Mr. Todd has accrued several notable accolades. Recognized as the National Deaf Cross Country Coach of the Year in 1989 and the Outstanding Young Alumni by Wofford College in 1992, he was presented with the International Service to Mankind Award by Sertoma International in 2001. Furthermore, he was inducted into the Hall of Fame for the South Carolina chapter of the Road Runners Club of America in 1999, the USA Track & Field, Inc., in honor of a Lifetime of Achievement in 2006, and the United States Association of Blind Athletes as a coach in 2009. Likewise, Mr. Todd was selected for inclusion in the eighth edition of Who's Who in American Education and both the 24th and 25th editions of Who's Who in the South and Southwest.

A Lifetime of Achievement in **Education**

Lloyd Ultan

Professor
Fairleigh Dickinson University
NEW YORK, NY UNITED STATES

P rior to embarking upon his professional path, Lloyd Ultan earned a Bachelor of Arts, cum laude, from Hunter College in 1959 and a Master of Arts from Columbia University in 1960. He began his career in the Edward Williams College at Fairleigh Dickinson University, holding the ranks of an associate, an assistant professor, and an associate professor. Since 1981, he has excelled as a professor at Fairleigh Dickinson University.

During this time, Mr. Ultan has found success as a consultant in his field and a guest lecturer at numerous institutions, including Herbert H. Lehman College, Bronx Community College, the College of Mount Saint Vincent, The City College of New York, Fordham University and the Albert Einstein College of Medicine, among others. Interested in history from a young age, he has succeeded in his field due to his desire to share knowledge with others as well as the support he has received from family and colleagues. After studying the history of the United States and several other countries, he decided to explore the history of the Bronx, where he grew up. A celebrated educator, Mr. Ultan is particularly proud of the encouragement he was able to give a particularly bright student who had been discouraged earlier in his academic career.

Currently recognized as a distinguished professor for scholarship and research at Fairleigh Dickinson University, Mr. Ultan has been honored by several professionally relevant organizations throughout his career's duration. He is an honorary member of Neumann-Goldman Post No. 69, and he has been inducted into the Bronx Jewish Hall of Fame for Lifetime Achievement. Moreover, he has received several certificates in his field, among numerous other instances of recognition.

The Bronx Borough Historian since 1996, Mr. Ultan has also contributed to his community as the president of the 91 Van Cortlandt Owners Corp., a founder of the Bronx Council on the Arts and a member of the board of directors for the National Shrine of the Bill of Rights. Other organizations and committees he has been involved with include the Historic Preservation Committee of St. Ann's Episcopal Church, the Bronx Borough President's Bicentennial Advisory Committee, the Bronx Day Commission and the Bronx Civic League. He has served the Bronx County Historical Society in several capacities, including as the president.

Mr. Ultan's creative contributions to his field are numerous and include "The Bronx County Building's Historical Murals: An Artistic Legacy," "The Northern Borough: A History of the Bronx" and "Presidents of the United States, Volume VI of Roots of the Republic." He also co-authored such works as "A Historical Sketch of the Bronx" and "The Bronx: The Ultimate Guide to New York City's Beautiful Borough." A prominent scholar in his field, Mr. Ultan has participated in symposia and panel discussions for The Bronx Museum of the Arts, the State University of New York Empire State College, the Southern New York State Symposium on the Bronx River, Saint Ann's Episcopal Church and the 125th anniversary of the Bronx Park system.

From 1992 to 1993, Mr. Ultan excelled as a vice president of the Teaneck chapter of the American Association of University Professors and the secretary of the Council of Fairleigh Dickinson University chapter of the American Association of University Professors. He has also been involved with such organizations as the New York City Committee on Cultural Concerns, the New York City Department of Cultural Affairs' Program Guidelines Committee, the New-York Historical Society and the American Historical Association. A member of Sigma Lambda, Alpha Chi Alpha and Phi Alpha Theta, he was appointed to the New York City Mayor's Task Force on Spontaneous Memorials in 2002.

Demonstrating considerable knowledge and professional expertise, Mr. Ultan has accepted a number of awards, including Fairleigh Dickinson University's 50-Year Award in 2014, Bissel Gardens' Award of Honor in 1999, the Bronx County Historical Society's Edgar Allan Poe

Award for Literary Excellence in 1996, the Bronx Landmarks Education Award in 1995 and Edward Williams College's Outstanding Teacher of the Year Award in 1994, among several others. He was also selected for inclusion in the Alumni Association of Hunter College Hall of Fame in 1974 and was presented with a New York State Regents college teaching fellowship in 1959. Due to his considerable professional contributions, Mr. Ultan has been featured in numerous editions of Who's Who in America, Who's Who in American Education, Who's Who in the East and Who's Who in the World.

A Lifetime of Achievement in **Education**

Donna R. Vocate, PhD

Speech-Language Educator

DENVER, CO UNITED STATES

With more than two decades of experience and several books to her credit, Donna R. Vocate, PhD, has enjoyed a rich career as a speech-language educator. Her interest in speech and education was encouraged at a young age by a teacher in her hometown. Growing up in rural Kansas, Dr. Vocate always loved to read and exhibited a keen interest in journalism, as well as investigating words and how sentences were put together. Going to school in a small schoolhouse, her teacher, who also taught her mother, would bring her books, and this kind act opened her eyes to the wide world of speech and language.

Prior to beginning her professional career, Dr. Vocate gained a solid foundation at the University of Colorado, where she earned a Bachelor of Arts in 1962. Following this accomplishment, she subsequently attended the University of Denver, where she completed coursework to obtain a Master of Arts in 1977 and Doctor of Philosophy in 1980. A lifelong learner, Dr. Vocate gained further skills and knowledge at the Harvard University Graduate School of Education management development program in 1999.

Well-equipped with a strong educational background, Dr. Vocate began her career as an assistant professor at Eastern Montana College, now known as Montana State University Billings. She succeeded in this position from 1980 to 1983 before going to the University of Colorado Boulder, where she thrived as an assistant professor from 1983 to 1990. Dr. Vocate then served as a professor at Boston University from 1990 to 1992, prior to accepting a position at Arkansas Tech University, in Russellville, where she excelled as a professor from

1990 until 2003. A dedicated educator, she counts the most rewarding aspect of her profession to be the ability to connect with her students.

In addition to her professional responsibilities, Dr. Vocate served as a director of the Young Scholars Summer Session at the University of Colorado from 1988 to 1993. She currently retains a position as a faculty research associate at the Institute of Cognitive Science at the University of Colorado Boulder, a role she accepted in 1984. The institute includes three research centers aimed at enhancing the understanding of human cognition, learning and development, in addition to encouraging the formation of interdisciplinary partnerships.

Recognized as a leader in her field, Dr. Vocate is a prolific author who has shared her expertise by contributing articles to various professional journals. In 1987, she published "The Theory of A.R. Luria," a book that takes a closer look at the work of notable neuropsychologist Alexander Romanovich Luria. She is also the author of Intrapersonal Communication: Different Voices, Different Minds, a textbook released in 1994 for graduate students and professionals that explores intrapersonal communication, in addition to offering applications and pedagogical guidance.

To stay up to date on changes in the field, Dr. Vocate maintains affiliation with the International Communication Association, the Western Speech Communication Association, the American Association of University Women and the Honors Speech Communication Association. She further lent her leadership to the National Speech Communication Association as the chairman of the speech and language science division from 1985 to 1986, and as the chair of the National Communication Association's speech and language sciences and international divisions.

Dr. Vocate was born on July 15, 1941, in Smith County, Kansas, to Ancel L. Garrett and Eva Covey Garrett. She enjoyed many years of marriage to Gilbert E. Vocate before his passing. Dr. Vocate currently resides in Denver, Colorado.

A Lifetime of Achievement in **Education**

Rebecca Ann Wilson

Educator (Retired)

SHEPHERDSTOWN, WV UNITED STATES

Rebecca Ann Wilson began her career at Shepherd College, where she majored in home economics and minored in English and earned a Bachelor of Arts in secondary education in 1967.

While at Shepherd College, she was a member of the Miller Hall dorm council and a member of the Shepherd College concert and pep bands for four years. She was president of the Home Economics Club, student assistant in the English department and a member of the Sigma Sigma Sigma Sorority.

From West Virginia University, she gained her certification in special education and, to maintain her teaching and substitute teaching certification, she completed 27 postgraduate hours in education, psychology and administration. During 1997 and 1998, she attended three national developmental disabilities seminars and accumulated nine hours of continuing education in the spectrum of developmental disabilities through the Office of Continuing Medical Education at Johns Hopkins University.

With more than 10 years of professional experience, Mrs. Wilson was a teacher with the Jefferson County Schools from 1967 to 1972, where she taught reading, English, special education and home economics. While teaching at Charles Town Junior High School, she was the student government sponsor. She was a substitute teacher in grades seven through 12 from 1975 to 1979.

In addition to her primary roles, she was appointed by the West Virginia state superintendent of schools to serve as a parent member of the West Virginia Advisory Council for the Education of Exceptional Children, which, with the assistance of the West Virginia State Board of Education, advises the state legislature, the state Board of Education, the state superintendent of schools and the public, concerning the unmet needs of exceptional children and to make such recommendations as it deems proper. During her second three-year appointment, she served as chair of the council.

Appointed by the governor of West Virginia, Mrs. Wilson served as a member of the Governor's Schools of West Virginia advisory board, which advised its governing body, the West Virginia Department of Education and the Arts, regarding site selections and program offerings. It selects students and faculty for each of the schools, including the Governor's School for Math and Science, the School for the Arts and the Governor's Honors Academy.

A respected voice in her areas of interest, Mrs. Wilson has been an active leader in her community. She was on the board of directors of the Shepherdstown Day Care Center as well as the advisory board of the Jefferson Center and the Outreach Committee to Expand Recognition in the Community, and the board of directors of the Jefferson County Special Olympics. She served on the board of directors of the Potomac Center in Romney, West Virginia, the only residential intensive training facility for children with intellectual and development disorders and accompanying behavioral problems.

With her children in school, she was a member of the Shepherdstown Elementary Association and enjoyed being homeroom mother for over 11 years. She was also a member of the Parent Teacher Organization of Shepherdstown Junior High School, a member of the Jefferson High School Band Boosters and a chaperone on many field trips, team sports away games, and marching band and concert band competitions and trips. During those same years, she was a member of the steering committee for the creation of a TV studio at the Jefferson County Board of Education office, the Jefferson High School vocational advisory council and the board of directors for the Alliance for Technology Access. Prior to a building and school expansion program, Mrs. Wilson was tapped by the Jefferson County Board of Education to be on a 25-member citizens advisory committee, which was charged with identifying future facilities, locations and services needed for the rapidly growing student population and providing those findings to the board in both an oral and printed report.

A Lifetime of Achievement | **Rebecca Ann Wilson**

As an elected member of the Jefferson County Board of Education, she represented her home district, which is Shepherdstown, West Virginia. In addition to her job as a board member, she was Board of Education liaison to business partner signings and also liaison to the Eastern Panhandle Children's Summit, sponsored by United Way. Beyond that, she continued to work through the Martinsburg Family Resource Center to sponsor events for children in accordance with the ideals set forth in America's Promise, headed by Colin Powell. She was also a member of the board of directors of Regional Education Service Agency 8, which is a regional public multiservice agency that is authorized by state law to develop, manage and provide services and programs to local education agencies, such as public schools.

Outside of her profession, Mrs. Wilson is a member of Trinity Episcopal Church and a member of the Order of the Eastern State #155, both in Shepherdstown. She is a Maryland 4-H All Star and has been a 4-H leader, a member of the Jefferson County Leaders Association, and a judge at county fairs in Harford County and Howard County, Maryland, and the Jefferson County Fair in West Virginia. She has also judged at public school social studies fairs and science fairs in Jefferson County.

She is a lifetime member of the American Association of University Women and the Sigma Sigma Sigma Sorority; a charter member of the National Women's History Museum, the Jefferson County Special Olympics board of directors and the Homemakers Club, a county outreach education service; a convention member of the International Association of Jazz Educators, the Shepherd University Emeritus Club and the Jefferson County Cotillion Club; and an honorary citizen of George Washington's Mount Vernon. As a member of the General Federation of Women's Clubs, she served as president of the GFWC Shepherdstown Women's Club for three terms, president of the GFWC West Virginia Eastern District for one term, West Virginia LEADS delegate and a member of GFWC Woman's Club of Martinsburg.

Notably profiled in the 73rd edition of Who's Who in America, Mrs. Wilson was raised on a dairy farm near Jarrettsville, Maryland. She gives credit to her loving parents, Nancy Ann Yingling Wiley and Bertram Bradford Wiley, for being excellent role models with common sense and high standards laced with a sense of humor. In 1967, she married David Lloyd Wilson. She has two wonderful daughters, Laura

Beth Wilson and Amy Lynn Wilson Hardy. One of the best parts of her life includes spending time with her grandchildren, Ian Bradford Hardy and Isabel Katherine Hardy.

Sil Louis Arata Sr.

Packaging Engineer (Retired)
Hewlett-Packard Company
PHILOMATH, OR UNITED STATES

With 40 years of experience to his credit, Sil Louis Arata Sr. is currently retired, having excelled with the Hewlett-Packard Company as a packaging engineer from 1981 to 1999. Prior to this appointment, he worked as a packaging engineer for the John Fluke Manufacturing Company in 1979. Previously, he held a number of positions with Tektronix, Inc., including as a packaging engineering manager from 1972 to 1978, the manager of engineering development support from 1969 to 1972, and a packaging engineer from 1961 to 1969. Mr. Arata began his career as a production foreman for Signet Controls from 1959 to 1960 and an inspector with the Hyster Corporation from 1960 to 1961.

Before embarking on his professional path, Mr. Arata enlisted in the U.S. Navy, serving from 1949 until his honorable discharge in 1952. Following this accomplishment, he pursued an education at Clark College, completing coursework in pre-engineering in 1954. He continued his academic efforts at Oregon State University, earning a Bachelor of Science in industrial engineering in 1959. Mr. Arata concluded his studies with coursework in packaging at Purdue University in 1963, coursework in electronics at Multnomah College in 1966, and coursework in marketing at Portland State University in 1967.

Beyond his responsibilities within the field, Mr. Arata has participated in numerous endeavors outside of his professional circles. In 1966, he contributed to the East County Multnomah Republican

Central Committee as a captain. A seminar leader for the Fall Equipment Production Show in Seattle, Washington, in 1979, he previously held the role of a judge for the Society of Packaging and Handling Engineers Show in 1973, the North Star Packaging Competition in 1974, and a West Pack Packaging Expo in 1987. Mr. Arata found success as an educator as well, having provided his wealth of knowledge as an instructor of packaging technology at Mount Hood College in 1972.

In addition to his primary vocation, Mr. Arata remains affiliated with various organizations in relation to his areas of expertise. He has maintained his involvement with the Society of Packaging and Handling Engineers since 1964, holding many administrative posts for committees, chapters, boards and programs during this time. Between 1976 and 1981, he was also active with the Institute of Packaging Professionals as the chairman for the national honors awards committee, the vice president of the Western region, a member of the national packaging committee, a chairman for the recertification committee and a judge. A member of Sigma Phi Epsilon, the National Packaging Fraternity, Mr. Arata was a loaned executive for the United Way in 1971 and a fundraising chairman for Junior Achievement in 1976.

In light of his exceptional undertakings, Mr. Arata has accrued several accolades throughout his impressive career. He has been recognized as an honorary lifetime member of the Institute of Packaging Professionals, which remains the highlight of his remarkable career. He was presented with fellowships from the Institute of Packaging Professionals and the Society of Packaging and Handling Engineers. Likewise, Mr. Arata was selected for inclusion in the first edition of Who's Who in Science and Engineering, the 29th edition of Who's Who in Finance and Industry, and multiple editions of Who's Who in the West and Who's Who in the World.

Inadvertently entering his profession after defining the design packaging of a product with which his company had been struggling, Mr. Arata was further mentored by Dr. Zuzi of Cornell University, Dr. Golf of Michigan State University, and Dr. Raphael of the Rochester Institute of Technology. He notably remembers the challenge of making companies realize packaging was a part of their product, and he proudly crafted packaging for Hewlett-Packard that was nearly indestructible. Looking toward the future, Mr. Arata hopes to continue enjoying his retirement while cementing his legacy as an accurate, open-minded and responsible figure in his industry who always shared credit with his colleagues.

A Lifetime of Achievement in **Engineering**

John W. Barrier

Director (Retired)
ClearFuels Technology Inc.
CLOVERDALE, AL UNITED STATES

With more than 40 years of experience to his credit, John W. Barrier is currently retired, having excelled as a director of ClearFuels Technology Inc. in Honolulu, Hawaii, from 2002 to 2013. During this time, he held the same position with Frontier Fuels LLC from 2005 to 2010 and Metropolitan Energy Systems, Inc., from 2000 to 2010. Prior to these appointments, he served the Tennessee Valley Authority in Muscle Shoals, Alabama, as a program manager from 1986 to 2000, a project manager from 1985 to 1986, a process development leader from 1982 to 1986, and a chemical engineer from 1976 to 1982. Mr. Barrier began his career as a process engineer for the Monsanto Company in Decatur, Alabama, from 1972 to 1976.

Before embarking on his professional path, Mr. Barrier pursued an education at the University of Tennessee, earning a Bachelor of Science in chemical engineering in 1972. He concluded his academic efforts at the University of Tennessee in 1975, graduating with a Master of Science in engineering administration. In addition to these accomplishments, Mr. Barrier completed his training through the management development program through the Monsanto Company from 1972 to 1976 and the management training program through the Tennessee Valley Authority from 1984 to 1988.

Beyond his responsibilities within the field, Mr. Barrier has participated in numerous endeavors outside of his professional circles. He has contributed to the board of directors to the Heritage Christian

University since 2004, the board of advisers for the Aina Institute since 2000, and the president's advisory board for the Freed-Hardeman University since 1997. Working on the adjunct faculty for the department of science and engineering at Calhoun Community College from 1973 to 1976, he held the role of an adjunct instructor at Faulkner University from 1980 to 2000 and Heritage Christian University from 1992 to 2010. A consultant on environmental science and energy, Mr. Barrier found success with his written works as well, authoring over 150 technical reports and publications and over 50 speeches for national and international conferences.

In addition to his primary vocation, Mr. Barrier remains affiliated with various organizations in relation to his areas of expertise. From 2001 to 2005, he dedicated his significant knowledge to the U.S. Department of Energy as an adviser and a nonpaid adviser. Mr. Barrier was also active as an Army social worker in the 330th Military Police Detachment of the U.S. Army Reserve in Sheffield, Alabama, from 1972 to 1978, at which point he attained his honorable discharge.

In light of his exceptional undertakings, Mr. Barrier has accrued several accolades throughout his impressive career. In 1979, he was recognized among the Outstanding Young Men in America. Accepting several awards for his achievements in management and engineering, he was notably presented with a Technology Achievement Award from the U.S. Department of Energy in 1985. Likewise, Mr. Barrier was selected for inclusion in multiple editions of Who's Who in America, Who's Who in Science and Engineering, Who's Who in the South and Southwest, and Who's Who of Emerging Leaders in America.

Attributing his success to his reach, mentors and the opportunities to work alongside great organizations, Mr. Barrier was inspired by his encouraging teachers, his inherent passion in chemistry, and his desire to benefit society through his hard work in energy, energy research and energy policy. Proud of his patriotism and integrity, he has developed a series of technologies for energy production with a number of federal agencies, including those for renewable fuel production, coal conversion, power production, emission control and system integration. Having traveled to more than 30 countries around the world over the course of his career, he emphasizes the importance of being dependable, loyal, strategic, committed to working hard, and seeking graduate studies for success within his field. Looking toward the future, Mr. Barrier hopes to continue volunteering, spreading his expertise, and cementing his legacy as an honest, fair, confident and motivated figure in chemical engineering.

Looking toward his future, Mr. Barrier plans to enjoy retirement with his family, his wife Janet, his four children and his seven grandchildren. Since 1997, he has maintained his involvement and continues his volunteer work with the Double Springs Church of Christ in Double Springs, Alabama, as a mission's minister.

Richard C. Chou
Mechanical Engineer (Retired)
MONTEREY PARK, CA UNITED STATES

Richard C. Chou has enjoyed an illustrious career as a mechanical engineer, emerging as an innovative leader in dynamic motion systems. With nearly 40 years of experience to his credit, he most recently excelled as the president of NuSat International Ltd. for six years, until 2000. Prior to thriving in this position, Mr. Chou contributed to ITT-Gilfillan, located in Van Nuys, California, as a senior member of the technical staff from 1985 until his departure in 1993. He launched his career at The Franklin Institute, based in Philadelphia, Pennsylvania, a world-class museum and science education center, where he found success as a principal engineer from 1961 to 1985.

A native of Beijing, China, Mr. Chou initially became interested in pursuing a career in engineering as a child tinkering with machines. He was also greatly influenced by his father, a general in the Chinese army who taught his son how to make the most out of the least amount of equipment. Shortly after arriving to the United States in 1956, Mr. Chou commenced his academic efforts with Purdue University, a world-renowned research university located in Indiana, where he received a Bachelor of Mechanical Engineering in 1959. Continuing his studies, he earned a Bachelor of Science in applied mathematics at Milton College in Wisconsin in 1961 and completed postgraduate coursework at the University of Pennsylvania in Philadelphia in 1963.

Renowned for his knowledge and leadership, Mr. Chou has lent his expertise to several professional organizations. A member of Sigma Xi,

A Lifetime of Achievement | **Richard C. Chou**

he maintains affiliation with the Alumni Association Board of the Frances Payne Bolton School of Nursing at Case Western Reserve University in Cleveland. Mr. Chou is further affiliated with the National Defense Association, a nonprofit educational organization that identifies key issues of national security and utilizes the knowledge of its 85,000 individual members and 1,600 corporate members to address them.

In a career marked by several achievements, Mr. Chou is proud to have developed groundbreaking technology for major corporations. Among the highlights of his professional life are designing motion systems for dynamic space flight simulators as well as playing a role in the creation of a driving simulator for Mercedes-Benz. Additionally, he was grateful for the opportunity to work with the National Aeronautics and Space Administration, which led to him receiving the Space Act Award from the organization in 1998. Prior to this accomplishment, Mr. Chou was presented the German Industry Innovation Award in 1986. In light of his exceptional undertakings, he has been selected for inclusion in multiple editions of Who's Who in America and Who's Who in Science and Engineering, as well as the 21st edition of Who's Who in the West and the 20th edition of Who's Who in the World. He was notably profiled in the 73rd edition of Who's Who in America. In recognition of Mr. Chou's remarkable leadership and notable achievements to the field, he has also been named the recipient of the Albert Nelson Marquis Lifetime Achievement Award. The prestigious award is considered one of the highest distinctions available through Marquis Who's Who.

Mr. Chou was born on February 7, 1934, to Kuan-Shih and Chi-Chung Chang Chou. He and his wife, Roseanna Chou, have enjoyed many happy years of marriage and currently reside in California. They are the proud parents of three children, Henry, Jerry and Karol, and doting grandparents of one grandson who was married in May 2019.

A Lifetime of Achievement in **Engineering**

Simon A. Ginzburg, PhD

Lead Engineer (Retired)
MITRE Corp.
BOXBOROUGH, MA UNITED STATES

With 50 years of industry experience to his credit, Simon A. Ginzburg, PhD, is currently retired, having excelled as a lead engineer for the MITRE Corp. in Bedford, Massachusetts, from 1999 to 2009. He previously provided engineering and technical guidance for the federal government in 1958. The MITRE Corp. has dedicated its efforts to helping governments around the globe to resolve issues on the battlefield, in hospitals, in cyberspace and beyond through the operation of federally funded research and development centers.

Prior to this appointment, Dr. Ginzburg held the position of a senior member on the technical staff for Racal-Datacom, Inc., in Boxborough, Massachusetts, from 1992 to 1997. Previously, he served as a principal engineer for the Digital Equipment Corporation in Littleton, Massachusetts, from 1985 to 1992. Relocating to the United States in 1980, Dr. Ginzburg further worked in the same capacity for Wang Laboratories in Lowell, Massachusetts, from 1981 to 1985.

Dr. Ginzburg began his career at the Central Research Institute of Communications in Moscow, Russia, for which he was active as an engineer, a senior engineer, and a principal engineer and senior scientist between 1969 and 1980. Before embarking on his professional path, he pursued an education at the Institute of Radio-engineering and Electronics in Moscow, earning a Master of Science in 1961. Following this accomplishment, he concluded his studies with a Doctor of Philosophy at the Institute of Radio-engineering and Electronics in 1969. Dr. Ginzburg published 40 papers in the field of radio engineering and has been awarded four United States patents.

Beyond his responsibilities within the field, Dr. Ginzburg has participated in numerous endeavors outside of his professional circles. He has found much success with his written works, having authored "Waveguides with Discrete Correction" in 1975, two editions of "Statistical Communication" in 1977 and 1979 and authored "Lightwave Transmission Systems" in 1980. Having attended the Cambridge Symposium on Fiber Optics and Integrated Optoelectronics in 1987, he further contributed to "Waveguides for Communications" as an editor in 1980. In the past, Dr. Ginzburg remained active with a number of athletic events, including cross-country skiing, long-distance biking, running, swimming, hiking and triathlons.

In light of his exceptional undertakings, Dr. Ginzburg has accrued four patents from the U.S. Patent and Trademark Office. He obtained his first patent in 1990, which was granted for a method and an apparatus for the transmission of local area network signals over unshielded twisted pairs. Subsequently, he garnered patents for a method and an apparatus for equalization for the transmission over a band-limited channel in 1991 and a method and an apparatus for transmission of communication signals over two parallel channels in 1992. Dr. Ginzburg accrued his final patent in 1993, which was for a method and an apparatus for the transmission of local area network signals over a single unshielded twisted pair. He was notably profiled in the 73rd edition of Who's Who in America.

The son of Aaron Samuel and Broha Moisha Ginzburg, Dr. Ginzburg is the proud father of three children: Irina, Natasha and Michael. He has welcomed three grandchildren, Anthony, Jacklyn and Michelle, into his family as well. A current member of the Republican Party, Dr. Ginzburg initially became involved with his primary vocation due to his interest in radio techniques in his youth.

A Lifetime of Achievement in **Engineering**

Francis T. Jones, PhD

Chemistry Professor (Retired)
Stevens Institute of Technology
RIDGEFIELD, NJ UNITED STATES

After earning a Bachelor of Science from The Pennsylvania State University in 1955, Francis T. Jones, PhD, went on to earn a Doctor of Philosophy from the Polytechnic Institute of Brooklyn, now known as the New York University Tandon School of Engineering, in 1960. Upon graduating, he searched for postdoctoral work in radiation chemistry. This proved difficult because it was during the Cold War and radiation information remained top secret in the United States. Luckily, he was offered a postdoctoral GEC fellowship at the High Energy Radiation Laboratory of the University of Leeds in England from 1960 to 1962. Reflecting on his academic career, Dr. Jones is grateful for the mentorship he received from his chemistry teachers over the years. Additionally, he notes that the best advice he ever received was from his music teacher.

He began his career as a research scientist at the Union Carbide Corporation in Tuxedo, New York, from 1962 to 1964. He was also a faculty participant at the Oak Ridge National Laboratories in Tennessee in 1965. Since 1964, Dr. Jones has been on the faculty of the Stevens Institute of Technology in Hoboken, New Jersey. He progressed from assistant professor to professor from 1964 to 1971, and served as department head of chemistry and chemical engineering from 1979 to 1990; department director of chemistry, chemical biology and biomedical engineering from 2000 to 2008; and director of chemistry and chemical biology from 2008 to 2015. He acted as a chemistry professor from 1971 to 2015.

He was appointed secretary of the faculty of the Stevens Institute of Technology from 1971 to 1979, and was awarded an honorary Master of Engineering in 1975.

Dr. Jones has maintained an active interest in both chemistry and music — his second field of interest — and has made significant contributions to both fields. His doctoral dissertation required constructing a gauge to measure para-hydrogen, one of the forms of hydrogen gas. In Leeds, he developed a technique to measure the spectrum of an unstable species created by ionizing radiation in a low temperature glassy matrix. On a much larger scale, at Stevens Institute he created a new undergraduate major now named chemical biology, which has since been widely imitated at other universities. The graduate program leading to master's and doctoral degrees in chemical biology soon followed.

Among his contributions to music were the digital-analog interface to connect an electronic organ to the pipe organ, making the voices of both instruments simultaneously accessible to the performer. For this development, Dr. Jones received the Episcopal Church's Trinity Award in both 1991 and 1995. He has given numerous public recitals demonstrating this instrument. He has previously been selected for inclusion in such honors publications as the 24th edition of Who's Who in the East, which was published in 1992. Civically, he has been an organist and choir director of Trinity Episcopal Church in Cliffside Park, New Jersey, from 1990 to 2006. Additionally, he maintains memberships with prestigious organizations in order to remain an active presence in the field. Notably, he is an emeritus member of the American Chemical Society.

Dr. Jones was born on October 19, 1933, in Pottsville, Pennsylvania, to mother Marion Amelia Kagel Jones and father Francis Thomas Jones. He later married Nuran on January 3, 1981, and together, they are the proud parents of two daughters: Dr. Anne Jones, a physician, and Marian Jones, an architect. They have three grandchildren. In his free time, he enjoys music.

A Lifetime of Achievement in **Engineering**

Richard G. Merrell

Electronics Systems Engineer (Retired)

HEBRON, IL UNITED STATES

With several decades of professional experience to his name, Richard G. Merrell has enjoyed a successful career as an electronics systems engineer. From 1999 to 2003, he was an electronic engineering manager with GFI Genfare. Before accepting this post, he acted as an electronic systems engineer with Baxter Healthcare Corp. from 1997 to 1998, a technical recruiter for TSC Management Services Group from 1993 to 1996, technical recruiter for Executive Search Network from 1991 to 1992, electronic engineering manager for Zenith Electronics Corp. from 1981 to 1991, and electronic engineering manager for Oak Industries from 1978 to 1981.

From 1968 to 1978, Mr. Merrell served as a senior consultant engineer with Zenith Electronics Corp. His first professional role was as an electronic engineer with Motorola Inc. from 1962 to 1968. Outside of his primary endeavors, he was a part-time instructor with the Illinois Institute of Technology in Chicago, Illinois, from 1974 to 1982. Furthermore, he has contributed many articles to professional journals and has co-authored numerous technical papers. Impressively, he has 28 patents in the field.

As a high school student, Mr. Merrell had a teacher who was an electrical engineer. Inspired by this teacher, he decided to go down the same professional path. Continuing this passion into adulthood, he sought to expand his knowledge through the pursuit of a formal education at a number of esteemed academic institutions. He first attended Valparaiso Technical Institute in Valparaiso, Indiana, and earned a Bachelor of Science in electrical engineering in 1962. He continued his studies at the Illinois Institute of Technology in Chicago, Illinois, obtaining a Bachelor of Science in electrical engineering, with distinction, in 1970. Ultimately, he achieved a Master of Science in electrical engineering from the Illinois Institute of Technology in 1974. Before beginning his academic career, he was ranked as seaman apprentice in the U.S. Navy from 1954 to 1955.

An active presence in the field, Mr. Merrell formerly maintained membership with the administrative committee of the Consumer Electronics Group of the Institute of Electrical and Electronics Engineers, where he was a senior member. Further associated with community organizations, he has dedicated his time to serving as a volunteer for the McHenry County Conservation Group and a coach for girls' softball and little league baseball in Hebron, Illinois, from 1984 to 1991. With the Illinois District 19 Board of Education in Hebron, Illinois, he served as vice president from 1991 to 1993, having been a member from 1985 to 1993 and again from 1995 to 1997.

In light of his professional successes, Mr. Merrell has gained recognition in the form of myriad awards and accolades. Notably, he was voted Best of the Year for Technical Paper, which was titled "Vertical Hold Control Sync System," by the Institute of Electrical and Electronics Engineers in 1976. In addition, he has previously been selected for inclusion in such honors publications as the 24th and 25th editions of Who's Who in the Midwest and the 73rd edition of Who's Who in America.

Mr. Merrell was born on January 16, 1937, in Bald Knob, Arkansas, to mother Callie I. Beavers Merrell and father Leroy G. Merrell. He later married Aprildawn D. Messerschmidt on June 22, 1963, and together, they are the proud parents of two children, Christopher G. and Kelly E. Moreover, they have three grandchildren named Kiera, Cole and Gage. In his free time, he enjoys camping, fishing, traveling, exercising and spectator sports.

Leticia Rustia Miranda

Chemical Engineer & Consultant (Retired)

MATTHEWS, NC UNITED STATES

Having accrued more than 40 years of experience, chemical engineer Leticia Rustia Miranda is well-regarded as a leader in her industry. Not only has she thrived in a variety of positions, but she has also played a key role in designing products that have been sold internationally. Following a rewarding career, Ms. Miranda retired from consulting in chemical engineering in 2001.

A Philippines native, Ms. Miranda grew up the youngest of six children and was inspired to go into engineering by her brother, who was a civil engineer. After graduating as the valedictorian of the St. Joseph School in 1953, she attended the University of Santo Tomas in Manila on a scholarship. She graduated magna cum laude from the institution of higher education, widely recognized as one of the best schools in the Philippines, with a Bachelor of Science in chemical engineering in 1957. Ms. Miranda promptly accepted a position at her alma mater as an assistant professor, and passed on her knowledge to students for more than 10 years before immigrating to the United States in 1970.

After briefly serving as an assistant programmer at Tokheim Corp. in Fort Wayne, Indiana, Ms. Miranda continued her professional journey and offered her expertise as an analyst programmer with Duke Power Co. in Charlotte, North Carolina, from 1979 to 1989. During this time, she obtained a Master of Science from the University of North Carolina, which greatly enhanced her ability to affiliate in the field for which she held the most passion: engineering. To this end, Ms. Miranda departed from Duke Power Co. and subsequently joined the staff of Joy Energy Systems as a process engineer, an appointment she held until 1990.

Ms. Miranda found further success at Process Heat Inc., where the company's owner gave her freedom to exercise her expertise. Working alongside an electrical engineer, her valuable skills as a chemical engineer yielded the 96% VOC destruction thermal oxidizer, whose design allowed fumes in chemical facilities to produce steam. The device was so successful that it was sold hundreds of times to various companies throughout the world, particularly in Venezuela and Mexico. It even earned Ms. Miranda a Gold Medal from the University of Santo Tomas in 2007. She is also responsible for designing a Federal Drug Administration approved steam dryer for prescription drugs.

After her affiliation with Process Heat concluded, Ms. Miranda briefly worked as a design engineer for Aeroglide in Cary, North Carolina, until 1997, whereupon she shared her extensive knowledge by consulting independently with different organizations until her retirement. For her professional achievements in the field, she has been listed in the 29th edition of Who's Who in Finance and Industry as well as presented with the prestigious Albert Nelson Marquis Lifetime Achievement Award. To remain informed on developments in her field, Ms. Miranda maintains membership with the National Society of Professional Engineers, the only organization dedicated to addressing concerns of professional engineers from all backgrounds.

Ms. Miranda was born on April 7, 1936, in Peñaranda, Philippines, to Roman Rustia and Caridad Ortiz Rustia. Now a North Carolina resident, she has been happily married to her husband, Florinio, for over 50 years, and together, they are the proud parents of five children, Nathaniel, Earl, Xavier, Harvey and Sergio. Outside of her professional concerns, Ms. Miranda's avocations include skating and gardening.

John R. Pate, BCCC, BE

President
John Pate & Associates LLC
ROGERS, AR UNITED STATES

Utilizing more than five decades of experience, John R. Pate, BCCC, BE, is a distinguished engineer who has been serving as president of John Pate & Associates LLC in Rogers, Arkansas, since 2000. Prior to this appointment, he served in the same capacity for Environmental Enterprises Inc., in Little Rock, Arkansas, from 1973 to 2000. Mr. Pate commenced his career as an engineer for Trane Inc. in La Crosse, Wisconsin, from 1966 to 1973. Alongside his primary endeavors, Mr. Pate was a former member of the principal's advisory council at the Liebert Corp. in Columbus, Ohio, as well as a former contract trainer of energy auditors at the Arkansas Energy Office.

Prior to establishing himself as a trusted voice in the field, Mr. Pate sought to expand his knowledge through the pursuit of a formal education at a number of esteemed academic institutions. He first attended Lipscomb University in Nashville, Tennessee, where he earned a Bachelor of Science in liberal arts in 1965. He continued his studies at Vanderbilt University in Nashville, Tennessee, ultimately achieving a Bachelor of Engineering in 1966.

To remain up to date on recent developments within the industry, he has maintained affiliation with numerous professional organizations in relation to his areas of expertise, including the American Society of Heating, Refrigerating and Air-Conditioning Engineers, where he is a lifetime member and previously served as chapter president in the early

1970s. In addition, Mr. Pate has been associated with the Association of Energy Engineers, the Data Processing Management Association, the Little Rock Engineers Club, and the Arkansas Council of Engineering and Related Societies, where he served as chairman in 1979.

When he is not involved in his professional pursuits, Mr. Pate enjoys giving back to his community as a board member of the Arkansas Engineering Foundation and member of the Arkansas State Energy Task Force. Likewise, he is a past instructor at the College of Engineering at the University of Arkansas at Little Rock and former general chairman of the Governor's Prayer Breakfast. He was a commissioner on the Benton County Planning Board. Also involved in his local church, Mr. Pate is a deacon of the Roman Catholic Church and a board-certified hospice chaplain.

Author of the autobiography "Blest," Mr. Pate has notably been published at Phillip Monroe Publishing. See www.homilystarters.com for more information. As a testament to his success, he has accrued several accolades over the course of his career, having been named to the Hall of Fame of the Arkansas chapter of the American Society of Heating, Refrigerating and Air-Conditioning Engineers, which he considers to be a highlight of his career. In addition, the society honored him with an Ernest N. Pettit Award and a Lincoln Bullion Award in 1973. In light of all his accomplishments, Mr. Pate has been highlighted in the first edition of Who's Who of Emerging Leaders in America, the 20th edition of Who's Who in the South and Southwest, and multiple editions of Who's Who in Science and Engineering.

Mr. Pate was born on July 17, 1942, in Memphis, Tennessee, to mother Edith Sawyer Pate and father Stoy Pate. He later married Sandra Snell, PhD, on December 16, 1961, and together, they are the proud parents of two children named Phil and Eric. Moreover, they have six grandchildren and six great-grandchildren. In his free time, he enjoys participating in such activities as boating.

A Lifetime of Achievement in **Engineering**

Jack Andrew Wagner Jr.

Electrical Engineer (Retired)

CHATTANOOGA, TN UNITED STATES

As a child, Jack Andrew Wagner Jr. was inspired by his father, who worked as a chemical engineer. He recalls walking down an alley with friends when he was in elementary school and noticing people putting things in the garbage that were not actual garbage. He sorted through the items and took home an old record player with a built-in radio. His father encouraged this curiosity by helping him order the necessary parts to repair it. Carrying this passion into adulthood, he decided to pursue a formal education in order to prepare for his professional path.

Mr. Wagner began his academic pursuits at The University of Tennessee, Knoxville. He graduated from the esteemed academic institution in 1972 with a Bachelor of Science in electrical engineering. Subsequently, he obtained a certification as a registered professional engineer in the states of Tennessee, Alabama, Georgia and Kentucky. In addition, he is a certified data professional.

Upon earning his degree and certifications, Mr. Wagner accepted a position as the manager of distribution engineering with the Chattanooga, Tennessee, Electric Power Board. He remained in this role from 1972 to 2003. Later, he was briefly employed by the Tennessee Valley Authority from 2003 to 2004. Upon leaving this post, he began service with Sargent & Lundy in 2004, remaining there for the following 11 years until his retirement in 2015.

Outside of his primary endeavors, Mr. Wagner has dedicated his time and knowledge to serving his community in various roles over the years. Notably, he has acted as the co-chair for the Chattanooga Regional Engineering and Science Fair. An active presence in the field, he maintains memberships with a number of prestigious organizations, including Eta Kappa Nu and the Chattanooga Engineers Club. With the Chattanooga Engineers Club, he found success as the president for one year in 1998.

In light of his professional achievements, Mr. Wagner has gained recognition in the form of a number of awards and accolades. For his many remarkable contributions to the industry, he has previously been selected for inclusion in numerous editions of such honors publications as Who's Who in Science and Engineering as well as Who's Who in the South and Southwest. He was notably profiled in the 73rd edition of Who's Who in America. Though these recognitions are impressive, he considers the highlight of his career to be putting together information management systems. Reflecting on his years in the field, he is grateful for the mentorship of many of his engineering co-workers.

Mr. Wagner was born on July 18, 1949, in Borger, Texas, to mother Marjory Willson Wagner and father Jack Andrew Wagner. He considers his parents to be the biggest mentors in his life because they motivated and inspired him over the years. He grew up alongside two brothers named Clifford and Mark. He later married Linda Mae Beavers on September 4, 1971, and together, they are the proud parents of three children named Melinda Mae Hamby, Lance Andrew Wagner and Julie Elaine Knight.

Moreover, Mr. Wagner has seven grandchildren named Isabelle Elaine Hamby, Emma Katherine Hamby, Harrison Howard Hamby, Elena Frances Wagner, Laurel Beth Knight, Linda Eden Knight and Sebastian Glen Knight. In his free time, he enjoys magic and flower gardening. He considers the highlight of his career to be his ability to influence his grandchildren with science and magic, and is very proud of having instilled some curiosity in their minds over the years. In his own youth, Mr. Wagner reached the rank of Eagle Scout in the Boy Scouts of America.

Kurt V. Wipior

Supervisor
Technical Publications Engineering
Mitsubishi Aircraft Corporation
NORMANDY PARK, WA UNITED STATES

With more than 40 years of professional experience, Kurt V. Wipior has excelled as the supervisor of technical publications engineering at Mitsubishi Aircraft Corporation in Renton, Washington, since 2017. Prior to attaining this position, he found success for over two decades with Boeing Commercial Airplanes in Seattle, Washington, serving in the posts of a propulsion specialist from 1990 to 1996, the lead propulsion engineer from 1996 to 1998 and the manager of customer support engineering from 1998 to 2002. Mr. Wipior held several other administrative roles with Boeing between 2002 and 2015, including as a manager of process analysis and compliance from 2002 to 2004, manager of regulatory/ICA compliance from 2004 to 2009, and senior manager of support and service domain leader from 2009 to 2015. Subsequently, he acted as a senior manager of regulatory/ICA compliance with Boeing Commercial Airplane Group in Seal Beach, California, from 2015 to 2017.

An expert in the development and delivery of aircraft maintenance solutions, software development oversight and application portfolio leadership, Mr. Wipior began his career as a design assistant at Julian Designs in Miami, Florida, from 1976 to 1978. Following this opportunity, he sought to expand his knowledge in the field through the pursuit of a formal education. He first attended Embry-Riddle Aeronautical University in Daytona Beach, Florida, where he earned a Bachelor of Science in aeronautical science in 1982. Mr. Wipior continued his studies at the same esteemed academic institution and ultimately achieved a Master of Science in aviation management in 1984. Subsequently, he obtained a certification as a Six Sigma green belt in 2001. He further holds certification in value stream and accelerated integrated workshop.

Growing up in a family that was very involved in aviation, Mr. Wipior always knew he wanted to have a career working with aircraft. His father was a World War II fighter pilot and went on to become a charter pilot. He also owned a DC-3 for a period of time. Initially intending to work for Eastern Air Lines, Mr. Wipior received a fascinating job offer from the Dee Howard Company in San Antonio, Texas, now known as VT San Antonio Aerospace. Initially active as a senior technical writer from 1984 to 1986, he continued his efforts with the company as a publications supervisor from 1986 to 1990. During this time, Mr. Wipior notably worked under contract with Boeing to modify 747 aircraft to be the private aircraft for the king of Saudi Arabia. This work is what initially drew him to accept the position.

Mr. Wipior was born on August 1, 1960, in Miami, Florida, to mother Marjorie Alva Johnson Wipior and father Henry George Wipior. In his free time, he enjoys participating in such activities as flying, taking photos and traveling. Impressively, he is a private pilot. Looking to the future, he plans to pass along his knowledge and mentor others at Mitsubishi. His goal is to rebuild their commercial aircraft industry. He is grateful for the mentorship he himself received from A. Wallace, who taught him how to do the technical publications engineering work early on in his career. He also taught him to create documentations to support maintenance on aircraft. He considers the highlight of his career to be all of the work he completed in supporting the safety of the flying public.

A Lifetime of Achievement in **Finance / Financial Services**

Michael Braude

President & Chief Executive Officer
Kansas City Board of Trade
SHAWNEE MISSION, KS UNITED STATES

With nearly 40 years of experience to his credit, Michael Braude is currently retired, having excelled as the president and the chief executive officer for the Kansas City Board of Trade in Missouri from 1984 to 2001. Prior to this appointment, he held the position of the executive vice president for American Bank in Kansas City, Missouri, from 1973 to 1984. Previously, he served at the Mercantile Bank of Kansas City as the vice president from 1966 to 1973. Mr. Braude began his career as the vice president of Commerce Bank in Kansas City, Missouri, from 1962 to 1966.

Before embarking on his professional path, Mr. Braude pursued an education at the University of Missouri, earning a Bachelor of Science in 1957. He concluded his studies at Columbia University in 1958, graduating with a Master of Science. Following these accomplishments, Mr. Braude accepted an honorary doctorate from Baker University in 2004.

Beyond his responsibilities within the field, Mr. Braude has participated in numerous endeavors outside of his professional circles. He has contributed to the board of directors for the Midwest Trust Company, the Kansas City Life Insurance Company, MGP Ingredients, Inc., and the Hodgdon Powder Company. He further worked as the mayor of the city of Mission Woods, Kansas, from 1982 to 1984. Having penned a number of articles for journals, including a weekly column in the Kansas City Business Journal for more than 10 years, Mr. Braude found

A Lifetime of Achievement | **Michael Braude**

much success with his written works, having authored "Managing Your Money" in 1975 as well as 12 children's books.

In addition to his primary vocation, Mr. Braude remains affiliated with various organizations in relation to his areas of expertise. From 1982 to 1984, he had maintained his involvement as the president of the Metropolitan Community College Foundation in Kansas City, Missouri. He was also active as a trustee for the Kansas Public Employee Retirement Systems from 2001 to 2012 as well as for Baker University from 2006 to 2010. Moreover, Mr. Braude is a member of the University of Missouri Alumni Association.

In light of his exceptional undertakings, Mr. Braude has accrued several accolades throughout his impressive career. In 2000, he was presented with a Faculty Alumni Award from the University of Missouri. Likewise, Mr. Braude was selected for inclusion in multiple editions of Who's Who in Finance and Business, Who's Who in Finance and Industry, Who's Who in America, Who's Who in the Midwest and Who's Who in the World.

Passionate for his profession, Mr. Braude was further inspired by Sam Wenberg, a professor at the University of Missouri, as well as his 10-year-old nephew, whose questions regarding the stock market eventually led to his career as a children's author upon the publication of "Shelby Goes to Wall Street." Defined by his determination and desire to succeed, Mr. Braude is the husband of Linda Miller, with whom he has proudly raised two sons and welcomed four grandchildren into their immediate family.

A Lifetime of Achievement in **Finance / Financial Services**

Alfonso G. Finocchiaro, PhD

President
Alfie Holdings, LLC
CALDWELL, NJ UNITED STATES

Alfonso G. Finocchiaro, PhD, has established himself as a leader in the finance industry, building a prolific career for himself over the last 50 years. He currently serves as the president of Alfie Holdings LLC, a role he assumed after finding success as the chairman of both FINAB International Corporate Management Services Ltd. from 2000 to 2016 and BPD Bank in New York City from 2005 to 2009. Prior to these positions, Dr. Finocchiaro found success as a director, contributing to Southern Financial Bank in Virginia from 1997 to 2004, the Banco Portugues do Atlantico Overseas from 1993 to 1996, the International Strategy Services from 1990 to 1996, and BPA Futures Cayman from 1989 to 1996.

Dr. Finocchiaro was active overseas as well, working for the Banco Portugues do Atlantico in their Lisbon, Portugal, and Brazil offices as an adviser to the board of directors from 1996 to 1997 and as the vice chairman from 1993 to 1996. Prior to assuming these roles, he thrived at the company's New York City office as the executive vice president and the American regional director from 1978 to 1995. Earlier in his career, Dr. Finocchiaro garnered expertise as the president and the general manager of Connecticut Bank International in 1977 to 1978 and as the vice president of Chemical Bank from 1966 to 1977 in New York City.

Outside of his primary professional endeavors, Dr. Finocchiaro thrived as the director of BPD International Bank from 1997 to 2005 and as an adviser to the board of directors of Banco Internacional do Funchal in Lisbon, Portugal, from 1997 to 2007. He also served on the board of directors for Southern Financial Bank from 1997 to 2004 and of IMAG since 2005. Well-regarded as an expert in his field, Dr. Finocchiaro has contributed his expertise and leadership to several professional organizations, including the European American Chamber of Commerce in the United States, of which he has been active on the board of directors and as the vice president, the International Management and Development Institute, and the Global Leadership Institute, of which he served on the board of directors. Dr. Finocchiaro further maintained involvement as the vice president and on the board of directors of the American Portuguese Society and as the president of the Portugal-US Chamber of Commerce, where he remains affiliated on the board of directors.

Dr. Finocchiaro's professional journey began in his home country of Italy, where he obtained a Doctor of Philosophy in political science at the University of Catania in Sicily in 1958. After serving as a lieutenant in the Carabinieri, an Italian military component that carries out civil law enforcement, he immigrated to the United States in 1960. To further his education, Dr. Finocchiaro attended Pace University in New York City, obtaining a Master of Business Administration in international finance in 1967. He additionally attended management courses by Harvard Business School faculty.

In 1988, Dr. Finocchiaro was named a Decorated Commander from the Order Infante D. Henrique in Portugal and also received a leadership award from the International Management and Development Institute. In recognition of his many achievements and contributions to his industry, he has been included in multiple editions of Who's Who in Finance and Industry, Who's Who in America, Who's Who in the East and Who's Who in the World. Dr. Finocchiaro is also the recipient of the Albert Nelson Marquis Lifetime Achievement Award, presented to individuals who have demonstrated exceptional success in their field. An active member of the Portuguese community, he considers the highlight of his career to be attending President Ronald Reagan's White House dinner as a guest, along with his wife and the then-president of Portugal, António Ramalho Eanes. Dr. Finocchiaro had the additional privilege of meeting Pope Francis.

Dr. Finocchiaro was born on August 20, 1932, in Catania, Italy, to Giovanni and Giuseppina Cavalieri Finocchiaro. He and his wife, Diana

Louise Cavagnolo, are the proud parents of John Paul and Carol Anne. In his free time, Dr. Finocchiaro enjoys playing the piano, listening to music, traveling, and staying up to date with foreign affairs.

A Lifetime of Achievement in **Finance / Financial Services**

Alicia Johnson Foster, CPA

Accountant & Founding Partner (Retired)
Abrams, Foster, Nole & Williams, CPA
BALTIMORE, MD UNITED STATES

With 35 years of experience to her credit, Alicia Johnson Foster, CPA, is currently retired, having excelled as a founding partner of Abrams, Foster, Nole & Williams, CPA, an African American CPA firm in Baltimore, Maryland, from 1983 to 2013. Ms. Foster was the audit partner and served as quality control and educational training partner during her 30-year tenure. Prior to this, she served as an audit manager for Taylor, Williams & Associates, CPA, from 1982 to 1983. Previously she worked at Alexander Grant & Company, CPA, as an auditor in 1979 to 1982. Ms. Foster began her career at Morgan State University, for which she held the positions of an accountant from 1978 to 1979 and an instructor in evening school from 1979 to 1985.

Before embarking on her professional path, Ms. Foster pursued her higher education at Morgan State University, earning a Bachelor of Science in accounting in 1978. Following this accomplishment, she passed the CPA exam and became certified as a public accountant in the state of Maryland in 1979. Subsequently, Ms. Foster concluded her studies at the University of Baltimore in 1981, graduating with a Master of Science in finance.

Beyond her responsibilities within the field, Ms. Foster has participated in numerous endeavors within her professional circles. Since 1985, she has contributed to the Maryland Association of Certified Public Accountants in a number of capacities as a board member, including as chairperson of the Quality Higher Education Committee. She worked with the Peer Review Compliance Assurance Committee for the association for several years and was very proud of the accomplishments of that committee. She also worked with the American Institute of Certified Public Accountants and served on several committees, notably the Peer Review Committee, and she served as a peer reviewer for the institute for several years.

Ms. Foster was so enthusiastic about working within her field that in 1996 she was awarded with her appointment to the Maryland State Board of Public Accountancy and served in a number of capacities, including recognition as the first African American woman board chair from 2000 to 2002. While on this board, she also joined and served on committees of the National Association of State Boards of Accountancy and furthered her commitment to her profession by gaining a broad range of knowledge and experience in the field of public accounting across the country. Joining and participating with a large number of committed professionals heightened her interest and enthusiasm in the field of accountancy.

Ms. Foster's civic activities were diverse and extensive. Serving on the board and committees of the National Association of Black Accountants from 2001 to 2008, she participated in the annual scholarship program, assisting with raising scholarship funds for minority students in the field of accounting. She has conducted many presentations for accounting seminars and workshops as a member of the accounting advisory boards for Morgan State University and the University of Baltimore. She has served on the Capital Region Minority Supplier Development Council in Baltimore, the North Central Baltimore Health Corporation as treasurer, the Baltimore City Private Industry Council, the Forest Park Senior Citizens Board, and the Maryland Governor's Workforce Investment Board as a member from 2002 to 2008, serving as vice chair for two years. Ms. Foster is a member of the First Baptist Church of Baltimore and served as treasurer for many years.

In light of her exceptional undertakings, Ms. Foster has accrued numerous accolades throughout her impressive career. The recipient of a Recognition for Outstanding Services from the Morgan State University Accounting Club, she was honored with the Earl Graves Advancement Award and the Academic Honors Award from the Financial Executives Institute at Morgan State University. She has also received recognition from the Maryland Association of Certified Public

Accountants. She was notably presented with a Theta Award, citations for serving on the Board of Accountancy, the Woman of the Year in Business Award from the Alpha Zeta chapter of the Zeta Phi Beta Sorority, Inc., and a Professional Achievement Award from the National Association of Black Professional Women's Clubs. Likewise, Ms. Foster was selected for inclusion in the 16th edition of Who's Who of American Women, and is the recipient of the esteemed Albert Nelson Marquis Lifetime Achievement Award.

Through her many years of committee work with the Maryland Association of Certified Public Accountants, Ms. Foster is proud of her achievements and especially her participation in changes to the Maryland Public Accountancy Act, the requirements for out-of-state experience for reciprocal licensure in Maryland and the procedures for non-CPA firms to obtain permits in Maryland.

Ms. Foster was drawn toward accounting in her formative years. However, unexpected financial obstacles forced her to focus on her family and her three children during her academic efforts. As time passed, Ms. Foster was able to continue her journey and complete her educational pursuit. Inspired and motivated by her mentor and instructor at Morgan State University, Christanta Ricks-Johns, CPA, she fondly recalls her appointment to the Maryland State Board of Public Accountancy and the board for the Maryland Association of Certified Public Accountants, as well as her 30 years tenure as a founding partner of Abrams, Foster, Nole & Williams, CPA. Looking toward to the future, Ms. Foster hopes to enjoy her well-deserved retirement while informally working to advise the next generation of accounting professionals.

A Lifetime of Achievement in **Finance / Financial Services**

Alan I W Frank

President & Chairman of the Board
Alan I W Frank Corporation
PITTSBURGH, PA UNITED STATES

Driven by a desire to save a piece of personal history that has worldwide appeal, Alan I W Frank has set himself apart as a noted preservationist. With more than six decades of professional experience to his credit, he is the longtime president and chairman of the board of the Alan I W Frank Corporation in Pittsburgh, Pennsylvania. He established the Alan I W Frank House Foundation in an effort to continue to preserve his historic family home. The nonprofit aims to maintain the landmark for future generations to learn from, as well as provide visitors a tangible connection to some of the greatest architects of the 20th century.

Designed by esteemed architects Walter Gropius and Marcel Breuer, the Alan I W Frank House is a monument to modernist architecture. Featuring four floors, an indoor swimming pool, nine bedrooms, over 10 bathrooms, a rooftop dance floor and a signature curved, three-level staircase, the Alan I W Frank House has been widely recognized as an architectural marvel that highlights happy, healthy living. Completed in 1940, the home remains largely unchanged, containing the same furniture, fabrics and textures as it did when the Frank family first moved into the 17,000-square-foot residence. With its groundbreaking design, the home served as both a private residence and a destination for members of Pittsburgh's arts and education community.

Mr. Frank earned a Bachelor of Arts from Harvard University in Cambridge, Massachusetts, in 1954 and a Bachelor of Laws at Columbia University in the City of New York in 1960. Following these accomplishments, he was licensed to practice law by the New York Bar and the Pennsylvania State Bar. Mr. Frank began his career as the president of the National Petroleum Corp. in 1954, subsequently continuing to cultivate his expertise through roles with Columbia University's $200 Million Campaign in the Pittsburgh area, the Rensselaer Polytechnic Institute, Harvard College, and the Pittsburgh History and Landmarks Foundation. Early on in his career, he spent two years as a special agent with the U.S. Army Counter Intelligence Corps from 1955 to 1957.

For excellence in his career, Mr. Frank has been the recipient of a number of honors and accolades over the years. Notably, he is a patentee in his field and was presented with a Medal of Honor from the city of Los Angeles. In light of his many achievements, Mr. Frank has been selected for inclusion in Who's Who in Finance and Business, Who's Who in Finance and Industry, Who's Who in America, Who's Who in the East and Who's Who in the World. He is also the recipient of the prestigious Albert Nelson Marquis Lifetime Achievement Award.

Mr. Frank is the youngest child of Robert and Cecelia Frank. His father, an engineer and inventor who built Copperweld Steel Company, and his mother, a devoted member of the Pittsburgh community, were actively involved in the construction of the Alan I W Frank House, working with the architects over several years. Dedicating decades to maintaining the home and its original furniture, Mr. Frank recently worked on the book "The Alan I W Frank House: A Modernist Masterwork by Walter Gropius and Marcel Breuer," which was slated for publication in October 2019. Born on March 6, 1932, in Pittsburgh, Mr. Frank is the father of two daughters, Darcy Frank-Mackay and Kimberly Frank-Shaw.

A Lifetime of Achievement in **Finance / Financial Services**

Robert Truman Handy

Financial Adviser & Representative
ViaQuest Financial Group
DICKINSON, TX UNITED STATES

With more than 60 years of experience to his credit, Robert Truman Handy has excelled as a financial adviser and representative for the ViaQuest Financial Group in Houston, Texas, since 1999. Prior to this appointment, he held the position of the executive director for the Brazoria County Historical Museum in Angleton, Texas, from 1992 to 1999. From 1988 to 1999, he was active as the president for Development Resources International. Mr. Handy additionally worked as the executive director of the Houston World Trade Association from 1984 to 1988.

Previously, Mr. Handy served as the founder and the executive director for the Gulf Coast World Affairs Council from 1976 to 1984. He further held the post of the director of international programs at the College of the Mainland in Texas City, Texas, from 1975 to 1976. He began his career as the director of continuing education and community services at the College of the Mainland from 1972 to 1974. Before embarking on his professional path, Mr. Handy completed service in the U.S. Navy from 1959 to 1962, attaining the rank of the electrician's mate second class prior to his honorable discharge.

Following his military service, Mr. Handy pursued an education at Portland State University, earning a Bachelor of Science in history and political science in 1969. He concluded his studies at the aforementioned academic institute in 1971, graduating with a Master of Arts in American diplomatic history. In addition to these accomplishments,

A Lifetime of Achievement | **Robert Truman Handy**

Mr. Handy has obtained a Series 7 and 65 certification from the Financial Industry Regulatory Authority.

Beyond his responsibilities within the field, Mr. Handy has participated in numerous endeavors outside of his professional circles. From 1994 to 1998, he contributed to the adjunct faculty for Alvin Community College. A member of the advisory board for the Center for International Studies at the University of St. Thomas since 2010, he has held roles on the La Marque Aid and Guidance Council and the La Marque Economic Development Council between 1979 and 1980. The publisher and editor for the Journal of Foreign Affairs and the international editor for In Between Magazine, Mr. Handy found much success as a book reviewer for the Houston Chronicle and a feature writer for Northwest Magazine as well.

Moreover, Mr. Handy was selected as a delegate for the European Community Visitors Program, traveling to Czechoslovakia, Belgium, Germany, France and England in 1981. Representing the US-China Peoples Friendship Association for a three-week briefing tour of the People's Republic of China in 1979, he further organized and led the first Southern U. S. legal delegation to research the legal system of the People's Republic of China in 1988. Mr. Handy was also appointed to Team 1992 for the European Community Visitors Program in 1989.

Furthermore, Mr. Handy remains affiliated with various organizations in relation to his areas of expertise. Since 1999, he has maintained his involvement as the vice chairman of the Friends of History at Portland State University. He was also associated with the Galveston County Community Action Council as a member of the board of directors in 1973 as well as the Galveston County Council of Chambers as the chairman in 1982. Mr. Handy was a member of the American Association for State and Local History, the North Galveston County Chamber of Commerce and the Dickinson Historical Society, for which he has provided his time and resources on the board of directors.

In light of his exceptional undertakings, Mr. Handy has accrued several accolades throughout his impressive career. Recognized as the chairman of the Stephen F. Austin Statewide Bicentennial Celebration Commission by Texas Governor Ann Richards in 1993, he was instrumental in establishing the Bernard V. Burke History Scholarship Endowment Fund at Portland State University. Likewise, he was featured in multiple editions of Who's Who in America, Who's Who in the South and Southwest, and Who's Who in the World. Looking toward the future, Mr. Hardy hopes to retire and write his memoir in addition to a book regarding the internationalization of Houston.

A Lifetime of Achievement in **Finance / Financial Services**

James Joseph Odorizzi

Financial Adviser
Troverco
COLLINSVILLE, IL UNITED STATES

With a propensity for helping individuals and corporations understand their finances, James Joseph Odorizzi has enjoyed a rich career as a food company executive. Throughout the course of his professional journey, he has garnered a reputation for his ability to see the big picture, a trait that has allowed him the opportunity to provide valuable guidance to a myriad of businesses. Currently, Mr. Odorizzi contributes his services as a financial adviser to Troverco, a food service firm that manufactures fresh sandwiches and snacks. Previously, he found success as the chief financial officer of Landshire, an esteemed food brand that supplies sandwiches and breakfast items to schools, convenience stores, restaurants and various retailers across the country. Mr. Odorizzi thrived in this position from 1977 to 2010.

Prior to finding his niche in food services, Mr. Odorizzi gained valuable experience in the accounting sector. From 1976 to 1977, he was an associate at Teel, Heller & Wenzel, a certified public accounting firm based out of Belleville, Illinois. He previously acted as a supervisor at Ernst and Ernst, CPAs, in St. Louis. Having utilized his financial acumen to contribute as a staff accountant with the U.S. Army Audit Agency from 1969 to 1970, Mr. Odorizzi was further active in the same capacity with the Army during his service throughout Vietnam from 1970 until his honorable discharge in 1972.

Possessing a natural talent for numbers, Mr. Odorizzi was introduced to the business world at a young age. His father — a first-generation Italian immigrant — owned a beer distribution company, and Mr. Odorizzi would help him by delivering products to customers and offering his advice on pricing and other business matters. Seeing his aptitude and passion for math, Mr. Odorizzi's father encouraged him to become an accountant. He followed his father's wise advice and attended Southern Illinois University Edwardsville, earning a Bachelor of Science in business administration in 1969 and graduating second in his class. To remain up to date with changes in his industry, he maintains affiliation as a member of the American Institute of Certified Public Accountants and the Illinois CPA Society.

Beyond his primary professional endeavors, Mr. Odorizzi is a well-respected source of guidance to the St. Peter and Paul Catholic Church, of which he is a member and serves on its finance council. Previously, he was a member of the audit committee for the city of Collinsville, Illinois. Furthermore, he has held the post of the treasurer for a number of organizations, including the Collinsville Metropolitan Exposition Auditorium and Office Building Authority, the Collinsville Education Scholarship Foundation, the Collinsville Baseball Softball League and the Knights of Columbus, in addition to his children's local grade school soccer association.

Mr. Odorizzi has been recognized on numerous occasions for his excellence in the field. He has been highlighted with features in multiple editions of Who's Who in Finance and Industry and is also the recipient of the prestigious Albert Nelson Marquis Lifetime Achievement Award, presented to individuals who have demonstrated exceptional leadership and made a difference in their industry. With decades of success to his credit, Mr. Odorizzi attributes his success to the support and encouragement of Theresa Koehne, his wife of 50 years. In addition, he is the proud father of four children — Gregory, Lisa, Michael and Kathryn — and a doting grandfather of eight grandchildren. A second-degree black belt in taekwondo, Mr. Odorizzi is also an avid golfer and enjoys gardening in his free time.

A Lifetime of Achievement in **Finance / Financial Services**

Hobart Robinson

Management Consulting Company Executive (Retired)

PONTE VEDRA BEACH, FL UNITED STATES

After accruing more than 30 years of practiced industry experience, Hobart Robinson moved from his role as director of administration for McKinsey & Company in Stockholm, Sweden, in 1989 to director of administration in New York. He retired on July 1, 1998. Early in his career, he joined Exxon Mobil Corp., formerly known as Mobil Chemical Co., as a market analyst in 1964. During interviews for the job, he was told that if he accepted the job, he would be involved in analyzing new investments in phosphate mines in the Fort Meade area of Florida. Once out of business school, he and his classmates were the first to have the ability to calculate internal rate of return and net present value, which quickly became the way to evaluate investment opportunities. Throughout his career, he has gained a plethora of expertise as a financial analyst with Polaroid Corp., as the executive vice president at the Simplex Wire & Cable Co., and as president and chief executive officer of Brink's Inc.

An active presence in the field, Mr. Robinson has maintained memberships with such prestigious organizations as the Sawgrass Country Club and the Tournament Players Club in Ponte Vedra Beach, Florida. Equally involved in civic work, he was associated with the Williams College Alumni Fund as vice chair from 1999 to 2004 and class agent from 1998 to 2015. From 1980 to 1981, he was the president of the American Club in Copenhagen, Denmark, and a director of the Fulbright Commission in Copenhagen. Outside of his primary endeavors, he acted as the director of Burlington No. Air Freight Inc. in Newport Beach, California, from 1982 to 1984.

Looking back on his career, Mr. Robinson considers the highlight of his career to be when the Berlin Wall came down when he was living in Stockholm. With some colleagues, he opened an office in St. Petersburg, then in Moscow, Warsaw, Prague, the Czech Republic and Budapest, Hungary, all within an 18-month period. They called it the "Wild East." He believes that the most rewarding aspect of his profession is the variety of problems to be addressed.

Prior to establishing himself as a trusted voice in the field, Mr. Robinson sought to expand his knowledge through the pursuit of a formal education at a number of esteemed academic institutions. He first attended Williams College, where he completed coursework and obtained a Bachelor of Arts in 1959. Taking a break from academia, he joined the U.S. Naval Reserve in Newport, Rhode Island, in 1959, serving as a lieutenant for the following three years. He continued his studies at the prestigious Columbia University, where he ultimately achieved a Master of Business Administration upon graduating in May 1964.

In light of his many successes, Mr. Robinson has gained recognition in the form of various awards and accolades. He has previously been selected for inclusion in such honors publications as the 32nd and 33rd editions of Who's Who in the World, the 38th through 42nd editions of Who's Who in the South and Southwest, and the 39th edition of Who's Who in the East. He was also listed in 25 editions of Who's Who in America, which were published between 1986 and 2016. Reflecting on his accomplishments, he attributes much of his success to his mentor, Ron Daniels, at McKinsey & Company, who was the New York office manager and later became managing director of the firm.

Mr. Robinson was born on October 8, 1937, in Quincy, Massachusetts, to mother Charlotte Elizabeth Hall Robinson and father Hobart Krum Robinson. He later married Gerd Ingela Janhede on October 17, 1964, and together, they are the proud parents of three children named Steven Whitney, Karina Jill and Peter Danforth. Moreover, he has six grandchildren. In his free time, he enjoys golfing, singing in his local chorus, and studying genealogy and history. Looking to the future, he plans to continue enjoying his retirement. The advice he can offer the next generation or others aspiring to work in his profession is to know your function and your industry.

A Lifetime of Achievement in **Finance / Financial Services**

William D. Rutherford

Investment Executive
Rutherford Investment Management
PORTLAND, OR UNITED STATES

When, at 10 years old, William D. Rutherford first heard his father talking about a money-making machine called the stock market, he was instantly intrigued. Through his modest silver-dollar-a-week earnings, he was able to scrape together $200 and make his first investment. The rest is history.

With 50 years of investment experience behind him, Mr. Rutherford remains a self-proclaimed lifelong learner, infusing his client services with the many lessons gathered from leading businesses and governments to international success. He launched Rutherford Investment Management in 1994 with the mission of providing institutional quality investment management to the long-term investor. The firm prides itself in not only growing clients' wealth over time, but growing their investment prowess too, attributing its performance largely to effective client education.

As much a teacher as a learner, Mr. Rutherford has shared his expertise through a variety of corporate leadership roles: chief executive officer of Fibreboard Asbestos Compensation Trust, director of special projects for Metallgesellschaft Corporation and chairman of the board of Metro One Telecommunications while it was one of the fastest growing public companies in the U.S. In the early '90s, he served as president of the Société Générale Touche Remnant, the international investing subsidiary of Société Générale, France's largest publicly traded bank, and as a member of the board of directors. In the years prior, he held positions as president, chief executive officer and member of the board at the ABD International Management Corporation, the international investment management arm of Dresdner Bank, at the time Germany's second largest bank and one of the world's largest banks.

Having served in the Oregon House of Representatives from 1977 to 1984, he subsequently led Oregon into international equity investing as its state treasurer, becoming the first public fund to do so and serving as a model for other states to follow. In 1986, he also became chairman of the Oregon Investment Council, leaving the Oregon PERS significantly overfunded and positioned to remain so.

Mr. Rutherford's life trajectory was heavily shaped by his invaluable experience as a young boy working in the family business and eventually handling its finances. His professional pursuits kicked off with a Bachelor of Science at the University of Oregon followed by a degree from Harvard University Law School. After completing 10 years of active and reserve duty in the U.S. Army, he began practicing law. Eventually, he returned to his childhood home of McMinnville, Oregon, to launch his own legal practice in 1971.

Beyond his professional endeavors, Mr. Rutherford has also stayed active in the community, having served on the Portland Opera Association board of directors, as president of the McMinnville Chamber of Commerce and head of its award-winning downtown redevelopment, and as a trustee for the Oregon Nature Conservancy. He currently serves on the board of the Palm Springs Air Museum and on the investment committee of the Oregon Community Foundation. In 2006, he penned "Who Shot Goldilocks?" an engaging look at why the 90s Goldilocks era collapsed.

Although Mr. Rutherford has accrued several accolades throughout his career, such as the Contribution to Individual Freedom Award from the American Civil Liberties Union in 1981 and inclusion in multiple editions of Who's Who, he is most proud of his long-term philanthropic commitments. These include a fund he set up to aid in protecting Cascade Head, a prominent geographical location on the Oregon coast that sees 30,000 annual visitors. To build a bridge of understanding among cultures and facilitate mutual problem-solving, he created and funds an initiative at the University of Oregon that has resulted in the Middle Eastern studies minor. Beyond that, Mr. Rutherford has made significant donations to his alma maters, end-of-life palliative care research and public school music programs.

A Lifetime of Achievement | **William D. Rutherford**

As a teenager, before any of this came to pass, he took a career test that determined he should become a social worker. Given Mr. Rutherford's life's work as a trusted adviser educating and empowering individuals, organizations and communities, perhaps that test was accurate after all in predicting a legacy of service. He was notably profiled in the 73rd edition of Who's Who in America.

A Lifetime of Achievement in **Finance / Financial Services**

Marc A. Schoen

President (Retired)
A Pension Store, Inc.

LAWRENCEVILLE, GA UNITED STATES

With more than 50 years of experience to his credit, Marc A. Schoen has emerged as a leader in the field of pensions and benefits. In addition to serving as a certified financial adviser, he is an enrolled retirement plan agent and expert in flexible compensation, knowledge that allowed him to assist a wide variety of clients. Mr. Schoen served as the president of A Pension Store, Inc., in Miami, Florida, from 1973 until his retirement in 2004. He formerly thrived as an agent at a private practice, at Prudential Financial and at Fidelity Mutual Life Insurance from 1966 to 1973. Mr. Schoen also has experience as an assistant buyer at Allied Stores in Miami, Florida, a post he held from 1965 to 1966.

Prior to his career in insurance, Mr. Schoen contributed as a consultant at Criterion Funds, Inc., in Houston, Texas, from 1983 to 1987 and at TMG Holding, LLC, in Chicago, Illinois, from 2004 to 2006. To prepare for his future endeavors, he attended the University of Miami, where he received a Bachelor of Science and Bachelor of Business Administration in 1963. He also served with the U.S. Navy from 1957 to 1962. Mr. Schoen's impressive career accomplishments include authoring more than 250 columns for leading business publications and associations. In addition to spending almost 10 years as a newspaper columnist, he has shared his expertise on "Business News and Views You Can Use," a radio program. He further contributed as a commentator on the television program, "Main Street Wall Street." Well-regarded as a leader in the field, Mr. Schoen has appeared before members of the U.S. House Ways and Means Committee, in addition to speaking before the coordinator and instructor of the American Society of Pension Professionals and Actuaries and the International Association for Food Protection.

Mr. Schoen stands out in the field as a knowledgeable source who sees his peers in the industry as friends, rather than competitors. To stay up to date with changes in the field, he remains a member of the South Florida Employee Benefits Council, the National Association of Insurance and Financial Advisors, the Employers Council on Flexible Compensation, and the Million Dollar Round Table. Further, he is a Life Underwriter Training Council fellow and an associate member of the American Society of Pension Professionals and Actuaries. Outside of his professional affiliations, Mr. Schoen has volunteered as a scoutmaster with the Boy Scouts of America in Miami from 1966 to 1990. He is also a member of the area Rotary and Masons.

Throughout the course of his career, Mr. Schoen has been honored several times for his achievements. He was the recipient of the Community Service Award from Prudential Financial in 1968 and named an Outstanding Young Man of the Year in 1967. His accomplishments have been recognized in several Marquis Who's Who publications, including numerous editions of Who's Who in America, the 25th and 26th editions of Who's Who in Finance and Industry, and more than 10 editions of Who's Who in the World.

Mr. Schoen was born on May 30, 1938, to A. Robert and Ruth D. Schoen in Worcester, Massachusetts. He has been married to Joanne S. Schultz since June 24, 1962, and together, they are the proud parents of four children: Elliot, Aaron, Jennifer and Matthew. Additionally, their family includes eight grandchildren. In his free time, Mr. Schoen enjoys stamp collecting, as well as camping and hiking.

A Lifetime of Achievement in **Finance / Financial Services**

Alan Roger Shaw

Market Analyst & Stock Brokerage Company Executive (Retired)

GREENPORT, NY UNITED STATES

With more than four decades of professional experience to his name, Alan Roger Shaw has enjoyed a lengthy and successful career as a market analyst and stock brokerage company executive. Currently enjoying retirement, he has spent the majority of his career at companies located throughout New York City. His most recent role was as a senior vice president and managing director of Smith Barney in New York City for over two decades. He began there in 1980 and held these titles until his retirement from the industry in 2004.

Prior to accepting this position, Mr. Shaw excelled as the first vice president of Smith Barney, Harris Upham & Co. in New York City from 1975 to 1980. Previously, he acted as the vice president of Harris Upham & Co. in New York City from 1973 to 1975. With the same company, he had also served as the assistant vice president from 1971 as well as an analyst from 1958 to 1971, which was his first professional role.

Prior to establishing himself as a trusted voice in the field, Mr. Shaw sought to expand his knowledge through the pursuit of a formal education at a number of esteemed academic institutions. He first attended Susquehanna University, a private liberal arts university that is located in Selinsgrove, Pennsylvania. He completed coursework at the school in 1957. From there, he continued his studies at Adelphi University, a private university with campuses all over New York, including Garden City, Manhattan, Hudson Valley and Suffolk County. He completed coursework there for three years from 1963 until 1966. After achieving success in the field, he was the recipient of an honorary Doctor of Laws from Susquehanna University in 1999.

In order to remain an active presence in the field and up to date with developments in the profession, Mr. Shaw maintains memberships with many prestigious organizations in his areas of interest. Moreover, he has dedicated his time and knowledge to serving many of the groups in positions of leadership. Notably, he is a member of the Chartered Market Technicians Association, now known as the CMT Association, where he also served as a president in 1974. He is further associated with both the New York Society of Security Analysts and the New York Athletic Club.

Currently, Mr. Shaw is involved with the Securities Industry Association Institute as a member. Previously, he found success with the organization as a trustee for six years beginning in 1986 until his departure from this role in 1992. In addition, he has served the Unqua Corinthian Yacht Club in Amityville, New York, as a member. Throughout his time there, he also spent two years as a commodore from 1988 to 1990. Outside of his primary endeavors, he has contributed his knowledge to others through his role as a teacher at the New York Institute of Finance in New York City from 1966 to 2004. He was notably profiled in the 73rd edition of Who's Who in America.

Mr. Shaw was born on July 7, 1938, in Brooklyn, New York, to mother Vera Dimmick Shaw and father Sewall Shaw. He later married Barbara Ann Phillips-Cole on September 28, 2013. Currently, he is the proud father of three children named Stephen S., Todd J. and Bradley C. In his free time, he enjoys doing crossword puzzles and jigsaw puzzles. His other interests include reading and model trains. Looking to the future, he plans to continue enjoying his retirement.

Robert Charles Tengdin

Chairman Emeritus
Allison-Williams Company
MINNEAPOLIS, MN UNITED STATES

With more than 65 years of experience to his credit, Robert Charles Tengdin has been designated as a chairman emeritus of the Allison-Williams Company since 2018. Prior to this appointment, he excelled in a number of positions with the aforementioned company, such as the chairman from 1980 to 2017, the president from 1975 to 1980, and an executive vice president from 1969 to 1975. Previously, he served the Allison-Williams Company as the director from 1960 to 1969, the vice president from 1959 to 1960, and the assistant vice president from 1956 to 1959. Mr. Tengdin began his career on the staff of the Allison-Williams Company in 1952.

Before embarking on his professional path, Mr. Tengdin completed service in the U.S. Air Force from 1949 to 1950. He pursued an education at St. Olaf College, obtaining a Bachelor of Arts in 1952. Mr. Tengdin concluded his studies at The Wharton School at The University of Pennsylvania in 1962, graduating from the Institute of Investment Banking.

Beyond his responsibilities within the field, Mr. Tengdin has participated in numerous endeavors outside of his professional circles. From 1960 to 1962, he contributed to the special study group for Edina Public Schools in Minnesota. He formerly held the role of a director with the American Trustee Life Insurance Company. Mr. Tengdin found further success as a board member for the American Swedish Institute.

In addition to his primary vocation, Mr. Tengdin remains affiliated with various organizations in relation to his areas of expertise. In

1979, he maintained his involvement with the U.S. Ski and Snowboard Association as a member of the Alpine competition committee. He is also active with the Interlachen Country Club, where he has been the men's tennis singles champion 11 times. Moreover, Mr. Tengdin is also a member of the Minneapolis Club.

In light of his exceptional undertakings, Mr. Tengdin has accrued several accolades throughout his impressive career. In 2015, he was recognized as a Distinguished Alumnus by St. Olaf College. Notably, he has won the Master's Alpine Skiing Championship in his age group in Canada, the United States, Norway and Sweden. He was runner-up for the World Title in his age group in 2010. Mr. Tengdin was selected for inclusion in the 24th edition of Who's Who in Finance and Industry, which was published in 1985.

Initially, Mr. Tengdin planned to work for Procter & Gamble upon his graduation, but fortunately, he was introduced to the owners of Allison-Williams, who changed his perspective on the importance of municipal bonds and the financing of public debt. He built a wealth of knowledge that allowed him to build great relationships with financial institutions around the country. Equipped with communication skills that fostered many of his personal and professional ties, he has been further blessed by God to have been in the right place at the right time while making good friends throughout his industry. Mr. Tengdin is also well-versed in regional investment banking, for which he deals strictly with financial institutions throughout North America and handles privately placed debt.

Additionally, Mr. Tengdin was inspired by multiple role models, including his football coach at St. Olaf, Ade Christenson; his mentor, Kermit B. Sorum; and Safeco's Dick Campbell. The son of Elmer and Agnes Tengdin, he is the proud father of three children, David, Douglas and Daniel, who has sadly passed away. After his first wife, Fern, died, he married his wife, Dorothy, in 2010. He has also welcomed 16 grandchildren into his extended family. Looking toward the future, Mr. Tengdin hopes to continue enjoying his semiretirement while cementing his legacy as an authority in the field of finance.

A Lifetime of Achievement in **Finance / Financial Services**

Tony Vecchiotti
Vice President
Northwoods Insurance Corp.

WEBSTER, NY UNITED STATES

P rior to establishing himself as a trusted voice in the field, Tony Vecchiotti sought to expand his knowledge through the pursuit of a formal education at a number of esteemed academic institutions. He first attended Nazareth College in Rochester, New York, where he earned a Bachelor of Management Science in 1981. Subsequently, he was certified as a licensed agent in the state of New York in 1982. After working as a sales manager for Prudential Financial in Fairport, New York, from 1982 to 1992, he went on to work as a commercial account executive for the Barker, Heslip, Bradshaw Agency in Rochester from 1992 to 1997 and a personal lines manager for the Riedman Insurance Corp. and Brown & Brown of New York in Rochester from 1997 to 2003. Mr. Vecchiotti is currently president of North Coast New York in Geneva, a role he has held since 2004, and vice president of Northwoods Insurance Corp. in Rochester, Geneva, Binghamton and Williamsville, New York, a role he has held since 2006.

In addition to his primary endeavors, Mr. Vecchiotti worked as an instructor of insurance for the Independent Insurance Agents & Brokers of New York from 1997 to 2005 and worked with the Center for Professional Advancement from 1992 to 1998. Since 2003, he has been the president of the Honeoye Lake Park Association as well as chairman of the public affairs committee for the New York state chapter of the March of Dimes. He also served the aforementioned society from 1995 to 1999 as chairman of the Finger Lakes chapter. Impressively, Mr.

Vecchiotti's service to March of Dimes led to an award being named after him, and he was named Volunteer of the Year in 1996 and 2006.

Mr. Vecchiotti's decision to pursue insurance stemmed from his initial interest in sales. He has since cultivated a successful career, and he notably purchased the three offices of the Riedman Insurance Corp. that remained after they were bought by Brown & Brown of New York. He was named Rochester Insurance Professional of the Year in 2006 by the Individual Insurance Agents & Brokers of New York and the Rochester Chartered Property and Casualty Underwriters Society, and he was named Citizen of the Year by the Monroe County Fire Chiefs Association in 2002. Notable for his considerable contributions to his industry, Mr. Vecchiotti co-authored the National General Insurance examination in 2011.

Interested in keeping abreast of industry developments, Mr. Vecchiotti belongs to the Independent Insurance Agents of Monroe County, where he has served as director from 1996 to 2007, and the Independent Insurance Agents & Brokers of New York, where he has served as the president from 1999 to 2000 and director from 2000 to 2001. He is further associated with American Mensa. He has previously been selected for inclusion in such honors publications as the 37th edition of Who's Who in Finance and Business, the 62nd through 70th editions of Who's Who in America, and the 26th and 27th editions of Who's Who in the World.

Mr. Vecchiotti was born on March 16, 1960, in Rochester, New York, to mother Julia D. Vecchiotti and father Anthony Vecchiotti. He later married Leslie A. Elliott on February 16, 1985, and they are the proud parents of three children, Julianna C., Anthony E. and Vico S. He later married the late Elizabeth A. Presley on April 20, 2014, and has been married to Linda J. Tompkins since August 1, 2016. In his free time, he enjoys participating in such activities as bicycling, boating and golfing.

A Lifetime of Achievement in **Government / Public Service**

Thomas Patrick Costin Jr.

Owner
M. Jaffe Company
NAHANT, MA UNITED STATES

With more than 70 years of experience to his credit, Thomas Patrick Costin Jr. has excelled as the owner of the M. Jaffe Company in Danvers, Massachusetts, and in Brooklyn, New York, since 1979. Moreover, he has found success as the owner of the Jesmond Nursing Home, the Greenleaf House, and the Town & Country Nursing Home in Massachusetts since 1968. From 1961 to 1992, he was active as a postmaster in the post office in Lynn, Massachusetts. During this time, Mr. Costin flourished as the owner of the Sterling Machine Company from 1966 to 1992 and the Sole Tech Company from 1979 to 1992.

The section center manager for the post office in Lynn from 1971 to 1981, Mr. Costin previously worked as a labor management negotiator for the Post Office Department in Washington, D.C., from 1963 to 1967. He further held the positions of the co-founder and the owner of Mount Pleasant Hospital in Lynn from 1962 to 1965. Prior to this appointment, he served as the mayor of the city of Lynn, Massachusetts, from 1955 to 1961. Mr. Costin began his career as a member of the Lynn City Council from 1947 to 1955, at which point he was noted as the youngest man ever elected to this post at the age of 21.

Before embarking on his professional path, Mr. Costin pursued an education at Boston College, earning a Bachelor of Science in government in 1951. He continued his academic efforts at New England Law, obtaining a DDL degree in 1958. Following these accomplishments, he procured a Master of Education in 1962 from Salem State University. Mr. Costin concluded his studies at the University of Massachusetts in 1986, graduating with a Doctor of Laws.

Beyond his responsibilities within the field, Mr. Costin has participated in numerous endeavors outside of his professional circles. He held the role of a chairman for the Lynn Business Partnership's Transportation Committee and Rebuild Lynn After Fire from 1981 to 1982. A trustee of the North Shore Medical Center Union Hospital from 1956 to 1984, he further contributed to the Lynn Development Board and the board of trustees at the University of Massachusetts from 1980 to 1985. From 1944 to 1946, Mr. Costin completed service as a corporal in the U.S. Marine Corps.

In addition to his primary vocation, Mr. Costin remains affiliated with various organizations in relation to his areas of expertise. He had maintained his involvement with the United Postmasters and Managers of America as the national president from 1968 to 1969 and 1984 to 1985. He was also associated with the Massachusetts chapter of the American Cancer Society from 1980 to 1982 as the co-chairman, during which time he raised over $7 million in charitable donations. Moreover, Mr. Costin has been a member of the board of directors for the Lynn Business Education Foundation from 1992 to 1995, the Greater Lynn Chamber of Commerce since 1986, and the Lynn Business Partnership since 1991.

In light of his exceptional undertakings, Mr. Costin has accrued several accolades throughout his impressive career. He was notably presented with the Outstanding Young Man Award from the Junior Chamber of Commerce in 1955, the Post Office Developmental Honor Award for Meritorious Service in 1964, the Citation of Merit from the National Beautification Program in 1965, the Post Office Developmental Honor Award in 1981 and 1982, the Irishman of the Year Award in 1986, and the Heritage Hero Award from the Essex National Heritage Commission in 2009. Recognized as an Outstanding Young Man by the Greater Boston Junior Chamber of Commerce in 1956, he was celebrated with five commendations from U.S. presidents, including two from John F. Kennedy, two from Lyndon B. Johnson and one from Richard Nixon. Appointed as a Knight of Malta in 1992 and inducted into the Classical High School Hall of Fame in 1993, Mr. Costin was selected for inclusion in multiple editions of Who's Who in the East.

A Lifetime of Achievement | **Thomas Patrick Costin Jr.**

A personal friend of Jack Kennedy, whom he met after being profiled in The Boston Globe regarding his exemplary military and political experiences, Mr. Costin was eponymously honored in 2019 with the Thomas P. Costin Jr. Post Office Building in Lynn. Additionally featured in The Daily Item in 2018, he was the vice president of Essex Heritage for the National Park Service in 1992. He is particularly proud of passing a mandate that workers for the city of Lynn could not be fired for alcoholism without first being offered medical help. Married to Noel Spinney Costin since 1998, Mr. Costin is the proud father of five wonderful children.

A Lifetime of Achievement in **Government / Public Service**

L. Karen Darner

Member (Retired)
Virginia House of Delegates
Virginia General Assembly

School Speech Pathologist (Retired)

ARLINGTON, VA UNITED STATES

L. Karen Darner has devoted her professional career to helping others, both in the United States and abroad. Now retired, she has enjoyed a rich and varied career as a state legislator and school speech pathologist. Originally working for the Special School District of St. Louis County, Missouri, as a speech pathologist and hearing clinician between 1968 and 1971, Ms. Darner then devoted another 35 years to the Arlington Public Schools as a speech pathologist. Taking two years off during her tenure, she entered the Peace Corps as a speech pathologist and audiologist. In 1991, Ms. Darner began a second career as a member of the Virginia House of Delegates of the Virginia General Assembly, where she remained until 2004. She credits her success in the legislature to her desire to know more about Arlington, as well as to her time spent in the Peace Corps, which taught her more about herself and the importance of learning about others.

Holding numerous leadership positions over the years, Ms. Darner was active with the League of Women Voters, the Arlington County Civic Federation, the Mental Health Association of Northern Virginia and the Arlington Community Temporary Shelter, now known as Doorways, the Marjorie Hughes Fund for Children, and the American Association of University Women, among other organizations.

She served on the boards for Community Resources, Inc., and the Arlington Committee of 100, and she has been active with the Rape Victim Companion Program through Arlington's Commission on the Status of Women. Ms. Darner formerly co-chaired a special task force of the Arlington Community Foundation, was a representative of the American Association of University Women in Nairobi, Kenya, and served on the advisory board of her alma mater, the University of Illinois. She was also a Brownie Scout leader during the mid-1980s for three years. Ms. Darner is a long-standing member of the Virginia and Arlington Education Association, the Arlington Commission on the Status of Women, the Virginia Relay Board for the Deaf and Hard of Hearing, and the Virginia Commission on Youth.

During the summer of 1985, Ms. Darner attended a United Nations Conference for Women to commemorate the end of the International Decade of Women. In February 2010, she was part of a team that provided teacher training in Liberia through the Liberia Orphan Education Project. She later participated in mission work in Honduras with the Honduras Independence Bilingual School in 2017. Ms. Darner has also helped with voter registration through the League of Women Voters in addition to working on a federal grant with the American Speech-Language-Hearing Association to develop programs to collect data on children during diagnostic time and treatment.

Ms. Darner has been recognized several times for her professional accomplishments and civic efforts. She received the inaugural Mary Hatwood Futrell Award for distinguished work and advocacy in education from the Virginia Education Association, the Journal Cup Award for community activism from the Arlington Civic Federation, and the Spirit of Community William T. Newman Award from the Arlington Community Foundation. In addition, Ms. Darner was selected as Teacher of the Year for Randolph Elementary School in 2007. She has been showcased in approximately a dozen editions of Who's Who in America, Who's Who in the South and Southwest, and Who's Who of American Women. Earning both a Bachelor of Science and Master of Science from the University of Illinois in 1967 and 1968, respectively, Ms. Darner has been a licensed speech pathologist in Virginia since 1976, when state licensure began in Virginia.

A Lifetime of Achievement in **Government / Public Service**

William H. Garrigan III

Firefighter & Paramedic

NEW LENOX, IL UNITED STATES

A respected member of his community, William H. Garrigan III has led a heroic career as a firefighter and paramedic for over 25 years. Prior to establishing himself as a trusted voice in the field, he sought to expand his knowledge through the pursuit of a formal education. He first attended the College of DuPage in Glen Ellyn, Illinois, where he earned an Associate of Arts in 1975. Subsequently, he completed paramedic training at Loyola University Medical Center in 1976 and became a student at Northern Illinois University between 1976 and 1977. He concluded his academic pursuits with a Bachelor of Science from Southern Illinois University in 1987. Furthermore, Mr. Garrigan received certifications in CPR, firefighting, fire service instruction, and the operation of a fire apparatus.

At the commencement of his career, he worked with the North Palos Fire Department in Illinois as a paramedic and firefighter between 1977 and 1978. A short time later, he was hired in the same role with the Oak Brook Fire Department in Illinois between 1979 and 2006. During this time, Mr. Garrigan simultaneously contributed as an assistant coordinator of emergency medical services, further progressing to a full coordinator with the Oak Brook Fire Department from 1983 to 1997. In 2007, Mr. Garrigan became the owner and principal of EmbroidMe in New Lenox, Illinois, as well as a proprietor and promotional marketer for Fully Promoted, a company that focuses on branded products and marketing services.

Other career-related endeavors to Mr. Garrigan's credit include his involvement with the committee for paramedic education with the village of Downers Grove in Illinois since 1990 and the public safety education committee with the village of Oak Brook since 1987. Civically, he has dedicated his time as an advancement chairman for Troop 669 with the Boy Scouts of America in Palos Park, Illinois, during 1994 and as a trainer and coach for the Palos Panthers Soccer Club in 1999. Since 1986, he has served as an Advanced Cardiovascular Life Support provider with the Heart Association of South Cook County in Illinois.

Mr. Garrigan is a former U.S. Navy hospital corpsman, having served from 1974 to 1980. For his commitment to the community, he has received acknowledgment from the Department of Public Health with the state of Illinois in 1987. Likewise, he was recognized for his dedication and service by the village of Oak Brook in 1989. A member of the National Association of Emergency Medical Technicians, he maintains professional alignment with the Illinois Professional Firefighters Association, the North Palos Firefighters Association and Dive Rescue International, among others.

Mr. Garrigan was born on April 5, 1954, in Evergreen Park, Illinois, to mother Mary Jane O'Connell Garrigan and father William Garrigan Jr. He later married Melissa Ann Vaughan on August 2, 1980, and together, they are the proud parents of three children named William, Vaughan and Amanda. Moreover, they have one grandchild. In his free time, he enjoys participating in such activities as golfing, water skiing, scuba diving and swimming. He also likes music, theater and performing arts. He has previously been selected for inclusion in such honors publications as the 12th edition of Who's Who in the World and the 23rd through 42nd editions of Who's Who in the Midwest. He has also been listed in six editions of Who's Who in America.

A Lifetime of Achievement in **Government / Public Service**

John W. Jaacks

Lieutenant Colonel (Retired)
U.S. Air Force
RANCHO PALOS VERDES, CA UNITED STATES

With decades of experience in the Air Force to his credit, Lt. Col. John W. Jaacks currently provides his leadership prowess as the president of Christ Lutheran Church and School in Rancho Palos Verdes, California. Prior to accepting his role as an educational leader, he followed through on his childhood dream of becoming a fighter pilot, enlisting in the Air Force in 1950. Lt. Col. Jaacks was subsequently commissioned as a second lieutenant and advanced through the grades to lieutenant colonel.

From 1952 to 1955, Lt. Col. Jaacks served as a navigator fighter-interceptor officer at the Elmendorf Air Force Base in Alaska, later on becoming a squadron operations officer and an interceptor pilot at Youngstown Air Force Base between 1957 and 1960. He was assigned to serve with the Dutch Air Force to Holland, where he served as an interceptor pilot and the chief of avionics and aircraft maintenance at Soesterberg Air Force Base from 1962 to 1965. In 1967, Lt. Col. Jaacks returned to the United States, where he was assigned to the Space Launch Vehicles Directorate of the Space and Missile Systems Center at the Los Angeles Air Force Base until his retirement in 1973.

As a registered professional engineer and commercial pilot, Lt. Col. Jaacks was also an F18 Radar Integrated Logistics Systems program manager at the Hughes Aircraft Co. in El Segundo, California. Civically involved as well, he contributed as the chairman of the Southwest Exploring Division and as vice president of the Los Angeles Area Council of the Boy Scouts of America. He is the past president of the Palos Verdes Center for the Performing Arts, in addition to previously finding success as the president of the Palos Verdes Sunset Rotary Club and as a Rotary assistant district governor.

While serving in the U.S. Air Force, Lt. Col. Jaacks pursued formal education at various universities across the United States. He first attended the University of Illinois, receiving a Bachelor of Science in industrial administration in 1949 and a Bachelor of Science in industrial engineering in 1962. He attended the University of Southern California, where he earned a Master of Business Administration in 1970, as well as master's degrees in liberal arts in 1984 and in professional writing in 1993. His master's thesis was "Contrails: Memoirs of a Cold Warrior," which was subsequently published.

To remain current with industry developments, Lt. Col. Jaacks maintains affiliation with the Air Force Association, the American Institute of Aeronautics and Astronautics, and the Institute of Industrial and Systems Engineers. He also remains involved with the University of Southern California and University of Illinois Alumni Associations, the Phi Kappa Psi Fraternity, and is a member of Chi Gamma Iota Veteran's Fraternity, a scholastic honor society.

As a testament to his success, Lt. Col. Jaacks has earned a number of accolades over the years. The U.S. Air Force honored him with the Meritorious Service Medal. The Boy Scouts of America presented him with the Award of Merit, the Exploring Spurgeon Award, the Silver Beaver Award and the President's Leadership Award. Rotary International recognized him with a District Outstanding President Award and the Lions Club gave him the Volunteer of the Year Award. Furthermore, Lt. Col. Jaacks was named the Los Angeles County Public Housing Authority Volunteer of the Year and was highlighted in the 25th edition of Who's Who in Finance and Industry and the 20th through 23rd editions of Who's Who in the West.

A Chicago, Illinois, native, Lt. Col. Jaacks has been married to Marilyn Joyce Walker for more than 65 years. Together, they are the proud parents of three children: John W. II, Jeffrey A., and Holly S., and doting grandparents of Peter, Jason and Benjamin. In his free time, Lt. Col Jaacks enjoys writing, playing tennis and growing orchids, in addition to attending theater and opera performances.

A Lifetime of Achievement in **Government / Public Service**

Marie A. Langan

Housing Specialist (Retired)
PHOENIX, AZ UNITED STATES

Driven by a desire to be independent and care for her children, Marie A. Langan has become a respected leader in Connecticut's housing industry. She initially became involved with environmental health when she decided to join the Federal Work Incentive Program. After demonstrating academic aptitude by easily passing her General Educational Development exam, Ms. Langan enrolled in an environmental training course and came out third in her class. She was chosen as one of two government employees to conduct fieldwork identifying polluted waters.

Ms. Langan draws upon an educational background at Asnuntuck Community College in Enfield, Connecticut, and New Hampshire College. After beginning her career as an environmental health assistant for the town of Manchester, Connecticut, from 1975 to 1978, she flourished as a code enforcement officer for the town of Enfield, Connecticut, a housing code enforcement officer for the town of Wallingford, Connecticut, and a housing specialist for the judicial department of the state of Connecticut in New Haven. Ms. Langan also worked as a member of the uniform relocation assistance act interim study subcommittee of the Connecticut General Assembly's planning and development committee from 1985 to 1986 and as a member of the uniform statewide housing code interim study committee and the planning and development committee from 1989 to 1990. Her efforts were honored by Community Mediation Inc. in 1990 with a recognition plaque.

A Lifetime of Achievement | Marie A. Langan

Ms. Langan has dedicated herself to community organizations as well, serving as a member of and the head coach for the Enfield Lancers from 1977 to 1978 and was recognized with a Plaque of Appreciation due to her volunteer involvement. She also participated on the board of directors for Big Brothers Big Sisters Enfield Inc. from 1978 to 1982 and was involved with the Enfield Day Care Center Inc. from 1978 to 1982. Professionally, Ms. Langan belongs to the Connecticut Association of Housing Code Enforcement Officials, Inc., for which she has held the posts of the secretary, the treasurer, the president and a member of the board of directors over a 25-year period. The aforementioned association honored her exemplary efforts with a plaque of appreciation in July 1997 and by establishing a scholarship in her name presented to officers who exemplify vision, leadership and community, and are looking to further their education.

Ms. Langan credits her background as the key to her success. Although she did not have a college degree like many of her peers, she believes she was able to better empathize with those she was serving and offer them referrals to resources of which they were not previously aware. In recognition of her many contributions in housing and civic endeavors, Ms. Langan was selected for inclusion in the first edition of Who's Who in Media and Communication as well as the 17th and 18th editions of Who's Who of American Women. She also received the Albert Nelson Marquis Lifetime Achievement Award.

Ms. Langan was born on June 5, 1943, in Cohoes, New York, to Armand Rosario Thyot and Marie Rose Lemay. She is the mother of four children, Judith Marie Langan, Daniel Noel II, Theresa Marie and Amanda M. Estrada. In her free time, Ms. Langan relaxes by reading, doing needlecrafts, quilting and taking photographs, as well as restoring turn-of-the-century homes. A lifetime member of the French-Canadian Genealogists Society of Connecticut and the American-French Genealogical Society, she also enjoys researching her family's history.

A Lifetime of Achievement in **Government / Public Service**

Myles James McTernan

Lieutenant Colonel (Retired)
U.S. Air Force
FOLSOM, CA UNITED STATES

Lt. Col. Myles James McTernan is a retired U.S. Air Force service member with more than 45 years of career distinction. In order to avoid being drafted before he was ready to serve, he enrolled in courses at the University of Massachusetts and completed a Bachelor of Business Administration in 1969. Upon graduation, he joined the U.S. Air Force as a commissioned second lieutenant. Mr. McTernan later returned to school, earning a Master of Business Administration from Golden Gate University in San Francisco in 1978. Golden Gate University's MBA program blends foundational skills of core business disciplines with essential soft skills such as effective communication, executive presentations and team building.

From 1969 until 1985, Mr. McTernan steadily rose through the U.S. Air Force ranks to that of a lieutenant colonel, operating as a B-52D navigator and radar navigator on more than 120 bombing missions. From 1985 to 1991, he served as the chief training and operations officer for the U.S. Air Force navigator training program at Mather Air Force Base in California. After more than 20 years of military service, he retired from the U.S. Air Force in 1991.

Following Mr. McTernan's retirement, he worked as a correctional officer for the city of Folsom between 1991 and 1992. The city is known for Folsom State Prison, California's second-oldest prison after San Quentin State Prison and the first in the U.S. to have electricity. Folsom was also one of the first maximum security prisons in the nation. In 1994, Mr. McTernan became a human resources representative for IBS and Output Technologies, a subsidiary of DST Systems Inc., where he would remain until his retirement in 2015.

Mr. McTernan is active in the Folsom Chamber of Commerce, where he has been a volunteer since 1986. In 1991, he was named as the Chamber of Commerce's Volunteer of the Year in recognition of his service. He is also the recipient of the Albert Nelson Marquis Lifetime Achievement Award, the highest honor presented by Marquis Who's Who. Furthermore, Mr. McTernan is a member of the Military Officers Association of America, formerly known as the Retired Officers Association, the Military Order of the Purple Heart and DAV, a nonprofit that supports disabled American veterans.

In 2013, Mr. McTernan was the subject of a captivating story, "Last Man Out," included in the collected works of the book "Into Hostile Skies: An Anthology." Comprised of four stories about the B-52 strategic bomber and the intrepid crews who flew it, the book highlights one of Mr. McTernan's most harrowing yet memorable experiences during his time serving in the Vietnam War. When his aircraft was damaged in flight, Mr. McTernan and the crew were ordered to bailout from the B-52 — except his seat had also sustained damage and could only partially eject him. He was forced to manually bailout through an open escape hatch and stayed afloat in the open sea far away from his other crew members. Despite suffering serious injuries and having looming fears of an unsuccessful rescue, Mr. McTernan and the crew were later able to recount their incredible story of survival.

Mr. McTernan was raised in an Irish Catholic family, which he credits with helping him learn right from wrong. His parents worked hard to provide for him and his siblings, shielding the children from ever knowing their financial struggles. He had an older brother named Bernard J. McTernan, a full colonel in the U.S. Army, and two older sisters. Moving forward, Mr. McTernan hopes to complete his bucket list. He is married to his loving wife of 11 years, Donna Snyder McTernan, and is the proud father of two wonderful children, Sabrina D. Ford and Jason M. Purdy.

A Lifetime of Achievement in **Government / Public Service**

Diana "Dee" Miskill

Commander (Retired)
U.S. Navy Reserve

Lieutenant (Retired)
U.S. Navy

ORRS ISLAND, ME UNITED STATES

Marquis Who's Who, the world's premier publisher of biographical profiles, is proud to present Diana "Dee" Miskill with the Albert Nelson Marquis Lifetime Achievement Award. An accomplished candidate, Ms. Miskill celebrates many years' experience in her professional network. She has been recognized for myriad achievements and leadership qualities that she has demonstrated in her field. As in all Marquis Who's Who biographical volumes, individuals profiled are selected based on the current reference value. Factors such as position, noteworthy accomplishments, visibility, and prominence in a field are all taken into account during the selection process.

For over 40 years, Ms. Miskill excelled as a veteran and a civilian volunteer. Her U.S. Navy career began in 1970 serving on active duty in Fighter Squadron 101 at Naval Air Station Oceana in Virginia Beach, Virginia. Her next duty station was human resources in Norfolk, Virginia. She left active duty in 1976 as a lieutenant and joined the Naval Reserve. Over the next 15 years, she served in multiple reserve units stationed in Virginia, Maine and Massachusetts. During this time, she was promoted to commander and retired in 1993.

Concurrent with her military duties, Ms. Miskill volunteered much of her time and energy in the local community in Brunswick, Maine.

She was very active with the Mid Coast Chapter of the American Red Cross, chairing the advisory committee for the Naval Air Station Brunswick, working local blood drives, and being a member of the Red Cross Chapter board of directors. She eventually accepted the position of director of development for the chapter for a year. As a member of the board, she co-chaired two highly successful annual Red Cross balls. During the period from 1992 to 1994, she served as the senior adviser to the base commanding officer at Naval Air Station Sigonella in Sicily.

From 1995 to 1998, Ms. Miskill was hired by Mid Coast Health Services in Brunswick as the public information specialist. She was responsible for newsletters, advertisements and materials for their monthly TV show, and assisting all hospital departments with their graphic design needs.

Other noteworthy activities include: monthly preparing meals for a local homeless shelter for over 20 years, serving as administrative assistant for a summer swim program for eight years, providing graphic design services to her town recreation department for several years, and producing newsletters for the Merrymeeting Audubon Chapter, on which she also serves on the board of directors, and the Orr's Island Library.

In recognition of her accomplishments, she was awarded a Navy Commendation Medal for her work at an international intelligence conference and the Clara Barton Honor Award for Meritorious Volunteer Leader from the American Red Cross. Likewise, Ms. Miskill has been featured in numerous editions of Who's Who in Finance and Business, Who's Who in Finance and Industry, Who's Who in America, Who's Who in the World and Who's Who of American Women.

Ms. Miskill initially pursued studies at Marymount Junior College in Arlington, Virginia, from 1966 to 1967. She then transferred to Adelphi University in Garden City, New York, where she completed her education with a Bachelor of Arts in sociology in 1970. She currently maintains affiliations with Autism Speaks, the National Organization for Women, Friends of Fallingwater, Maine Audubon, the World Wildlife Fund, and the National Parks Conservation Association.

A Lifetime of Achievement in **Government / Public Service**

Edward George Schwier

Captain (Retired)
U.S. Navy

RICHLAND, WA UNITED STATES

With more than 40 years of experience to his credit, Capt. Edward George Schwier is currently retired, having worked for Fluor Daniel Hanford in Richland, Washington, as a manager from 1996 to 2012. Prior to this appointment, he held the positions of a commanding officer for the Naval Warfare Assessment Division in Corona, California, from 1993 to 1995 and a comptroller for Norfolk & Charleston Naval Shipyards from 1990 to 1993. The director of operations for the Staff of Commander Joint Task Force in the Middle East from 1989 to 1990, he previously served as a flag secretary, an aide, and a commander for the Atlantic Fleet of the Naval Surface Force from 1982 to 1984. Moreover, Capt. Schwier has excelled as the founder of Building Leaders and Teams.

Capt. Schwier garnered a number of impressive military titles between 1969 and 1982, having been active as a commanding officer of the USS Aylwin and the main propulsion assistant for the USS Eugene A. Greene. Subsequently, he flourished as an engineer officer for the USS Reasoner and the staff commander for Destroyer Squadron 15 in Yokosuka, Japan. Additionally, Capt. Schwier held the post of an executive officer on the USS Estocin.

Before embarking on his professional path, Capt. Schwier pursued an education at the U.S. Naval Academy in Annapolis, Maryland, earning a Bachelor of Science in aeronautical engineering in 1969. He concluded his studies at the Naval Postgraduate School in Monterey, California,

A Lifetime of Achievement | **Edward George Schwier**

graduating with a Master of Science in weapons systems technology in 1980. In addition to these accomplishments, Capt. Schwier has been certified as a manager and a quality engineer as well as a weapon system acquisition manager and a surface warfare officer.

Beyond his responsibilities within the field, Capt. Schwier has participated in numerous endeavors outside of his professional circles. In 1969, he began his military service when he was commissioned as an ensign by the U.S. Navy. Over the next 20 years, he advanced through the grades to the rank of captain. Retiring as a captain in the command of the Naval Warfare Assessment Division, Capt. Schwier found success with his written works as well, contributing as an author for multiple military publications.

In addition to his primary vocation, Capt. Schwier remains affiliated with various organizations in relation to his areas of expertise. He has maintained his involvement with Chapter 395 of the National Management Association, for which he had participated on the Columbia Basin area council. He was also associated with the Richland Desert Wind Toastmasters Club 7308. Furthermore, Capt. Schwier was a member of the Knights of Columbus.

In light of his exceptional undertakings, Capt. Schwier has accrued several accolades throughout his impressive career. From 1968 to 1969, he was recognized as a Trident scholar by the U.S. Naval Academy. Highlighted as a Distinguished Toastmaster, he was honored as the Comptroller of the Year by the American Society of Military Comptrollers in 1993. Likewise, Capt. Schwier was selected as the Member of the Year by the National Management Association in 2004.

Finding his training and experiences in the U.S. Naval Academy to be challenging yet rewarding, Capt. Schwier attributes his success to being a constant learner and a voracious researcher who was in the right place at the right time. In 1988, he was the victim of a near-fatal automobile accident, from which he made a miraculous recovery and left the hospital less than a month following the accident. Coincidentally, Dr. John Staeheli, who later replaced Capt. Schwier's hips and knees, was the surgeon who led the joint team that was instrumental in saving his life.

Mentored by Cmdr. Richard Dietz, Capt. Schwier considers himself an expert on anti-warfare technology, leadership, communications, engineering, and various elements of war. He has been a public speaker and a teacher on community service issues as well as in developing leadership skills to better navigate a path toward success. Looking toward the future, Capt. Schwier hopes to remain in the Columbia Valley of Washington, where he teaches communications and maintains his community outreach.

A Lifetime of Achievement in **Government / Public Service**

Thomas Michael Thompson

Technical Data Department Manager (Retired)
Naval Surface Warfare Center
Naval Sea Systems Command
U.S. Navy
BAKERSFIELD, CA UNITED STATES

Driven by a desire to help others, Thomas Michael Thompson has emerged as a leader in the fields of logistics and foreign military sales, as well as in psychology. After accruing nearly 30 years of practiced experience in various defense positions, he retired from active, full-time professional pursuits in 1994. Mr. Thompson spent the majority of his career at the Naval Surface Warfare Center, part of the Naval Sea Systems Command of the U.S. Navy, in Port Hueneme, California. Over the course of more than two decades, he was part of a team that helped to design, build, deliver and maintain ships and systems for the U.S. Navy. He thrived in various positions, including as the technical data department manager from 1990 to 1994, the division manager from 1986 to 1990, the assistant for logistics and tech operations from 1983 to 1986, the logistics management specialist from 1972 to 1983 and the inventory management specialist from 1969 to 1972.

Earlier in his professional journey, Mr. Thompson worked at Sharpe Army Depot, a defense logistics agency facility, located in Lathrop, California. He briefly served as a supply specialist in 1967, before becoming a supply systems analyst in 1968. Mr. Thompson began his career by enlisting in the U.S. Army as a supply specialist in Weapons Command in 1966. As he reflects on the many successes of his professional journey, Mr. Thompson has been most proud of his time as a liaison with foreign militaries and governments, which were aided by his accrued

A Lifetime of Achievement | **Thomas Michael Thompson**

knowledge in the field. He credits Eleanor Nanke, the Army Weapons Command in Rock Island, and Thomas P. Meyers as the greatest influences on his career.

To prepare him for a career of service, Mr. Thompson earned a Bachelor of Arts in political science from Seattle University, a Jesuit Catholic university located in Washington state, in 1965. Outside of his work in the military, he has dedicated himself to helping families and couples. He obtained a Master of Arts in counseling psychology from the University of San Francisco in 1989 and is a licensed marriage and family therapist in the state of California. In order to remain aware of changes in psychology and therapy, Mr. Thompson is affiliated with the California Association of Marriage Family Therapists. Outside of his professional endeavors, he remains involved with the Solera at Kern County Homeowners Association in Bakersfield, California.

For his excellence in the field, Mr. Thompson was honored with the Department of the Navy Meritorious Civilian Service Medal in 1994, an accomplishment he counts as one of the highlights of his career. The prestigious award, consisting of a certificate and a citation, is presented to civilian Navy employees in recognition of commendable service or contributions of high value for the Navy or Marine Corps. It is the third highest Navy civilian award. Additionally, Mr. Thompson was featured in the 24th edition of Who's Who in the West in 1993. In recognition of his exceptional leadership and contributions to his industry, he has also been presented with the prestigious Albert Nelson Marquis Lifetime Achievement Award.

Mr. Thompson was born on December 3, 1943, to Henry Clay Harman and Marion Margaret Lee Thompson in Eureka, California. In his free time, he enjoys reading, traveling, plate collecting, music and tutoring. In the near future, Mr. Thompson intends to experience the continued growth and success of his career.

A Lifetime of Achievement in **Government / Public Service**

Karon Lynette Uzzell-Baggett, OTD

Director (Retired)
Career Development Center
Tennessee State University

Lieutenant Colonel (Retired)
U.S. Air Force

NASHVILLE, TN UNITED STATES

Lt. Col. Karon Lynette Uzzell-Baggett, OTD, OTR/L, SHRM-SCP, SPHR, a retired lieutenant colonel, served as the director of the career development center at Tennessee State University in Nashville from 2011 to 2014, having previously been a commander of the U.S. Air Force ROTC detachment at the school from 2008 to 2011. She previously dedicated her time and knowledge to the Office of Security Cooperation-Afghanistan as well as such bases as Maxwell Air Force Base, Sheppard Air Force Base, Andrews Air Force Base, Spangdahlem Air Force Base, Murted Air Base and Langley Air Force Base.

Prior to establishing herself as a trusted voice in the field, Lt. Col. Uzzell-Baggett sought to expand her knowledge through the pursuit of a formal education at a number of esteemed academic institutions. She first attended the University of North Carolina at Chapel Hill, where she earned a Bachelor of Science in 1986. Taking a break from academia, she served as a commissioned second lieutenant in the U.S. Air Force in 1986, later earning the rank of captain in 1990. From there, she continued her studies at the University of Maryland University College in College Park, where she completed postgraduate coursework from 1993 to 1996. In 2019, she completed doctoral coursework in occupational therapy at Belmont University in Nashville, a pursuit that has brought her great joy in life. She plans to practice in various settings.

An active presence in the field, Lt. Col. Uzzell-Baggett maintains memberships with such prestigious organizations as the Southern Poverty Law Center, the Society for Human Resources Management, and the Human Resources Certification Institute. She is further associated with the American Occupational Therapy Association and the Military Officers Association of America, with which she has a life membership. Civically, she has been a board member of the middle Tennessee chapter of the Military Officers Association of America since 2012 and a memorial volunteer for Women in Military Service since 1993.

In light of her professional achievements, Lt. Col. Uzzell-Baggett has gained recognition in the form of various awards and accolades. She has previously been selected for inclusion in such honors publications as the 51st through 70th editions of Who's Who in America, the 26th and 27th editions of Who's Who in the East, and the 19th through 28th editions of Who's Who of American Women. She has also been featured in the 21st, 24th and 27th through 33rd editions of Who's Who in the World. Reflecting on her career, she considers the highlight of her career to be the time she spent commanding several units as a minority female. She worked with many wonderful people, whether they were at the cadet level or senior level. She has always been proud of her father's military service, which inspired her to do her part to serve the nation.

Lt. Col. Uzzell-Baggett was born in April 1964 in Goldsboro, North Carolina, to mother Ernestine Smith Uzzell and father Jesse Lee Uzzell. She later married Ronald Walter Baggett on July 26, 1990. Currently, she is the proud mother to one child named Kathleen "Katey," who is a scholar, and stepmother to three stepchildren named Christina, Brian and Adam. All three of her stepchildren have followed in her footsteps and gone into the Army and Air Force. In her free time, she enjoys participating in such activities as exercising, sewing and gardening.

A Lifetime of Achievement in **Government / Public Service**

Robert D. Walz

Lieutenant Colonel (Retired)
U.S. Army

KANSAS CITY, MO UNITED STATES

Before spending nearly 40 years with the U.S. armed forces in service to his country, Robert D. Walz pursued a formal education. He first attended the University of South Dakota, where he earned a Bachelor of Arts in history and government in 1966. He continued his studies at the same esteemed academic institution and ultimately achieved a Master of Arts in government with a minor in history in 1968. From there, he was commissioned as a battery officer for the 3rd Battalion of the 320th Field Artillery Regiment stationed in Fort Bragg, North Carolina. He was transferred within a year to the 2nd Battalion of the 320th, where he was a fire support officer in Vietnam. After his return to the United States, Mr. Walz was named as commander of Battery A for the 1st Battalion of the 17th Artillery in Fort Sill, Oklahoma.

In 1972, having accrued recognition for his skills in strategic analysis, Mr. Walz was appointed to the position of assistant professor of military science at The University of Vermont. He remained on the faculty for two years before going overseas once more, this time occupying the role of staff officer for the 1st Battalion of the 38th Artillery at Camp Stanley in South Korea. He went on to contribute his inexhaustible services to the military in various capacities through the remainder of the 1970s and 1980s, gradually transitioning toward education. At the Command and General Staff College in Fort Leavenworth, Kansas, he was the only instructor specializing in China — long a fascination of his — for the latter half of the 1980s. Mr. Walz retired as a civilian in 2007, having taught such foreign luminaries as the second highest ranked officer in the Army of the Netherlands and a former defense minister of the Republic of Georgia.

During his involvement with the armed forces, Mr. Walz garnered numerous recognitions in return for a sterling record of excellence, including a Legion of Merit, a Bronze Star, a Meritorious Service Medal, several Army Commendation Medals and five Air Medals. Impressively, he was also named the Civilian Instructor of the Year by the Command and General Staff College. He has previously been selected for inclusion in many honors publications, including the 10th and 11th editions of Who's Who in the World, the 22nd and 25th editions of Who's Who in the Midwest, and the 73rd edition of Who's Who in America.

Mr. Walz was born on May 15, 1944, in Great Falls, Montana, to mother Jean DeHaven Walz and father Robert Chaussee Walz. He later married Merrill Ann Martin on January 25, 1967, and together, they are the proud parents of one child named Juli Ann. Moreover, they have one grandchild named David. Now free to dedicate his energies to pursuits outside the military, he has devoted himself to a long-standing passion: trains. In addition to being an avid builder of model railroad equipment and locomotives, he has authored or helped author 15 books on the Santa Fe railroad system, and holds membership with The Santa Fe Railway Historical and Modeling Society as its secretary, publication coordinator, and member of the board of directors, positions he has been in since 2013. Mr. Walz also associates with the National Railway Historical Society and the Railroad Artifact Preservation Society, where he was a former member of the board of directors.

A Lifetime of Achievement in **Information Science**

Melanie L. Freese, MLS

Associate Professor of Library Services
Hofstra University
NORTH BALDWIN, NY UNITED STATES

In the late 1960s, Melanie L. Freese, MLS, began her career as an elementary school teacher in Roosevelt and Massapequa, New York. After obtaining support from a staff member at the academic library at Adelphi University, she found herself drawn to the field of library sciences. Starting in 1972, she worked with Adelphi University as an assistant to the social work librarian, assistant to the acquisitions librarian and biographical searcher, reserve librarian and circulation assistant for the university's library. Subsequently, she gained valuable expertise with Hofstra University as a senior catalog librarian, assistant dean and chairwoman of technical services.

Throughout her career, Ms. Freese has presented numerous training workshops on cataloging and classification for both faculty and staff. Additionally, she has reviewed materials for "Libraries Alive," a publication of the National Church Library Association. She authored chapters that have appeared in the ninth volume of Library and Archival Security in 1989, and in the 66th volume of PNLA Quarterly. Despite all of these accomplishments, the highlight of her career was establishing a library for the residents of the Wayside Home School for Girls in 1993.

Before establishing herself as a trusted voice in the field, Ms. Freese pursued a formal education at a number of esteemed academic institutions. She first attended Hofstra University, where she earned a Bachelor of Education in elementary education in 1967 and a Master of Education in elementary education in 1969. She continued her studies at Long Island University Post and ultimately achieved a Master of Library Science in 1977. Subsequently, she obtained certifications as a public librarian in 1977 and a teacher of nursery through sixth grade in the state of New York in 1969.

An active presence in the field, Ms. Freese maintains memberships with such prestigious organizations as the American Library Association and the Nassau County Library Association, where she has served on the board of directors and the institutional services committee. Utilizing the knowledge she has gained over many years, she has authored many books, including "Fostering Communication and Understanding at Hofstra University's Axinn Library" in 2002, "Charles Leonard Woolley, 1880-1960" in 1989, and "Missing Links: Smart Barcodes and Inventory Analysis at Hofstra University's Axinn Library" in 1989.

Due to her excellence in library sciences, Ms. Freese has been recognized as Woman of the Year through the Business and Professional Women of Nassau County Inc. in 1994. She has further been presented with a Distinguished Service Award from St. Peter's Lutheran Church in Baldwin, New York, in 1993. Notably, the International Biographical Centre in Cambridge, England, honored her with an International Order of Merit in 1980 and a Twentieth Century Award for Achievement in 1994. Though these honors are impressive, she considers the most rewarding part of her career to be giving her students access to the projects she works on. She attributes her success to her education and work ethic.

Notably profiled in the 73rd edition of Who's Who in America, Ms. Freese was born on May 12, 1945, in Mineola, New York, to mother Agnes Jensen Freese and father Dr. Walter C. Freese. In her free time, she enjoys participating in such activities as knitting, doing needlework, crocheting and playing the piano. Looking to the future, she plans to be retired within five years. Currently, she is mentoring a younger colleague who is learning to catalog materials for the music library at Hofstra University.

Miriam C. Giebel

Genealogical Researcher
Librarian (Retired)
LEMONT, IL UNITED STATES

With more than six decades of professional experience to her name, Miriam C. Giebel has enjoyed a successful career as a genealogist and librarian. Since 2002, she has been an independent genealogical researcher. She previously served at the Chicago Heights Public Library as a webmaster from 2000 to 2001, a volunteer coordinator, and an extension and reference librarian from 1974 to 1999. Before accepting these roles, she was an assistant librarian at the Headquarters Library of the American Library Association in Chicago from 1964 to 1967.

Earlier in her career, Ms. Giebel acted as a librarian for the Little Company of Mary School of Nursing in Evergreen Park, Illinois, from 1963 to 1964. Previously, she was the technical services librarian at the Chicago Heights Public Library from 1959 to 1963. Her first professional role was as an assistant in the acquisitions department of the Marquette University Library in Milwaukee, Wisconsin, from 1956 to 1958. Reflecting on her career, she considers the most rewarding aspect of her career to be working with others.

Prior to establishing herself as a trusted voice in the field, Ms. Giebel sought to expand her knowledge through formal education at a number of esteemed academic institutions. She first attended Marquette University, where she completed coursework and earned a Bachelor of Science in 1956. She continued her studies at Rosary College and ultimately achieved a Master of Science in library science upon graduating from the school in 1960. Subsequently, she became a certified paralegal through Roosevelt University in 1992. In addition, she received a certificate in family history research through Brigham Young University in Provo, Utah, in 1992.

An active participant in the field, Ms. Giebel has maintained memberships with several prestigious lineage organizations. She has been serving as the honorary president of the Illinois Society of the Daughters of 1812 since 1999. Additionally, she has been the registrar of the Illinois branch of the National Society of Sons and Daughters of Pilgrims since 2011. She is a life member of the National Society of the Daughters of the American Revolution, the National Society of the Daughters of the Civil War 1861-1865, the Illinois Cameo Society of the Daughters of the American Revolution and The Society of Indiana Pioneers.

In light of her many accomplishments in the field, Ms. Giebel has gained recognition in the form of various awards and accolades over the years. Notably, she has previously been selected for inclusion in such honors publications as the 34th edition of Who's Who in Finance and Business, the 26th edition of Who's Who in the West, the 15th through 26th editions of Who's Who in the World and the 20th through 28th editions of Who's Who of American Women. She has also been featured in the 52nd through 63rd and 67th through 70th editions of Who's Who in America. She attributes her success to doing her best as well as her parents, who always emphasized the importance of education.

Ms. Giebel was born on October 10, 1934, in Williamsburg, Iowa, to mother Helen Gertrude Wright Donahoe and father John Timothy Donahoe. She later married William Herbert Giebel on September 30, 1967, and together, they are the proud parents of one child named Sara Ann Giebel-Ward. Moreover, they have two grandchildren named Jenna Ward and Andrew Ward. In her free time, she enjoys participating in such activities as reading, surfing the web, and doing personal genealogical research. Looking to the future, she plans to write a book and travel to Ireland.

A Lifetime of Achievement in **Information Science**

Virginia Lee Kinney

Librarian & Educator (Retired)

PLEASANT HILL, OH UNITED STATES

With nearly 55 years of professional experience, Virginia Lee Kinney excelled as a librarian with the Miami County Public Library from 1978 to 2011 and the Newton Local School in Pleasant Hill, Ohio, from 1984 to 2002. In addition to her primary roles, she worked as an instructor of GED preparation for Troy Continuing Education from 1988 to 2009, an instructor of English as a second language from 2004 to 2009, and an instructor in the Newton Local School Chapter 1 Program from 1978 to 1988. Ms. Kinney previously served as a teacher with Barnesville Elementary School from 1961 to 1962 and with Union Local Head Start in 1965. She began her career as an instructor with the Ohio State University County Extension Agent from 1959 to 1960 and a teacher with the Lamar Elementary School in Harlingen, Texas, from 1957 to 1958.

To prepare her for her professional endeavors, Ms. Kinney initially pursued an education at The Ohio State University in Columbus, earning a Bachelor of Science in home economics in 1956. She has also completed coursework with Ohio Wesleyan University, Muskingum College, Urbana University and the University of Dayton. Following these accomplishments, Ms. Kinney found success with her written works, authoring such publications as "The Life and Times of Johnny Appleseed from A to Z" in 2008 and "The Commemorative History Book of Newton Township" in 2003, among several others.

A respected voice in her areas of interest, Ms. Kinney has been affiliated with a number of professional and civic organizations. She is a member of the American Hereford Women as well as the Miami County Association of Family and Consumer Science. She was previously associated as a trustee of the Bradford Railroad Museum, the Miami County Republican Women, the Johnny Appleseed Society, the Human Ecology Alumni Society and the Astrobuds Garden Club.

Ms. Kinney has also been active with The Ohio State University Alumni Association; the Ohio CowBelles, as state president in 1985; the Red Hat Society; the Epworth Park Cottage Owners; the Antique Automobile Club of America; and the Plymouth Owners Club. Further, she has contributed her talents and expertise as a member of the Miami County Barn Survey Project, as a board member for the Oakes-Beitman Historical Museum and as a judge for 4-H projects. She has also compiled a series of 15 history books for the village of Belmont, Ohio.

Throughout her career, Ms. Kinney has been celebrated for her myriad contributions to the field. She has been accepted into such renowned honor societies as Phi Upsilon Omicron and Alpha Delta Pi, of which she previously served as state president. Likewise, Ms. Kinney has been celebrated in numerous publications, including Who's Who in Finance and Business, Who's Who in America, Who's Who in American Education and Who's Who of American Women. Her professional accomplishments and contributions to the field have also been commemorated with the prestigious Albert Nelson Marquis Lifetime Achievement Award.

Ms. Kinney's most recent accomplishment was presenting the project to the Ohio House of Representatives to vote for the sugar cookie as Ohio's state dessert. For her efforts, she received a certificate of special recognition from the Ohio General Assembly and the House of Representatives. The final step for the project to be completed is to have it accepted by the Ohio Senate.

Ms. Kinney was born on October 21, 1934, to James Jeffrey Groves and Mary Virginia Groves in Barnesville, Ohio. She has been married to her husband, Royce Bentley Kinney, for more than 60 years and together, they are the proud parents of four children, Charlotte, Robert, Margaret and Mary Elizabeth. She also has eight grandchildren: Brookelen, Heidi, Dustin, Victoria, Benjamin, Michael, Luke and Arianna, as well as five great-grandchildren: Dallas, Ryan, Briella, Rylie and Carson. In her free time, Ms. Kinney enjoys creating history booklets, exploring her family's genealogy, traveling and reading.

A Lifetime of Achievement in **Information Science**

Barbara Pickthorn

Librarian & Educator
Cameron University
LAWTON, OK UNITED STATES

Over a career spanning more than 30 years, Barbara Pickthorn has emerged as a leader in the fields of education and library science. She has spent her entire career at Cameron University, a public institution of higher education located in Lawton, Oklahoma. Since 2016, Ms. Pickthorn has served as the interim assistant director of the university's library, overseeing the collection and guiding a staff of nearly a dozen librarians and librarian associates as well as providing valuable assistance to students seeking books, archival information and educational resources.

Ms. Pickthorn's hands-on experience managing other areas of the library prepared her well for her current role. Prior to assuming her present position, she excelled as the assistant director of library services from 1990 to 2015, previously finding success as the assistant director of public services from 1988 to 1990. Furthermore, as an assistant professor, she served as the chair of the faculty council from 1997 to 1998 and advanced to the rank of associate professor in 2002.

Ms. Pickthorn achieved faculty status at Cameron University as librarian and instructor in 1979 and advanced to assistant professor in 1981. She then became the assistant director of technological services at the Cameron University Library in 1983. Outside of her primary professional responsibilities, she contributed as the chair of the Oklahoma Chapter of the Association of College and Research Libraries from 1988 to 1991. The professional organization provides a valuable network for academic and research librarians, as well as strives to promote library service throughout the state of Oklahoma.

Well-regarded as an expert in her field, Ms. Pickthorn was inducted into Phi Kappa Phi in 2006 and served as secretary from 2005 to 2008 and enrollment officer from 2008 to 2015. She was also inducted into Alpha Delta Kappa, an international honor organization for women educators, in 1976. Serving Alpha Delta Kappa as chapter president from 1978 to 1980 and 2004 to 2006, she was also Oklahoma State Alpha Delta Kappa president from 2008 to 2010. A member of the Friends of Libraries in Oklahoma, also known as FOLIO, Ms. Pickthorn has also been involved with the Oklahoma Library Association, where she spent time as the chair of SMART, the Supervisors, Managers and Administrators Committee from 2006 to 2008.

In addition to her work with the library system, Ms. Pickthorn is an accomplished musician. A talented cellist, she spent several years playing with the Lawton Philharmonic Orchestra, from 1975 to 1982 and in 2008, and served on the Lawton Philharmonic board in 1977. She currently lends her talents to the Oklahoma Baptist Symphony as well as the Cameron Civic Symphony, comprised of Cameron University students and community members. Ms. Pickthorn additionally served on the Lawton Arts and Humanities Council from 2017 to 2019. A devoted Baptist, she is very active in her church and teaches Sunday school.

Ms. Pickthorn's fascination in library science began in childhood, as she exhibited an early interest in organizing and working with her junior and high school libraries. To further expand upon her love of the organizational aspect of library resources, she attended the University of North Texas in Denton, where she earned her Bachelor of Arts in 1967 and a Master of Library Science in 1974. Later in her career, Ms. Pickthorn furthered her education at Cameron University in Lawton, Oklahoma, obtaining a Master of Science in 1992.

Ms. Pickthorn has been the recipient of several awards in recognition of her many contributions to her community and industry. In 2003, she was named a Phi Kappa Phi inductee, and she additionally received the Meritorious Service Award in 2010. In 2007, she and the Phi Eta Sigma chapter received a literacy grant from Phi Kappa Phi, which was called "Books for Kids" and was used to purchase books that were put in the backpacks given to students who were food insecure.

Likewise, the Oklahoma Chapter of the Association of College and Research Libraries presented Ms. Pickthorn with the Outstanding Service Award in 1993. Her many accomplishments have also earned her inclusion in the 27th and 28th editions of Who's Who of American Women, as well as the esteemed Albert Nelson Marquis Lifetime Achievement Award. The prestigious designation is the highest honor presented by Marquis Who's Who, awarded to individuals who have demonstrated exceptional leadership and made a difference in their field.

A Lifetime of Achievement in **Law / Legal Services**

Janet L. Bassitt

Attorney (Retired)

ROSELLE, IL UNITED STATES

J anet L. Bassitt, a retired attorney, earned her Doctor of Jurisprudence from the John Marshall Law School in Chicago. Prior to law school, she graduated from the University of Illinois at Chicago in 1976, earning her Bachelor of Arts, with honors, in psychology. She began her career as a lawyer in 1981, with the entertainment and media law firm of Attorney D. M. Ephraim in Chicago. During law school, Ms. Bassitt had published a professional article in the Illinois Bar Journal addressing the medicolegal association between law and psychology as they formed an "Involuntary Act" defense; she also served as a writer for the law school newspaper, Decisive Utterance, and was an elected officer in the Lincoln Chapter of Phi Alpha Delta Law Fraternity. When she was growing up, Ms. Bassitt lived in Macomb, Illinois, and attended school from kindergarten through high school at the Laboratory School of the Western Illinois State Teachers College, now Western Illinois University. She is a descendant of Revolutionary War Patriot Abijah Flagg.

Visually challenged herself, Ms. Bassitt, during law school, volunteered as a soundbooth reader for Recording for the Blind Chicago, now known as Learning Ally, recording law books for use by blind law students. She completed her Illinois Supreme Court Rule Internship with the Homicide Task Force of the Cook County Illinois Office of the Public Defender at the Criminal Courts Building in Chicago.

Subsequent to her 1981 admission to practice law in Illinois, Ms. Bassitt was admitted to practice in the U.S. District Court for the

Northern District of Illinois, the U.S. Court of Appeals for the 7th Circuit, the U.S. Tax Court and the Supreme Court of the United States. She operated her own private law practice between 1982 and 2004 in suburban Chicago, serving the Illinois counties of Cook, DuPage, Will, Kane, McHenry and Lake. In 1985, Ms. Bassitt was honored to research and author a full volume practice guide for the Illinois Institute for Continuing Legal Education titled "Attorney Conduct." While in practice for herself, she served as pro bono attorney for the State Appellate Defender, representing indigent persons on appeal in criminal cases, when appointed by the Illinois Appellate Court. She worked periodically as an instructor for the Women's Program associated with Harper College in Palatine, Illinois, and also contributed to the United Way of Schaumburg-Hoffman, Illinois, as a member of the board of directors. She remains a longtime member of both the American Bar Association and the Illinois State Bar Association.

Beyond her responsibilities within the field of law, Ms. Bassitt has participated in numerous endeavors previous to and outside of her professional circles. As an Illinois elementary school student, high school student and adult, she worked tirelessly raising funds for the March of Dimes effort to cure polio; and later, when she lived in the state of Washington, she served two years as chair of the Mothers' March for March of Dimes in Wenatchee in 1971 and 1972. While still in high school, she headed a chapter of Rainbow for Girls, which successfully raised and contributed funds to the Masonic Hospital for Children in Chicago, which provided free specialized orthopedic care and burn treatment to children.

In high school, she was elected to serve as a representative from her high school for a Saturday teen panel radio program discussing current teen issues and broadcast by radio station WKAI. Her first job as a teenager was as a long-distance telephone operator for General Telephone of Illinois, then as a switchboard operator for the new McDonough District Hospital in Illinois, and ultimately as a career nurse assistant for the hospital, authorized to work on the medical floor, surgical floor, delivery room and baby nursery, including the task of mixing all of the hospital's daily baby formula requirements.

Between 1961 and 1966, when her young family moved to Nashville, Illinois, Ms. Bassitt authored a human interest column for the Nashville News newspaper. During those years, Ms. Bassitt continued her dedication to raising funds to find a cure for tuberculosis, a cure for polio, and, after the availability of the polio vaccine, helping to distribute the new vaccine to the entire community. She was also active in helping to raise funds to build a much-needed hospital in the area. The hospital was built, and she excelled as the founder of the Washington County Medical Scholarship Fund in 1964, for the purpose of encouraging new medical school graduates to come work in the new hospital in the county seat and charming small town of Nashville, Illinois, with a population of 3,000.

In the late 1960s, when her husband was going through graduate school, the Bassitt family of five moved to a different state, agreeing that Mr. Bassitt would complete his graduate studies first and then Ms. Bassitt could proceed with her studies. During this time, she helped by selling Avon products, taking in sewing and ironing, babysitting the children of other graduate students and clerking part time in an upscale dress shop. Her efforts earned enough to feed the family, while Mr. Bassitt earned enough from a student assistant job to cover the rent and automobile. When her husband completed his studies, the family moved to Wenatchee, Washington, where Mr. Bassitt was employed by the Junior College and Ms. Bassitt worked full time as an orthodontic assistant and also as the manager of the 20-unit townhouse complex where the family lived, helping to repay her husband's student loans.

Three years later, the family returned to Illinois. In Illinois, Ms. Bassitt worked for one year as a teaching assistant for Schaumburg School District 54 in their new Illinois "Open Space" pilot program for grades one through three. She also concurrently operated her own medical transcription business from home in the evenings, typing for several hospitals in Chicago that delivered and picked up their work twice weekly. Throughout the years, as her three children were growing up and going through school, Ms. Bassitt was active with them as room mother, Girl Scout troop leader, Boy Scout den mother, teachers' helper, Friday activity instructor, seamstress of cheerleaders uniforms and more. Then, it was her turn at more schooling, and she started classes at the University of Illinois at Chicago, then on to the John Marshall Law School, where classes were offered morning, afternoon and evening, opening doors for mothers and full-time employed persons to create a flexible class schedule.

In those years, there were no commercial child care options available. The three Bassitt children were all in school by then and all had learned to cook, sew and care for pets, which made them wonderful helpers. Mr. Bassitt had a time-demanding job, but handled the house repairs and automotive problems; he had been warned of a possible heart condition and his student loan was looming large, which meant it was important for Ms. Bassitt to continue her studies; the entire family pulled together. While going through her law studies, Ms. Bassitt also worked weekends as a radiology transcriptionist for a local hospital.

In light of her exceptional undertakings, she has accrued several accolades throughout her impressive career. She was recognized by Western Illinois University with an honor in their annual yearbook as a winner of their 1957 Personalities Contest. She was invited to the Recognition Day for Alumni Authors by the Western Illinois University Alumni Association in 1985 and the inclusion of her book in the university's archives.

Honored for her work regarding the perpetuation of democracy and the appreciation of what so many have sacrificed for the goal of freedom and peace in the world, Ms. Bassitt, at age 14, was awarded a college scholarship as winner of an "I Speak for Democracy" Broadcasters of America student oratorical contest. In 1957, she was a medal winner in the Illinois State Speech Contest for her original poetry, and over several years was also a First Place Band winner in the annual Illinois State Music Contest, playing flute and piccolo.

Some years ago, Mr. Bassitt passed away, and Ms. Bassitt retired from traveling the counties representing clients in court. Her interest has now turned toward sound legal actions that show promise for blocking behavioral corruption; toward achieving the cure for epidermolysis bullosa, the very painful rare genetic condition that can affect all people, all races, male and female; toward developing better systems for educating those who struggle with dyslexia; and toward a better understanding of the human "accidental savant" ability.

A Lifetime of Achievement in **Law / Legal Services**

Robert W. "Joe" Bishop, Esq.

President & Founder
Bishop Friend PSC

LOUISVILLE, KY UNITED STATES

Robert W. "Joe" Bishop, Esq., the president and founder of Bishop Friend PSC, has focused his practice in recent years on employment law, contracts and class action litigation. He and his firm have worked on numerous employment cases and class actions involving varied subject matters, including antitrust, securities, personal injury, products liability, consumer protection, ERISA, wage and hour, and civil rights. Mr. Bishop is a life member of the Multi-Million Dollar Advocates Forum. He also has been selected to the Kentucky Super Lawyers List every year since 2012.

Mr. Bishop was born in Atlanta, Georgia. Growing up in a military family, his childhood years were marked by travel, both abroad and within the United States, from Clark Air Force Base in the Philippines to the suburbs of London, to the Washington, D.C., area. He attended Wallop Boys School in Surrey, England, and graduated from Yorktown High School in Arlington, Virginia, where he was a member of the National Honor Society, earned athletic letters in soccer and tennis, and was captain of the tennis team. He attended Duke University, where he was a member of Sigma Alpha Epsilon fraternity, and earned a letter in soccer. He also attended the National Law Center at The George Washington University, and the University of Kentucky, where he earned his Bachelor of Arts in political science, graduating Phi Beta Kappa, and his Doctor of Jurisprudence from the College of Law, graduating Order of the Coif.

Mr. Bishop was admitted to practice law in 1976 in Ohio, hired out of the University of Kentucky Law School by one of the 10 largest law firms in the country, Squire, Sanders & Dempsey, in Cleveland, Ohio. He returned to and was admitted to practice in Kentucky in 1981, among other things, in order to work on an antitrust case in which his firm were lead counsel for the governmental entities. Mr. Bishop was chairman of the federal practice section of the Louisville Bar Association. He has been lead counsel in many noteworthy cases, with verdicts, judgments and settlements on behalf of joined plaintiffs, individual plaintiffs, and both opt-in and opt-out plaintiffs in class actions.

Mr. Bishop is admitted to U.S. District Courts in Kentucky, Ohio and Texas; the 3rd, 4th, 6th, 7th and 9th U.S. Circuit Courts of Appeal; and the Supreme Court of the United States. He is a member of the federal, Kentucky, and Louisville bar associations, and was active in his community in the city of Louisville as a coach, and as a board member of the Louisville Central Community Centers. His enjoyment of watching, playing and coaching soccer led Mr. Bishop to become an officer and director of the Greater Louisville Soccer League, and one of the original founders, owners, officers and board members of the Louisville Thunder Professional Indoor Soccer Team.

A celebrated Marquis listee, Mr. Bishop has also been featured in approximately 25 editions of Who's Who, including Who's Who in America, Who's Who in American Law and Who's Who in the World. For his leadership and contributions, he has also been named the recipient of the Albert Nelson Marquis Lifetime Achievement Award.

Notably profiled in the 73rd edition of Who's Who in America, Mr. Bishop has been married to and in love with his wife and best friend, Cynthia Graham Bishop, for nearly 50 years. Together they are the proud parents of Jessica Levesque, Joshua Davis Bishop, Amanda Joyce Bishop and Alexandra Kelt Bishop, all of whom are college graduates, three of whom have obtained one or more graduate degrees, and all of whom are successfully pursuing postgraduate careers in business, science, humanitarian ventures and/or the arts. Cynthia and Joe are also the doting grandparents of four grandchildren, Ganyon, Torin, Freyja and Dot.

Outside of his work in the courtroom, Mr. Bishop has enjoyed climbing, rowing, sailing, cycling, hiking, hanging out with his family and friends, and reading. Looking toward the future, he, together with his law partners, hope to continue to expand their firm's class action practice and employment work within Kentucky and across the country.

A Lifetime of Achievement in **Law / Legal Services**

David Sinclair Bouschor

Judge (Retired)
Minnesota District Court
DULUTH, MN UNITED STATES

Supported by nearly 40 years of practiced experience, David Sinclair Bouschor excelled as a judge for the Minnesota District Court in Duluth from 1978 until his retirement in 1995. Prior to this appointment, he briefly served as a judge for St. Louis County in Minnesota between 1977 and 1978. From 1960 to 1976, he contributed as an attorney for the city of Proctor, Minnesota, while simultaneously working at a private practice in Duluth between 1958 and 1977. In 1976, he founded both Clan Sinclair USA and the Duluth Scottish Heritage Association.

Before embarking on his professional endeavors, Judge Bouschor sought to expand his knowledge through the pursuit of a formal education at a number of esteemed academic institutions. He first studied at Northwestern University in Evanston, Illinois, and graduated with a Bachelor of Science in 1952. He continued his studies at the William Mitchell College of Law in St. Paul, Minnesota, where he completed further coursework and ultimately achieved a Doctor of Jurisprudence in 1958. Subsequent to graduating with his law degree, he was admitted to the Minnesota State Bar Association in 1958.

An active member of his community, Judge Bouschor served of counsel for the Proctor Public Utilities Board for Proctor Public Schools and as special municipal judge for the city of Duluth. Additionally, he devoted his time as the past president of the Learning Disabilities Association of Minnesota, a member of the board of governors for the St.

Andrew's Society of Minnesota, a member of the advisory board for the Duluth Salvation Army, and the past chairman of the United Day Activity Center. For his civic involvement and contributions, he was presented with the Outstanding Eagle Scout Award from the Boy Scouts of America and honored in the City of Proctor Hall of Fame in 1959.

An active presence in the field, Judge Bouschor maintains affiliation with several prestigious organizations, including the Minnesota District Judges Association and the Minnesota Bar Association. An avid lover of all things Scottish, he is a member of numerous related organizations, including the Clan Sinclair Association, the Royal Order of Scotland, the Scottish Rite of Freemasonry, and Scottish-American Military Society. He also maintained association with the Sons of the American Revolution, the Sovereign Military Order of the Temple of Jerusalem, Rotary International, and the Elks and the Masons, where he was a grand high priest and grand master.

In addition, Judge Bouschor has previously been selected for inclusion in such honors publications as Who's Who in American Law and Who's Who in the Midwest. He considers the highlight of his many professional years to be having achieved many of the goals he set out for himself. He attributes his success to the role model his father was. His father was also a judge, and he practiced law at the same time. From the age of 5, Judge Bouschor knew he wanted to grow up and be just like his father.

Judge Bouschor was born on November 23, 1930, in Duluth, Minnesota, to mother Eleanor Sinclair Bouschor and father Royal George Bouschor. He later married Gloria Lee Wetters on August 15, 1953, and together, they are the proud parents of four children named Denise, David Jr., Charles and Diana. David Jr. and Denise are both lawyers. Moreover, they have seven grandchildren and two great-grandchildren. In his free time, he enjoys participating in such activities as playing the bagpipes and studying history.

A Lifetime of Achievement in **Law / Legal Services**

Shelley A. Bower, Esq.
Attorney
CATSKILL, NY UNITED STATES

With 35 years of experience to her credit, Shelley A. Bower, Esq., has excelled as a lawyer focusing on family law and labor law out of her private practice since 2016. Prior to this appointment, she held the position of the director of strategy and planning for GPJ from 2014 to 2015. From 1997 to 2013, she was active in a number of posts at IBM, including as a principal and a consultant for the IBM Global Consultant Service Manufacturing Industries. During this time, Ms. Bower worked with the IBM Software Group as a customer relationship management principal from 2001 to 2002, an executive from 2001 to 2002, an offering manager in the Lotus division from 2002 to 2005, and a software program director from 2005 to 2013.

Previously, Ms. Bower served the Oracle Corporation as a principal from 1996 to 1997 and C.T. Male Associates as both the director of planning and development and the corporate counsel from 1995 to 1996. A consultant for Electronic Data Systems in Southfield, Michigan, from 1992 to 1995, she was associated with General Motors as an engineer of technology and the director of corporate training and program administration in Troy, Michigan, from 1988 to 1992. From 1986 to 1988, she flourished as a division manager for Property Professionals in Saugerties, New York. Ms. Bower began her career with Cadillac in Detroit, Michigan, as an employee in training from 1984 to 1985 and the supervisor for equal employment opportunities from 1985 to 1986.

Before embarking on her professional path, Ms. Bower pursued an education at Michigan Technological University, earning a Bachelor of

Arts in 1977. She concluded her studies at the Michigan State University College of Law, formerly known as the Detroit College of Law, in 1984, graduating with a Doctor of Jurisprudence. Following these accomplishments, Ms. Bower has been admitted to practice law by the New York State Bar Association.

Beyond her responsibilities within the field, Ms. Bower has participated in numerous endeavors outside of her professional circles. She has found much success with the Catskill Education Foundation, having contributed on the board of directors as a corresponding secretary since 2018, the president in 2013, and a founding member in 2005. Furthermore, she remains affiliated with various organizations in relation to her areas of expertise, such as the National Association of Female Executives. In light of her exceptional undertakings, Ms. Bower was selected for inclusion in the 30th edition of Who's Who in Finance and Industry as well as multiple editions of Who's Who in Finance and Business, Who's Who in America, Who's Who in the East, Who's Who in the World and Who's Who of American Women. She was notably profiled in the 73rd edition of Who's Who in America.

Attracted to the field of law by the idealistic call of the profession as well as her exposure to multiple industries beforehand, Ms. Bower notably aided major corporations in resigning their labor organizational and strategic processes as a consultant. She attributes her success to her determination and the ability to question directions and requirements to achieve an outcome that works for everyone in order to open a discussion and find a resolution. The highlight of her career was working with people from many different backgrounds around the world, having conducted her business with many bright and kind people. Looking toward the future, Ms. Bower hopes to continue in her law practice, build upon her local community, and cement her legacy as a fair and balanced professional.

A Lifetime of Achievement in **Law / Legal Services**

Arnie Rolf Braafladt

Attorney (Retired)

JACKSONVILLE, OR UNITED STATES

With more than 35 years of experience to his credit, Arnie Rolf Braafladt has enjoyed a successful career in labor and employment law. Prior to beginning his professional journey, he earned a Bachelor of Arts in political science and journalism, magna cum laude, from Humboldt State University in Arcata, California, in 1974. He followed this accomplishment with a Master of Arts in urban studies from Occidental College in Los Angeles in 1976 and a Doctor of Jurisprudence from Willamette University in Salem, Oregon, in 1978. Highly qualified in his field, Mr. Braafladt has been admitted to practice law in Oregon, California and Washington, as well as before the U.S. District Court for the Northern District of California, the U.S. Court of Appeals for the 9th Circuit and the U.S. District Court of Oregon.

After starting out as a law clerk to the presiding justice for the Washington Supreme Court in 1979, Mr. Braafladt went on to work as the deputy legislative counsel for the Oregon Legislature, a partner with Shields & Braafladt and an associate with Howser & Munsell. He has also worked as a lawyer and a labor relations manager with the Oregon Executive Department, and a staff attorney and the senior staff counsel for the California School Employees Association. Mr. Braafladt most recently worked for the California School Employees Association as the deputy chief counsel, serving in this capacity from 2007 until his retirement in 2017. Outside of his professional endeavors, he has also served as a lecturer of media law at Humboldt State University and contributed legal counsel to the Lumberjack student newspaper. Interested in contributing to his field, Mr. Braafladt was the associate editor of the Willamette Law Journal from 1977 to 1978 and has had several articles published in professional journals.

Mr. Braafladt's career was shaped by a fellowship in San Francisco and his exposure to a diverse urban environment. Drawing upon an early interest in law, he is particularly proud of the work he has done to support school employees who were at risk of being contracted out, along with his work representing the Humboldt State newspaper. Demonstrating considerable professional expertise, Mr. Braafladt has been the recipient of numerous awards and recognitions, including the Freedom of Information Award as given by the Northern California chapter of the Society of Professional Journalists in 1987. He was also a fellow of the Coro Foundation from 1974 to 1975, the recipient of the Bill Farr Freedom of Press Award in 1987, and a member of the executive committee of the labor and employment law section of The State Bar of California from 2004 to 2007. He was an adviser to the executive committee from late 2007 to 2012. In recognition of his leadership experience and contributions to the field, Mr. Braafladt has also been included in numerous honors publications, including the fifth edition of Who's Who in American Law, the 20th edition of Who's Who in the West, the first edition of Who's Who of Emerging Leaders in America and the 73rd edition of Who's Who in America. Additionally, he is the recipient of the prestigious Albert Nelson Marquis Lifetime Achievement Award.

Interested in maintaining professional connections, Mr. Braafladt is a past member of the California Trial Lawyers Association and the Association of Trial Lawyers of America, and a current member of the Humboldt State University Alumni Association, the American Constitution Society, the Green and Gold Key Society, and several bar associations. He has been lead counsel on numerous cases in his field, including Bostean v. Los Angeles Unified School District in 1998 and California School Employees Association v. Lucia Mar Unified School District in 2001. Also interested in civic outreach, Mr. Braafladt has been involved with the Redwood Community Action Agency, the Humboldt County Democratic Central Committee, the Democratic National Committee Leadership Circle, and various political campaigns.

A Minnesota native, Mr. Braafladt currently lives in Oregon. He is the proud father of Nicole Yvonne Farrell and Sarah Arlene Shaffer, and doting grandfather of Cedar, Sage and Dahlia. Since retiring from the California School Employees Association, Mr. Braafladt has been traveling to conferences in an effort to learn new topics. In his free time, he enjoys camping and hiking.

A Lifetime of Achievement in **Law / Legal Services**

Darwin Bünger, JD
Attorney
BURLINGTON, IA UNITED STATES

Darwin Bünger, JD, began his career in law in 1966 as an associate with Wunschel & Schechtman, then as a partner with Kurth & Bünger from 1969 to 1991, before going on to hold the same title with Crowley & Bünger from 1992 to 2012 and Crowley, Bünger & Schroeder from 2012 to 2014. From there, he became a senior partner with Crowley, Bünger, Schroeder & Prill from 2014 to 2015. From 2014 to 2016, he excelled as a senior partner with Crowley, Bünger & Prill from 2014 up until 2017, when the firm decided it would be a good time for him to retire. He did not agree with this, which led him to begin his own firm, where he has been a solo practitioner since 2018. Civically, Mr. Bünger has dedicated his time to such organizations as the Church Council, where he has been both member and president. He also acted as president of Bart Howard Foundation Inc. from 2013 to 2018, and the University of Iowa I Club.

Prior to establishing himself as a trusted voice in the field, Mr. Bünger sought to expand his knowledge through the pursuit of a formal education at a number of esteemed academic institutions. He first attended Wartburg College in Waverly, Iowa, where he completed coursework and went on to obtain a bachelor's degree in history and business. During this time, one of his fellow undergraduate students encouraged him to enter the field of law. Mr. Bünger did not grow up in a family of lawyers and would not have made the decision without his friend's guidance. Feeling at a crossroads, he took a test to see if he would qualify. When he passed the test, he realized he was meant to enter the field. He continued his studies at The University of Iowa in Iowa City, where he ultimately achieved a Doctor of Jurisprudence upon graduating in 1966.

In light of his professional achievements, Mr. Bünger has gained recognition in the form of various awards and accolades over the years. Notably, he was named an AV Preeminent Attorney in 2011 and 2014. In addition, he was honored with an ILTA Public Justice Award in 1997. Though these acknowledgements are impressive, he considers the highlight of his career to be in the 1990s, when he and his partner acquired verdicts one year apart that were in excess of $1 million and the $14.5 million verdict with co-counsel in December 2018. Outside of financial successes, he is tremendously proud of the ways he has influenced the lives of others in positive ways. He enjoys being able to give people a sense of relief.

Reflecting on his career, Mr. Bünger is grateful for the many mentors who have both motivated and inspired him. He attributes his success to a man named David Harris who was a judge for the district court in the area. He was in when Mr. Bünger first started practicing and he ultimately became a Supreme Court justice. He was a very good guide for him as a young lawyer. Moreover, many of the judges he worked with over the years gave him confidence, information and knowledge.

Mr. Bünger was born in New Hampton, Iowa, to mother Vera R. Bünger and father William H. Bünger. He later married Judith K. Bünger, who has since passed away. His present wife is Robyn Hortie of Canada. He is the proud father of three children named Chad William Bünger, Michele Ann Sovers and Jason William Bünger. In his free time, he enjoys participating in such activities as golfing, painting, reading and tending to his roses.

A Lifetime of Achievement in **Law / Legal Services**

James C. Carpenter

Partner
Steptoe & Johnson PLLC
NEW ALBANY, OH UNITED STATES

Accruing more than four decades of professional experience, James C. Carpenter has excelled as a partner of Steptoe & Johnson PLLC since 2010. His practice is focused on the areas of complex business, commercial and banking litigation. Mr. Carpenter began his professional career as an associate of Knepper, White, Arter & Hadden in Columbus, Ohio, in 1975, remaining in this position for five years before becoming chief of staff for U.S. Representative Robert Shamansky in Washington, D.C., between 1981 and 1982. He later served as a partner of Carlile, Patchen & Murphy from 1982 to 1996 and Lane, Alton & Horst, LLC, from 1996 to 2006. Mr. Carpenter subsequently found success as a managing partner at Carpenter Lane, LLC, from 2006 to 2010.

Prior to embarking on his professional path, Mr. Carpenter pursued a formal education at Ohio University, graduating with a Bachelor of Arts, summa cum laude, in 1972. He also served as a captain of the tennis team. He concluded his studies at The Ohio State University in Columbus, Ohio, where he obtained a Doctor of Jurisprudence in 1974. After receiving these academic honors, Mr. Carpenter was admitted to practice law in a number of state and federal courts, including the Ohio State Bar Association, the U.S. District Courts for the Southern and Northern Districts of Ohio, the U.S. Tax Court, the U.S. Court of Claims, the Supreme Court of the United States, and the U.S. Courts of Appeals for the 3rd and 6th Circuits.

Active in his local community, Mr. Carpenter worked as a trustee of the Columbus Area Leadership Program from 1985 to 1991, for which he also held the post of the president, and the League Against Child Abuse in Columbus, Ohio, from 1989 to 1990. Since 2017, he has maintained his involvement as an elder at the New Albany Presbyterian Church. Outside of his primary responsibilities, Mr. Carpenter remains updated of trends in his field through affiliations with numerous related organizations. A fellow of the Columbus Bar Association, he has been affiliated with the American Bar Association, the Million Dollar Advocacy Forum and Phi Beta Kappa. Likewise, Mr. Carpenter has been a fellow and a board member of the litigation section of the Ohio State Bar Association since 2015.

Among Mr. Carpenter's many accomplishments was his involvement in creating a mentorship program for the Columbus Bar Association, where he worked alongside Supreme Court Justices to provide guidance for lawyers. In light of his exceptional undertakings, he was recognized annually among the Super Lawyers between 2006 and 2010. A charter fellow of the Construction Lawyers Society of America, he has been honored among the Best Lawyers in America since 2011 and was selected by Best Lawyers as its Central Ohio Lawyer of the Year in civil litigation in 2017 and again in 2019. Featured in America's Top 100 High Stakes Litigators, Mr. Carpenter was also selected for inclusion in the fifth edition of Who's Who in American Law and the second through fourth editions of Who's Who of Emerging Leaders in America. Additionally, his accomplishments have earned him the Albert Nelson Marquis Lifetime Achievement Award.

Born on November 20, 1949, in Louisville, Kentucky, Mr. Carpenter is married to Mary Jane McDowell and is the proud father of four daughters, Katheryn Elizabeth Gibson, Elizabeth Anne Hendrickson, Caroline Jane Carpenter and Abigail Rose Carpenter. He also has five grandchildren: Reid, Ethan, Charlotte, Llyod and William. In his free time, Mr. Carpenter enjoys staying active through cycling, golf and mountain hiking, as well as exercising his creativity with poetry and photography.

A Lifetime of Achievement in **Law / Legal Services**

William N. Clark

Attorney & Partner
Redden, Mills, Clark & Shaw, LLP
MOUNTAIN BROOK, AL UNITED STATES

Since 1974, William N. Clark has been an attorney and a partner at Redden, Mills, Clark & Shaw, LLP, in Birmingham. Working for the aforementioned firm as an associate from 1972 to 1974, he also served for one year as a law clerk with the U.S. Court of Appeals for the 5th Circuit. The firm, which dates back more than 50 years, notably handles matters of criminal defense, driving under the influence, white-collar crime, civil litigation, divorce and family law, and appeals.

During his career at the firm, Mr. Clark became a leading attorney in the state of Alabama, focusing much of his practice on criminal defense and family law. While serving as the chair of the firm's indigent defense committee, he was able to increase the rate paid by point counsel. He was also instrumental in recommending a statewide public defender program and a state indigent commission. As a result, there is now a state indigent commission that oversees indigent defense, as well as public defender programs in Birmingham. An adjunct professor of evidence, criminal procedure and business fraud at the Hugh F. Culverhouse Jr. School of Law at The University of Alabama, Mr. Clark also devoted 15 years as a member of the advisory committee on criminal procedure at the Supreme Court of Alabama between 1979 and 1994.

Active in his local community, Mr. Clark participated on the board of directors for the Boys & Girls Club of Central Alabama and the Kiwanis Club of Birmingham. Contributing on the board and as the chair of the YMCA of Greater Birmingham, he also chaired the Vulcan District Boy Scouts of America. Furthermore, he found success as the president of The University of Alabama Law School Foundation, the Birmingham Bar Foundation, the Birmingham Bar Association and the Alabama State Bar Association. Since 1993, he has been teaching the adult Sunday school at the Highlands United Methodist Church.

Earning a Bachelor of Science from the U.S. Military Academy at West Point in 1963, Mr. Clark later received a Doctor of Jurisprudence from the Hugh F. Culverhouse Jr. School of Law at The University of Alabama in 1971. He has since been licensed by the Alabama State Bar and admitted to practice by the U.S. District Court for the Northern District of Alabama, the U.S. Courts of Appeals for the 5th and 11th Circuits, and the Supreme Court of the United States. An elected fellow of the American College of Trial Lawyers, Mr. Clark also maintains his professional affiliation with the National Association of Criminal Defense Lawyers and The American Law Institute.

Serving over 35 years in the U.S. Army and the U.S. Army Reserve, Mr. Clark retired in 2000 as a major general. Stationed in Germany and Vietnam from 1963 to 1968, he was later presented with a Distinguished Service Medal, a Vietnamese Cross of Gallantry Bronze Star, an Army Commendation Medal, a Meritorious Service Medal and an Air Medal, among several other prestigious recognitions.

Born in Meridian, Mississippi, Mr. Clark originally planned on studying engineering upon his arrival at West Point, which was very common there. Although he did find the subject fascinating, he enjoyed two semesters of constitutional law and military law. Following his return from Vietnam, Mr. Clark decided to further pursue a legal career as an attorney.

In 1981, Mr. Clark was presented with the Alabama State Bar Award of Merit for his service as the chair of the state bar committee on indigent defense. He was also the recipient of a Roderick P. Beddow Distinguished Service Award from the Alabama Criminal Defense Lawyers Association and Lifetime Achievement Awards from the Birmingham Bar Association and the Greater Birmingham Criminal Defense Lawyers Association. Likewise, Mr. Clark has been recognized among the Best Lawyers in America in the areas of criminal defense and domestic relations, the Super Lawyers and in dozens of editions of Who's Who in America, Who's Who in American Law, Who's Who in the South and Southwest, and Who's Who in the World. He was notably profiled in the 73rd edition of Who's Who in America.

A Lifetime of Achievement in **Law / Legal Services**

Edward Xavier Clinton Sr.

Attorney
Clinton Law Firm
CHICAGO, IL UNITED STATES

With nearly 65 years of experience to his credit, Edward Xavier Clinton Sr. has excelled as an attorney operating out of his private practice, the Clinton Law Firm, in Chicago, Illinois, since 1992. Prior to this appointment, he held the position of a partner at Keck, Mahin & Cate from 1965 to 1992 and at Hough, Young & Coale from 1957 to 1965. Previously, he served with the securities department for the state of Illinois from 1956 to 1957. Moreover, Mr. Clinton began his career as an associate for Schultz & Biro from 1955 to 1956.

Having always wanted to be a lawyer since his childhood, Mr. Clinton enlisted in the U.S. Army as a law recruit in 1953. Stationed at Fort Riley in Kansas, he was honorably discharged from active duty as a corporal in 1955 following two years of service. Mr. Clinton has proudly been a part of myriad notable cases, including the legal process of aiding the AHSC to become a publicly traded company on the New York Stock Exchange, during which time he had the good fortune of working with the founder of AHSC, Foster G. McGaw.

Before embarking on his professional path, Mr. Clinton pursued an education at DePaul University, completing coursework between 1949 and 1950. He concluded his studies at the John Marshall Law School in 1953, graduating with a Doctor of Jurisprudence. Following these accomplishments, Mr. Clinton was admitted to practice law by the Illinois State Bar Association in 1953, the U.S. District Court for the Northern District of Illinois in 1955, the U.S. Court of Appeals for the 7th Circuit in 1955, and the Supreme Court of the United States in 1995.

Beyond his responsibilities within the field, Mr. Clinton has participated in numerous endeavors outside of his professional circles. A speaker in his field, he notably contributed to the John Marshall Law School as a securities instructor from 1965 to 1974. A former arbitrator for the New York Stock Exchange, he also held roles on the board of directors for Records Management Services from 1966 to 1997, the pastoral council for Holy Name Cathedral from 1989 to 1994, the advisory board for the Steppenwolf Theatre Company from 1988 to 1989, the advisory board for the Chicago Opera Theater from 1983 to 1988, and the advisory board for Little Sisters of Poor. Mr. Clinton is particularly proud of his decades-spanning involvement with the Children's Care Foundation, a multimillion-dollar charity for which he worked as general counsel, the director, the vice president, an advisory board member, and the president since 2015.

Mr. Clinton found success with his written works as well, having authored many articles for professional journals. Alongside his son, Edward X. Clinton Jr., he penned "Federal Regulation of Securities" and "State Regulation of Securities," both of which were supplements for "Illinois Business Law Series: Vol. III: Miscellaneous Operating Issues" in 2008. Mr. Clinton has also provided his wealth of knowledge to the Federal Civil Procedure Blog and the Clinton Law Firm Blog.

In addition to his primary vocation, Mr. Clinton remains affiliated with various organizations in relation to his areas of expertise. From 1985 to 1995, he had maintained his involvement on the board of directors for the Executives' Club of Chicago. He was an active member of the American Bar Association, the National Lawyers Association, the 7th Circuit Bar Association, The Chicago Bar Association and the Lawyers Club of Chicago. Mr. Clinton was further associated with the Evanston Golf Club, The Union League Club, the Knights of Columbus and The American Legion.

In light of his exceptional undertakings, Mr. Clinton has accrued several accolades throughout his impressive career. He was notably celebrated with an Albert Nelson Marquis Lifetime Achievement Award. Furthermore, he was presented with a John Jewell scholarship and a postgraduate scholarship from the John Marshall Law School in 1953. Likewise, Mr. Clinton was selected for inclusion in multiple editions of Who's Who in America and Who's Who in American Law.

A Lifetime of Achievement in **Law / Legal Services**

H. Fred Cook

Attorney

HOUSTON, TX UNITED STATES

Leading a prolific career, H. Fred Cook has accrued 15 years of experience as a lawyer and an investor. His most recent position was as a shareholder for the real estate firm Wilson Cribbs & Goren, P.C., where he focused on litigation, construction and mediation. Prior to joining this well-respected firm, Mr. Cook served as a principal attorney with Hirsch & Westheimer, P.C., in Houston from 1990 to 1997 and as an associate attorney for Weycer, Kaplan, Pulaski & Zuber, P.C., in Houston between 1985 and 1990. Mr. Cook began his professional journey as an associate with Childs, Fortenbach, Beck & Guyton in Houston from 1982 to 1985.

A graduate of Wabash College in Crawfordsville, Indiana, Mr. Cook earned a Bachelor of Arts, magna cum laude, in 1979. He continued his education at Vanderbilt University in Nashville, Tennessee, securing a Doctor of Jurisprudence in 1982. While at this prestigious university, Mr. Cook contributed his talents as the associate editor of the Vanderbilt Journal of Transnational Law, an internationally recognized and widely cited legal journal focused on comparative and international law. He further served as the president of the Vanderbilt International Law Society, helping to promote opportunities for students to gain hands-on experience and professional expertise regarding transnational conflicts.

A well-respected lawyer with years of practice to his credit, Mr. Cook has dedicated himself to assisting others through his work in the legal industry. He was admitted to the State Bar of Texas in 1982, specializing in litigation, alternative dispute resolution and construction law. Mr. Cook gained further licensure by the U.S. District

Court for the Southern District of Texas in 1983 and the U.S. Court of Appeals for the 5th Circuit in 1990. Additionally, he was admitted before the U.S. District Court for the Western and Eastern Districts of Texas in 1990.

In order to remain current with legal trends, Mr. Cook maintains a professional relationship with the American Bar Association and the Houston Bar Association, where he served in the litigation section of both organizations. Regarded as an expert in his field, Mr. Cook's career has been marked by numerous highlights, including representing the developers of the Ashby High-Rise in Houston, an important land use case. In light of his many accomplishments, Mr. Cook has been presented an AV rating through Martindale-Hubbell since 1997. His achievements in the legal industry and contributions to his community have further been commemorated with the prestigious Albert Nelson Marquis Lifetime Achievement Award.

Mr. Cook was born on March 24, 1957, in Panama City, Florida, to Harold Fredrick Cook and Marilyn Rae Mouser Snider. He has been married to Julia Cook for more than 35 years, and together, they are the proud parents of two daughters, Claire Lyn and Karen Elizabeth. In addition to his many contributions to the legal industry, Mr. Cook has also lent his talents and expertise to helping his community. He has volunteered his time as a deacon for the St. Andrew's Presbyterian Church in Houston, a member of the Caring for Children Foundation in Bellaire, Texas, the director of the Texas Conference of Churches, and the commissioner to the General Assembly of the Presbyterian Church. Mr. Cook has also provided pro bono representation for the St. Andrew's Presbyterian Church. Outside of his professional duties, he enjoys swimming, reading, chess and backgammon.

A Lifetime of Achievement in **Law / Legal Services**

June Resnick German, Esq.

Attorney

DIX HILLS, NY UNITED STATES

For the past 50 years, June Resnick German, Esq., has excelled in the field of law. At the start of her career, she worked for the Mental Health Information Service, an agency under the aegis of the Appellate Division, First Department, New York State, protecting the rights of mentally ill persons. She began as a staff attorney, then rose to the positions of senior attorney and supervising attorney from 1968 to 1977.

Ms. German litigated cases to guarantee rights to mentally disabled persons, including a landmark case that established that in New York, civil involuntary patients have a right to treatment, a right to be treated in a facility that is least restrictive of their liberty and a right to remain in a civil facility. She has also pursued litigation to establish rights for mentally ill persons involved in the criminal justice system. In addition, she has collaborated on amicus curiae briefs to the Supreme Court of the United States in the fields of mental health and environmental law. She has participated in the development of and later taught a course in human behavior and the law for members of the Judiciary of New York. Since 1985, she has maintained a private solo practice in Huntington, New York.

During the course of her illustrious career, Ms. German has had the honor of representing an orphanage in Guatemala. She considers this case to be one of the highlights of her career. It all began with a "Sixty Minutes" program in which the orphanage director, she believed wrongfully, was accused of misbehavior. Based on the allegation that the director was engaged in mail fraud, the United States commenced a forfeiture proceeding to seize the funds that had been donated to the orphanage.

Ms. German represented the corporation that ran the orphanage in an attempt to recover these funds. After the district court ruled against the orphanage, she appealed to the U.S. Court of Appeals for the 2nd Circuit, which reversed the ruling. Not only was the money returned, but costs, legal fees and interest were recovered as well. The recovered funds were sufficient to provide all the funding needed to care for the several hundred orphans for many years.

Prior to establishing herself as a trusted voice in the field of law, Ms. German pursued her education at the University of Pennsylvania, where she earned a Bachelor of Arts in 1965. She then continued her studies at the New York University School of Law, where she received a Juris Doctor in 1968.

Ms. German has co-authored "Mental Illness, Due Process and the Acquitted Defendant," published in 1979, and has been a contributing author to Bioethics and Human Rights, as well as contributing to other professional journals in the fields of psychiatry and law. An active presence in the community, she maintains membership with the Suffolk County Bar Association. She serves as a member of the citizen's advisory committee to the Dix Hills Water District and has served on various additional advisory committees to the town of Huntington. She further serves as a board member on the Huntington Tennis Association.

Reflecting on her career, she is grateful for the mentorship of her uncle William Weintraub, Esq., who practiced law for 60 years in Brooklyn; Simon Rosenzweig, Esq., director of the Mental Health Information Service for which she worked; and Stanley L. Shapiro, Esq., with whom she collaborated on several cases. She is especially grateful to her parents for their strong commitment to education.

Her father, Irving Resnick, was a chemical engineer recruited by the Manhattan Project. He solved complex problems concerning the use of gaseous diffusion to enrich uranium. Her mother, Stella Resnick, taught early education. Her mother, ahead of her time, always taught her that a woman could do anything that she wanted to do and could pursue any profession she desired.

In light of her professional accomplishments, Ms. German has gained recognition in the form of various awards and accolades. Notably, she was honored with the Golden Anniversary Award by the Suffolk

County Bar Association, celebrating 50 years of practice in 2018. She has previously been selected for inclusion in such honors publications as Who's Who in America, Who's Who in American Law, Who's Who in the East and Who's Who in the World.

Looking ahead, she intends to experience continued success in her career. In her free time, she enjoys participating in such activities as playing tennis, playing the piano, hiking and traveling, as well as spending time with her family.

A Lifetime of Achievement in **Law / Legal Services**

Douglas M. Halsey

Attorney & President
Douglas M. Halsey, P.A.
MIAMI, FL UNITED STATES

With over 40 years of experience, Douglas M. Halsey has established himself as a respected voice in the environmental law field. He is currently the president of Douglas M. Halsey, P.A., a firm based in Miami, Florida, that addresses environmental and land use law issues. Prior to establishing his own practice, Mr. Halsey was a partner at White & Case LLP, where he was the head of the firm's environmental practice until his retirement in June 2017. Prior to that position, he was the founder and managing partner of Halsey & Burns PA in Miami from 1997 until 2000, and his own private practice from 1989 to 1997. Earlier in his career, he served as a partner at Thomson, Bohrer, Werth & Razook in Miami from 1985 to 1988 and as an associate at Paul & Thomson from 1979 to 1985.

Mr. Halsey earned his bachelor's degree at Columbia University in New York City in 1976 and his Doctor of Jurisprudence, cum laude, from the University of Miami in 1979. In that same year, he was admitted to practice law in the state of Florida and later by the U.S. Courts of Appeals for the 5th and 11th Circuits and the U.S. District Courts for the Southern and Middle Districts of Florida. He has also been admitted to practice in New York and the District of Columbia.

Over the last four decades, Mr. Halsey has tried numerous cases in state and federal court and related appellate matters, with a special focus on cost recovery claims and land use disputes involving wetlands and endangered species. His clients have included manufacturers, developers, financial institutions and property owners looking for guidance and legal representation. He has experience litigating under the Clean Water Act; the Comprehensive Environmental Response, Compensation and Liability Act; the Resource Conservation and Recovery Act; the Clean Air Act; the National Environmental Policy Act; and parallel state and local government regulatory schemes. In 2003, following 11 years of litigation in federal and state courts, Mr. Halsey obtained for property owners in Monroe County, Florida, the largest recovery in United States history for a "temporary taking."

Mr. Halsey represents industrial and developer clients before environmental agencies on regulatory and permitting matters on a local, state and national level. His many years of experience include representing the largest solid waste company in the United States, as well as coordinating wetlands and endangered species permitting and complex land use matters in environmentally sensitive areas of Florida and other jurisdictions.

Mr. Halsey also advises environmental risks associated with business transactions. He is frequently called upon to work with transactional lawyers in multibillion-dollar acquisitions, financings, stock and bond offerings and land development deals. Much of his corporate work has been in the real estate, power, pharmaceutical, and oil and gas industries. A well-known leader in his field, in 1993 and 1994, he served as the chairman of the environmental and land use section of The Florida Bar. In addition, Mr. Halsey regularly speaks at seminars on various federal and state environmental and land use issues.

In addition to his professional contributions, Mr. Halsey maintains his affiliation with various volunteer organizations. He has been an active member of the United Way of Miami-Dade County's Alexis de Tocqueville Society since 1995. Further, he has served as the chairman of the Children's Home Society in Florida from 2000 to 2002 and of Foster Care Review Inc. in Miami, Florida, from 1998 to 2000. Mr. Halsey's legal efforts on behalf of children in the foster care system were recognized by The Florida Bar President's Pro Bono Service Award in 1991. In recognition of his achievements in the legal field and for his community leadership, he has been included in numerous editions of Who's Who publications, including Who's Who in Finance and Industry, Who's Who in America, Who's Who in American Law and Who's Who in the World. A resident of Miami, Mr. Halsey and his wife of more than 40 years, Amy Halsey, have two children as well as two grandchildren.

A Lifetime of Achievement in **Law / Legal Services**

David R. Hayes Sr., Esq.
Law Clerk
U.S. District Court for the Western District of New York

BUFFALO, NY UNITED STATES

A tenured attorney of 30 years, David R. Hayes Sr., Esq., has excelled as a law clerk for the U.S. District Court for the Western District of New York, serving U.S. Magistrate Judge Hugh Scott in Buffalo, New York, since 2004. Formerly focusing his practice in civil litigation and pretrial activities, his experience includes working as an assistant corporate counsel for the city of Buffalo from 1995 to 2003 and as a law clerk for the U.S. Court of Appeals for the 2nd Circuit in New York City from 1989 to 1990. Mr. Hayes additionally built his career as an associate attorney at Paul, Weiss, Rifkind, in New York City from 1988 to 1989 and Phillips Lytle in Buffalo from 1991 to 1995.

An active presence in the field, Mr. Hayes maintains memberships with various prestigious professional organizations. He is notably a long-standing member of the Bar Association of Erie County, the Federal Bar Council, the New York State Bar Association and Phi Beta Kappa. Since 2016, he has served on the board of directors for the Mount Olive Development Corporation, and he is also a member of the Minority Bar Association, where he acted as vice president from 1996 to 1997. Locally, he was appointed to the board of directors of New Refuge House Inc. in Buffalo from 1992 to 2002.

In light of his many contributions to the industry over the years, Mr. Hayes has gained recognition in the form of multiple awards and accolades. He was recognized as Volunteer of the Year by the Tatonka District of the Greater Niagara Frontier Council of Boy Scouts of America in 2015 and was recognized with his family by the Tatonka District in 2018 as Scouting Family of the Year. He was previously honored in 1999 with a Legal Service Award by the Minority Bar Association of Western New York. Likewise, Mr. Hayes has previously been selected for inclusion in such honors publications as the 59th edition of Who's Who in America and the 10th and 13th editions of Who's Who in American Law.

Ever since he was a young child, Mr. Hayes always took an interest in law. While in grade school, he particularly enjoyed the subject of social studies. He carried this passion into adulthood and decided to pursue a formal education in an effort to prepare himself for his professional path. He first attended Howard University and earned a Bachelor of Arts in 1985. He continued his studies at Yale University in New Haven, Connecticut, where he ultimately achieved a Doctor of Jurisprudence in 1988. Subsequently, he was admitted to practice law by the New York State Supreme Court in 1989, the U.S. Court of Appeals for the 2nd Circuit in 1995 and the U.S. District Court for the Western District of New York in 1991.

Reflecting on his career, Mr. Hayes is grateful for the mentorship of his current boss, U.S. Magistrate Judge Hugh Scott. He admires the way he handles cases with careful attention to coming to the right decisions. Richard Griffin, a former partner at Phillips Lytle in Buffalo, was also a mentor. Mr. Hayes was born on November 25, 1963, in Rochester, New York, to mother Jeanette Arlene Quintyne and father Ralph. Married to Paula Hayes since 2018, he is the proud father to four children named Ashtin Pendleton, David Hayes Jr., Samuel Hayes and Andrew Hayes. In his free time, he enjoys participating in such activities as bicycling and collecting stamps.

A Lifetime of Achievement in **Law / Legal Services**

Roberta Karmel

Of Counsel (Retired)
Kelley Drye & Warren LLP
NEW YORK, NY UNITED STATES

Roberta Karmel began her career as an enforcement attorney, then branch chief, then assistant regional administrator of the Securities and Exchange Commission in New York from 1962 to 1969. After this opportunity, she served as an associate with Willkie Farr & Gallagher LLP in New York City from 1969 to 1972. From 1972 to 1977, she was a partner with Roger & Wells in New York City.

Ms. Karmel was further associated with the Securities and Exchange Commission in Washington, D.C., as commissioner from 1977 to 1980. She was the first woman appointed to that position. Following this appointment, she served as partner and then of counsel at Roger & Wells in New York City from 1980 to 1986 and then worked as a professor at the Brooklyn Law School from 1985 to the present. From 1987 to 1994, she became a partner with Kelley Drye & Warren LLP in New York City. She maintained involvement of counsel with Kelley Drye & Warren LLP from 1995 until 2002.

Prior to embarking on her professional path, Ms. Karmel earned a Bachelor of Arts from Radcliffe College in Cambridge, Massachusetts. Following this accomplishment, she received a Bachelor of Laws from New York University in New York City in 1962. In 1998, she was awarded an honorary Doctor of Humanities from King's College in New York City. She received her bar certification from the state of New York in 1962 and was admitted to practice by the U.S. District Court for the Southern and Eastern Districts of New York in 1964, the Supreme Court of the United States, and U.S. Court of Appeals for the 2nd and 3rd Circuits.

Ms. Karmel was an adjunct professor of law at the Brooklyn Law School from 1973 to 1977 and from 1982 to 1985. She has been a full professor at the Brooklyn Law School since 1985. She has also been co-director of the Block Center for the Study of International Business Law at the Brooklyn Law School, a trustee of the SEC Historical Society, a fellow of the American Bar Association, and a former trustee and chair of the Practising Law Institute. She authored the books "Regulation by Prosecution" in 1982 and "Life at the Center: Reflections on Fifty Years of Securities Regulation" in 2014. Additionally, she is a regular contributor of articles to professional journals. From 1980 to 2016, she was a columnist on securities regulation for the New York Law Journal.

Ms. Karmel is a member of the American Bar Association, the American Law Institute and the Financial Women's Association of New York, Inc. She is also an honorary member of the Alpha Iota chapter of Phi Beta Kappa. She has been the recipient of the William O. Douglas Award from the Association of Securities and Exchange Commission Alumni, the Direct Women Award from the Sandra Day O'Connor Board of Excellence, and the Margaret Brent Women Lawyers of Achievement Award from the American Bar Association. Ms. Karmel has previously been selected for inclusion in multiple editions of Who's Who in the East, Who's Who in American Law, Who's Who of American Women, Who's Who in American Education and Who's Who in America.

Ms. Karmel was born on May 4, 1937, in Chicago to mother Eva E. Elin Segal and father J. Herzl Segal. She married S. David Harrison on October 29, 1995. Previously, she was married to Paul R. Karmel from 1934 to 1994, and they were the proud parents of four children named Philip, Solomon, Jonathan and Miriam.

A Lifetime of Achievement in **Law / Legal Services**

Louis Mangano

Attorney

ELMWOOD PARK, NJ UNITED STATES

With several decades of professional experience to his name, Louis Mangano has enjoyed a successful career as a lawyer. Demonstrating dedication to his work, he has been serving as a private practice attorney in Elmwood Park, New Jersey, since 1981. Previously, he contributed his time and knowledge to working with the Elmwood Park Police Department from 1966 to 1983. Outside of his endeavors in law, he has been an adjunct professor at Fairleigh Dickinson University in Rutherford, New Jersey, from 1973 to 1975. Moreover, he held the same role with Jersey City State College for the same period of time. From 1983 to 1984, he excelled as an assistant professor at William Paterson College, now William Paterson University, in Wayne, New Jersey. He was also an adjunct professor at William Paterson University for the years 1980 to 1982 and 1984 to 1986.

Prior to establishing himself as a trusted voice in the field, Mr. Mangano sought to expand his knowledge through the pursuit of a formal education at a number of esteemed academic institutions. He first attended Seton Hall University in South Orange, New Jersey, and earned a Bachelor of Science in business administration in 1970. During his time there, he was named to the dean's list. He continued his studies at the John Jay College of Criminal Justice, where he obtained a Master of Arts in criminal justice in 1973. Impressively, he completed his thesis for this degree. Ultimately, he returned to Seton Hall University and achieved a Doctor of Jurisprudence upon his graduation from the school in 1979.

Subsequently, Mr. Mangano obtained numerous bar admissions. In 1981, he was admitted to practice law by the state of New Jersey as well as the U.S. District Court for the District of New Jersey. Four years later, he earned admission to practice law by the Supreme Court of the United States. Before embarking on his academic or professional path, he served with the U.S. Army from 1959 to 1961. During this time, he was an X-ray technician while he was stationed in Giessen, Germany.

Outside of his primary responsibilities, Mr. Mangano also maintains an active presence in his community. He was an attorney for the borough of Elmwood Park from 2005 to 2007. He also dedicated his time to serving the Elmwood Park Board of Education. He notably excelled as a member of the school board, trustee, and president from 1980 to 1983 and again from 1989 to 1993.

In light of his many professional accomplishments and contributions to the field, Mr. Mangano has gained recognition in the form of various awards and accolades. Notably, his achievements include trying a publicly televised case in 1992, Pagano v. United Jersey Bank. This was a landmark decision by the Supreme Court of New Jersey in 1995. In this case, he was the attorney for Linda Pagano, who was suing United Jersey Bank in order to receive the money her late mother had deposited 20 years prior when the bank was operating under a different time. The bank had initially refused to fulfill the request because they had no record of it, though Pagano herself had her mother's record of the transaction.

Mr. Mangano was born on September 19, 1939, in Passaic, New Jersey, to mother Mary Mangano and father Salvatore Mangano. He later married Arlene M. Triolo on September 20, 1964. Together, they are the proud parents of four children named Kenneth L., Eileen M., Louis M. and Michael S. Moreover, they have four grandchildren named Kaitlyn, Nicholas, Marco and Isabella.

A Lifetime of Achievement in **Law / Legal Services**

Allan Mantel

Partner
Mantel McDonough Riso, LLP
NEW YORK, NY UNITED STATES

With more than 30 years of experience to his credit, Allan Mantel has built a reputation as one of America's premier matrimonial and business attorneys. He is renowned for his ability to help his prominent and high net worth clientele navigate divorce, custody, prenuptial and estate matters successfully, as well as his strong negotiation skills, which often result in favorable settlements. Before embarking on his professional path, Mr. Mantel attended New York University, where he earned his Bachelor of Arts in 1973. He continued his studies at the University at Buffalo School of Law, a part of the State University of New York system, receiving his Doctor of Jurisprudence in 1976. He was admitted to practice law by the New York State Bar Association and the U.S. District Courts for the Southern and Eastern Districts of New York in 1977.

Mr. Mantel began his legal career as an associate with the prestigious matrimonial firm of Rosenthal & Herman, PC, in New York City that same year, and was appointed as a named partner of Rosenthal, Herman & Mantel, PC, in 1984. He thrived in that capacity until his departure in 1994. From 1995 until 1999, Mr. Mantel continued his legal career as a partner, and as the head of the matrimonial department with the firm of Hofheimer Gartlir & Gross, LLP, in New York City.

In 1999, Mr. Mantel became a founding partner of Stein Riso Mantel McDonough, LLP, in New York City, a position he held until 2019. In 2019, his law firm was reorganized and renamed Mantel McDonough

Riso, LLP, where he continues with his active legal career. Many of his reported cases have established new legal precedent in matrimonial law, and have been widely discussed and debated by his peers.

Following rigorous peer evaluation, and meeting the highest competence and ethical standards, Mr. Mantel was recognized as a fellow of the American Academy of Matrimonial Lawyers in 1987, and as a fellow of the International Academy of Family Lawyers thereafter. He was elected and served as the president of the New York Chapter of the American Academy of Matrimonial Lawyers from 2007 to 2008. As further testament to his success, Mr. Mantel, again by peer selection, has been the recipient of the highest, AV Preeminent, rating from Martindale-Hubbell for more than 30 years. Likewise, he has been celebrated among the Best Lawyers of America, Super Lawyers of New York City and Ten Leaders since 2008.

For his accomplishments in the field of matrimonial law, Mr. Mantel has been selected for inclusion in multiple editions of Who's Who in America, Who's Who in American Law, Who's Who in Finance and Industry, Who's Who in the World and Who's Who of Emerging Leaders in America. He has also been honored with the Albert Nelson Marquis Lifetime Achievement Award. Recognized as an expert in his field, Mr. Mantel has contributed as a member of the dean's advisory council of the University at Buffalo School of Law since 2004.

Mr. Mantel also volunteered his time and efforts as a board trustee for the Brotherhood Synagogue from 2002 to 2014. Born on June 27, 1951, in New York City to Bernard and Ruth Mantel, he is married to Janet Mantel, with whom he has two children, Bernard and Elizabeth. In his free time, he enjoys gardening, boating, tennis, golf and photography, as well as history.

A Lifetime of Achievement in **Law / Legal Services**

Harry L. Munsinger

Attorney & Owner
Law Office of Harry L. Munsinger
SAN ANTONIO, TX UNITED STATES

With more than 25 years of professional experience in the field, Harry L. Munsinger has established himself as a respected voice in the legal community. Distinguishing him from his peers in the industry is his unique background in both law and psychology, which allows him to better empathize and understand the legal and emotional aspects of divorce, family law and estate planning. Mr. Munsinger began his illustrious career as the counsel for Bretton and Hall in San Antonio, Texas, where he thrived from 2008 to 2012. He has since found success as the owner of the Law Office of Harry L. Munsinger, where he focuses on estate planning and collaborative divorce. Renowned for his professionalism and skill, Mr. Munsinger has helped numerous couples come to an amicable and cooperative completion to their marriage.

Prior to opening his law firm, Mr. Munsinger served as an adjunct professor of law at The University of Texas at Austin School of Law and at the St. Mary's University School of Law in San Antonio. To prepare him for his professional career, Mr. Munsinger earned a Bachelor of Arts at the University of California, Berkeley. Following this accomplishment, he went on to earn a Doctor of Philosophy in experimental and clinical psychology from the University of Oregon in 1958, subsequently continuing his education at Duke University in North Carolina, where he earned a Doctor of Jurisprudence and was a member of the Duke Law Journal. Mr. Munsinger was also a postdoctoral fellow at

Yale University in New Haven, Connecticut, where he gained further hands-on experience in a world-class setting. In addition to his certification as a credentialed collaborative professional from the nonprofit organization Collaborative Divorce Texas, he is admitted to practice law in cases represented in the Texas Western District Court, the Texas Southern District Bankruptcy Court, the 5th Circuit Court of Appeals, and the United States Supreme Court.

In addition to his courtroom and psychological experience, Mr. Munsinger is also a seasoned writer who enjoys utilizing the written word as a way to organize his thoughts. Well-regarded as an authority in his field, he is the author of "Texas Divorce Guide: Everything You Need to Know About Divorce in Texas," which was published in 2017. In the book, he shares a detailed look at 10 signs a couple should consider when deciding whether or not to move forward with a divorce, as well as methods to deal with the emotional repercussions of ending a marriage. Mr. Munsinger provides helpful suggestions for readers, such as how to find the right divorce lawyer, navigating custody disputes successfully, and telling children about an impending divorce. A prolific author, he has also published several textbooks, such as "The Fundamentals of Child Development" and "Principles of Abnormal Psychology" in addition to writing more than 40 articles about psychology and legal matters. His literary prowess was recognized with a writing award in 2013.

A respected leader in the legal community, Mr. Munsinger served two terms as the president of Collaborative Divorce San Antonio, a group of lawyers, finance professionals and mental health experts looking to increase awareness of the collaborative divorce approach. Furthermore, he continues to contribute his guidance as a member of the board of trustees of Collaborative Divorce Texas. In his free time, Mr. Munsinger enjoys spending time with his grandchildren. He has notably been profiled in the 73rd edition of Who's Who in America.

A Lifetime of Achievement in **Law / Legal Services**

In Memoriam

James Francis O'Rorke Jr.

Lawyer (Retired)

NEW YORK, NY UNITED STATES

A lifelong New York resident who had amassed more than five decades of experience in the law, James Francis O'Rorke Jr. retired from working of counsel for seven years with Skadden, Arps, Slate, Meagher & Flom in 2014. He had previously excelled at the aforementioned New York City-based law firm as a partner between 1972 and 2006, during which time he handled real estate acquisitions, multistate mortgage financing transactions, construction loans, litigation and foreclosures, among many other legal matters. Prior to these appointments, he had practiced as a partner with Davies, Hardy, Ives & Lawther between 1969 and 1972. Mr. O'Rorke began his impressive legal career as an associate for Davies, Hardy & Schenck from 1962 to 1969.

Before embarking on his professional path, Mr. O'Rorke pursued an education at Princeton University, earning a Bachelor of Arts, cum laude, from the Woodrow Wilson School of Public and International Affairs in 1958. He concluded his studies at Yale University in 1961, graduating from Yale Law School with a Bachelor of Laws. Following these exemplary accomplishments, he was admitted to practice law by the New York State Bar Association in 1962. Furthermore, Mr. O'Rorke was always deeply grateful to the mentors he had who provided him with support, inspiration and guidance throughout his education and career.

A Lifetime of Achievement | **James Francis O'Rorke Jr.**

Beyond his primary responsibilities in the field, Mr. O'Rorke participated in numerous endeavors within his professional circles. He notably contributed to the advisory board for the Chicago Title Insurance Company. He additionally held directorial positions with the Keen Company from 2001 to 2012, the James Lenox House Association from 1998 to 2002 and the Clinipad Corporation. Mr. O'Rorke had found further success as a trustee of the George Gustav Heye Center at the National Museum of the American Indian from 1977 to 1980.

Mr. O'Rorke was also affiliated with various organizations in relation to his areas of expertise. He remained involved with the American Bar Association and the Association of the Bar of the City of New York, for which he was formerly engaged on the committee on state legislation and the committee on federal legislation. Moreover, he was a member of the American College of Real Estate Lawyers, the Princeton Club of New York, and the Key and Seal Club. Furthermore, he was a noted supporter of Doctors Without Borders. Throughout his career, Mr. O'Rorke won numerous awards for his pro bono work.

In light of his exceptional undertakings, Mr. O'Rorke was selected for inclusion in multiple Who's Who publications such as Who's Who in Finance and Business, Who's Who in Finance and Industry, Who's Who in America, Who's Who in American Law, Who's Who in the East and Who's Who in the World. Likewise, he had been presented with an AV Preeminent Peer Review Rating from Martindale-Hubbell. Sadly, Mr. O'Rorke passed away from natural causes in December 2019 at the age of 84; his obituary was published in The New York Times, and he is survived by his loving wife of 55 years, Carla Phelps.

Having been renowned as a reliable and intellectual figure within his practice, Mr. O'Rorke took pride in sharing his wealth of knowledge with his colleagues. They also attributed his success to his warm and humorous personal demeanor. In his spare time, Mr. O'Rorke greatly enjoyed the theater and restaurant scene in New York City in addition to reading mystery novels, photography, American Indian artwork, and vacationing in Arizona and Montana.

A Lifetime of Achievement in **Law / Legal Services**

Benjamin K. Phipps

Senior Partner
The Phipps Firm
TALLAHASSEE, FL UNITED STATES

Benjamin K. Phipps is the senior partner of the Florida law firm, The Phipps Firm, where he has worked in private practice since 1965. In addition to his work with the private sector, he has lent his wide range of expertise to numerous governmental entities. Mr. Phipps was the counsel for the tax committee of the Florida House of Representatives from 1966 to 1972, counsel to the speaker from 1973 to 1974, and a member of the advisory committee to the Florida House on Tax and Finance from 1983 to 1984. He was also a member of the Florida Taxpayer's Bill of Rights Task Force from 1989 to 1991.

Deciding to become a lawyer at age 13, Mr. Phipps began his legal career in 1955, earning a Bachelor of Science in commerce from the University of Virginia before obtaining a Bachelor of Laws in 1958. Following these accomplishments, he served in the U.S. Army from 1958 to 1964, rising to the rank of captain in the artillery. Mr. Phipps was licensed to practice law by The Florida Bar in 1964 and has since been admitted to practice in the U.S. District Court for the Northern District of Florida, the U.S. Courts of Appeals for the 5th and 11th Circuits, the U.S. Court of Claims and the U.S. Tax Court.

Recognized for his experience in tax law, Mr. Phipps was named as Legal Elite by Florida Trend Magazine, Best Lawyers in America by U.S. News, Best Attorneys in Florida by The Wall Street Journal, and as AV Preeminent by Martindale-Hubbell. Beginning in 1975, he was active in the tax section of The Florida Bar, holding every office and becoming chairman from 1985 to 1986. He also was chairman of the editorial board of the Florida Bar News & Journal. Mr. Phipps has remained a member of the state and local tax committee of the American Bar Association. He is a member of Sigma Alpha Epsilon, Phi Alpha Delta and Pi Delta Epsilon.

Well-regarded in his field, Mr. Phipps has contributed numerous articles regarding legal matters to professional journals and newspapers, as well as shared his knowledge as a columnist for the Tallahassee Democrat. The only lawyer in Florida to hold CMI designation in property taxation from the Institute of Professionals in Taxation, he is experienced in state and local tax. Since 1990, Mr. Phipps has personally briefed or argued more than 30 appellate tax cases, more than any other lawyer representing taxpayers in the state of Florida.

Mr. Phipps has been involved with historic preservation all his life and chaired the Historic Tallahassee Preservation Board from 1970 to 1991. He remains involved with the Tallahassee Trust for Historic Preservation, where he has acted as a treasurer since 1998. He also serves as counsel for the Museum of Florida History Foundation and served on the museum board from 1988 to 2000.

Mr. Phipps has been recognized on numerous occasion for his leadership and contributions to the community. He was awarded the Tallahassee Historic Preservation Award for "outstanding personal achievement in furthering historic preservation." Furthermore, he has been recognized in several honors publications, including multiple editions of Who's Who in America, Who's Who in American Law, Who's Who in the South and Southwest, Who's Who in the World, and Who's Who in Finance and Industry. Notably profiled in the 73rd edition of Who's Who in America, Mr. Phipps is also the recipient of the prestigious Albert Nelson Marquis Lifetime Achievement Award, presented to individuals who have demonstrated exemplary leadership and made notable contributions to their field.

A Lifetime of Achievement in **Law / Legal Services**

John W. Pope

Judge (Retired)

BELEN, NM UNITED STATES

With 40 years of experience to his credit, Judge John W. Pope has enjoyed a rewarding career in law and currently shares his expertise as a lecturer in the field. Interested in law since childhood, he pursued an education at The University of New Mexico in Albuquerque, where he earned a Bachelor of Arts in 1969 and a Doctor of Jurisprudence in 1973. Demonstrating unmatched credentials in his industry, Mr. Pope was licensed to practice law by the State Bar of New Mexico and has been admitted to practice by the U.S. District Court for the District of New Mexico and the U.S. Court of Appeals for the 10th Circuit.

Starting out as a law clerk at the New Mexico Court of Appeals in Santa Fe in 1973, Mr. Pope went on to work as an associate at Chavez & Cowper in 1974 and a partner with Cowper, Bailey & Pope from 1974 to 1975. As his career progressed, he established a private law practice in Belen, New Mexico, working in this capacity from 1976 to 1980, and eventually served as a partner with Pope, Apodaca & Conroy from 1980 to 1985. Mr. Pope then worked as the director of litigation for the city of Albuquerque from 1985 to 1987 and as a judge for the state of New Mexico from 1987 to 1992. He concluded his career as a judge for the 13th Judicial District Court of New Mexico from 1992 until his retirement in 2013.

Mr. Pope started working toward the goal of becoming a judge while he was in law school, and he is particularly proud of the design contributions he made to the Valencia County Courthouse in 2010. In addition to his primary professional accomplishments, he has served as a lecturer in his field, and has contributed his skills to The University of New Mexico in Albuquerque as an instructor and a professor of law. Mr. Pope has also dedicated his time to the state central committee for the New Mexico Democratic Party, as the state chair for Common Cause New Mexico, as the president of the Valencia County Historical Society, with New Mexico Legal Aid and the Supreme Court Jury, among other instances of civic involvement.

Due to his professional excellence, Mr. Pope is the three-time recipient of the Outstanding Judicial Service Award from the State Bar of New Mexico, first in 1996, and subsequently in 1997 and 2005. He has also been named Citizen of the Year by the city of Belen and honored with the Champion of Justice Award by New Mexico Legal Aid. Mr. Pope's accomplishments have further been recognized in numerous editions of Who's Who in America, Who's Who in American Law and Who's Who in the West, as well as the 18th edition of Who's Who in the World and the sixth edition of Who's Who in American Education.

For his contributions to the field and leadership, Mr. Pope has further been recognized with the prestigious Albert Nelson Marquis Lifetime Achievement Award. Twice recognized with an Excellence in Teaching Award in 1998 and 2002, he belongs to the Albuquerque Bar Association and the Valencia County Bar Association. A San Francisco, California, native, Mr. Pope is the proud father of three children, Justin, Ana and Lauren. In his free time, he enjoys swimming, golf, photography and historical research.

A Lifetime of Achievement in **Law / Legal Services**

C. E. Schmidt

Managing Partner
C. E. Schmidt & Associates, PLLC
HOUSTON, TX UNITED STATES

With nearly four decades of professional excellence to his credit, C. E. Schmidt has excelled as the managing partner of C. E. Schmidt & Associates, PLLC, based out of Houston, Texas, since 1996. At his highly rated law firm, he and his fellow attorneys exclusively handle divorce cases, family law, mediations, adoptions, suits affecting the parent-child relationship and probate matters. Renowned for his professionalism, Mr. Schmidt has a proven track record for resolving cases for his clients through settlement and mediation as well as serving same as a strong trial advocate at the courthouse.

Prior to obtaining his current position, Mr. Schmidt worked as a real estate attorney and an associate at Coppock & Teltschik LLC from 1980 to 1982 and in a private practice from 1983 to 1988. Following this experience, he thrived as a partner at Schmidt & Rothenberg from 1989 to 1995. A well-respected leader in his industry, he holds a Bachelor of Science in economics from Brigham Young University located in Provo, Utah, and a Doctor of Jurisprudence from the Maurice A. Deane School of Law at Hofstra University, located in Hempstead, New York. Mr. Schmidt is licensed to practice law in all the courts in both the state of Texas and the state of New York and before the U.S. District Courts for the Western and Southern Districts of Texas.

Mr. Schmidt pursued his vocation in the legal field out of a desire to help families find solutions to their conflicts. While initially considering a career as a judge, he realized he preferred the flexibility of serving as a trial lawyer and having the ability to seek out win-win scenarios. In order to remain abreast of changes in the legal field, Mr. Schmidt has maintained an affiliation with the Texas Bar College, where he became a fellow in 2001. He is likewise a member of both the Texas and New York State Bar Associations. For his outstanding efforts in the legal industry, he has been presented with the Albert Nelson Marquis Lifetime Achievement Award. His professional contributions and commitment to excellence have also been previously commemorated in the 71st edition of Who's Who in America and in Who's Who in American Law.

Though his career has been filled with many highlights, Mr. Schmidt is especially proud to have built a law firm that will continue to exist even after his eventual retirement. He enjoys offering his clients hope, helping them focus on the positive in their lives and the benefits of moving forward unhindered by past disappointments and the attendant emotional baggage. On a personal level, Mr. Schmidt has found meaning and purpose also in serving the local community as a scoutmaster for over 25 years.

Mr. Schmidt credits his father, Norbert G. Schmidt, a businessman who was a success in business but simultaneously was an empathetic employer and manager, as his biggest inspiration and hero. Mr. Schmidt has been married to Loriann Michelle Schmidt, since 1984, a fellow attorney, who has joined him both in the practice of law as his legal partner and as a lifetime companion. Together, they are the parents of three children: Laura Kristen Ashdown, Jonathan Eric Schmidt and Anna Michelle Erkman.

Mr. Schmidt abides by the belief that family should always come first and that education is a critical component in one's ability to be of service to the community. An expert in his field, he gives credit for his success as a result of acting upon the foundation of values built on biblical principles. He advises those considering a career in the legal field to know the area of practice they want to engage in prior to attending law school. In the coming years, Mr. Schmidt is committed to contributing to the continued growth and success of his law firm.

A Lifetime of Achievement in **Law / Legal Services**

Hon. Jon J. Shindurling

Senior Judge
Idaho Supreme Court
IDAHO FALLS, ID UNITED STATES

With more than 40 years of experience to his credit, the Hon. Jon J. Shindurling has excelled as a senior judge as assigned by the Idaho Supreme Court since 2015. Prior to this appointment, he held the position of a district judge for the Idaho 7th Judicial District from 2000 to 2015. During this time, he worked as a drug court judge from 2001 to 2015 and an administrative district judge for the Idaho Supreme Court and Idaho 7th Judicial District between 2009 and 2014. Moreover, Judge Shindurling flourished as the chief deputy for Bonneville County in Idaho from 1995 to 2000.

From 1994 to 2000, Judge Shindurling additionally served Bonneville County as the deputy prosecuting attorney. Previously, he was active as a partner at the Wright Law Offices in Idaho Falls, Idaho, from 1990 to 1993. He further held the role of the field director for the School of Urban and Wilderness Survival in Shoshone, Idaho, from 1988 to 1990. Judge Shindurling began his career as a partner for the May & May Law Offices in Twin Falls, Idaho, from 1977 to 1988.

Before embarking on his professional path, Judge Shindurling pursued an education at Brigham Young University, completing coursework between 1965 and 1971. He continued his academic efforts at Arizona State University, earning a Bachelor of Arts in English language and literature in 1972. He concluded his studies at the University of Idaho in 1977, graduating with a Doctor of Jurisprudence. Following these accomplishments, Judge Shindurling was admitted to practice law by the Idaho State Bar.

Beyond his responsibilities within the field, Judge Shindurling has participated in numerous endeavors outside of his professional circles. Providing his legal experience to the felony sentencing committee for the Idaho Supreme Court for 10 years, he contributed to the continuing legal education committee for the Idaho Law Foundation from 1985 to 1988 and the civil jury instructions committee for the Idaho Supreme Court from 1987 to 1989 and in 1996. He held the post on the board of directors for the Magic Valley YFCA from 1988 to 1990 and the Idaho Falls Opera Theatre from 1993 to 1999. Judge Shindurling found success with his written works as well, authoring an article published in The Advocate.

In addition to his primary vocation, Judge Shindurling remains affiliated with various organizations in relation to his areas of focus. He has maintained his involvement with the Idaho State Bar in a number of capacities, including on the bar examination grading committee since 2003, the fee disputes resolution committee since 1991, the chairman committee from 1980 to 1982, and the bar examination committee from 1979 to 1982. He was also associated with the Boy Scouts of America as a member of the executive board for the Snake River Council from 1979 to 1990. Furthermore, Judge Shindurling is also a member of the Church of Jesus Christ of Latter-day Saints.

In light of his exceptional undertakings, Judge Shindurling has accrued several accolades throughout his impressive career. In 2012, he was celebrated with the Kramer Award for Outstanding Court Management from the Idaho Supreme Court. He was further presented with an Outstanding Leadership Award from the Eagle Rock American Inn of Court and the Outstanding Service Award from the Idaho State Bar. Likewise, Judge Shindurling was selected for inclusion in multiple editions of Who's Who in America and Who's Who in American Law.

Fostering his interest in law as a child during his visits to his grandfather's attorney, Judge Shindurling was further inspired by his mentor, the late trial lawyer, James J. May, as well as Judge Ted Wood. A compassionate and civil advocate in his legal areas, he is incredibly proud of designing a dual-diagnosis court that handled both substance abuse issues and mental health issues known as the Wood Pilot Project, which has been very successful for over a decade. Valuing one's engagement with community service, he also enjoys recreationally singing in his community choir, an activity in which he has partaken for over 50 years. Looking toward the future, Judge Shindurling hopes to continue his professional excellence in his current role while cementing his legacy as someone who was fair and intelligent.

A Lifetime of Achievement in **Law / Legal Services**

Alvin L. Snowiss

Partner
Snowiss, Steinberg & Faulkner LLP
LOCK HAVEN, PA UNITED STATES

With nearly 65 years of experience to his credit, Alvin L. Snowiss has spent the last 44 years of his career practicing law in the areas of trust and estate planning and real estate. Since 1994, he has excelled as a partner at Snowiss, Steinberg & Faulkner LLP in Lock Haven, Pennsylvania. Prior to this appointment, he held the position of a partner with Lugg, Snowiss, Steinberg & Faulkner from 1974 to 1994. Previously, he served Lugg & Snowiss as a partner from 1960 to 1974. Mr. Snowiss began his career as a lawyer operating out of his private practice in Lock Haven from 1955 to 1960.

Before embarking on his professional path, Mr. Snowiss pursued an education at the University of Pennsylvania, earning a Bachelor of Arts in 1952. He concluded his academic efforts at the aforementioned university in 1955, graduating with a Doctor of Jurisprudence. Following these accomplishments, he was admitted to practice law by the Pennsylvania Bar Association in 1956, the U.S. District Court for the Middle District of Pennsylvania in 1958 and the Supreme Court of the United States in 1972. Mr. Snowiss subsequently was inducted as an honorary member of the Alumni Society of The Pennsylvania State University in 1998.

Beyond his responsibilities within the field, Mr. Snowiss has participated in numerous endeavors outside of his professional circles. He served Clinton County, Pennsylvania, as solicitor from 1964 to 1972, a state committeeman for the Clinton County Republican Committee from 1967 to 1980 and a member of the board of governors for the Clinton County Community Foundation from 1970 to 1997. He further held the role of a board member for Lock Haven Trust Co., which became Mellon Bank Central, for more than 25 years and served as chairman of the advisory board for the Palmer Museum of Art at Penn State. Mr. Snowiss found success as a lecturer as well, speaking about American artwork and estate administration and planning at a number of local universities.

From 1963 to 1986, Mr. Snowiss was active as a member, and part of that time as the vice president for the board of trustees, of the Annie Halenbake Ross Library in Lock Haven, Pennsylvania. He additionally held multiple posts at the Lock Haven Hospital for 32 years, including the chairman of the board and the president from 1982 to 1986. Moreover, Mr. Snowiss flourished as a member of the executive committee for the Pennsylvania Republican Committee from 1967 to 1980. He also belonged to the Clinton County Country Club for 63 years, where he played golf during that time and won several accolades.

In addition to his primary vocation, Mr. Snowiss remains affiliated with various organizations in relation to his areas of expertise. A delegate to the Pennsylvania Bar Association and to the American Bar Association from 1990 to 1992, he had maintained his involvement with the Pennsylvania Bar Association as a zone delegate from 1976 to 1982, the zone governor from 1983 to 1986, the treasurer from 1987 to 1990 and a member of the board of governors for six years. He was also associated with the Pennsylvania Bar Foundation as one of the founding members and a member of the board of directors from 1984 to 1995, and president of the Clinton County Bar Association in 1975 and 1976. Mr. Snowiss was a member of his Masonic lodge since 1953 and Kiwanis International from 1955 to 2000, during which time he held the title of the president for the Lock Haven chapter in 1966 and 1967. He was also a member of the Williamsport Consistory and the Jaffe Shrine.

In light of his exceptional undertakings, Mr. Snowiss has accrued several accolades throughout his impressive career. He was notably recognized as a fellow of The American College of Trust and Estate Counsel, the American Bar Foundation and the Pennsylvania Bar Foundation. He and his wife, Jean, were both honored by Penn State in 1994 and 2002 at luncheons hosted by the president of the university for their contributions to Penn State and the Palmer Museum of Art. Mr. Snowiss has also been honored by the Annie Halenbake Ross Library at a public library open house. Likewise, he was selected for inclusion in many editions of Who's Who in Finance and Industry, Who's Who in America and Who's Who in American Law.

Furthermore, Mr. Snowiss had garnered experience in management with his father's business, which handled fur for textile mills, after his father's sudden death, and in the legal field in a law office during his college years, as a title abstractor. Attributing his success to his love of the law and ability to get along with others, he prides himself on his professional honesty and his efforts to take his clients seriously and help them whenever possible. A former public speaker on estate law, he has represented clients in a variety of cases, including those in general law, murder and perjury.

He is an avid art collector who has exhibited at the Palmer Museum of Art, and he was the first chairman of and instrumental in establishing "Law Day" in Clinton County to better expose the public to different subjects pertaining to the law. Mr. Snowiss served for six years as a member of the Alumni Society of the University of Pennsylvania; he also served on the executive committee for fundraising at Penn State in 1994. He served for 15 years on the executive committee of the Clinton County Industrial Corp., was a first-time recipient of the Pennsylvania Bar Association Cultural Heritage Award, and, together with his wife, Jean, established scholarships for worthy students from Clinton County at Penn State. Mr. Snowiss hopes to continue cementing his legacy as a conscientious lawyer devoted to his practice.

A Lifetime of Achievement in **Law / Legal Services**

James Kevin Toohey

Partner (Retired)
Johnson & Bell, Ltd.
CHICAGO, IL UNITED STATES

Now retired, James Kevin Toohey is a tenured attorney of 50 years, who most recently found success as a partner at Johnson & Bell, Ltd., in Chicago. Focusing his practice on business law, litigation and toxic tort, he also thrived as the co-chair of the firm's toxic tort defense group. Mainly representing manufacturers in products liability, toxic tort and commercial breach of contract and breach of warranty claims from alleged failure of product performance, Mr. Toohey was well-versed in defending clients in asbestos litigation matters and class action litigation cases against major automotive manufacturers. Further, he is renowned for his work as a lead trial counsel in both state and federal courts across several states.

Prior to joining Johnson & Bell in 2005, Mr. Toohey was a partner at McGuireWoods LLP from 2003 to 2005 and Ross & Hardies in Chicago from 1978 to 2003. Earlier in his career, he found success as an assistant U.S. attorney for the Northern District of Illinois from 1971 through 1974 under U.S. Attorneys William J. Bauer and James R. Thompson, primarily handling a wide variety of civil suits and petitions for injunctions in which the United States was named defendant. Mr. Toohey launched his professional journey as an associate with Taylor, Miller, Magner, Sprowl & Hutchings in Chicago in 1970.

Inspired to pursue a career in law by his father, who was an attorney, Mr. Toohey attended the University of Notre Dame, receiving a Bachelor of Business Administration with a major in accounting in 1966. From there, he went to Northwestern University School of Law, receiving a Juris Doctor in 1969. That same year, Mr. Toohey received his license to practice law in Illinois. Subsequently, Mr. Toohey received certifications to practice in the Northern, Central and Southern Districts of Illinois, the 7th and 8th Circuit Courts of Appeals, and the U.S. Supreme Court. Mr. Toohey is an active member of the Illinois Society of Trial Lawyers, the Illinois State Bar Association and the Illinois Association of Defense Counsel. Well-regarded for his experience in his field, he has also published articles in various legal journals and served on the faculty of Harris-Martin Asbestos Seminars.

Mr. Toohey has recorded an unbroken string of defense verdicts over four decades for Volkswagen AG and Volkswagen Group of America, Audi AG, BMW AG and BMW of North America, Mercedes-Benz USA, and Ford Motor Company in automotive crashworthiness cases. He also represents Volkswagen, Audi, BMW and Mercedes-Benz in class-action cases — the most prominent of which was the complete defense victory on behalf of Audi AG and Volkswagen Group of America against a putative national class of plaintiffs who claimed that the 1978-1985 Audi 5000s accelerated without driver input. With countless cases to his credit, Mr. Toohey considers the highlight of his career to be earning a victory for a burn victim in a lawsuit against Ford.

Outside of his professional endeavors, Mr. Toohey is a dedicated member of his local community. He was actively involved in the initial organization of the Chicago Area Runners Association, serving in 1978-1980 as an original board member, helping to draft its bylaws, contributing as the editor and the principal writer of its 24-page quarterly, and creating the CARA Race Circuit and the Shamrock Shuffle, listed as the ninth largest run in the U.S. with a field limited to the first 30,000 registrants. He has also served on the Parish Council of St. Mary of the Wood and was active in the Edgebrook-Sauganash Athletic Association, contributing on the board, acting as a league commissioner, organizing annual player drafts and coaching. He has additionally coached girls softball and basketball.

Mr. Toohey played fullback on the Notre Dame Rugby football team, which was undefeated through the 1964-65 season, and played for the Chicago Lions Rugby team while attending law school. He played competitive Chicago 16-inch softball from his youth until retiring on his 70th birthday after playing in two playoff games. He continues to compete in his parish bowling league and to play golf at Evanston Golf

Club and at PGA Village courses in Port St. Lucie, Florida. Mr. Toohey has been happily married to Anne Margaret Boettingheimer since 1983. He is the proud father of Julie Colleen, Jeanne Christine, James Robert, Kevin John and Casey Anne, as well as the doting grandfather of six grandchildren.

A Lifetime of Achievement in **Media / Entertainment**

Thomas Bruce Birkenhead

Theater Producer

Professor Emeritus
Brooklyn College

NEW YORK, NY UNITED STATES

With 50 years of experience to his credit, Thomas Bruce Birkenhead has led an illustrious career as a theater producer and an educator. Prior to embarking on his professional journey, he attended Brooklyn College, a part of the City University of New York, where he obtained a Bachelor of Arts in 1954 and a Master of Arts in 1958. He concluded his studies at The New School for Social Research, where he completed the coursework necessary to obtain a Doctor of Philosophy in 1963.

Dr. Birkenhead began and concluded his career at his alma matter, thriving as a lecturer and then a professor of economics at Brooklyn College from 1957 to 1975. Subsequently, he lent his leadership and expertise to the School of Social Sciences as the dean from 1972 to 1975 before assuming the role of professor emeritus in 1975. In addition to his guidance in the classroom, Dr. Birkenhead has been a valuable member of the New York theater industry. He has contributed as a management consultant for the Keystone Musical Arts Center, in addition to finding success as the business manager for Theatre II in Glen Cove from 1970 to 1974.

Devoted to the theater industry, Dr. Birkenhead has provided invaluable support to several plays and shows. He was the co-manager for "Children of a Lesser God," "Brighton Beach Memoirs," "Ain't

Misbehavin', New York and Japan," "Master Harold and the Boys," and "Barbara Cook in Concert" among several others. Likewise, he was the general manager for the Cape Cod Melody Tent, a playhouse in Massachusetts, from 1969 to 1971, and productions such as "Dream a Little Dream: The Mamas and the Papas Musical" and "Long Day's Journey Into Night, London and Tel Aviv" in New York City. The secretary and treasurer of Highly Entertainment for over five years, Dr. Birkenhead further contributed as the co-producer for the 1995 Tony Award broadcast on NHK Japan.

Outside of his primary professional endeavors, Dr. Birkenhead has been affiliated with numerous civic organizations. A member of the U.S. Olympic Committee, he is a founding member and a sponsor of the Brooklyn College shooting team. Committed to preserving history, Dr. Birkenhead has additionally been involved with the U.S. Holocaust Memorial Museum in Washington, D.C., the American Air Museum in Britain, and the U.S. Naval Memorial. He has also lent his efforts as a board of trustees member of the pension and welfare fund of the Association of Theatrical Press Agents and Managers, further helping the group with Broadway contracts in 2006. To pursue his interests, Dr. Birkenhead maintains membership with the National Rifle Association, the U.S. Naval Institute, the Marine Corps Heritage Foundation and Habitat for Humanity. Additionally, he is associated with the Groucho Club in England, the World Jewish Congress, the Victorian Society, and the Friends of Israel Defense Force.

Dr. Birkenhead has been awarded numerous recognitions for his accomplishments in the field. Brooklyn College named a scholarship in his honor, and he was further the recipient of a teaching award from the City University of New York in 1999. He has also been listed in myriad honors publications, including multiple editions of Who's Who in America, Who's Who in Entertainment, Who's Who in the East and Who's Who in the World. Profiled in the 73rd edition of Who's Who in America, Dr. Birkenhead is further the recipient of the prestigious Albert Nelson Marquis Lifetime Achievement Award, presented to individuals who have demonstrated exceptional leadership and made notable contributions to their field.

A Lifetime of Achievement in **Media / Entertainment**

Richard A. Carvell

Assistant Professor (Retired)
Arkansas State University
JONESBORO, AR UNITED STATES

For more than 35 years, Richard A. Carvell excelled in the field of broadcasting, culminating in his most recent roles as assistant professor, chairman of the department of radio and television, and director of broadcasting at Arkansas State University in Jonesboro from 1988 to 2008, where he also served as instructor of radio and television from 1972 to 1988. Earlier in his career, he joined the U.S. Air Force and served as captain in the United States and Vietnam between 1967 and 1971 before transferring to radio station KASU in Jonesboro, Arkansas, as news director from 1971 to 1972, operations manager from 1972 to 1975 and station manager from 1976 to 1988.

Outside of his primary endeavors, Mr. Carvell has been a consultant for various educational and broadcast organizations and has served as a panelist at professional conferences and workshops. In a career filled with highlights, he is especially proud of the success his students have achieved both in broadcasting and other fields. Additionally, he recalls fondly his experiences in Vietnam, where he volunteered as a squadron civic action officer working with an orphanage. Reflecting on these years, he is grateful for the mentorship he received from Hi Mayo, the manager of KBRI, as well as Charles Rasberry, his boss at Arkansas State University, among many others.

Prior to establishing himself as a trusted voice in the field, Mr. Carvell sought to expand his knowledge through the pursuit of a formal education at a number of esteemed academic institutions. He first attended

Hendrix College, where he completed coursework from 1962 to 1964. He continued his studies at Arkansas State University and obtained a Bachelor of Science in radio journalism in 1966. He ultimately achieved a Master of Science in radio and television upon graduating from the University of Illinois in 1972.

An active presence in the field, Mr. Carvell has maintained memberships with a number of prestigious organizations, including the Disabled American Veterans, The American Legion, the Arkansas American Legion Boys State Commission, the Broadcast Education Association, and the Association for Education in Journalism and Mass Communications. With the Arkansas School Boards Association, he acted as the region director from 1991 to 1993, vice president in 1994 and president in 1996. The organization honored him with the Dr. Daniel Pilkinton Award for Outstanding Service to Education in Arkansas in 1994. He is further associated with the National School Public Relations Association as a member and former president of the Arkansas chapter in 1997.

With a plethora of knowledge at his disposal, Mr. Carvell wrote and produced a number of programs for the Indian Sports Network, East Arkansas Cablevision, Arkansas Educational TV Network, Voice of America and National Public Radio. In light of his professional experience, he earned a plethora of grants from the Corporation for Public Broadcasting and numerous other agencies between 1976 and 1988.

Mr. Carvell was born on December 18, 1943, in Brinkley, Arkansas, to mother Charlotte Allen Carvell and father Robert Carvell. Married to Pearl Elizabeth Granderson from August 1964 until 1975, he later married Linda Sue Rhoads on September 3, 1977. Currently, he is the proud father to four children named Richard Jr., David, Jonathan and James, as well as one stepson named Dean Collins. Moreover, he has five grandchildren named Cassey Collins, Morgan Carvell, Meredith Carvell, Lydia Carvell and Norah Carvell. In his free time, he enjoys practicing photography.

A Lifetime of Achievement in **Media / Entertainment**

Ron Daley

Theater Director

ARGYLE, WI UNITED STATES

L ooking back, Ron Daley sees many parallels in his life with that of Donald Trump. Born in Washington, D.C., in 1945, at the end of the war, he was always made aware of that. His mother, Dorothy Krouse Daley, was a kind, caring woman who worked as a public health nurse and frequently shared the horrors of her experience with Mr. Daley. His father, a hard task master who demanded achievement, regretted that we won the war. They lived in Chicago.

To continue the parallel, Mr. Daley won the oratorical contest at school, the science fair and the entertainment competition. None of his honors pleased his father, who wanted military excellence. Mr. Daley then enrolled at Culver Military Academy, where he still holds the longest tenure on the drill team. At Culver, he began to read Salinger, Camus and Sartre. He recognized the ostracism he had received as a Protestant in a Catholic neighborhood. His father had been excommunicated for marrying a Protestant.

This ostracism carried on at Culver, where Mr. Daley was not favored because his family was lower-middle class. He was, however, welcomed by the Jewish students and oddly enough by the Catholic students, who were often seen as poor. He was Gene Siskal's bridge partner.

After Culver, Mr. Daley's politics swung from right to left, reading Dos Passos, Hemingway, Conrad and Melville. He attended Carleton College, where again he was ostracized as everyone else was a valedictorian. In 1965, his mother committed suicide. He left Carleton to return home to help his sister graduate. In 1967, he graduated from North Park University, and Gen. Hershey rescinded all draft deferments.

With a number of 195 and no bone spurs, he enrolled at Roosevelt University, where he was lucky enough to study with Lorenzo Turner, Charles Hamilton and St. Claire Drake. Graduating in 1968 in English and philosophy, Mr. Daley began teaching at Malcolm X College, where he worked with the Modern Language Association, CCCC and the Black Panther Party. This last kept Gen. Hershey off his back.

In 1970, Mr. Daley left Malcolm X College to teach at Orange County Community College in Middletown, New York. During this time, he became involved in theater, first through politics — the Berrigans — then through the works of Bertolt Brecht. When the war ended, he attended Syracuse University, where he was Arthur Storch's assistant in the development of the Syracuse Stage.

Finally, Mr. Daley appeared in New York, where he struggled as a theater ombudsman — at this point the parallel with Trump closes — working in many positions: light design, set design, technical director, etc. He finally made it to director. He received accolades for his work on "The Lesson," "Journey's End," "The Au Pair Man" and "Knight of the Burning Pestle," which received an Outer Critics Circle nomination. In 1983, he took over the reins at the National Shakespeare Company after founder Philip Meister passed away. Nationally, he won the NCHC Award for best show for "Hamlet" and next year came in second for "Macbeth."

In 1985, Mr. Daley took over Shakespeare in the Park of New York and directed the first professional production of "The Spanish Tragedy," written in the late 1500s, in the United States. He has been cited for Best Show in Madison for "The Fat Zip," "Desire," "White People" and "In the Matter of John David Hutchins." He has directed many others in the last 20 years and written 17 more.

In 1986, Mr. Daley married Ginny Bean. The following year, they moved to Wisconsin. He and his wife have three sons: Jackson, Bryan and Geoffrey. Mr. Daley is a member of the Stage Directors and Choreographers Society and the Dramatists Guild of America.

A Lifetime of Achievement in **Media / Entertainment**

Leslie Grainger-Haynes

Foreign Language Video Producer

TAOS, NM UNITED STATES

Leslie Grainger-Haynes is a language and translation professional with more than 40 years of excellence in the entertainment industry and private sectors. Inspired by her mother, who was an American Airlines stewardess in the '40s and started the Taos Travel Agency in the '60s, Ms. Grainger-Haynes was shaped by early travel experiences and wanted to be able to communicate with people around the world. Her comprehensive education began at the Kent School for Girls in Denver and provided her with the basis to pursue her extensive career in the language industry. She then completed coursework at higher education institutions across the globe. These included The University of New Mexico in 1970; the University of Colorado from 1971 to 1973, completing a Bachelor of Arts in 1990; the Instituto Allende in San Miguel de Allende, Mexico, in 1972; the University of Manchester in England in 1974; and the Sorbonne University in Paris from 1977 to 1978.

In Nashville, Tennessee, Ms. Grainger-Haynes served as a studio interpreter for producer Billy Sherrill, working with Baby Records of Italy for two years, on two albums and one movie. She also worked for Buckhorn Music, where she translated "One Day at a Time" which was recorded and released in Quebec, Canada. Upon opening her company, International Translation Services, her first project was to translate and produce a song for recording artist Crystal Gayle in French. Ms. Grainger-Haynes, through her company, also translated and produced

George Gobel in three languages for a Mr. Transmission television ad for foreign release.

Ms. Grainger-Haynes considers the project she was hired to do by Mainichi Broadcasting, Tokyo, to be the crowning glory of her brilliant career. She flew to Colorado to meet a 12-man television crew from Tokyo to produce a 30-minute television show featuring John Denver and Japan's pop star, Mao Daichi, singing "Country Roads Take Me Home." She then flew to Nashville with the television crew to interview Pee Wee King and Redd Stewart, who wrote "The Tennessee Waltz," and to record with Patti Page and Mao. This project included interpreters in Japanese, which International Translation Services provided. She also provided professional translation and interpretive services to the entertainment and television industry, Nissan Manufacturing, U.S. Tobacco and many other companies and government entities from 1980 to 1986. She served on the Human Relations Board for four years.

She married and moved to Denver, Colorado, where she formed International Translation Services, which provided translation, interpretive services and foreign language video production. Her clients included the Denver Mayor's Office, engineering firms, gas and oil exploration companies, medical device producers, mining companies, telecommunications providers, Procter & Gamble and many other Fortune 500 companies between 1990 and 2010. International Translation Services produced their marketing and training videos into foreign languages for the world market.

As a testament to her success, Ms. Grainger-Haynes was selected for inclusion in the 27th edition of Who's Who in the West in 1999, and has now been selected for the Albert Nelson Marquis Lifetime Achievement Award. Upon retiring to Taos, New Mexico, she continued her translation work pro bono for families searching for the graves of downed P-51 pilots who led the Normandy invasion. She translated the French records, many handwritten accounts found in churches in France, for American and Canadian families. She also translated the thank-you letters, which were sent back to the French. She lives on her family property, 50 acres, overlooking Taos, where she collects fossils and cholla cacti to create fanciful statuettes. Her interests include farm-to-table canning and cooking. She developed the pet food pantry for the elderly for her Episcopal Church.

A Lifetime of Achievement in **Media / Entertainment**

Richard Stewart Mason

President
Telemark Dance Records

Editor Emeritus
Dance Week

Founder
Rancho Bernardo High School Friends of the Library

SAN DIEGO, CA UNITED STATES

With more than 50 years of experience in editing and publishing to his credit, Richard Stewart Mason has become an authority in his industry. He began his career path as the branch chief of the CIA from 1948 to 1972 and the vice president of Telemark Dance Records from 1962 to 1972. Mr. Mason currently serves as the president of Telemark Dance Records, editor emeritus of Dance Week and the founder of Rancho Bernardo High School Friends of the Library. Outside of his primary endeavors, he sporadically served the U.S. government as a Russian interpreter in the 1960s.

Mr. Mason served as an ensign-lieutenant commander at the U.S. Naval Supply Corps Reserve. Civically, he acted as a Sunday school teacher and president of the PTA from 1953 to 1973. From 1979 to 1983, he found success as the president of the U.S. Amateur Ballroom Dancers Association in McLean, Virginia. Moreover, he started a poetry contest in 2012 that remains active to this day.

Prior to establishing himself as a trusted voice in the field, Mr. Mason sought to expand his knowledge through the pursuit of a formal education at a number of esteemed academic institutions. He first attended the University of Texas, attaining a Bachelor of Arts in 1947.

He then enrolled at Johns Hopkins University and ultimately achieved a Master of Arts upon graduating in 1948. From there, he completed postgraduate coursework at American University from 1969 to 1970.

Mr. Mason excelled as the editor and publisher of the U.S. Ballroom Dancing Yearbooks from 1973 to 1975, the Potomac Ballroom Newsletter beginning in 1986 and the World Amateur Dancer Magazine from 1982 to 1983. His greatest career achievements include starting a weekly newsletter called Dance Week in McLean, which he continued for 23 years. He is also proud of founding Telemark Dance Records, a record producing firm in McLean, and organizing the Rancho Bernardo High School Friends of the Library.

In light of his many achievements in the field, he has received a number of accolades throughout his career. Mr. Mason received the Recognition Award from the Northeast chapter of the U.S. Amateur Ballroom Dancers Association in 1984 and the Lifetime Achievement Award from the U.S. Dance Foundation in 1987. Likewise, he was named Outstanding Volunteer of the Year by PUSD and inducted into the Rancho Bernardo Hall of Fame in 2014. In addition, he has previously been selected for inclusion in such honors publications as the second and third editions of Who's Who in Entertainment, which were published in 1992 and 1997, respectively.

Mr. Mason was born on December 31, 1921, in State College, Pennsylvania, to mother Elizabeth Mason and father Charles Russell Mason. Married to Sheila Myrtle Farquharson from 1945 to 1992, he is the proud father of two children named David Stewart Mason and Marion Elizabeth Strandh. Moreover, he has four grandchildren and nine great-grandchildren. In his free time, he enjoys participating in such activities as ballroom dancing, studying foreign languages and gardening. In the future, Mr. Mason hopes to continue to promote trade between the United States and Ukraine. He just set up a website for his music publishing firm and is currently working on a CD with Telemark Dance Records.

A Lifetime of Achievement in **Media / Entertainment**

Molleen Matsumura

Senior Editor & Director
ALIN Foundation

Network Project Director
National Center for Science Education

BERKELEY, CA UNITED STATES

With a passion for writing since she was a young girl, Molleen Matsumura has been a gifted writer for all of her life. Going on to attend lectures by Paul Kurtz, where she learned more about secular humanism, she eventually became quite well-known in the field. She wanted to advocate for what she believed in. Prior to establishing herself as a trusted voice in the field, she sought to expand her knowledge through the pursuit of a formal education. She attended the University of California, Berkeley, where she earned a Bachelor of Arts in 1970.

Ms. Matsumura has flourished as the senior editor and director of the ALIN Foundation in Berkeley since 1981. The foundation, which was established by her husband, Dr. Kenneth Matsumura, in 1962, is one of the oldest biotech organizations in the world. The association has notably developed several lifesaving treatments for heart attacks, cancer, diabetes and liver failure. Additionally, Ms. Matsumura has contributed as the network project director for the National Center for Science Education in El Cerrito, California, since 1993.

An active presence in the field, Ms. Matsumura has maintained memberships with numerous prestigious professional organizations, including the American Association of University Women, the American Civil Liberties Union, and the Americans United for Separation of Church and State, where she has been a member of the national advisory council since 1992. Civically involved as well, she has devoted her time as a member of the Feminists for Free Expression.

Recognized as an expert in the industry, she served the Free Inquiry magazine in Buffalo as an editorial associate from 1989 to 1995 and an associate editor beginning in 1995. She also held the title of editorial associate with the Missing Link newsletter between 1989 and 1995. In 1995, she contributed her knowledge and time to the role of editor with Voices for Evolution. She also co-authored "Japan's Economy in World Perspective," which was published in 1983, "Sex in China," which was published in 1991, and "Mother-to-be: Pregnancy and Birth for Women with Disabilities," which was published in 1991. Furthermore, she has contributed numerous articles to professional journals.

In light of her professional successes and accomplishments, Ms. Matsumura has gained recognition in the form of various awards and accolades over the years. Notably, she was the recipient of the Distinguished Service Award from the Council for Secular Humanism in 1993. In addition, she has previously been selected for inclusion in such honors publications as the 20th edition of Who's Who of American Women and the 73rd edition of Who's Who in America. Though these recognitions are impressive, she considers the highlight of her career to be her work in preserving evolution education in the United States for future generations.

Ms. Matsumura was born on May 1, 1948, in Riverside, California. She later married Kenneth Naoyuki Matsumura, and together, they are the proud parents of two children named Miriam Ellen and Maja. Maja was a child they adopted from Bosnia. Moreover, they have two wonderful grandchildren. Reflecting on her career, Ms. Matsumura is proud of having been the one person who knew right from wrong, and she never deviated from it. The advice she can offer fellow members or those aspiring to work in her field is to never get discouraged. There will be good and bad days; keep persevering.

A Lifetime of Achievement in **Media / Entertainment**

Lucy Rosenthal

Writer & Editor
Educator

NEW YORK, NY UNITED STATES

Photo: Robert Daniel Ullmann

Lucy Rosenthal's professional achievements have been in the intertwined fields of writing, education and editing. She has been engaged with writers and writing in all phases of her career.

Ms. Rosenthal is the author of two critically acclaimed novels, titled "The Ticket Out," which was published in 1983, and "The World of Rae English," published in 2014. She has edited several anthologies as well, including "Great American Love Stories" in 1988, "The World Treasury of Love Stories" in 1995 and "The Eloquent Short Story: Varieties of Narration" in 2004. Her reviews and articles have appeared in The Washington Post, The New York Times, Ms. Magazine, Saturday Review and Michigan Quarterly Review, among others. Two of her plays were produced at the Eugene O'Neill Memorial Theater in 1966 and 1967.

Ms. Rosenthal's 30 years as an educator were spent mainly at Sarah Lawrence College, on the faculty of its noted creative writing program from 1988 to 2016, teaching on both the undergraduate and graduate levels. She joined the college as guest faculty in 1988 and became a member of the regular writing faculty in 1996; she was awarded tenure in 2001. In 2016, she stepped down in order to write full time and is now among the writing department's emeriti faculty. She taught in the writing programs of New York University from 1986 to 1994 and Columbia University from 1990 to 1997 as well. She has brought to her teaching the perspective and skills of an experienced editor and critic, acquired during a long career in book publishing.

Ms. Rosenthal's positions in the publishing industry include 14 years at the Book of the Month Club from 1973 to 1987, initially as an editor. In 1974, she was appointed to the club's influential editorial board of judges, becoming the third woman to serve on that board in the club's then 50-year history. The judges' function was to choose the club's monthly selection to offer to its vast membership of subscribers. As the first market judgment for a book, the selection had major impact. This imprimatur — Book of the Month selection — was key to a book's launching and integral to its success. Ms. Rosenthal saw her own role on the board as including advocacy of books by women, especially those issuing from the burgeoning women's movement of the 70s, and to track emerging younger writers as well. From 1979 to 1987, Ms. Rosenthal served as the club's senior editorial adviser.

From 1957 to 1973, she worked as a freelance editorial consultant for various book publishing houses on hardcover and paperback books, and for literary agents.

She was a member of the 1980 Pulitzer Prize biography jury, served on the board of the American Book Awards from 1980 to 1981, and on the admissions committee of the Iowa Writers' Workshop at The University of Iowa, where she also studied from 1965 to 1968.

Ms. Rosenthal is a recipient of a Pulitzer fellowship in critical writing in 1968, a University of Michigan undergraduate Hopwood Award, and several residencies at the Virginia Center for the Creative Arts. She is a member of PEN America, the Authors Guild, the Authors League, the Women's Media Group, where she was a board member from 1979 to 1981, Phi Beta Kappa and Phi Kappa Phi. She earned a Bachelor of Arts from the University of Michigan in 1954, a Master of Science in journalism from Columbia University in 1955 and a Master of Fine Arts from the Yale School of Drama in 1961.

A Lifetime of Achievement in **Media / Entertainment**

H. Donald Winkler

Historical Researcher & Writer

GATLINBURG, TN UNITED STATES

During his retirement years, H. Donald Winkler is excelling as a historical researcher and writer, producing such works as "Stealing Secrets: How a Few Daring Women Deceived Generals, Impacted Battles, and Altered the Course of the Civil War" and "Lincoln and Booth, More Light on the Conspiracy." He also authored "The Women in Lincoln's Life: How the Sixteenth President Was Shaped by Fascinating Women Who Loved, Hated, Helped, Charmed, and Deceived Him," its sequel, "Lincoln's Ladies," and "Civil War Goats and Scapegoats: The Good, the Bad, and the Ugly."

Peer reviews noted that these "first-rate, fascinating books" reflect extensive research "that provide new insights and invaluable contributions about Lincoln's life and the Civil War era." His "Stealing Secrets" drew favorable comparison with the works of Ian Fleming, author of the James Bond novels. Mr. Winkler's reputation resulted in two speaking engagements at Ford's Theatre in Washington, D.C., where Lincoln was assassinated, at the Carl Sandburg Home National Historic Site, and other Lincoln venues.

In the late 1950s, Mr. Winkler began his first career as the executive administrator of the National Conference of Methodist Youth and the editor of its national magazine, Concern, which inspired young people to become informed about and involved in national and international affairs. An executive of the Anti-Defamation League of B'nai B'rith praised Mr. Winkler for "promoting intergroup understanding and witnessing most effectively on important social problems."

That experience was followed by a 38-year career as a university public relations executive, a field in which Mr. Winkler became one of the leading professionals. He developed imaginative programs, wrote presidential speeches, and served as news writer and director, special events planner, arid writer, editor, and designer of persuasive publications that won 84 national awards. He was inducted into the Virginia Communications Hall of Fame in 1995, the only person from his profession ever to be chosen. In 2013, his undergraduate alma mater, McKendree University, gave him a Lifetime Achievement Award for excellence in literature and communication.

The institutions he served included North Dakota State University; Randolph-Macon Woman's College; The George Washington University; California State University (CSU), Fresno; Longwood University; and the East-West Center (EWC), a U.S. State Department-affiliated think tank in Hawaii. At EWC, Mr. Winkler founded and edited an international, issues-oriented magazine, which was chosen as the nation's best educational magazine. At CSU Fresno, Mr. Winkler was one of only about a dozen persons awarded both academic and administrative tenure in the entire 23-campus California State University and Colleges system. At Longwood, he co-edited a journal for the best writings and art of Virginia high school students. It won a dozen national awards and was cited as a national model by the then vice president of the United States.

"Winkler's skills in management enabled him not just to know what ought to be done, but to do it," wrote Virginia Carter, then senior vice president of the Council for Advancement and Support of Education (CASE), the professional organization in the field. She said he is "a leading thinker and writer about public relations and one of the very few persons who understand what PR can do for an institution." CASE cited him "for professional efforts which have benefited not only his institutions but have strengthened the entire fabric of American education." CASE chose Mr. Winkler as a national consultant to evaluate PR programs at colleges and universities, as an adviser to its national certification program, and as a program director and speaker at its national conferences.

Mr. Winkler has also received commendations from such luminaries as the chief justice of the United States, the press secretary to the president of the United States, the head of the Voice of America, the president of NBC, and the editor-in-chief of United Press International, who wrote that "Winkler enjoyed the towering respect of the press, radio and TV corps." Active in community life, Mr. Winkler has chaired United Way campaigns; produced, directed and judged Miss America scholarship pageants; and served as a public relations consultant to various community and regional businesses and groups. Mr. Winkler was a 30-year member of The National Press Club and is a 50-year member of the Society of Professional Journalists, Sigma Delta Chi. He belongs to numerous professional organizations. He holds a master's degree in journalism and government from Ohio University.

A Lifetime of Achievement in **Medicine & Health Care**

Marilyn K. Bither

Emergency Nurse (Retired)

BROOMFIELD, CO UNITED STATES

Marilyn K. Bither has dedicated her career to helping patients seeking emergency medical care, embracing the challenge of assisting those in need. With more than 50 years of professional experience to her credit, she most recently served as a parish nurse with East Woods Community Church in Vancouver, Washington, from 2012 until her retirement in 2014. Prior to this position, Ms. Bither was a health direct nurse with Brim Healthcare, now known as HealthTechS3, since 1995.

She also found success as an emergency nurse, a critical care nurse and an educator with Redwood Memorial Hospital and a telenurse of emergency service at the General Hospital in Eureka, California, from 1992 to 1995. Earlier in her career, Ms. Bither thrived as a staff nurse and an interim nurse manager at St. Joseph's Hospital Emergency Department from 1980 to 1995 and a staff nurse at Seaside Hospital from 1963 to 1980. She has additionally contributed her time and knowledge as an emergency care consultant, a paramedic and emergency medical technician, and a member of several emergency care and prehospital task forces in the state of California.

Ms. Bither's desire to pursue a nursing career began at a young age, inspired by her upbringing and her family, including her sister, who was a nurse, and her mother, who always aspired to go into the field. Prior to embarking on her professional path, she began her studies at the Deaconess Hospital School of Nursing, where she obtained a diploma in 1962. Continuing her studies with Humboldt State University in Arcata, California, Ms. Bither went on to earn a teaching certificate in 1984. A registered nurse in the state of California, she is also certified as an emergency nurse and an instructor for advanced cardiac life support, pediatric advanced life support and basic life support, and was the northern California advanced cardiac life support representative for several years.

A respected voice in her areas of interest, Ms. Bither has been an active leader in her community. She has previously been affiliated with the Emergency Nurses Association, the International Order of the Rainbow for Girls, the Order of the Eastern Star and the Presbyterian Church of the USA from 1995 to 2019. A former CPR instructor for the American Heart Association, Ms. Bither was a first aid instructor with the National Safety Council, and a United States delegate to Russia and Eastern Europe for People to People International, a nonprofit organization that encourages people across borders to exchange ideas and expand their understanding through international experiences. Widely recognized for her expertise, she has also authored and edited educational programs in the field of nursing.

Throughout her career, Ms. Bither has been recognized for her contributions. The recipient of the Star of Life Award from North Coast Emergency Medical Services, she was named State Officer by the California Jaycees and Nurse of the Year by the Humboldt Nurses Interest Group. In light of all her accomplishments, Ms. Bither has been featured in numerous honors publications, including multiple editions of Who's Who in America. She is also the recipient of the prestigious Albert Nelson Marquis Lifetime Achievement Award, presented to individuals who have demonstrated extraordinary professional leadership and excellence in their field.

A Spokane, Washington, native, Ms. Bither was born on September 3, 1941, to Orville Christopher and Harriet Frances Bolen Shiek. She and her late husband, Richard Eugene Bither, enjoyed 60 years of marriage together and are the parents of Michele Rae and the late Bruce Allen. She is also the proud grandmother of Andrew, Douglas, Benjamin and Mollymae. In her free time, Ms. Bither enjoys sewing, crocheting prayer shawls for her church, creative writing, swimming and cycling.

A Lifetime of Achievement in **Medicine & Health Care**

B. Thomas Brown, MD, MBA

Urologist
DAYTONA BEACH, FL UNITED STATES

B. Thomas Brown, MD, MBA, is a physician who has been known for his work in general urology and male sexual dysfunction. Practicing at the Daytona Beach Urology Clinic between 1978 and 1990, he also spent 10 years at the Tomoka Correctional Institute in Daytona Beach from 1985 to 1995 and 24 years at Atlantic Urological Associates from 1990 to 2014. Affiliated with numerous hospitals, he notably served as chief of staff and chief of surgery at Memorial Hospital in Ormond Beach, Florida, and chief of urology at Halifax Health Medical Center of Daytona Beach. Dr. Brown also taught as a longtime clinical assistant professor of family practice medicine at the University of South Florida in Tampa beginning in 1979.

Dr. Brown was a student at Johns Hopkins University from 1966 to 1969 and went on to earn a Doctor of Medicine from the West Virginia University School of Medicine in 1973 and a Master of Business Administration from the University of South Florida in 1997. He completed a surgical internship and residency in medicine at West Virginia University and a second residency in urology at the University of Miami. He is a board-certified urologist and holds a medical license and certification in both West Virginia and Florida.

During his medical career, Dr. Brown has been active with the Accreditation Association for Ambulatory Health Care, Inc., as a surveyor. He has served on numerous committees and boards, including as chairman of the committee on applicants for the central

Florida chapter of the American College of Surgeons since 1998 and on the board of directors of the southeastern section of the American Urological Association since 1994. Dr. Brown has also served his local community in a variety of ways with such organizations as the American Cancer Society, the United Methodist Church and I-Care, and continues to serve as president of the board of directors for the Volusia County Cooperative Health Group.

Dr. Brown has conducted extensive clinical research and has also been published in his field. He has co-authored several articles in scholarly journals, including the Journal of Urology, the West Virginia Medical Journal, and European Urology. He has published several abstracts as well.

Named West Virginia 4-H All Star by the American Urological Association in 1977, Dr. Brown was also awarded Best Guest Feature by a Physician, receiving Second Place at the 21st Annual FMA County Medical Society Publications Contest in 1998. He has previously been selected for inclusion in numerous honors publications, including seven editions of Who's Who in America, two editions of Who's Who in Medicine and Healthcare, one edition of Who's Who in Science and Engineering, six editions of Who's Who in the South and Southwest, and two editions of Who's Who in the World.

Notably profiled in the 73rd edition of Who's Who in America, Dr. Brown was born on September 30, 1948, in Beckley, West Virginia, to mother Nancy Jo Ballengee Brown and father Benjamin Porter Jr. Dr. Brown contracted polio at the age of 3. Spending nine months in the hospital, he grew to love the physicians he was surrounded by and soon after decided that he, too, wanted to someday become a doctor. He was also inspired and motivated by his mother, who was a biology and physiology teacher, and his uncle, who was a physician. He is now the proud father of two amazing and successful children, Elizabeth Timbrook Brown, MD, and J. Schuyler Brown, JD. They are his greatest blessings.

A Lifetime of Achievement in **Medicine & Health Care**

Theodora M. Capezio

Nurse (Retired)

MONKTON, MD UNITED STATES

An expert in the field of medical surgical nursing, Theodora M. Capezio has made a lasting impact on the lives of her patients as well as those with developmental disabilities. She is a retired medical and surgical nurse who celebrated more than three decades in the field before retiring in 2006. Formerly affiliated with the prestigious Mercy Medical Center in Baltimore, Maryland, Ms. Capezio found success as a staff nurse in the medical and surgical unit and in the outpatient surgery unit. Prior to her tenure in Baltimore, she contributed as a staff nurse at Stella Maris Hospice, located in Towson, Maryland. Earlier in her career, Ms. Capezio shared her talents and expertise as a clinical instructor.

With a career full of highlights to look back on, Ms. Capezio's greatest accomplishment was her role in founding Pennsylvania-Mar Human Services, an organization that provides residential and daytime services for the mentally disabled in southern Pennsylvania and northern Baltimore County. Today, the organization, known as Penn-Mar Human Services, continues to flourish, providing educational, vocational and residential programs as well as social services to more than 400 individuals with developmental disabilities. The award-winning agency operates nearly 50 residential homes and numerous learning opportunities, as well as helps those with intellectual disabilities find employment. Outside of her groundbreaking work with Penn-Mar Human Services, Ms. Capezio has been affiliated as a member of Sigma Theta Tau, an international nursing honor society.

A Lifetime of Achievement | Theodora M. Capezio

Prior to beginning her professional path in nursing, Ms. Capezio pursued an education. She first acquired a diploma at Mercy Hospital in 1958. Following this accomplishment, she attended Notre Dame of Maryland University, where she earned a Bachelor of Science in nursing in 1990. A well-respected leader in her field, Ms. Capezio is a registered nurse in Maryland.

Ms. Capezio has earned multiple awards and recognitions for her commitment to improving the lives of her patients and the disabled. A celebrated Marquis listee, she has been featured in the fourth and fifth editions of Who's Who in American Nursing and the 25th edition of Who's Who of American Women. For her professional accomplishments and contributions to the field of nursing, Ms. Capezio has also been presented with the prestigious Albert Nelson Marquis Lifetime Achievement Award.

Ms. Capezio was born on September 1, 1937, to Vincent and Mary Regina Goulden Rybikowsky in Baltimore, Maryland. She was inspired to pursue a career in nursing from a young age after admiring a local nurse who lived in her neighborhood and went to work in a cap and apron. Afforded the opportunity to live out her dream in health care and being able to impact people's lives has been a very rewarding experience. She credits the Sisters of Mercy for motivating her along her journey to success, particularly Sister Mary Thecla, a member of Mercy Medical Center's pastoral care department who was renowned for her selflessness, compassion and ability to comfort.

Formerly married to the late Marion James Capezio, with whom she enjoyed more than 25 years of marriage, Ms. Capezio is the mother of six sons: Timothy, Jeffrey, Gregory, Matthew, Dennis and Mark. She is the proud grandmother of Jeffrey Nicholas, Brandon, Victoria, Ashley, Kirk, Gelly "Gel", Megan, Sean and Joshua, and stepgrandmother to Buddy, in addition to being a great-grandmother. In her free time, Ms. Capezio enjoys collecting Victorian cards and courting pictures.

A Lifetime of Achievement in **Medicine & Health Care**

Edward Sawyer Cooper, MD

Professor Emeritus
Department of Medicine
University of Pennsylvania
PHILADELPHIA, PA UNITED STATES

With 70 years of experience to his credit, Edward Sawyer Cooper, MD, has been designated as a professor emeritus of the department of medicine at the University of Pennsylvania since 1996. Previously, he excelled at the University of Pennsylvania as a professor in the Perelman School of Medicine from 1973 to 1996 and an associate professor in the department of medicine from 1970 to 1973. During this time, he worked at the Philadelphia General Hospital as the chief of the medical service in the University of Pennsylvania division from 1973 to 1976 and the Mercy-Douglass Hospital as a consultant in the department of medicine from 1969 to 1974. Prior to these appointments, Dr. Cooper held a number of positions with the Philadelphia General Hospital, including as the president of the medical staff from 1969 to 1971, a senior attending physician from 1968 to 1976, and both the co-founder and the co-director of the Stroke Research Center from 1968 to 1974.

From 1965 to 1996, Dr. Cooper served in the department of medicine at the Hospital of the University of Pennsylvania as an attending physician. He further flourished in the department of medicine at the University of Pennsylvania as an assistant professor from 1964 to 1970 and an associate in medicine from 1958 to 1964. He was additionally active as the program director for the department of medicine at the Mercy-Douglass Hospital from 1957 to 1969 and an attending physician in the department of medicine at Philadelphia General Hospital from 1957 to 1968. Notably, Dr. Cooper began his career as an intern, a resident and a National Institutes of Health fellow in cardiology at the Philadelphia General Hospital between 1949 and 1957.

Before embarking on his professional path, Dr. Cooper pursued an education at Lincoln University, earning a Bachelor of Arts, with high honors, in 1946. He concluded his studies at Meharry Medical College in 1949, graduating with a Doctor of Medicine with the highest honors. Moreover, he is a diplomate of the National Board of Medical Examiners and the American Board of Internal Medicine. Following these accomplishments, Dr. Cooper obtained an honorary master's degree from the University of Pennsylvania in 1972 and an honorary Doctor of Science from Meharry Medical College in 2011.

Beyond his responsibilities within the field, Dr. Cooper has participated in numerous endeavors outside of his professional circles, including on committees, subcommittees, and task forces for the University of Pennsylvania between 1969 and 1996. Holding a number of roles with the University of Pennsylvania Health System and the Hospital of the University of Pennsylvania, he has significantly contributed to Independence Blue Cross since 1974, The Rockefeller University since 1992, the West Philadelphia Empowerment Zone in 1996, the National Institutes of Health and a number of governor advisory committees between 1973 and 1980. Furthermore, Dr. Cooper completed service with the U.S. Air Force, appointed to the rank of captain as well as the chief of the medical service for the U.S. Air Force Hospital in the Philippines between 1954 and 1956.

Dr. Cooper found much success with his written works, having provided his skills and resources to the editorial boards for the Journal for Cerebrovascular Risk, Heart Disease and Stroke, the Journal of the National Medical Association, Excepta Media and Stroke. The co-author of "Stroke in Blacks," he has penned myriad articles and papers published in professional journals and chapters for books. Featured in a number of Who's Who publications, Dr. Cooper was honored as America's Leading Black Internal Medicine Specialist by Black Enterprise magazine in 1988 and for a Lifetime of Achievement by Ebony magazine in 1993. He was the first African American president of the American Heart Association, as well as member of the board of trustees of the Hospital of the University of Pennsylvania, The Rockefeller

University, The College of Physicians of Philadelphia, and the board of directors of Independence Blue Cross.

In addition to his primary vocation, Dr. Cooper remains affiliated with various organizations in relation to his areas of expertise. An honorary member of the International Society on Hypertension in Blacks, he has held multiple administrative posts for the Inter-Society Commission for Heart Disease Resources, the National Medical Association, American Health Education for African Development, The College of Physicians of Philadelphia, and the American Heart Association, Inc. He was also associated with the Philadelphia County Medical Society, the American Foundation for Negro Affairs, the American College of Physicians, the American Society of Hypertension, and the Medical Society of Pennsylvania. Likewise, Dr. Cooper was a member of the Association of Black Cardiologists, the American Association for the Advancement of Science, the American Association of University Professors, the Alpha Omega Alpha Honor Medical Society and AAMP Inc.

In light of his exceptional undertakings, Dr. Cooper has accrued several accolades throughout his impressive career. A fellow of The College of Physicians of Philadelphia and the American College of Physicians, he has been celebrated on many occasions by the Lincoln University, the American Heart Association, Inc., Meharry Medical College, and the University of Pennsylvania, which bestowed him with a number of eponymous honors. Inducted into the National Black College Alumni Hall of Fame Foundation, the African American Biographies Hall of Fame, the South Carolina Black Hall of Fame, and the Legion of Honor of the Chapel of Four Chaplains, Dr. Cooper has been presented with the Burr Prize for Best Research from the Philadelphia General Hospital, the Mercy-Douglass Memorial Lecture Award from the Medical Society of Eastern Pennsylvania, the Distinguished Service Award from Frontiers International, the Strittmatter Award from the Philadelphia County Medical Society, the Presidential Award from the Association of Black Cardiologists, and the Distinguished Service Award to Mankind and Medicine from the Palmetto State Medical, Dental, and Pharmaceutical Association, among countless other awards. Accepting additional recognition from Harvard University, the city of Philadelphia, the New Orleans Medical Association, the American Academy of Neurology Research and Education Foundation, and the Shanghai Medical College of Fudan University, Dr. Cooper is proud to have raised a family of doctors, with three children, three grandchildren and his late wife, Jean Marie, all having held Doctor of Medicine degrees, one with a doctorate of psychology. One son died with Hodgkin's disease; another grandson is a businessman.

A Lifetime of Achievement in **Medicine & Health Care**

Richard L. Coulson, PhD

Medical Education Consultant
College of Health
Clayton State University
FAYETTEVILLE, GA UNITED STATES

With nearly 55 years of experience to his credit, Richard L. Coulson, PhD, has excelled as a medical education consultant in the College of Health at Clayton State University since 2014. Prior to this appointment, he worked for Saint Louis University as a professor and the chair of physician assistant education from 2013 to 2014, Gordon College as a professor and an instructor of anatomy and physiology from 2010 to 2012, and the Geisinger Commonwealth School of Medicine as a founding professor in physiology and an evaluation director from 2008 to 2009. He was further active as a professor and a director of instructional development and assessment at Clayton State University from 2006 to 2008 as well as a professor on the Carbondale campus for the Windsor University School of Medicine from 2004 to 2006. Moreover, Dr. Coulson held many positions at Southern Illinois University between 1978 and 2004, including the director of assessment, a professor in the department of educational psychology and special education, a professor in the department of physiology, a professor in the cognitive science division of the department of medical education, and a professor of physiology, medical education and educational psychology.

Previously, Dr. Coulson flourished at Temple University in a number of capacities such as the assistant professor of medicine in cardiology from 1976 to 1978, an associate director of cardiology laboratories from 1976 to 1978, a research assistant for the professor of medicine from 1974 to 1976, and a postdoctoral cardiac fellow in 1974. He additionally flourished at University College London, as a postdoctoral research associate in the department of physiology in 1973, a research associate from 1972 to 1973, and a research assistant from 1971 to 1972. Between 1968 and 1971, he held the posts of a research assistant and a teaching assistant at the University of Toronto. Dr. Coulson began his career as a research assistant in the University of Calgary from 1965 to 1967 and a teaching assistant in the University of Alberta from 1967 to 1968.

Before embarking on his professional path, Dr. Coulson pursued an education at the University of Toronto, completing coursework from 1964 to 1965. He continued his academic efforts with a Bachelor of Science in zoology, botany and philosophy at the University of Calgary in 1967. Following these accomplishments, he obtained a Master of Science in physiology and biophysics at the University of Alberta in 1968. Dr. Coulson concluded his studies at the University of Toronto, graduating with a Doctor of Philosophy in physiology and bioengineering in 1971.

Beyond his responsibilities within the field, Dr. Coulson has participated in numerous endeavors outside of his professional circles. The co-inventor of the cognitive flexibility theory and the chief financial officer for Cognitive Flexibility Inc., he has notably contributed to the Educational Consortium for Artificial Intelligence Inc., the University of California, Davis, the Campaign for Better Health Care, and multiple school boards and committees for academic institutes. Also integral to the discovery of catecholamine depletion in cardiac hypertrophy and the depression of cardiac activation by nitroglycerine, Dr. Coulson held the roles of the president, the vice president, the chief executive officer, and an environmental consultant for North American Minerals Recovery Ltd. between 1964 and 2002.

Dr. Coulson found success with his written works as well, having authored articles for medical and scientific journals as well as chapters for books. An editorial consultant for the Institute of Physics, he was also the editor for Transactions, the refereed scientific journal of the Illinois State Academy of Science, from 1980 to 1983. A presenter in the field, Dr. Coulson also dedicated his time and resources as a reviewer for the American Journal of Physiology, the Journal of Applied Physiology, Circulation, Physics in Medicine & Biology, and Life Sciences, among others.

In addition to his primary vocation, Dr. Coulson remains affiliated with various organizations in relation to his areas of expertise. A grant reviewer for the March of Dimes and the American Heart Association, he had maintained involvement with divisions C and I of the American Educational Research Association. A founding member of the International Association of Medical Science Educators and the Philadelphia Academy of Cardiology, he was also associated with the American Mathematical Society, the American Physiological Society, the Canadian Microcirculation Society, the Canadian Physiological Society, and the European Microcirculation Society. Furthermore, Dr. Coulson was a member of the International Society for Heart Research, the Illinois Academy of Science, the Cognitive Science Society, the Biophysical Society and the Canadian Scottish Regiment.

In light of his exceptional undertakings, Dr. Coulson has accrued several accolades throughout his impressive career. Honored as a Medical Research Council student by the University of Toronto from 1968 to 1969, he was recognized as a Queen Elizabeth scholar by the University of Calgary in 1965 and an Edward Christie Stevens scholar by the University of Toronto in 1968. The recipient of numerous grants, he accepted a Young Investigators Award from the Deborah Heart Foundation in 1976 and an Outstanding Paper Award for Police Studies in 1997. Selected for inclusion in the eighth edition of Who's Who in American Education, Dr. Coulson was presented with a research fellowship from the Medical Research Council of Canada and University College London from 1971 to 1973, a fellowship from the Canadian Heart Fund and Temple University from 1973 to 1974, and a fellowship from the American Heart Association in 1976.

A Lifetime of Achievement in **Medicine & Health Care**

Richard J. Duma, MD, PhD

Physician & Educator

PALM COAST, FL UNITED STATES

With more than 50 years of professional experience, Richard J. Duma, MD, PhD, has emerged as a leader in the fields of medicine and academia. He most recently found success as a professor of microbiology and a tenured professor of infectious diseases and pathology at the Medical College of Virginia, also known as the Virginia Commonwealth University School of Medicine, both from 1975 to 1992. Having joined the faculty as a member from 1965 to 1967, Dr. Duma also served his fellows at Harvard Medical School-Massachusetts General Hospital, and prior to that, he was also at the University of Alabama Medical Center from 1959 to 1960 and 1962 to 1965, during which time he was the chief resident from 1964 to 1965.

Dr. Duma began his career as a student at Virginia Polytechnic Institute and State University, where he obtained a Bachelor of Arts from 1953 to 1955. He then joined the University of Virginia, completing a Doctor of Medicine from 1955 to 1959. Subsequently, he lent his knowledge and expertise to the U.S. Navy Reserve, serving with the Medical Corps from 1960 to 1962. He continued his studies at Virginia Commonwealth University, earning a Doctor of Philosophy in 1978. Dr. Duma is a licensed physician in the states of Florida and Virginia, and a diplomate of the American Board of Internal Medicine.

Alongside his primary endeavors, Dr. Duma was the chairman of the subcommittee on research at the U.S. Pharmacopeia Advisory Panel on Hospital Practices and was the executive director of the National Foundation for Infectious Diseases, where he also served as the vice president of the board of directors, in addition to holding the positions of the president, the trustee and the director emeritus. Likewise, he was the director of infectious diseases and infection control of Halifax Community Health System, where he remained as an editorial board member of Infectious Diseases in Clinical Practice in 2013.

A respected voice in his community, Dr. Duma has been affiliated with a number of professional organizations. He is a master of the American College of Physicians, and a fellow of the Infectious Diseases Society of America, the Royal Society of Tropical Medicine and Hygiene, the American Society of Tropical Medicine and Hygiene, the Florida Infectious Diseases Society, where he previously served as president in the late 1990s, and the Florida Department of Health Healthcare-Associated Infections. He is also a member of the American Clinical and Climatological Association, the American Association for the Advancement of Science, the American Federation for Clinical Research, the Virginia branch of the American Society for Microbiology, the American Society of Internal Medicine and the Virginia Society of Internal Medicine.

In addition, he has been active with the Richmond Society of Internal Medicine, the Southern Society for Clinical Investigation, the American Thoracic Society, The Royal Society of Medicine, the Medical Society of Virginia, the Richmond Academy of Medicine, the Academy of Medicine of Washington, D.C., the Medical Association of Florida, the Volusia County Medical Society, the Rotary Club of Daytona Beach, the Hammock Dunes Golf and Country Club, Sigma Xi and Tau Beta Pi. Dr. Duma also continues to serve as a member of the board of visitors of the Embry-Riddle Aeronautical University, an editor of the review panel for ImmunoFacts: Vaccines and Immunologic Drugs, and a member of the hospital-acquired infection advisory board for the Florida Department of Health.

In light of his many accomplishments and leadership in the field, Dr. Duma has been included in multiple editions of Who's Who in America, Who's Who in Medicine and Healthcare, Who's Who in the South and Southwest, and the 11th edition of Who's Who in Science and Engineering. He is also the recipient of the prestigious Albert Nelson Marquis Lifetime Achievement Award, presented to individuals who have made outstanding contributions to their industry. Dr. Duma has enjoyed more than six decades of marriage to Mary Alyce Fridley, and they have one child, Scott Lancet Duma. He is also the proud grandfather of Scott's three outstanding children: William, Benjamin and Katherine Duma.

A Lifetime of Achievement in **Medicine & Health Care**

Glen R. Elliott, PhD, MD

Chief Psychiatrist & Medical Director
Children's Health Council
PALO ALTO, CA UNITED STATES

For over 40 years, Glen R. Elliott, PhD, MD, has been dedicated to improving care of children and adolescents with severe psychiatric and behavioral disorders. He is currently serving as chief psychiatrist and medical director at the Children's Health Council. He initially embarked upon his academic career at Stanford University, where he leveraged his experience in chemistry toward the study of mental disorders, and subsequently earned both a Doctor of Medicine and Doctor of Philosophy. After completing a residency at Harvard Medical School, he returned to Stanford, where he did further training in child and adolescent psychiatry before joining the faculty as an assistant professor in 1986. In 1989, Dr. Elliott became director of child and adolescent psychiatry at the University of California, San Francisco, where he garnered an exemplary reputation for his clinical and research endeavors in attention deficit hyperactivity disorder, also known as ADHD, and autism, and for training the next generation of child and adolescent psychiatrists for over 17 years.

Dr. Elliott was honored with the status of professor emeritus in 2006, when he left to continue his career at the Children's Health Council. He also works part time at his alma mater, Stanford University, as the associate director of child and adolescent psychiatry and as an affiliated clinical professor with Stanford Medicine. An acclaimed thinker in his field, he wrote "Medicating Young Minds: How to Know if Psychiatric Drugs Will Help or Hurt Your Child" in 2006, and has received such honors as the Paul M. Howard Prize in 1984, recognition as the number one child psychiatrist in the United States by HealthTap in 2012, and the Al De Ranieri Lifetime Achievement Award in 2019, among many others. Although no longer directly involved in research, Dr. Elliott maintains association with multiple organizations pertinent to his field, including The American College of Psychiatrists, the American Board of Psychiatry and Neurology, and the American Academy of Child and Adolescent Psychiatry.

Adjacent to his professional career, Dr. Elliott serves as the director for Camp Opportunity in Santa Cruz, a nonprofit dedicated to helping children improve their self-esteem. Having a fond enjoyment for music, he is also director of the bell choir at his local church. Happily married to his wife, Janette, for many years, Dr. Elliott is the proud father of two sons, James and Mark Elliott.

A Lifetime of Achievement in **Medicine & Health Care**

Daniel L. Flugstad, MD

Orthopaedic Surgeon (Retired)

SEATTLE, WA UNITED STATES

Accruing 39 years of professional experience to his credit, Daniel L. Flugstad, MD, began his career as an intern and resident in the department of orthopaedics at the University of Washington in Seattle in 1980. He completed these positions in five years before receiving a fellowship in musculoskeletal oncology from the Harvard School of Medicine and the Massachusetts General Hospital from 1986 to 1987. During this time, he also served as a partner of the Virginia Mason Clinic in Seattle from 1985 to 1988. Dr. Flugstad subsequently transferred to the Polyclinic of Seattle in 1989, remaining there until 2018, and simultaneously, he was the chief of orthopaedic surgery at the Swedish Hospital in Seattle from 2001 to 2005, and has been an associate professor of orthopaedic surgery and a clinical faculty member of the University of Washington since 1985. He retired from clinical practice in June 2019.

In addition to this tenure, Dr. Flugstad has been a consultant of hospital privileges for the Virginia Mason Hospital Medical Center since 1985. Since 1989, he has also been a musculoskeletal oncology consultant for Group Health Cooperative and hospital privileges consultant for the Providence Hospital Medical Center and the Swedish Hospital Medical Center in Seattle. He additionally served at the Northshore Baptist Church on its board of overseers from 1992 to 2004, and has served on the Swedish Home Health Hospice Committee since 1996. Since 1990, Dr. Flugstad is further a member of the medical liaison committee of the Northwest Tissue Center and the orthopaedic implant selection committee of the Swedish Hospital, among others.

Prior to the start of his professional life, Dr. Flugstad pursued a formal education at the University of Washington, earning a Bachelor of Science in chemistry, summa cum laude, in 1976 and a Doctor of Medicine, with honors, in 1980. After completing his academic pursuits, he was certified by the National Board of Medical Examiners in 1981 and, in 1989, he became a diplomate of the American Academy of Orthopaedic Surgeons and was board-certified by the American Board of Orthopaedic Surgery, later becoming recertified in 2009 and 2017. Following this, Dr. Flugstad became a licensed physician in the state of Washington in 1991 and was recertified by the American Board of Orthopaedic Surgery in 2017.

Outside of his primary trade, Dr. Flugstad maintains involvement with numerous organizations related to his field, including the American Academy of Orthopaedic Surgery, the American Association of Tissue Banking, the Washington State Medical Society, the Christian Doctors Medical Society and the Musculoskeletal Tumor Society. Likewise, he is affiliated with myriad honor societies, including Alpha Omega Alpha, Phi Beta Kappa and Phi Lambda Upsilon. In light of his exceptional undertakings, Dr. Flugstad was annually named a Top Doctor by Seattle Magazine and Seattle Metropolitan Magazine from 2001 to 2018. Moreover, he was featured in the seventh edition of Who's Who in American Education, the eighth edition of Who's Who in Science and Engineering, and the 55th edition of Who's Who in America.

In his spare time, Dr. Flugstad has been known to enjoy skiing, boating, golfing, traveling, biking and participating in family activities. He is married to his loving wife of 44 years, Cheryl Ann Flugstad, with whom he has raised three wonderful sons: Matthew, a dentist; Nicholas, a plastic surgeon; and Jonathan, a business consultant at McKinsey. Dr. Flugstad is also a doting grandfather to eight beloved grandchildren, with a ninth on the way.

A Lifetime of Achievement in **Medicine & Health Care**

David William Furnas, MD

Professor Emeritus
University of California, Irvine
CORONA DEL MAR, CA UNITED STATES

With more than 45 years of professional experience, David William Furnas, MD, has been recognized as professor emeritus of the University of California, Irvine, since 2002. Prior to his retirement, he held a number of positions with the university, including clinical professor from 1980 to 2002, chief of plastic surgery from 1969 to 1999, professor from 1974 to 1980, and associate professor from 1969 to 1974. He was previously active with The University of Iowa as an associate and associate professor from 1968 to 1969, an assistant professor from 1966 to 1968, a senior resident and faculty associate from 1964 to 1965, and an associate from 1964 to 1968. Earlier in his career, Dr. Furnas was a registrar with the Glasgow Royal Infirmary from 1963 to 1964. He received a Doctor of Medicine from the University of California, San Francisco Medical Center, National Institute of Mental Health, and the Gorgas Hospital in the Panama Canal Zone in the Republic of Panama, among others.

Dr. Furnas was chief investigator on a National Institute of Health grant on the transplantation of forelimbs in puppies. He also authored and edited five textbooks. He is a member of the editorial boards for the Journal of Hand Surgery, the Annals of Plastic Surgery and the Journal of Craniofacial Surgery. He also acted as a reviewer for Plastic and Reconstructive Surgery. Additionally, he has dedicated his time and knowledge to various professorial roles, including at the Association of Plastic Surgeons of India and the Educational Foundation, where he was titled the Godrej visiting professor in Agra, India.

Prior to establishing himself as a trusted voice in the field, Dr. Furnas sought to expand his knowledge through the pursuit of a formal education. He first attended the University of California, Davis, for two years, then went on to the University of California, Berkeley, where he earned a Bachelor of Arts in 1952 and obtained a Doctor of Medicine in 1955 at the University of California, San Francisco. Subsequently, he became a diplomate of the Royal College of Surgeons of Canada as well as the American Board of Plastic Surgery in toxicology and pharmacology.

He then completed an internship at the University of California, San Francisco Medical Center from 1955 to 1956. Later, he served in the California Medical Corps of the U.S. Army Reserve of the state of California as a captain from 1957 to 1959 and later as a colonel from 1989 to the current time. He served as an associate professor of plastic surgery under professor and chairman of plastic surgery, Herbert Conway, a professor of surgery at the New York-Presbyterian/Weill Cornell Medical Center in Manhattan.

An active presence in the field, Dr. Furnas maintains memberships with organizations such as the American Medical Association, the California Medical Association, the Orange County Medical Association, the American Society of Plastic Surgeons and the American Society for Reconstructive Microsurgery. He is further associated with the Society of Head and Neck Surgeons, the American Cleft Palate-Craniofacial Association, the Society of University Surgeons, the Pacific Coast Surgical Association, and the International Society of Reconstructive Microsurgery. An honorary member of the British Association of Aesthetic Plastic Surgeons and the European Society of Plastic Surgeons, he was also involved through several leadership positions with the African Medical and Research Foundation. He is a member of the Royal Geographical Society of the United Kingdom as well.

Throughout his career, Dr. Furnas has been recognized for his contributions. The recipient of the Golden Apple Award, the Kaiser Permanente Award, and the Humanitarian Service Award for Black Medical Students from the University of California, Irvine, he was presented with the Senior Research Award by the Plastic Surgery Educational Foundation as well. He also received a certificate of special recognition from the U.S. Congress in 1998. Dr. Furnas has also been featured in multiple editions of Who's Who: Who's Who in Finance and Industry,

Who's Who in America, Who's Who in Medicine and Healthcare, Who's Who in Science and Engineering, Who's Who in the West and Who's Who in the World.

Dr. Furnas was born on April 1, 1931, in Caldwell, Idaho, to mother Esther Bradbury Hare Furnas and father John Doan Furnas. He later married Mary Lou Heatherly on February 11, 1956. Born in Harrisburg, Illinois, on September 25, 1933, she holds a Bachelor of Science from the University of Illinois Urbana-Champaign, and was a registered dietician at the University of California, San Francisco Medical Center. She was trained as a surgical technician at St. Joseph Hospital in Orange, California. Together they are the proud parents of three children named Heather Jean, MD, Brent David and Craig Jonathan. Moreover, he has three grandchildren named Jago, Siena and Diego Canales. His son-in-law Francisco "Paco," MD, is a graduate of Harvard University in Cambridge, Massachusetts.

A Lifetime of Achievement in **Medicine & Health Care**

Robert J. Gerety, MD, PhD

Chief Development Officer (Retired)
Medicine in Need
NATICK, MA UNITED STATES

With more than 40 years of industry experience to his credit, Robert J. Gerety, MD, PhD, served as the chief development officer of Medicine in Need in Cambridge, Massachusetts, from 2007 to 2012. He began his professional career as a research associate in the department of medical microbiology at Stanford University Medical School in 1969, remaining in this position for one year before completing an internship in pediatrics and residency at the school. Dr. Gerety then served separate one-year terms as a staff associate at the National Institutes of Health (NIH) Laboratory for Viral Immunology and the Food and Drug Administration (FDA) Bureau of Biologics before directing the FDA hepatitis branch in Bethesda, Maryland, from 1973 to 1984. Following this long tenure, he served the FDA as the associate director of medicine and science and the chief infectious diseases branch from 1984 to 1985.

Continuing on his professional path, Dr. Gerety accepted the posts of the executive director of virus and cell biology and the chief of clinical evaluation of vaccines and antiviral drugs at the Merck Research Laboratories in West Point, Pennsylvania, from 1985 to 1989. He subsequently served as the vice president, the president, and the chief executive officer for several companies in Massachusetts and California, including Biogen Inc., the Immulogic Pharmaceutical Corporation, ORAVAX, Cell Gate Inc., Inhale Therapeutic Systems and Nektar Therapeutics. In addition to these roles, Dr. Gerety chaired the product development team and taught medicine at the Thomas Jefferson Medical School in Philadelphia in 1985. A plenary lecturer at the International Symposium on Viral Hepatitis and Liver Disease in London in 1987, he also participated on the executive committee of the Nektar Business Review.

The medical director of the U.S. Public Health Service from 1970 to 1985, Dr. Gerety has celebrated many important career achievements. He significantly contributed to the development and/or approval of a vaccine against hepatitis A and B, many pediatric vaccines including Haemophilus influenza B and varicella, Biogen's beta interferon product to treat multiple sclerosis, also known as Avonex, and a direct thrombin inhibitor, more commonly known as Angiomax. Furthermore, Dr. Gerety holds several patents for the inactivation of a non-hepatitis A and B agent, a hepatitis B immune globulin used to inactivate the hepatitis B virus in injectable biological products, and the detection of non-hepatitis A and B associated antigen. Other patents to his credit include a heat treatment of a non-hepatitis A and B agent to prepare a vaccine, a hepatitis B core antigen vaccine made by recombinant DNA, a purified antigen from a non-hepatitis A and B causing factor, and a screening test for reverse transcriptase containing viruses in human blood.

Prior to the beginning of his illustrious career, Dr. Gerety pursued a formal education at Rutgers, The State University of New Jersey, earning a Bachelor of Arts, with special honors, in 1962. He then enrolled at Stanford University, obtaining a Master of Arts in 1966 and a Doctor of Philosophy in 1971. During this time, he graduated with a Doctor of Medicine from The George Washington University in 1970. Additionally, Dr. Gerety is a diplomate of the National Board of Medical Examiners.

A prolific writer, Dr. Gerety has contributed over 200 articles to scientific journals and held the post of an editor for "Non-A, Non-B Hepatitis" in 1981, "Hepatitis A" in 1984 and "Hepatitis B" in 1985. He was also an editorial board member for Biologicals between 1990 and 1994. A fellow of the Infectious Disease Society of America, Dr. Gerety remains aware of the latest trends in his field through his affiliations with the American Medical Association, the American Society for Microbiology, the American Academy of Pediatrics, and the American Association of Immunologists. Likewise, he has maintained his involvement with the William Beaumont Society, the Henry Rutgers Society, the International Association for Biological Standards, and the International Society of Interferon Research.

In light of his exceptional undertakings, Dr. Gerety received a Commendation Medal from the U.S. Public Health Service in 1975. A Henry Rutgers and NIH fellow, he also accepted an Outstanding Service Medal in 1982, the Patriotic Service Award from the U.S. Department of the Treasury in 1983, and the Distinguished Service Medal in 1985. Moreover, Dr. Gerety was selected for inclusion in several editions of Who's Who in America, Who's Who in Medicine and Healthcare, Who's Who in Science and Engineering, Who's Who in the East and Who's Who in the World.

A Lifetime of Achievement in **Medicine & Health Care**

In Memoriam

Robert E. Hammer, PhD

Psychologist (Retired)

FARIBAULT, MN UNITED STATES

Prior to his passing in 2021, Robert E. Hammer, PhD, led an illustrious career in psychology, emerging as a well-respected voice in the fields of special needs, research, counseling, behavioral management and consulting. After serving in the U.S. Air Force from 1950 to 1953, he obtained a job as a ballroom dancing teacher to supplement his GI Bill. While initially pursuing an education degree and then a business major, in order to accommodate his work schedule and the demands of administration, he switched his academic focus to psychology. In 1959, Dr. Hammer earned a Bachelor of Science, cum laude, in psychology from the University of Houston, achieving a Master of Arts in 1963. Following this accomplishment, he obtained a Doctor of Philosophy in special education administration from The University of Iowa in 1970.

Launching his career at the Houston Independent School District, Dr. Hammer found success as a teacher of students with intellectual disabilities and as a counselor and testing lab supervisor at the University of Houston counseling center from 1963 to 1965. During his time with the university, he developed protocols for the personnel departments to help lower staff turnover rates and provided corporate employee screening, including for NASA contractors. He continued his professional journey at the Mental Health Institute in Independence, Iowa, where he contributed in a variety of roles from 1965 to 1997.

Initially a licensed psychologist excelling in child psychology, Dr. Hammer was the director of the adolescent treatment unit and psychological services, and the acting director of the activity therapies department and the social services department. At the hospital, he served as preceptor and supervisor of physicians in psychiatric residency during their psychology department rotations and, furthermore, he served as a liaison between the department of human services, the department of corrections and the Attorney General's Office during the development of treatments for predatory sex offenders. Having amassed a wide breadth of expertise, he was subsequently active as a part-time consultant psychologist for Duffy Psychology Associates in Iowa City from 1997 until his official retirement in 2005. Simultaneously, he was also a private practice counseling and consultant psychologist, providing invaluable guidance and help to patients from 1974 to 2005.

To further connect people with mental health resources, Dr. Hammer was a domestic abuse and anger management specialist at Cedar House, Inc., an outpatient community-based mental health service located in Faribault, Minnesota, where he worked from 2006 to 2017. Well-regarded for his expertise, Dr. Hammer further contributed as the research director of the Division of Mental Health and Disability Services for the state of Iowa and as a substitute teacher for special education in multiple Minnesota school districts from 2006 to 2016.

Reflecting on a career that spanned nearly 60 years, Dr. Hammer loved developing programs and doing consulting work for populations of all ages. Highly respected for his industry prowess, he shared his knowledge through contributions to a number of professional journals. To remain up to date on changes in his field, Dr. Hammer maintained affiliation with several notable organizations, including the American Psychological Association, the National Association for Rural Mental Health, the American Society for Quality, the National Association of State Mental Health Program Directors, the Iowa Psychological Association and the Minnesota Psychological Association.

Beyond his primary professional affiliations, Dr. Hammer was active with the U.S. Chess Federation, the Barbershop Harmony Society, The American Legion, Disabled American Veterans and the Faribault Area Senior Center — of which he was a board member — among others. Spending 29 years as a voluntary fireman, he met the national standards to be certified as a "fire fighter one." He was also certified as a Red Cross water safety instructor and CPR and obstructed airway instructor.

He further contributed his leadership as a trustee of the North Grove Cemetery Association and as a member on a number of boards, including the Iowa Nursing Foundation and the District One Hospital. Dr. Hammer was additionally a talented singer, and had been involved with the men's gospel quartets at the First Baptist Church and the United Parish Church. He was active as an elder in both Presbyterian and Disciples churches, and as a lay speaker in the United Methodist Church.

Dr. Hammer was recognized on multiple occasions for his achievements. He has been featured in myriad honors publications, including Who's Who in America, Who's Who in Science and Engineering, Who's Who in Medicine and Healthcare, Who's Who in the Midwest and Who's Who in the World. Likewise, he was the recipient of the prestigious Albert Nelson Marquis Lifetime Achievement Award, presented to individuals who have demonstrated exceptional leadership and made a notable difference in their field.

A Lifetime of Achievement in **Medicine & Health Care**

Marjorie I. Hartog-Vander Aarde

Bureau Chief of Certification (Retired)
Quality Assurance Division
Montana Department of Public Health and Human Services

GREAT FALLS, MT UNITED STATES

With many years of experience to her credit, Marjorie I. Hartog-Vander Aarde is currently retired, having excelled as the bureau chief of certification in the quality assurance division for the Montana Department of Public Health and Human Services from 2000 to 2006. Previously, she worked as the chief executive officer and the chief operating officer for the Coalinga Regional Medical Center between 1997 and 2000. From 1993 to 1997, she was active as the director of human resources at the Montana Deaconess Medical Center. Moreover, Ms. Hartog-Vander Aarde further served the Montana Deaconess Medical Center as the vice president of human services from 1990 to 1993.

Prior to these appointments, Ms. Hartog-Vander Aarde held a number of positions at the Montana Deaconess Medical Center such as the assistant vice president, the assistant director of education, the critical care education coordinator, the head nurse in the critical care units, and a staff educator. Furthermore, she progressed from the post of a staff member to a charge nurse at the aforementioned medical center. She has also provided her wealth of knowledge as a consultant for the American Mission Hospital in Kuwait over the course of eight years. Ms. Hartog-Vander Aarde began her career as a staff nurse in the operating room of the emergency department at the Holland Hospital in Michigan.

A Lifetime of Achievement | **Marjorie I. Hartog-Vander Aarde**

Before embarking on her professional path, Ms. Hartog-Vander Aarde pursued an education at the Northwestern Classical Academy and Northwestern Junior College, completing coursework between 1956 and 1957. Earning a diploma from the Swedish Covenant Hospital in Chicago in 1960, she continued her academic efforts with a Bachelor of Science in nursing in 1975 at Montana State University. Following these accomplishments, she obtained a Master of Science in nursing at Texas Woman's University in 1982. Registered as a nurse in Montana, Michigan and Illinois, Ms. Hartog-Vander Aarde concluded her studies at the University of Colorado in 1990, graduating with a Master of Science in health care administration.

Beyond her responsibilities within the field, Ms. Hartog-Vander Aarde has participated in numerous endeavors outside of her professional circles. She contributed to the College of Nursing at Montana State University as an instructor. She additionally held the role of an executive board adviser for the Women's Guild of Christ at the Church on the Hill, a congregation of the Reformed Church in America. Ms. Hartog-Vander Aarde found success with the United Way of Cascade County as well, flourishing on the worship, education and music committee, the board of directors, the executive committee, the personnel committee, and the nominating committee, for which she was the chairperson.

In addition to her primary vocation, Ms. Hartog-Vander Aarde remains affiliated with various organizations in relation to her areas of expertise. She has maintained her involvement as a volunteer with the Family Promise of Great Falls. She was also associated with The Honor Society of Phi Kappa Phi and the Sigma Theta Tau International Honor Society of Nursing. Ms. Hartog-Vander Aarde was a member of the American Association of Critical-Care Nurses and a nominated member of the American College of Healthcare Executives.

In light of her exceptional undertakings, Ms. Hartog-Vander Aarde has accrued several accolades throughout her impressive career. Since 2008, she has been recognized as a fellow of the American College of Healthcare Executives. She was notably presented with the certificate of appreciation from the Montana Department of Health and Environmental Sciences and the Distinguished Service to Humankind Award from Northwestern College in 2015. Likewise, Ms. Hartog-Vander Aarde was incredibly proud of her tenure at Coalinga Medical Center, amassing a $1.7 million turnaround within a year without a single employee termination.

Initially desiring a career as a doctor but discovering nursing upon experiencing gender discrimination, Ms. Hartog-Vander Aarde was mentored by her mother, Gertrude, as well as her father-in-law, Bernard. Active in her church, for which she has performed in the choir and on the organ, she has remained resolute throughout her career, overcoming a tumor diagnosis on her knee with the support of her husband, Robert. For future medical professionals, Ms. Hartog-Vander Aarde suggests that they should remember that patients come first, including tending to their physical, emotional and spiritual well-being. She was notably profiled in the 73rd edition of Who's Who in America.

A Lifetime of Achievement in **Medicine & Health Care**

William Orris Houston, DDS

Oral and Maxillofacial Surgeon (Retired)

BOISE, ID UNITED STATES

Now retired from a distinguished career as an oral and maxillofacial surgeon in Boise, Idaho, William Orris Houston, DDS, spent 40 wonderful years in private practice until 2001. During his career, he was also affiliated as a staff member at the Saint Alphonsus Regional Medical Center in Boise from 1961 to 2001 and served as a board member on their foundation. He also found success as a staff member of St. Luke's Boise Medical Center. Furthermore, Dr. Houston contributed as a consultant in his field for the Boise Veterans Affairs Medical Center from 1961 to 2011.

With a lifelong interest in becoming a surgeon, Dr. Houston first studied at Saint Martin's University in Olympia, Washington, before acquiring a Doctor of Dental Surgery at Nebraska's Creighton University in 1955. Following his accomplishment, he notably served three years in the U.S. Air Force. Upon his honorable discharge, Dr. Houston completed postgraduate coursework at the University of Pennsylvania and the Geisinger Medical Center in Danville, Pennsylvania, and became a diplomate of the American Board of Oral and Maxillofacial Surgery.

An elected fellow of the American College of Dentists and the International College of Dentists, Dr. Houston has additionally been affiliated with several other professional organizations. Some of these include the American Dental Association, the Idaho State Dental Association, the American Association of Oral and Maxillofacial Surgeons and the Western Society of Oral and Maxillofacial Surgeons. Furthermore, Dr. Houston was elected as the charter president of the Idaho Society of

Oral and Maxillofacial Surgeons. Outside of his professional responsibilities, he has been involved in several civic organizations. He was active with his local Rotary Club and received a Paul Harris fellowship. Dr. Houston is also a 50-year member of the Knights of Columbus, and he served the Boise community as a member of the board of trustees for the Boise Independent School District from 1972 through 1982.

Throughout his career, Dr. Houston has been honored for his professional excellence and achievements in the field. In 1992, he received a St. George Medal from the American Cancer Society. Dr. Houston was also recognized as the Distinguished Citizen of the Week by the Idaho Statesman. He was later honored with the inaugural Distinguished Doctor of the Year Award from the St. Alphonsus Foundation in 2015. A celebrated Marquis listee, Dr. Houston has been featured in the 56th edition of Who's Who in America and the second and third editions of Who's Who in Medicine and Healthcare. He is also the recipient of the prestigious Albert Nelson Marquis Lifetime Achievement Award, presented to individuals who have demonstrated exceptional leadership and made notable contributions to their field.

Dr. Houston was born to William O. and Vera Loretta Hornback Houston, both early educators, on August 8, 1931, in Pueblo, Colorado. The early education he received at the Holy Cross Catholic Order of Nuns was instrumental in shaping his future, as the nuns increased his level of motivation and taught him at a young age to work hard to achieve his goals. Looking back on a career filled with accomplishments, Dr. Houston credits his success to his late wife Betty Jean, who provided him with unwavering support. Currently an Idaho resident, he is the proud father of two daughters, Kelly and Shelly. In his free time, Dr. Houston enjoys to go skiing, fishing and camping.

A Lifetime of Achievement in **Medicine & Health Care**

Nikzad S. Javid, DMD, MSc, MEd, FICD

Dentist

Professor Emeritus
University of Florida College of Dentistry
GAINESVILLE, FL UNITED STATES

Nikzad S. Javid, DMD, MSc, MEd, FICD, retired as professor emeritus in 2004 from the University of Florida College of Dentistry. From 2004 to 2014, he served as a prosthodontist and managing dentist in Fresno and Lancaster, California. He is a practicing dentist and prosthodontist of nearly five years who has been working for Cunning Dental Group in Montclair, California, since 2014. He is notably experienced with the "All-on-4" implant system. This system allows total oral rehabilitation with the placement of 12 fixed teeth on just four implants. This solution is an option for patients who already have a denture or have failing teeth and are looking for an alternative to standard dentures.

Previously, Dr. Javid taught as a professor at The Ohio State University. He taught in the College of Dentistry at the University of Florida for 23 years. During these years, he accepted the position of dean of the dental school at the University of Tehran in Iran and adviser of Ministry of Higher Education for nearly four years. The chancellor of the University of Tehran hired him and assigned him a task of correcting the College of Dentistry's financial disaster and upgrading dental education in Iran to the level of America's dental education. He was able to improve the level of income 10 times more than previous years. With this income, and collecting donations from private sources, Dr. Javid was able to change dental treatment units with modern equipment from Germany, America and Japan. He also attracted and hired more than 20 Iranian dentists specialized in the United States in the different specialties of dental education.

By changing the curriculum, Dr. Javid created 12 semesters of dental education for dental students, and with the help of the Ministry of Higher Education, he was able to provide scholarships for 19 dentists to specialize in the United States. Most important of all, he started seven advanced specialty programs. These specialists, after passing the specialty board, could be members of the academy of that specialty. Creation of specialty in dentistry happened for the first time in Iran by Dr. Javid. He was also the founder of a dental school at the University of Tabriz and named as the adviser and founder of the project.

Many Iranian dentists believe Dr. Javid revolutionized Iranian dentistry. During his career, he served as a consultant and lecturer in the field of prosthodontics and implants. He has authored several dentistry books as well, including "Stress Breaker in Partial Denture" in 1966 and "Cleft Palate Prosthetics" in 1968. He has also contributed numerous articles to professional journals and a chapter in a textbook named Essentials of Complete Denture Prosthodontics.

An elected fellow of the International College of Dentists and member of the International College of Prosthodontics, the American College of Prosthodontics and the American Academy of Maxillofacial Prosthetics, Dr. Javid is also a fellow of the Royal Society for Public Health in England and has served with various other organizations. He is a member and former director of the Iranian Dental Association and a member and former secretary-treasurer of the Iranian division of the International Association for Dental Research. Furthermore, Dr. Javid is a longtime member of the American Dental Association and the Iranian American Dental Association, where he was the recipient of an Honorary Lifetime Award in 2000.

The recipient of multiple teaching awards throughout his career, Dr. Javid was named eight times as Professor of the Year, Distinguished Professor of the Year and Outstanding Clinical Instructor of the Year, among others. He has also been included in approximately 30 editions of Who's Who, including Who's Who in America, Who's Who in Medicine and Healthcare, and Who's Who in the World.

Dr. Javid has held a Doctor of Dental Medicine from the University of Tehran since 1958, a Master of Science from The Ohio State University since 1971, and a Master of Education from the University of Florida since 1981. He has certifications in maxillofacial prosthetics as well as gnathology, which is the study of the masticatory system, or chewing. Dr. Javid notably served in the medical section of the Iranian Army. Married to Mahnaz Z. Javid, Dr. Javid has three children and three grandchildren. His wife is a retired educational counselor. His children work in the medical field; his daughter is graduating from the University of Florida College of Journalism and Communications, and one of his sons, Behrooz, is a prosthodontic dentist who has been utilizing the "All-on-4" implant system for more than 10 years. Dr. Javid's parents also both served in the medical field.

Federico R. Justiniani, MD, MACP

Internist (Retired)

Professor (Retired)
University of Miami
CORAL GABLES, FL UNITED STATES

With 55 years of experience in medicine to his credit, Federico R. Justiniani, MD, MACP, has become an authority in his industry. Retiring in 2010 as a professor at the University of Miami, he previously served as a program coordinator of the residency in internal medicine program and a director of medical education at Mount Sinai Medical Center in Miami Beach, Florida. During his tenure at the University of Miami, Dr. Justiniani excelled as an instructor of medicine from 1969 to 1972, an assistant professor from 1972 to 1982, an associate professor from 1982 to 1990 and a professor from 1990 until his retirement in 2010. He also spent time as a visiting professor and guest of honor for many congresses and courses in internal medicine at institutions throughout Latin America.

Prior to becoming a successful doctor and educator, Dr. Justiniani pursued higher education with a Bachelor of Science from De La Salle College in Havana, Cuba, in 1947 and a Doctor of Medicine from the University of Havana in 1954. He completed an internship and residency in internal medicine at the General Calixto García University Hospital between 1955 and 1961. Subsequently, he went on to fulfill an internship at St. Francis Hospital in Miami Beach in 1965 and a residency in internal medicine at Mount Sinai Medical Center between 1966 and 1969. He is additionally a diplomate of the American Board of Internal Medicine.

A Lifetime of Achievement | **Federico R. Justiniani**

A well-respected leader in his field, Dr. Justiniani has contributed to a number of publications in professional journals, including "Cocaine-associated rhabdomyolysis and hemoptysis mimicking pulmonary embolism" and "Massive rhabdomyolysis: A rare presentation of primary Vibrio vulnificus septicemia," both published in 1990. He was also notably the founder and director of the Annual Pan American Medical Seminar, sponsored by Mount Sinai Medical Center in Miami Beach. A five-day course on internal medicine, presented to Latin American physicians entirely in Spanish, the seminar was attended annually by roughly 200 people and ran for 30 consecutive years. Dr. Justiniani served as a lecturer for the Annual Pan American Medical Seminar every year since its inception.

In addition to his academic writing, Dr. Justiniani has also written extensively about his personal life in both English and Spanish. In 2015, he published "Memories, Memories," an illustrated autobiography detailing his family history, growing up in Cuba, his beginnings in medicine and immigrating to America. In 2016, he wrote his second book, a biography about his father, a judge in Havana who was involved in one of the biggest criminal cases in the country. The paperback book also details his father's childhood, education and family life. A prolific writer, Dr. Justiniani is currently working on his third book.

Outside of his professional responsibilities, Dr. Justiniani remains aware of the changes and advancements in his industry through relevant organizations. He is an active member of the Dade County Medical Association, the American College of Physicians and the National Association of Cuban American Educators. Previously, he was involved with the American Medical Association, the Florida Medical Association and several others. Currently an ex officio member of the executive committee for the National Association of Cuban American Educators, he also spent time in the roles of president, treasurer and vice treasurer.

Dr. Justiniani is scheduled to receive the National Association of Cuban American Educators' prestigious Educator of the Year Award in December 2019. In 2002, the American College of Physician named him a master, granting him the title MACP. Further recognized by the American Medical Association with a Physicians Recognition Award, he has also been featured in several editions of Who's Who in America, Who's Who in American Education, Who's Who in Medicine and Healthcare, Who's Who in Science and Engineering, Who's Who in the South and Southwest, and Who's Who in the World. Dr. Justiniani credits his success to his motivation and ability to work hard toward long and short-term goals.

Dr. Justiniani emigrated from Havana to the United States in 1964 and became a naturalized citizen in 1969. The son of Federico Luis and Margarita Longa Justiniani, he was happily married to the late Maria Suarez for more than 40 years. Apart from being a respected practitioner of medicine, he is a musician and composer of romantic Spanish songs. Dr. Justiniani is also an expert photographer, and his work can be viewed at his website, Justiniani Photography.

A Lifetime of Achievement in **Medicine & Health Care**

Alma Louise Young Kicklighter

Founder & Director (Retired)
Ghettreal Community Services
ST. PETERSBURG, FL UNITED STATES

Motivated by a desire to care for others, Alma Louise Young Kicklighter has dedicated her efforts toward nursing and public health education. Having completed nearly 60 years of professional service, she is currently retired, having thrived as the founder and the director of Ghettreal Community Services in St. Petersburg, Florida, from 2007 to 2016. In this role, Ms. Kicklighter taught about and tested for communicable diseases, providing invaluable education about HIV and AIDS to residents all over St. Petersburg. Her passion for preventive care has extended to area prisons, where she led a ministry that taught inmates about diseases.

Prior to founding Ghettreal Community Services, Ms. Kicklighter has found success in the medical field as a nurse, a profession she was inspired to pursue by her grandmother, who was a midwife. She flourished as a nursing teacher with the Pinellas County School Board in Largo, Florida, from 2000 to 2007 and a public health nurse supervisor with the Pinellas County Health Department from 1964 to 2000. Ms. Kicklighter additionally excelled in the department as the supervisor of epidemiology from 1979 to 1994 and as a public health nurse and a school consultant from 1959 to 1963.

Ms. Kicklighter initially pursued an education at the Florida Agricultural and Mechanical University in Tallahassee, where she earned a Bachelor of Science in nursing in 1958. Following this accomplishment, she continued her academic efforts, completing her postgraduate coursework at the University of South Florida in Tampa. Beginning her career while she was still a student, Ms. Kicklighter taught with the

A Lifetime of Achievement | **Alma Louise Young Kicklighter**

Columbia County School District in 1955 before accepting a position as a charge nurse in the medical, surgical and obstetrical wards of Mercy Hospital in St. Petersburg from 1958 to 1962.

A respected voice in her areas of expertise, Ms. Kicklighter is an active leader in her community. Recognized as Woman of the Year by the American Business Women's Association from 1978 to 1979, she is further affiliated with the American Nurses Association, the Florida Nurses Association, the Florida Public Health Association and the Staff Association of the Community Nursing Service. Furthermore, Ms. Kicklighter is associated with the RNs Club, Chi Eta Phi Sorority, Inc., and Delta Sigma Theta Sorority, Inc. Outside of her professional affiliations, Ms. Kicklighter has volunteered her time and resources to the St. Petersburg Citizens Council on Crime, as the past president of the Parent Teachers Association of Boca Ciega High School and as the St. Petersburg organizer of the Open Door Bible Study in 1980.

Throughout her career, Ms. Kicklighter has been celebrated for her civic and professional contributions. Notably, she received a plaque from the Equal Employment Committee in 1979. In light of all her accomplishments, Ms. Kicklighter has previously been featured in numerous honors publications, including multiple editions of Who's Who in American Nursing, Who's Who in Medicine and Healthcare, and Who's Who of American Women. In recognition of her outstanding achievements, Ms. Kicklighter has also been presented with the Albert Nelson Marquis Lifetime Achievement Award. She was notably profiled in the 73rd edition of Who's Who in America.

Ms. Kicklighter was born on January 12, 1933, in Live Oak, Florida, to Eugene and Mary Bell Ashley Young. She and her husband, Samuel Kicklighter, are the proud parents of four children, Carletta Ophelia, Harrell Alonzo, Samuel and June Renee. Their family also includes nine grandchildren and three great-grandchildren. Looking back on her exceptional career, Ms. Kicklighter attributes her success to a genuine desire to make others comfortable and happy. She has achieved many milestones, but considers being able to take care of patients who were suffering her greatest reward.

A Lifetime of Achievement in **Medicine & Health Care**

Mary Ann Chudy Levy, MD

Psychiatrist & Psychoanalyst

Clinical Professor of Psychiatry
Anschutz Medical Campus
University of Colorado

LAKEWOOD, CO UNITED STATES

Mary Ann Chudy Levy, MD, is a psychiatrist and psychoanalyst with more than 45 years of experience to her name. She has been a clinical professor of psychiatry at the Anschutz Medical Campus of the University of Colorado since 1972. She is a training and supervising analyst for the Denver Institute for Psychoanalysis, a nonprofit educational and research organization focused on increasing the quality of mental health education and treatment in Colorado. For excellence in her career, Dr. Levy was presented with a certificate of achievement from the University of Colorado in 2000 and has been cited in the 65th edition of Who's Who in America. A past president and current member of the Denver Psychoanalytic Society, Dr. Levy is also a long-standing member of the American Psychiatric Association and the American Psychoanalytic Association. She also regularly contributes articles to professional journals.

She has received multiple teaching awards during her long career and has given many presentations on different topics in a variety of settings. She received the Brandt Steele Award in 2001 for her community outreach efforts and teaching after she provided leadership in organizing the society to provide mental health services for the traumatized community after the Columbine High School shootings. Dr. Levy was responsible for organizing the response from the Denver Psychoanalytic Society to provide immediate emotional aid to the students and the school system from highly skilled volunteers, who continued their work with the community for over a year. She considers this to be the highlight of her career because of the positive impact she was able to have on the lives of others. She authored an article in the Journal of the American Psychoanalytic Association in February 2004 titled "Healing After Columbine: Reflections of Psychoanalytic Responders to Community Trauma" on her experience after the 1999 shooting.

Dr. Levy notes her interest in dealing with post-traumatic stress developed slowly. When Dr. Levy was very young, her father suffered a terrible illness and nearly died. He discharged himself from the hospital to treat himself at home when he was denied treatment by the hospital. Inspired by her father's strength and perseverance, but puzzled over his personality changes as a result of the trauma, Dr. Levy decided to pursue a career where she could help those who needed it. Notably, she earned a Doctor of Medicine from the University of Manitoba in Winnipeg in 1964, where she was one of only three women to graduate. She became certified in psychiatry through the University of Cincinnati in Ohio in 1968 and was later certified in psychoanalysis through the Denver Institute of Psychoanalysis in 1981, where she was the first woman to graduate from the program.

Dr. Levy is the daughter of Joseph Chudy and Sonia Rosedeba. She is widowed, following the death of her husband, Alan B. Levy, MD, to pancreatic cancer, after 43 years of happy marriage. Moreover, she has two grandchildren. In her free time, she enjoys taking poetry and writing classes. Reflecting on her career, she finds her profession to be very rewarding. She is particularly proud of working with patients to help them resolve their issues, which allows them to live happy lives. She recently traveled to Japan to give presentations on chronic trauma and help people move on from real-life events. Looking to the future, she plans to continue occasionally teaching at the University of Colorado Health Sciences Center.

A Lifetime of Achievement in **Medicine & Health Care**

Deepak K. Malhotra, MD, PhD

Nephrologist

Professor
College of Medicine and Life Sciences
The University of Toledo

TOLEDO, OH UNITED STATES

With more than three decades of professional experience to his credit, Deepak K. Malhotra, MD, PhD, has been active as a professor with the College of Medicine and Life Sciences at The University of Toledo in Ohio since 2003. He initially joined the university as an associate professor from 1997 to 2003. Before accepting this position, he previously served as an assistant professor at The University of New Mexico in Albuquerque from 1991 to 1997. Commencing his career in 1988, Dr. Malhotra spent three years as a fellow in renal diseases at the University of Colorado Health Sciences Center in Denver.

Dr. Malhotra further cultivated his skills through work with the Raymond G. Murphy VA Medical Center in New Mexico, Davita-Southland Dialysis in Ohio, and The University of Toledo Medical Center, where he is currently active as the chief of the division of nephrology and as a transplant nephrologist on the kidney transplant team. He has served on several institutional review boards for The University of Toledo as well. With his research expertise in molecular mechanisms of renal injury and mechanisms of cardiac dysfunction in renal disease, Dr. Malhotra is a regular contributor of articles to professional journals.

Prior to embarking on his career, Dr. Malhotra sought to expand his knowledge through the pursuit of a formal education. He attended Case

Western Reserve University in Cleveland and earned a Bachelor of Science in 1978. He continued his studies at the same esteemed academic institution and obtained a Doctor of Philosophy in 1984. Ultimately, he achieved a Doctor of Medicine upon graduating from the school in 1985. Following these accomplishments, he completed a residency in internal medicine at the Cleveland Clinic Foundation from 1985 to 1988. Subsequently, he became certified in internal medicine in 1989 and in nephrology in 1994. Reflecting on his academic years, he is grateful for the mentorship he received from his teachers throughout elementary school, college and medical school.

An active presence in his field, Dr. Malhotra maintains affiliation with several prestigious professional organizations, including the International Society of Nephrology, the American Society of Nephrology, and the American Society of Transplant Physicians International, now the American Society of Transplantation. He is further associated with the American College of Physicians, the American Chemical Society, and the American Association for the Advancement of Science.

Dr. Malhotra has been the recipient of a number of honors for his many achievements throughout the years. A grantee of the American Heart Association in 1994, he has most notably been honored with an endowed professorship in nephrology by The University of Toledo in 2014. In light of his accomplishments, he has previously been selected for inclusion in such honors publications as the 53rd, 55th, 57th and 73rd editions of Who's Who in America. He was also featured in the second and fourth editions of Who's Who in Medicine and Healthcare as well as the fourth and eighth editions of Who's Who in Science and Engineering.

Dr. Malhotra was born on March 7, 1956, in Amritsar, India, to mother Bimla Vijh Malhotra and father Om Parkash. He immigrated to the United States in 1958 at 2 years old. He later married Judith Maria Konfal on April 20, 1989, and together, they are the parents of two children named Nathan and Kristin. In his free time, he enjoys woodworking, practicing photography, and doing various home and automotive repairs.

A Lifetime of Achievement in **Medicine & Health Care**

Jacqueline C. Mashin

Registered Nurse (Retired)

SILVER SPRING, MD UNITED STATES

Driven by a constant curiosity, Jacqueline C. Mashin has enjoyed a rich and wide-ranging career spanning more than 45 years. Her desire to pursue nursing as a profession began when she was 11 years old and was realized at the MedStar Washington Hospital Center, the largest private hospital in Washington, D.C. Ms. Mashin thrived as a registered nurse at the hospital for more than 15 years, treating a diverse population of patients with dignity and respect until her retirement in 2009.

Prior to her role in the hospital, Ms. Mashin thrived in various government positions. She worked for the U.S. Department of the Interior in Washington, D.C., as a consultant from 1989 to 1993, and as the director of international communications and a special assistant to the commissioner from 1986 to 1989. Ms. Mashin previously found success as a special assistant to the deputy director at the Office of Management and Budget from 1983 to 1986, a confidential assistant to the director at the Office of Personnel Management from 1981 to 1983, and an assistant regional political director at the Office of the President-Elect from 1980 to 1981. Additionally, Ms. Mashin served as the vice president and a partnership owner of the Discount Linen Store in Silver Spring, Maryland, from 1979 to 1981 and as the executive assistant to the assistant executive director of the Air Force Association from 1974 to 1979. Prior to these appointments, she began her career as an administrative assistant with the Central Intelligence Agency from 1963 to 1966 and an assistant to the managing director of the Aerospace Education Foundation from 1966 to 1974.

A respected voice in her areas of interest, Ms. Mashin has been an active leader in her community. She is a member of the White House Volunteers, the Air Force Association, the U.S. Capitol Historical Society, and the Auxiliary Salvation Army. The president of the Layhill Civic Association, Ms. Mashin held the posts of the state chair of Maryland's Reagan Youth Delegation as well as the state treasurer and the office manager of the Reagan-Bush Headquarters of Maryland. Further, she has served as the chairman for the Maryland Federation of Republican Women on numerous occasions, in addition to volunteering her talents as a coordinator for the Maryland Republican Party in 1999. Ms. Mashin has additionally been affiliated with the Women's Committee National Symphony Orchestra, the Rock Creek Women's Republican Club, the Montgomery County Republican Party, the Wheaton Redevelopment Program, and the Maryland Board of Health and Mental Hygiene.

Ms. Mashin earned a Bachelor of Science in business administration and psychology from the University of Maryland in 1984 and a Bachelor of Science in nursing from The Catholic University of America in 1993. Additionally, she is a certified Realtor. For her many accomplishments and contributions to the field, Ms. Mashin has been celebrated in multiple editions of Who's Who in America, Who's Who in Medicine and Healthcare, Who's Who in Science and Engineering, Who's Who in the East, Who's Who in the World, and Who's Who of American Women.

Ms. Mashin was born in Chicago, Illinois, on May 11, 1941, to William Hermann and Ann Cook. She has two children, Joseph Glenn and Alison Robin, and is the proud grandmother of two grandchildren. In her free time, she enjoys golf and horseback riding. An avid traveler, Ms. Mashin is spending her retirement relaxing and traveling to her home in Argentina.

A Lifetime of Achievement in **Medicine & Health Care**

Sandra T. McBride, RN, MSN

Psychiatric Nurse
Western Mental Health Institute
RAMER, TN UNITED STATES

With nearly 35 years of experience to her credit, Sandra T. McBride RN, MSN, has helped countless patients and established herself as a leader in the field of psychiatric nursing. As a mental health nurse, she specializes in caring for individuals of all ages who experience mental distress. In addition to working with patients, she collaborates with their families, communities and other health care providers to provide well-rounded, comprehensive treatment. Ms. McBride has spent the majority of her career as a staff nurse at the Western Mental Health Institute, a psychiatric hospital run by the Tennessee Department of Mental Health and Substance Abuse Services that serves more than 20 counties throughout western Tennessee. Thriving in this role since 1992, she helps offer valuable, personalized services to patients, giving them the tools they need to successfully return to their communities.

Prior to this position, Ms. McBride worked briefly as a staff nurse at the U.S. Medical Center for Federal Prisoners in Springfield, Missouri, as well as took on a leadership role as the shift supervisor for the Tennessee Department of Correction at the West Tennessee High Security Facility in Ripley. Earlier in her career, she gained valuable hands-on experience as a staff nurse at Bolivar Community Hospital from 1988 to 1990. She launched her career as a nurse supervisor at Alcorn County Care, Inc., located in Corinth, Mississippi, in 1985 to 1987.

A Lifetime of Achievement | Sandra T. McBride

Ms. McBride has been certified as a licensed practical nurse since 1981 and is registered to practice in Mississippi and Tennessee. Prior to embarking on her professional path, she attended Shelby State Community College, now known as Southwest Tennessee Community College, where she earned an Associate of Applied Science in 1983. Following this accomplishment, she subsequently attended the University of North Alabama in Florence, completing the necessary coursework to obtain a Bachelor of Science in nursing in 1987. Ms. McBride continued her education at Union University in Jackson, Tennessee, where she received a Master of Science in nursing in 2001.

While now an esteemed medical professional, as a child, Ms. McBride often found herself in the patient's seat due to ear infections. The wonderful care she received inspired her at a young age to pursue a career in nursing, a profession she has found success in throughout the course of more than three decades because of her unwavering compassion. She has set herself apart from others in the industry by her ability to treat her patients and colleagues with respect and is motivated by a desire to see all those in her care become well and live healthy lives outside of the hospital. Despite facing challenges and those who doubted her ability, Ms. McBride has continually demonstrated professional aptitude and knowledge in her field. For her leadership, dedication and many accomplishments in her industry, she has been recognized among Marquis Who's Who Top Nurses.

Ms. McBride was born on September 13, 1958, in Corinth, Mississippi, to Clarence R. and Alice Ingram T., who were constant sources of encouragement. Currently a Tennessee resident, she has enjoyed many years of marriage to her husband, David, and together, they are the proud parents of three children, Angela, Aaron and Madison. Looking toward the future, Ms. McBride is hoping to retire and spend more time enjoying her hobbies, which include reading and foster parenting.

A Lifetime of Achievement in **Medicine & Health Care**

Don Lewis McCord, MD

Surgeon (Retired)

DALLAS, TX UNITED STATES

Don Lewis McCord, MD, is a retired general surgeon who formerly spent 30 years in private practice in Dallas. Retiring in 2016, he has helped countless patients during his nearly six decades in medicine. Some of Dr. McCord's noteworthy positions included serving as a section chief of general surgery at Medical City Dallas Hospital from 1990 to 1992 and an assistant chief of surgery at the U.S. Naval Hospital in Corpus Christi, Texas, from 1959 to 1962. He was also affiliated with a group practice in Clifton, Texas, from 1974 to 1986, and was previously in private practice in Hamilton, Texas, a role in which he thrived from 1962 to 1974. Additionally, Dr. McCord lent his expertise as a consultant in surgery at Hamilton General Hospital from 1988 to 1996 and De Leon Hospital in Texas. A portion of his tenure included being the only surgeon in the county, meaning he was always on call and working long hours.

Dr. McCord's interest in medicine began at a young age, as there were several physicians in his life while he grew up. The idea of becoming a doctor appealed to him, and after graduating from high school, he attended Abilene Christian University in Texas, receiving a Bachelor of Science in chemistry in 1949. Continuing his studies, he achieved a Doctor of Medicine, with honors, at the University of Texas in 1953. Additional educational pursuits include the completion of an internship at University Hospital in Ann Arbor, Michigan, and a residency in surgery at the U.S. Naval Hospital, located in Oakland, California.

A Lifetime of Achievement | Don Lewis McCord

Dr. McCord is board-certified by the American Board of Surgery. He notably served eight years in the U.S. Navy between 1954 and 1962, serving as the lieutenant commander. During this time, Dr. McCord spent a year at sea riding a destroyer, an experience that allowed him a different perspective on the problems that can arise on a naval ship and provided him the privilege of assisting many sick patients.

Well-regarded as an expert in his field, Dr. McCord is a fellow of the American College of Surgeons. To keep current on changes in his industry, he maintains affiliation with the American Medical Association, the Texas Medical Association, the Dallas County Medical Society, the Dallas Society of General Surgeons, Alpha Omega Alpha and the Flying Physicians Association, a group of physician-pilots who promote safety, education and human interest projects. In recognition of his many contributions to the field and his professional excellence, Dr. McCord has been featured in multiple editions of Who's Who in America, including the 73rd edition, Who's Who in Medicine and Healthcare, Who's Who in Science and Engineering, Who's Who in the World, and the 26th edition of Who's Who in the South and Southwest. He is also the recipient of the prestigious Albert Nelson Marquis Lifetime Achievement Award, presented to individuals who have demonstrated leadership and success in their industry.

Dr. McCord was born on August 25, 1929, in Vernon, Texas, to Thomas Garfield and Dola Cavender McCord. He married Barbara Gayle McCord on March 4, 1972, and together, the couple are the proud parents of Daniel Linsey, the late Elizabeth Ann, Melissa Ann Mares and Nicole Pryor, as well as the doting grandparents of one granddaughter. Residing in Dallas, in his free time, Dr. McCord enjoys helping others safely explore the skies as a flight instructor.

A Lifetime of Achievement in **Medicine & Health Care**

James Minard, PhD

Psychologist (Retired)

PORTLAND, OR UNITED STATES

J ames Minard, PhD, received a master's degree from the University of Washington in Seattle, with Irwin Sarason as his adviser, and a Doctor of Philosophy from the University of Colorado Boulder, with Michael Wertheimer as his adviser. The advisers had complementary orientations. His papers showed that often-ignored features of the environment can have significant effects and that emotions affect stimulus detection as well as purely verbal response preferences. With Daniel Bailey, he developed a computer program others also used. One paper showed high RFT error scores indicated repression, but also that moderate scores suggested vigilance. An evolutionary explanation was proposed.

In 1962 and 1963, he was an instructor in a doctoral program at the State University of New York Downstate Medical Center. It taught sciences to practicing physicians and sponsored a meeting of the world's sleep researchers. At the meeting, they decided to incorporate. Their yearly meetings provided the best information on the developing science.

He reviewed for "Science Books." From 1963 to 1971, he moved from instructor to assistant professor at the University of Pittsburgh. There, he and Donald Coleman, MD, showed newborn infants were the ideal subjects for much sleep research. They made a widely used film on infant sleep. "CBS Special Reports" and "PBS Innovation" filmed his work. The nation's narcoleptic organization invited him to lecture or hold a workshop at three yearly meetings. Others requested more.

Stimulated by results with the sleep of the newborn of schizophrenics, Dr. Minard moved to the Maryland Psychiatric Research Center in 1971, where access to those infants was superior. Results were promising. In 1973, he went to the New Jersey University of Medicine and Dentistry as an associate professor of pediatrics and psychiatry. He visited sleep centers across the country and presented papers in the United States, Mexico, Belgium and Germany.

Most years, Dr. Minard and his associates held one to four continuing medical education programs on sleep and its disorders, some funded. Yearly, he taught sleep science to the first-year medical students in six groups, allowing study of teaching methods. A popular method proved inferior though students liked it best. Prior to retirement in 1994, he completed the training and examinations required for certification in school psychology.

Featured in the 73rd edition of Who's Who in America, Dr. Minard is the son of Glen and Irene Minard, both educators. In 1959, he married Nancy Croyle, a librarian, editor and educator. They have two daughters, Annette and Kate, as well as four grandchildren: Devin and Patience Minard-King and Jackson and Samantha Thomas. His forthcoming book is "Sleep, Dreams and Shaolin Zen."

A Lifetime of Achievement in **Medicine & Health Care**

Georg Noren, MD, PhD

Neurosurgeon

Professor Emeritus
Brown University

BRISTOL, RI UNITED STATES

After accruing nearly four decades of clinical experience, Georg Noren, MD, PhD, retired from his position as a neurosurgeon and medical director of the Gamma Knife Center at Rhode Island Hospital in 2011, having been on staff since 1994. Earlier in his career, between 1979 and 1994, he was a staff member of the department of neurosurgery at the Karolinska Hospital in Stockholm, Sweden. His teaching as full professor of the residents at the Warren Alpert Medical School of Brown University in Providence, Rhode Island, included hands-on training in gamma knife radiosurgery. After retirement, he was appointed professor emeritus and continues to be involved in research focusing on gamma knife radiosurgery for the treatment of obsessive-compulsive disorder.

During his high school years in Sweden, Dr. Noren decided to become a doctor, the first in his family. After graduating from high school, he was admitted to the Karolinska Institute, the medical school in Stockholm, in 1963. He graduated with a Doctor of Medicine in 1971 and was licensed to practice medicine. During some early moonlighting, he had the opportunity to assist professor Herbert Olivecrona, the father of Swedish neurosurgery, in the operating room. Finding this specialty fascinating, he started his residency in neurosurgery at the Karolinska Institute in 1972 and became a specialist in neurosurgery in 1979.

At the time, the head of the department of neurosurgery at Karolinska Hospital, the main teaching hospital of the Karolinska Institute, was professor Lars Leksell. As a resident, Dr. Noren had become involved with Dr. Leksell's research, which mainly focused on the stereotactic system and gamma knife radiosurgery, a technique invented by Dr. Leksell. Dr. Noren was given the project of developing that technique for the treatment of a certain type of intracranial tumor, vestibular schwannoma, also known as acoustic neuroma. This resulted in his doctoral thesis, which he publicly defended at the Karolinska Institute in 1982. He was able to define the technique and subsequently, in 1989, the optimal minimum single dose of radiation, 12-13 Gy, for the effective treatment of these benign tumors. Since then, this practice has been accepted and used worldwide.

Dr. Noren is a member of the following prestigious organizations: the Congress of Neurological Surgeons, the World Society for Stereotactic and Functional Neurosurgery, the American Society for Stereotactic and Functional Neurosurgery, the International Stereotactic Radiosurgery Society and the Swedish Neurosurgical Society. In light of his excellence in the field of neurosurgery, he was awarded the Mahaley Clinical Research Award by the American Association of Neurological Surgeons in 1993 and the Pioneers in Radiosurgery Award at the 13th International Meeting of the Leksell Gamma Knife Society in Seoul, South Korea, in 2006. He was previously selected for inclusion in the 60th edition of Who's Who in America, published in 2005.

At age 14, Dr. Noren started playing the oboe and later the oboe d'amore, the English horn and, more recently, the bass oboe. As for his contribution to the community, he is a member of the Fall River Symphony Orchestra, the Ocean State Pops Orchestra and the Great Woods Symphony Orchestra at Wheaton College in Norton, Massachusetts.

Dr. Noren was born on October 24, 1943, in Stockholm, Sweden, to mother Elsa Norén and father Daniel Norén. He has been married to María del Pilar Avendaño Altimira, a Spanish neurosurgeon, since 2003. He has five adult children from two earlier marriages. Dr. Noren is a citizen of both the United States and Sweden.

A Lifetime of Achievement in **Medicine & Health Care**

Charles S. O'Mara, MD, MBA

Associate Vice Chancellor for Clinical Affairs
University of Mississippi Medical Center

RIDGELAND, MS UNITED STATES

Charles S. O'Mara, MD, MBA, is a vascular surgeon and health care administrative leader with over 40 years of professional experience to his credit. He is considered an authority in his field, and he currently serves as the associate vice chancellor for clinical affairs and a professor of surgery at the University of Mississippi Medical Center. He took on these roles at the university after decades of professional success in private practice as a highly rated and recognized vascular surgeon. Dr. O'Mara's current role at a prominent state-supported academic medical center allows him the opportunity "to give back in a way that has real meaning for many people, beyond just one patient at a time."

Dr. O'Mara began his career path at the University of Mississippi in Oxford, where he received a Bachelor of Science in 1970 and was awarded the Taylor Medal in Biology. He then graduated, summa cum laude, with a Doctor of Medicine from the Tulane University School of Medicine in 1973. From 1973 to 1979, he continued his medical training at The Johns Hopkins Hospital in Baltimore, where he was initially a surgical intern, then a resident, and finally the chief resident in surgery. Finishing a vascular surgery fellowship at Northwestern University in Chicago in 1980, Dr. O'Mara then returned to Johns Hopkins as an assistant professor of surgery, a staff surgeon, and the director of the Non-Invasive Vascular Laboratory.

In 1982, Dr. O'Mara returned to his home state of Mississippi and joined the Cardiovascular Surgical Clinic in Jackson, where he was a partner and a surgeon for the next 26 years. From 2008 to 2013, Dr. O'Mara was a vascular surgeon for Baptist Cardiovascular Surgery. In 2011, he completed a Master of Business Administration at The University of Texas at Dallas. In 2013, Dr. O'Mara started at the University of Mississippi Medical Center as a professor of surgery. He was the first to accept the role of a special adviser to the vice chancellor, Dr. James Keeton, and soon thereafter, he was appointed to his current position of an associate vice chancellor for clinical affairs.

In addition to his practice of surgery, Dr. O'Mara has contributed over 60 papers and articles to professional journals, as well as chapters to medical textbooks. At the University of Mississippi Medical Center, he has served in a leadership role for numerous important institutional initiatives. He has formerly participated on the board of directors for the Mississippi Baptist Health System, the Mississippi Baptist Medical Center, the MIND Center, and the Leukemia Society of Jackson, Mississippi. He has held the post as a president of the Southern Surgeons Club, the Callender Society, the Mississippi Chapter of the American College of Surgeons, and the Tulane Chapter of Alpha Omega Alpha. Dr. O'Mara is a fellow of the American College of Surgeons and a distinguished fellow of the Society for Vascular Surgery.

Over the course of his career, Dr. O'Mara has been honored and recognized for his work in numerous ways. He led the program that was ranked #1 in Mississippi for Vascular Surgery consecutively between 2011 and 2013, and he was the inaugural recipient of the Patient First Award at the Mississippi Baptist Medical Center. He is a four-time winner of the Richard M. Nowell Award from the Callender Society, having been presented with this accolade in 1990, 1992, 1996 and 2000, and while at Tulane Medical School, he received the Roche Award, the Dr. Walter G. Unglaub Memorial Award, the Oscar Creech Award and the Isador Dyer Memorial Prize. Moreover, Dr. O'Mara has been featured in multiple editions of Who's Who in America.

Dr. O'Mara and his wife, Susan, presently live in Ridgeland, Mississippi. The proud parents of four children, they have welcomed nine wonderful grandchildren into their family. Dr. O'Mara's personal interests include various outdoor activities, the visual arts, traveling and activities with his grandchildren.

A Lifetime of Achievement in **Medicine & Health Care**

Stephen M. Pastores, MD

Critical Care Physician
Memorial Sloan Kettering Cancer Center
NEW YORK, NY UNITED STATES

A critical care physician and intensivist with more than two decades of experience, Stephen M. Pastores, MD, is highly regarded for his expertise, professionalism and integrity. His noteworthy achievements include in-depth research on septic shock, the use and costs of critical care medicine, intensivist workforce, and the use of corticosteroids in critical illnesses. Today, Dr. Pastores finds success as the vice chair of education for the department of anesthesiology and the fellowship program director for critical care medicine at Memorial Sloan Kettering Cancer Center in New York City.

At the same time, Dr. Pastores is a professor of medicine and anesthesiology for Weill Cornell Medicine, a role that he has held since 2007. His previous roles have included that of an attending critical care physician with Memorial Sloan Kettering Cancer Center since 1999; the assistant director for the surgical ICU and the director of emergency services for the James J. Peters VA Medical Center in New York City; the attending critical care physician for Montefiore Medical Center; and the house officer for the department of surgery at the Cabrini Medical Center. In addition to these prominent roles, Dr. Pastores is well-regarded for his contributions as a member of the board of regents for the Society of Critical Care Medicine and a member of the editorial boards of Critical Care Medicine, CHEST, and the Journal of Critical Care. He was appointed the chancellor of the American College of Critical Care Medicine in 2019.

Dr. Pastores completed a Bachelor of Science from the University of Santo Tomas in Manila, Philippines, in 1978. Thereafter, he attended Lyceum-Northwestern University in Dagupan City, Philippines, where he achieved a Doctor of Medicine in 1982. In preparation for a career in medicine, Dr. Pastores completed a residency in internal medicine with the Metropolitan Hospital Center in New York City. After completing this three-year program, he became a chief resident for the center for one year.

Dr. Pastores then went on to complete a fellowship in pulmonary and critical care medicine at NYU Langone Medical Center in 1992 and a fellowship in critical care medicine at Mount Sinai Medical Center in New York City in 1993. His successes have led to him earning a Safar Global Partner Award from the Society of Critical Care Medicine, several Distinguished Service Awards from the Society of Critical Care Medicine and the title of Castle Connolly Top Doctor for five consecutive years. Furthermore, Dr. Pastores has been named to several honors publications, including multiple editions of Who's Who in America, Who's Who in Medicine and Healthcare, Who's Who in Science and Engineering, Who's Who in the East and Who's Who in the World. Highly esteemed in his field, he is also the recipient of the prestigious Albert Nelson Marquis Lifetime Achievement Award.

Dr. Pastores' career has blended clinical practice, research and education in a way that has allowed him to establish himself as a leader in his field. He has authored more than 200 peer-reviewed articles and book chapters and has shared his knowledge through lectures all over the world. With myriad accomplishments to his credit, he credits the institutions to where he did his postgraduate training and mentors he had along the way as crucial to his success. Dr. Pastores is a master of the American College of Physicians and a fellow of the American College of Critical Care Medicine and the American College of Chest Physicians (CHEST).

A Lifetime of Achievement in **Medicine & Health Care**

Stuart P. Pegg, MD

Professor Emeritus
The University of Queensland
BRISBANE, QUEENSLAND, AUSTRALIA

Stuart P. Pegg, MD, has been a professor emeritus at The University of Queensland in Brisbane, Australia, since 2001. On campus for five years, he specialized in teaching burn surgery methods to students. As a physician, Dr. Pegg held the role of director of surgery at the Royal Brisbane and Women's Hospital and surgical supervisor for 51 years beginning in June 1967. He previously held the role of surgical registrar at the Royal Berkshire Hospital in England from 1965 to 1966 and the Princess Alexandra Hospital in Brisbane from 1962 to 1964, and was a medical superintendent at Julia Creek in Queensland from 1958 to 1961. Throughout his career, Dr. Pegg has contributed chapters to several books. He has also authored or co-authored articles in numerous professional journals, including the Journal of Surgery, the Journal of Burn Care and Rehabilitation, and Intensive Care Medicine.

An honorary lifetime member of the International Society for Burn Injuries and a fellow of the Royal Australasian College of Surgeons, Dr. Pegg is also affiliated as a member of multiple other prestigious organizations. He is further affiliated with the Royal College of Surgeons, the Royal Australasian College of Medical Administrators, the Australian Medical Association, the American Burn Association and the South African Burn Society. An honorary member of The American Association for the Surgery of Trauma, he has spent time as the president of the Churchill Fellows Association of Queensland as well as the Australian and New Zealand Burn Association. Additionally, he was the vice president of the International Society for Burn Injuries from 1990 to 1998.

Honored in 2018 with The University of Queensland Vice-Chancellor's Alumni Excellence Award, Dr. Pegg previously received a 2003 G. Whitaker International Burn Prize in Sicily and received a Decorated Order of Australia. The major burns center in Queensland is at the Royal Brisbane and Women's Hospital and in 2003 was named the Professor Stuart Pegg Adult Burns Centre. The burns center at the Queensland Children's Hospital also bears his name. He has previously been selected for inclusion in many honors publications, including the second and third editions of Who's Who in Medicine and Healthcare, the fourth and eighth editions of Who's Who in Science and Engineering, the 73rd edition of Who's Who in America, and the 19th through 21st editions of Who's Who in the World.

Prior to establishing himself as a trusted voice in the field, Dr. Pegg sought to expand his knowledge through the pursuit of a formal education. He first attended The University of Queensland in Brisbane, where he earned a Bachelor of Medicine and a Bachelor of Science, both with honors, in 1956. One year later, he completed an internship in the Royal Brisbane and Women's Hospital. He paused his academics to serve as a major in the Australian Army Reserve from 1981 to 1987. Subsequently, he became registered in general and pediatric surgery by the Medical Board of Australia in 1964. He continued his studies at the same esteemed academic institution and ultimately achieved a Doctor of Medicine in 2006.

Dr. Pegg was born on March 13, 1932, in Gladstone, Queensland, to mother Eileen Standish Pegg and father Harry Thomas Pegg. He later married Gwenda Mary Smart on December 12, 1958, and together, they are the proud parents of three children named Michael Stuart, Susan Mary and David Andrew. In his free time, he enjoys working in his garden. He especially loves growing orchids.

A Lifetime of Achievement in **Medicine & Health Care**

Suzanne Zein-Eldin Powell, MD

Professor
Texas A&M University

Professor
Weill Cornell Medical College

HOUSTON, TX UNITED STATES

Suzanne Zein-Eldin Powell, MD, has enjoyed a rich and varied career in pathology, but believes the most rewarding aspect of her profession is the number of people she has trained and watched develop into pathologists of their own. She has served as the vice chair for education in the pathology department at Houston Methodist Hospital since 2009, in addition to sharing her knowledge with aspiring doctors as a professor of pathology and laboratory medicine at Texas A&M University and Weill Cornell Medical College. In addition to her teaching duties, Dr. Powell manages the pathology residency program at Houston Methodist Hospital and works as a consulting neuropathologist for the Harris County Medical Examiner's Office. She has also found success as an attending pathologist at the Texas Children's Hospital, Ben Taub Hospital and Houston Methodist Hospital.

While Dr. Powell has built a prolific career as a pathology professor, her early days were spent in a classroom of a different kind. After obtaining a Bachelor of Education in music education from Drake University in Iowa, she taught music for several years. However, influenced by her mother, a violinist and chemist, as well as her father, a psychiatrist, Dr. Powell decided to pursue medicine. In her free time, she still enjoys playing the piano and clarinet, as well as traveling and needlepoint. Since 2012, Dr. Powell has also lent her talents to the Houston Children's Chorus, and she credits her success to her passion for education and an internal drive to see projects through to completion.

Dr. Powell's knowledge has been an invaluable resource for numerous medical publications. She has participated on the editorial boards of Ultrastructural Pathology, Academic Pathology, Archives of Pathology and Laboratory Medicine, Advances in Anatomic Pathology, and Modern Pathology, in addition to acting as a reviewer for scientific journals. Dr. Powell has also written and contributed more than 100 articles to professional journals as well as chapters for medical books.

Well-respected among her peers, Dr. Powell plays an active part in the medical community. She holds a position on The American Board of Pathology's neuropathology test committee, on the board of directors for the United States and Canadian Academy of Pathologists, and as a chair for both the American Association of Neuropathologists and the College of American Pathologists. She is also a member of the Congress of Neurological Surgeons, the American Society of Clinical Pathologists, the Texas Society of Pathologists, the Texas Medical Association, the American Association of Neuropathologists and the American Medical Association, as well as Alpha Omega Alpha, a medical honor society. On a more local level, she provides her expertise to the Houston Neurological Society, the Harris County Medical Society, the Florida Society of Pathologists and the Florida Medical Association.

Dr. Powell's medical education began at West Virginia University, where she completed coursework and earned a Doctor of Medicine at the School of Medicine in 1988. She continued her training in the University of Florida Health Science Center's department of pathology, where she pursued her residency in anatomic and clinical pathology from 1989 to 1993, acting as resident liaison in the department of pathology from 1991 to 1993. Her success propelled her to the position of the chief resident of pathology in 1992, which was followed by a fellowship in neuropathology at the University of Florida College of Medicine from 1993 to 1995.

Dr. Powell's accomplishments in the medical field and classroom have been widely recognized. She was the recipient of the Outstanding Service Award and Resident Advocate Award from the College of American Pathologists in 2017 and 2011, respectively. Likewise, she has been honored among the Best Doctors in America from 2010 to 2012. In addition, Dr. Powell has been presented with the Outstanding Teacher

Award in Neuropathology from the University of Florida Health Center, in addition to being designated by Houston Methodist Hospital as an endowed chair in pathology education. Accepting a grant from the Baylor College of Medicine as a result of her Alzheimer's disease research, she was celebrated by the same academic institute as the Teacher of the Year in Anatomic Pathology for the 2000-2001 school year. Furthermore, Dr. Powell obtained the College of American Pathologists Foundation Scholars Program Fellowship Award.

A Lifetime of Achievement in **Medicine & Health Care**

Carol J. Schneider, PhD

Clinical Psychologist & Director
Colorado Center for Biobehavioral Health

ERIE, CO UNITED STATES

With several decades of professional experience to her name, Carol J. Schneider, PhD, has enjoyed a successful career as a psychologist. Since 1976, she has been the clinical psychologist and longtime director of the Colorado Center for Biobehavioral Health in Boulder. Prior to her tenure at the center, she spent 17 years as the founder and director of biofeedback at the Stress Management Clinic at the University of Colorado Student Health Service between 1970 and 1987. She also spent 45 years in academia at the School of Medicine at the University of Colorado as an assistant clinical professor in the department of psychiatry from 1970 to 2015 and as an adjunct professor in the department of psychology at the University of Colorado Boulder from 1972 to 1990.

Early, Dr. Schneider acted as a research psychologist for the Battered Child Treatment Project in Adams County, Colorado, for two years beginning in 1968. She also consulted at Michigan State University in the department of human development and family studies on the development of a questionnaire that is still in use today. Chapters in "The Battered Child" and "Helping the Battered Child and His Family" describe this work.

Outside of her primary endeavors, Dr. Schneider has contributed multiple articles to scholarly journals throughout her career. She has co-authored such works as "Bolder Bodies: A Physical and Emotional Wellness Guidebook" in 1977 and "The Challenge of Chronic Muscle

Pain" in 1989. She also wrote "Foundations of Biofeedback Practice" with Edgar S. Wilson, MD, in 1985. She and Dr. Wilson co-presented workshops on biofeedback and stress management all over the United States as well as in Europe, China and India for 10 years.

An active presence in the field, Dr. Schneider maintains memberships with numerous organizations, including the International Society for the Studies of Subtle Energies and Energy Medicine, where she served on the board of directors in 1990 and as president in 1994. She is a former member of the American Psychological Association and a former board member and president of the Association of Applied Psychophysiology and Biofeedback. In addition, she was on the board of directors of Boulder International Chamber Players from 1984 to 1990.

Prior to establishing herself as a trusted voice in the field of biofeedback, Dr. Schneider sought to expand her knowledge through the pursuit of a formal education at a number of esteemed academic institutions over the years. She first attended the University of Wisconsin and earned a Bachelor of Science in 1960. She continued her studies at the University of Colorado, where she obtained a Doctor of Philosophy in psychology in 1965.

In light of her professional achievements, Dr. Schneider has gained recognition in the form of many awards and accolades. The recipient of the James T. Lewis Prize in creative writing from the University of Wisconsin in 1957, she also received a grant from the Creative Research Council at the School of Medicine at the University of Colorado several years later in 1967. In light of all her accomplishments, she has been cited in the 63rd and 73rd editions of Who's Who in America and the 18th and 27th editions of Who's Who of American Women. Reflecting on her career, she is grateful for the mentorship of Ray Helfer, Harry Harlow, Johan Stoyva, Tom Budzynski, Charles Strobel and Alan Schore.

Dr. Schneider was born on May 5, 1938, in Appleton, Wisconsin, to mother Lorraine Hendrickson Joyce and father Richard Coppel Joyce. Married to Robert Schneider from 1963 to 1970, she had two children with her husband named Kayt and Jay. Moreover, they have four grandchildren named Keane, JR and twin girls Pace and Lane. In her free time, she enjoys participating in such activities as reading, hiking and playing classical piano.

A Lifetime of Achievement in **Medicine & Health Care**

Martin William Schwarze, DO

Clinical Professor of Medicine
Division of Cardiology
Saint Louis University Hospital
CHESTERFIELD, MO UNITED STATES

Supported by more than 40 years of practiced experience in medicine and academia, Martin William Schwarze, DO, rose through the academic ranks from instructor of medicine to assistant clinical professor before becoming a full clinical professor of medicine within the division of cardiology at Saint Louis University Hospital in 1999. He has also held the title of clinical professor at the Kirksville College of Osteopathic Medicine at the A.T. Still University since 1988. He has had the opportunity to teach medical students at both the Saint Louis University School of Medicine and the New England College of Osteopathic Medicine. Excelling in his role as the past director of noninvasive cardiology at Barnes-Jewish St. Peter's Hospital in the 1980s, he also served for a period of time as director of the cardiac rehabilitation program and ultimately as chief of staff. He also was the chief of cardiology at St. Luke's Des Peres Hospital from the early 1980s until 2009.

Alongside his primary care responsibilities, Dr. Schwarze served the Normandy Osteopathic Hospitals as the treasurer of the department of internal medicine for two years, and later became the chairman of the department of internal medicine, the director of the cardiac rehabilitation program and was the chief of staff at Barnes-Jewish St. Peter's Hospital. Likewise, he served St. Peter's Community Hospital as the director of the medical intensive care unit in the early 1980s. A contributor to a myriad of articles to professional journals, he recently published a paper on a case report of gabapentin-induced cardiomyopathy. He also authored a paper titled "Statins in the Elderly" in clinical geriatrics in 2004, as well as "Myocarditis" in the Journal of the American Osteopathic Association in 1990. Dr. Schwarze presented "Treatment of acute myocarditis with venous suppression therapy" at the American College of Cardiology Scientific Session in 1984. In addition, he had a fortunate opportunity to chair a number of national cardiology meetings throughout the country as well as sharing local programs for over 30 years on topics in the field of cardiology. Lastly, he has participated in a large number of pharmaceutical research studies on cardiovascular drugs, especially in the field of lipidology.

To prepare for his career, Dr. Schwarze pursued a formal education at Saint Louis University, where he received a Bachelor of Science in chemistry in 1968. Going on to earn a Doctor of Osteopathic Medicine from the Kirksville College of Osteopathic Medicine at A.T. Still University in 1973, he was licensed to practice medicine in the state of Missouri the following year. Board-certified in internal medicine cardiology, he is a diplomate of the American Osteopathic Board of Internal Medicine and the subspecialty of cardiovascular disease. Likewise, Dr. Schwarze is a fellow of the American College of Cardiology and a master fellow of the American College of Osteopathic Internists.

A former member of the board of governors of the Missouri chapter of the American College of Cardiology, Dr. Schwarze has maintained affiliation with numerous organizations throughout his career. He is a past present of the St. Louis chapter of the American Heart Association, as well as serving in other capacities during his 30 years on the board. He is also past present, vice president and secretary-treasurer of the St. Louis Cardiac Club. Earlier in his career, he sat on the patient care committee of St. Peter's Community Hospital and the future planning committee of the Normandy Osteopathic Hospitals. He is a member of the American Osteopathic Association, a past member of the St. Louis Metropolitan Medical Society, and a life member of the Missouri Association of Osteopathic Physicians and Surgeons.

In light of his exceptional undertakings, Dr. Schwarze has received numerous accolades and honors. Named Educator of the Year by the Normandy Osteopathic Hospitals in 1987, he received the Arthur E. Strauss Lifetime Achievement Award and the Hugh D. McCulloch Medical Honoree Award from the American Heart Association in 2003 and 2008, respectively. Listed in Best Doctors in St. Louis since 2008, he was presented with a Super Hero Award from the Barnes-Jewish St. Peters & Progress West Foundation in 2015 and was also named Educator of the Year in 1999, 2000 and 2006. He was notably profiled in the 73rd edition of Who's Who in America.

His hobbies include horticulture, model trains and antique cars. He has been married for 46 years and has two children, Julie and Brian, and two grandchildren, Mason and Lillie.

A Lifetime of Achievement in **Medicine & Health Care**

In Memoriam

Estherina Shems, MD

Child Psychiatrist (Retired)

WYNNEWOOD, PA UNITED STATES

D efying cultural expectations, Estherina Shems, MD, achieved her childhood dreams and established herself as a leading child psychiatrist. With more than four decades of experience to her credit, she retired in 2002 after a long and successful career in mental health care and academia, which she began as a child psychiatry affiliate at the Child Study Center in Philadelphia in 1961. In addition, Dr. Shems taught in the department of psychiatry at the Perelman School of Medicine at the University of Pennsylvania and the Irving Schwartz Institute for Children and Youth. She also held various staff and administrative positions at the Philadelphia Psychiatric Center and the Irving Schwartz Institute for Children and Youth. A former clinical associate in psychiatry at the University of Pennsylvania, Dr. Shems served as a consultant to early intervention programs for the Community Council for MH/MR, Inc., also in Philadelphia.

Throughout her career, Dr. Shems accepted numerous consulting and teaching posts in the field, including as an invited lecturer at the Institute of Pediatrics in the Chinese Academy of Medical Sciences in Beijing, China. On a local level, she excelled as the vice chairman of the Trust Fund of the Alumnae/Alumni Association of the Medical College of Pennsylvania. Furthermore, Dr. Shems served on the executive board of the Alumnae/Alumni Association of the Woman's Medical College.

An elected fellow of the American Psychiatric Association, Dr. Shems was previously active as the vice president of the Medical Women's International Association for North America, where she held several other roles. She further contributed to the American Medical Women's

Association, where she was a lifetime member, and a former member of the board of directors and of several committees and task forces. Prior to her passing, Dr. Shems was affiliated with the Psychiatric Physicians of Pennsylvania, the Philadelphia Psychiatric Society, The College of Physicians of Philadelphia and several honor societies.

The recipient of a Lifetime Achievement Award from the Virginia Foundation of Independent Colleges in 2002, Dr. Shems was presented with a Richard H. Thornton Award for Excellence in 1995 and the T. Gibson Hobbs Outstanding Alumni Award from the University of Lynchburg in 1969, among other accolades. She was also selected for inclusion in over two dozen editions of Who's Who, including Who's Who in America, Who's Who in Medicine and Healthcare, and Who's Who in the World. For her professional accomplishments, Dr. Shems was named the recipient of the prestigious Albert Nelson Marquis Lifetime Achievement Award. She was notably profiled in the 73rd edition of Who's Who in America. In 2009, she was additionally celebrated with an honorary doctorate in science from the University of Lynchburg.

Born in Tel Aviv, Israel, Dr. Shems grew up in a culture that considered females as less than first class. Knowing early on that she wanted to become a doctor, she never strayed from her passion for wanting to be more than she was told she could become. Relocating to the United States in 1950, she soon after earned a Bachelor of Science, cum laude, at the University of Lynchburg in 1954 and a Doctor of Medicine at the Woman's Medical College of Pennsylvania in 1958. She subsequently completed an internship at Lankenau Medical Center and a fellowship in adult psychiatry at the University of Pennsylvania between 1960 and 1963. Dr. Shems decided to focus her studies on psychiatry, as she believed that it was one of the fields of medicine that concentrated on the whole person.

Dr. Shems enjoyed 40 years of marriage to accomplished neurologist Donald Lewis Schotland, MD, before his passing in 2015. She was the proud daughter of Aaron Shems and Rachel Yehuda Shems. In her free time, Dr. Shems enjoyed traveling, photography, music and reading.

A Lifetime of Achievement in **Medicine & Health Care**

Stanley S. Siegelman, MD

Professor Emeritus of Radiology
Johns Hopkins University
BALTIMORE, MD UNITED STATES

Stanley S. Siegelman, MD, is a professor emeritus of radiology who taught at Johns Hopkins University in Baltimore, Maryland, for more than 40 years, beginning in 1973 and becoming emeritus in 2017. During his tenure, he was the director of diagnostic radiology at the university from 1973 to 1986. He formerly spent three years as an associate professor of radiology at the Albert Einstein College of Medicine in the Bronx, New York, from 1970 to 1973. Dr. Siegelman remains an active member of the clinical teaching faculty, and his priceless insights from an illustrious career continue to inspire residents on a daily basis.

An accomplished author in his field, Dr. Siegelman co-authored "The Lungs in Systemic Disease" in 1969 and "Computed Tomography of the Thorax" in 1984. Involved with a number of professional journals as well, he served as a consultant for the Journal of Urology between 1975 and 1983 and the editor of Radiology from 1986 to 1998. Furthermore, Dr. Siegelman has notably contributed more than 350 papers to various publications, as well as several monographs.

A founding member of the International Skeletal Society and the North American Society for Cardiovascular Radiology, Dr. Siegelman is also a fellow of the American College of Radiology. He is a member and the past president of the Society of Computed Body Tomography & Magnetic Resonance and a longtime member of the Association of University Radiologists, the Radiological Society of North America, where he received several magna cum laude awards between 1975 and 1981, the American Roentgen Ray Society and the Alpha Omega Alpha Honor Medical Society. Furthermore, Dr. Siegelman is an honorary member of the European Society of Radiology, the French Society of Radiology and the German Radiological Society.

Honored with multiple awards throughout his career, Dr. Siegelman has received Gold Medals from the Radiological Society of North America, the American Roentgen Ray Society and the Society of Computed Body Tomography & Magnetic Resonance. He was also the recipient of a Grubbe Memorial Award from the Chicago Radiological Society and a Harry Z. Mullins Teaching Award from the State University of New York Downstate Medical Center. In light of all his accomplishments, Dr. Siegelman has been cited in the 44th, 46th and 73rd editions of Who's Who in America. He has also been recognized with the Albert Nelson Marquis Lifetime Achievement Award.

Prior to embarking on his career, Dr. Siegelman received a Bachelor of Arts at Cornell University in Ithaca, New York, in 1953 and a Doctor of Medicine at the State University of New York in New York City in 1957. Joining the U.S. Army while he was in medical school, he interned at the Walter Reed Army Medical Center in Washington, D.C., from 1957 to 1958. Following these accomplishments, he spent three years at Fort Meade Hospital from 1958 to 1961. While he was there, he enjoyed many different positions and had the opportunity to explore the importance of radiology. Dr. Siegelman went on to complete a residency in radiology at the Montefiore Medical Center in New York City from 1961 to 1964 and became certified by the American Board of Radiology in 1965.

Dr. Siegelman was born on June 18, 1932, to Charles and Kate Siegelman in New York City. He was married to Doris Franklin Siegelman for nearly 40 years until her passing in 1995. Dr. Siegelman is the father of two sons, Bryan and Evan as well as five grandchildren, Daniel, Mathew, Dylan, Ariel and Joshua. He is also a great-grandfather to Nora Grace. He married Merle Ann Siegelman in 1999 and has three stepchildren, Jonathan, Sharon and Betty, as well as five stepgrandchildren, David, Elizabeth, Benjamin, Alexander and Adin. In his free time, Dr. Siegelman enjoys sports and reading.

A Lifetime of Achievement in **Medicine & Health Care**

Helene Tanous, MD

Radiologist (Retired)

HOUSTON, TX UNITED STATES

R etired from her full-time career as an assistant professor at The University of Texas Medical Branch at Galveston in 1990 after teaching on campus for three years, Helene Tanous, MD, was also a private practice diagnostic radiologist in Largo, Florida, between 1974 and 1980. In previous years, she worked as the director of medical student education in diagnostic radiology at the Ben Taub Hospital in Houston and a private practice physician specializing in radiology in Los Angeles. In academia, she excelled as an assistant professor of diagnostic radiology at the Baylor College of Medicine in Houston, an instructor of radiology at the Keck School of Medicine of the University of Southern California in Los Angeles and an assistant professor and the director of medical student education in diagnostic radiology at The University of Texas Medical Branch at Galveston. The chief of radiology at the Diagnostic Clinic in Largo, Florida, Dr. Tanous continued to teach as an assistant professor of diagnostic radiology as well as director of medical student education at the Morsani College of Medicine at the University of South Florida in 1980.

A member, past president and member of the board of directors of the L'Alliance Francaise of Tampa since 1984, Dr. Tanous is also a member and former member of the board of directors for the Federation of Alliances Francaises USA. She is further affiliated with the American Medical Association, the Southern Medical Association since 1974, and the Houston Committee on Foreign Relations as well. Within her community, Dr. Tanous has contributed a great deal of her time as the president and founder of Child Advocates Inc. between 1977 and 1985 and on the board of directors of the Florida Endowment for the Humanities from 1979 to 1983. Dr. Tanous has been a member of the Order of Salvador with the Salvador Dalí Museum in St. Petersburg, Florida, since 1992.

In 1988, Dr. Tanous was presented with a Knighthood-Chevalier des Palmes Academiques from the government of France at a luncheon in her honor. Likewise, she was presented with a Distinguished Alumni Award, the Golden Dome, from Marymount College of Fordham University. Moreover, Dr. Tanous has since been featured in more than 25 editions of Who's Who in America, Who's Who in the South and Southwest, Who's Who in the World and Who's Who of American Women. Dr. Tanous has made appearances on television as well as given many interviews to newspapers.

Earning a Bachelor of Arts at Marymount College in Tarrytown, New York, in 1961, Dr. Tanous soon after obtained a Doctor of Medicine at the University of Texas in Galveston in 1967. She later completed an internship at the County Hospital in Los Angeles, followed by residencies in radiology at Cedars-Sinai Medical Center in Los Angeles and the USC University Hospital in Los Angeles. Furthermore, Dr. Tanous is a diplomate of the American Board of Radiology.

A Lifetime of Achievement in **Medicine & Health Care**

Robert Lee Warren, DDS, MAGD

Dentist

Adjunct Professor of Operative Dentistry
School of Dentistry
University of North Carolina

BOONE, NC UNITED STATES

Supported by more than five decades of practiced experience in dentistry and education, Robert Lee Warren, DDS, MAGD, has served in a general dentistry practice in his hometown of Boone, North Carolina, since 1972. Alongside this endeavor, he has been an adjunct professor of operative dentistry at the School of Dentistry at the University of North Carolina since 2014, a post he also held from 1972 to 1979 and which he considers his civic duty. Dr. Warren began his career in 1965 as an instructor in biology and chemistry at West Wilkes High School in North Wilkesboro, a role he held for three years. He later served as an adjunct assistant professor of fixed prosthodontics at the School of Dentistry at the University of North Carolina from 1982 to 1984 and of operative dentistry from 1987 to 1997.

Dr. Warren's interest in dentistry was sparked in high school, and to prepare for his career, he pursued a formal education at Appalachian State University in Boone, where he received a Bachelor of Science in biology in 1965. He later completed postgraduate coursework at Duke University in Durham, North Carolina, in 1967 before transferring to the University of North Carolina, where he received a Doctor of Dental Surgery in 1972. With myriad accomplishments to his credit, Dr. Warren credits his Christian faith and a desire to pass on the knowledge his professors gave him as the motivators to his success.

A former member of the Watauga County Board of Education for more than 16 years, Dr. Warren maintains affiliation with several organizations in an effort to remain abreast of changes in the field. A leader in his industry, he formerly sat on the board of directors of the Academy of General Dentistry, and he holds membership with the American Dental Association, the North Carolina Dental Society, the University of North Carolina Alumni Association, where he is a lifetime member, and the Tar Heel Dental Study Club, where he serves as president. Dr. Warren is also a member of Delta Sigma Delta and the Boone Area Chamber of Commerce.

As a testament to his success, Dr. Warren received a mastership from the Academy of General Dentistry in 1997. In addition, the North Carolina Dental Society honored him with a Distinguished Service Award, and he was a National Science Foundation fellow of Duke University and the International College of Dentists. Impressively, he was also featured in the 20th edition of Who's Who in the South and Southwest, the 22nd edition of Who's Who in the World and the 58th through 61st editions of Who's Who in America. Furthermore, he is the recipient of the Albert Nelson Marquis Lifetime Achievement Award, presented to individuals who have demonstrated extraordinary leadership and made major accomplishments in their field.

Dr. Warren was born on July 20, 1943, in Boone, North Carolina, to John Floyd and Maude Elizabeth Roark Warren. He and his wife, Deborah Andrews, who served as the office manager of his practice, are the proud parents of three children, Blaire, Robert II and Debin, who have all pursued dentistry or dental hygiene careers. In his free time, Dr. Warren enjoys spending time with his family, sports cars, show horses and keeping up to date with the North Carolina Tar Heels basketball team.

A Lifetime of Achievement in **Medicine & Health Care**

Devora Whiting, RN

Nurse Case Manager (Retired)
Department of OB-GYN Maternal and Child Health
Division of Clinical Quality Systems
University of Maryland Medical System

BALTIMORE, MD UNITED STATES

After accruing 45 years of practiced industry experience, Devora Whiting, RN, retired from her work as a nurse case manager for the department of OB-GYN maternal and child health in the division of clinical quality systems of the University of Maryland Medical System in Baltimore, where she previously served as a community liaison nurse of discharge planning from 1973 to 1996. In the mid-1960s, she began in the field as a head nurse with Provident Hospital from 1965 to 1972, as a staff nurse in the pediatric intensive care unit at The Johns Hopkins Hospital from 1966 to 1968, and a community health nurse in the department of public health from 1968 to 1973.

Outside of her primary endeavors, Ms. Whiting gained valuable expertise working as a bereavement counselor with Resolve Through Sharing. She also worked as a discharge planning nurse for the high-risk mothers and babies in OB-GYN and oncology. She initially became interested in the field because when she was a little girl, there was an African American community health nurse in her neighborhood, Ms. Brown, who inspired her a lot. Reflecting on her career, she is also grateful for the mentorship and inspiration she received from Ms. Brooks and many of her teachers.

Prior to establishing herself as a trusted voice in the field, Ms. Whiting sought to expand her knowledge through the pursuit of a formal education at a number of esteemed academic institutions.

A Lifetime of Achievement | Devora Whiting

Because segregation was in place at this time, she had to attend an all-Black school. She first attended the Helene Fuld School of Nursing at Provident Hospital in Baltimore, where she completed coursework and earned a diploma in 1965. She considers her time spent there to be an influential time in her life. She continued her studies at Morgan State University and ultimately achieved a Bachelor of Science upon graduating in 1972. Subsequently, she became certified as a registered nurse in the state of Maryland.

An active presence in the field, Ms. Whiting has maintained memberships with such prestigious organizations as the Maryland Perinatal Association and the Maryland High Risk Infant Council. She is further associated with Chi Eta Sigma and Sigma Theta Tau. With the American Nurses Association, she is a certified community health nurse. Additionally, her membership as a diamond life member of Zeta Phi Beta earned her a Zeta of the Year Award in 1996.

In light of her professional accomplishments, Ms. Whiting has gained recognition in the form of various awards and accolades. She is especially proud of earning the Harriet Tubman Award, as well as being named Outstanding Community Health Nurse by the state of Maryland in 1985. In acknowledgement of her service to Provident Hospital, she was the recipient of the Provident Hospital Alumni 50 Year Medallion. Though these are impressive, she considers one of the highlights of her career to be receiving letters from the mothers with whom she worked.

Ms. Whiting was born on June 14, 1942, in Baltimore, Maryland, to mother Naomi Battle Jenkins and father Arthur B. Jenkins Sr. She married George W. Whiting on July 1, 1973, and together, they had two children named Tarik and Camile. George passed away in 2013. Looking toward the future, Ms. Whiting intends to continue enjoying her retirement.

A Lifetime of Achievement in **Medicine & Health Care**

Lou Ann Wieand, PhD

Professor Emeritus
Humboldt State University
SAN FRANCISCO, CA UNITED STATES

Lou Ann Wieand, PhD, is a celebrated leader in the field of psychology. Backed by more than three decades of professional experience, she holds the title of professor emeritus with Humboldt State University (HSU) in Arcata, California, and has helmed a private psychotherapy practice since 1989. She initially began working for HSU in 1982, holding the role of a professor until her retirement in 2014. Earlier in her career, Dr. Wieand cultivated her expertise as a research associate with the VA Loma Linda Healthcare System from 1980 to 1982 and as an assistant professor at the University of Redlands in California from 1979 to 1980.

Previously, Dr. Wieand earned a Bachelor of Arts in psychology from Manchester University in Indiana in 1963 and a Master of Arts in clinical psychology from Ball State University in Indiana in 1977. Concluding her studies with a Doctor of Philosophy in social personality psychology from the University of California, Riverside, in 1983, she was licensed as a psychologist in the state of California in 1989. Dr. Wieand has provided guidance to individuals transitioning into retirement and has begun offering couples therapy workshops through her practice. Furthermore, she has contributed her skills as a therapist for the San Francisco AIDS Foundation and as a board member for several substance abuse agencies. Dr. Wieand has also shared her expertise overseas, presenting in Cape Town, South Africa, in 2004 and teaching students psychology at the University of Macau in China as part of the Fulbright scholar teaching experience in 2006. Another highlight in her illustrious career was conducting research for four months as a scholar at the University of Oxford in England.

Dr. Wieand was motivated to pursue adult psychology and couples therapy after observing how much she enjoyed interactions between older populations. She has had a number of supportive mentors along her path to success. She credits Dr. Donald Colburn, a professor at Manchester University, for providing indispensable guidance and care through her academic years. Additionally, Robert Singer, a University of California, Riverside, professor, was very helpful in defining the social personality psychology work she was completing.

Alongside her primary endeavors, Dr. Wieand has authored a number of book chapters and has participated in research presentations at a variety of conferences on regional, national and international levels. Furthermore, she has excelled as a consultant for various mental health agencies and supervised marriage and family therapy interns in her private practice. In order to remain up to date with developments in her field, Dr. Wieand maintains affiliation with the American Psychological Association, the Society for the Psychological Study of Social Issues, the Association for Psychological Science, and the Society for the Scientific Study of Sexuality. She is also a member of the Commonwealth Club of San Francisco, a nonprofit organization that holds forums on public issues.

For her professional efforts, Dr. Wieand has received a number of accolades. Notably, she was inducted into the National Honor Society for excellence in her field. Additionally, she was selected for inclusion in multiple editions of Who's Who in America and recognized with the Albert Nelson Marquis Lifetime Achievement Award. Dr. Wieand is the mother of three children, Joel Brent, Brian Randal and Darin Michael, as well as the grandmother of four grandchildren, Daniel, David, Marissa and Harrison. A talented vocalist, she enjoys singing in regional and national chorales in her free time, traveling to competitions and shows overseas.

A Lifetime of Achievement in **Religion / Spiritual Services**

Rev. Rayann Burnham Cummings

Minister & Teacher
Mayflower Congregational United Church of Christ
FORT MYERS, FL UNITED STATES

With more than 40 years of industry experience to her credit, Rev. Rayann Burnham Cummings has been retired since 2004, having excelled as a minister and a teacher for the Mayflower Congregational United Church of Christ in Sioux City, Iowa, from 1998 to 2003. Prior to this appointment, she held the same positions for the First Federated Church of the United Church of Christ and the Unitarian Universalist Association in Beverly, Massachusetts, from 1989 to 1998 and the Deansboro Congregational United Church of Christ in Deansboro, New York, from 1984 to 1989. A distance education teacher of biblical studies at Empire State College, a part of the State University of New York system, from 1989 to 1992, she previously served as a teacher of English and social studies at Nathan Hale-Ray High School from 1968 to 1981. Ms. Cummings began her career as a teacher of social studies at Lyman Moore Middle School from 1960 to 1961.

Before embarking on her professional path, Ms. Cummings pursued an education at Gorham State College, now known as the University of Southern Maine, earning a Bachelor of Science in 1960. She continued her academic efforts with a Master of Arts in 1972 at the University of Connecticut. Following these accomplishments with postgraduate coursework at Sacred Heart University from 1977 to 1980, she graduated from the Andover Newton Theological School with a Master of Divinity in 1984. Ms. Cummings concluded her studies with postgraduate coursework at the Hartford Seminary from 1991 to 1994.

Beyond her responsibilities within the field, Ms. Cummings has participated in numerous endeavors outside of her professional circles.

A host for many exchange students for Rotary International between 1972 and 1981, she contributed to the Sioux City chapter of the American Interprofessional Institute as a member from 1999 to 2004, the board of directors for the Mary J. Treglia Community House as a program chair from 2001 to 2003, and the Republican Town Committee of East Hampton, Connecticut, as an active member from 1978 to 1980. A member and a secretary of the board of directors for Calico Kids Preschool from 2000 to 2003, she held the roles of a tutor for Literacy Volunteers of America since 2004 and a tutor for English as a second language for the Sioux City Community School District from 2000 to 2003. Ms. Cummings found success with her additional spiritual works, providing her skills and resources to the Ecumenical Discussion Group of Sioux City as the founder and a facilitator from 2002 to 2003, the Spiritual Leadership Coalition of Siouxland as a member and the chair from 2000 to 2003, the Interfaith Council of Beverly, Massachusetts, as the founder and a member from 1995 to 1998, and the New York State Council of Churches as a member of the board of directors from 1985 to 1989.

Furthermore, Ms. Cummings remains affiliated with various organizations in relation to her areas of expertise. From 2005 to 2012, she had maintained her involvement with the Friendship Force of Southwest Florida as a member of the board of directors for the public section. She was also active with the Girl Scouts of the United States of America as a lifetime member and a trainer for their Connecticut Trails Council from 1974 to 1979. Moreover, Ms. Cummings was a member of PEO International, the Lee County Genealogical Society, and the Fort Myers Congregational United Church of Christ.

In light of her exceptional undertakings, Ms. Cummings has accrued several accolades throughout her impressive career. She was notably presented with an award from the Beverly Citizen in 1996. Likewise, Ms. Cummings was selected for inclusion in the 63rd edition of Who's Who in America and multiple editions of Who's Who of American Women.

Working as a teacher at the time of her divorce, Ms. Cummings considered a career as a chaplain for youth offenders for her local police department before becoming inspired to enter the seminary. Motivating others to join the seminary as a result of her exemplary religious services, she is incredibly proud of having raised her children as a single mother and witnessing their subsequent success. Looking toward the future, Ms. Cummings hopes to continue enjoying her retirement and finding comfort in her faith.

A Lifetime of Achievement in **Religion / Spiritual Services**

Michael Ralph Ladra

Senior Pastor
Compass Church
SALINAS, CA UNITED STATES

Michael Ralph Ladra has brought his passion for the bible and love for people to his role as a minister. Growing up, his family was atheistic. However, when he began his formal education at Stanford University, he became a Christian. During his time there, he majored in philosophy and humanities. Throughout the course of his studies, Christianity began to make sense to him. During his last month in college, he felt a tug to go into ministry, and he never looked back. He wrote a dissertation titled "The Existentialism of Jean-Paul Sartre and His Cultural Influence" and graduated with a Bachelor of Arts in 1968. He continues to use his background in philosophy and history in his preaching.

After earning a bachelor's degree, Dr. Ladra attended the Princeton Theological Seminary, where he majored in theology and pastoral counseling. He graduated from the school in 1971 with a Master of Divinity. At this time, he was ordained to ministry by the Presbyterian Church. From there, he continued his studies at Fuller Theological Seminary in Pasadena, California, where he majored in church growth and graduated with a Doctor of Ministry in 1976. Later, he went on sabbaticals at Hebrew University of Jerusalem from 1997 to 1999 as well as at Merton College and Oxford University from 2001 to 2017.

Dr. Ladra began his career as an associate pastor with Park Boulevard Presbyterian Church in Oakland, California, from 1971 to 1975. For the following two years, he was the director of men's ministry at Bible

Study Fellowship in Oakland. In the decade that followed, he dedicated his time and service to the Corona Presbyterian Church in Denver, Colorado, as a senior pastor. Since 1987, he has been the senior pastor at Compass Church in Salinas, California. When he arrived at this church, there were only 300 people in worship. However, during his time there, it has grown significantly. They now have a 1,500-square-foot worship center that welcomes the 6,000 people who worship. Through this growth, they have saved many marriages and lives. He is tremendously proud of being part of that growth.

Notably, Compass Church changed its name from First Presbyterian Church in order to remove the denomination and thus create a broader appeal. Because of these changes, the church is now one of a few churches that is entirely integrated. The congregation is made up of varying races, economics backgrounds and ages. In the late 1990s, the church began a twice daily radio broadcast of sermons on KKMC and televised the Sunday sermon. The radio audience exceeds 120,000 and extends to three countries, and the television audience exceeds 90,000. Currently, six different worship services with varying music styles are offered at three different locations.

Dr. Ladra was born on October 14, 1946, in Glendale, Arizona, to mother Dorothy West and father Phil Harold. He later married Susie Elizabeth Ladra on June 21, 1969. Together, they had two children named Jennifer Michelle and Jonathan Clayton. Through the agonizing loss of his son, Jonathan, to mental illness and suicide, Dr. Ladra has been able to connect with those in his church who are struggling. His daughter, Jennifer, is married with two children, making Dr. Ladra the proud grandfather to two grandchildren named Tegan and Juliet. In his free time, he enjoys listening to music, woodworking, and English gardening and roses. Looking to the future, he plans to continue celebrating life every day.

A Lifetime of Achievement in **Research & Science**

Joseph A. Adamo, PhD

Biologist & Researcher (Retired)

Educator (Retired)

TOMS RIVER, NJ UNITED STATES

A well-respected leader in his field, Joseph A. Adamo, PhD, has enjoyed a noteworthy career in biology, research and academia. With a professional background in biology that spans 55 years, he spent much of his career at Ocean County College in Toms River, New Jersey, where he garnered valuable experience in a variety of roles ranging from professorial duties to directing the environmental center. Additionally, Dr. Adamo contributed as the head of the college's department of science from 1981 to 1991. Propelled by an inexhaustible drive to teach students, he also aligned with other institutions of higher learning, such as Drexel University and Rutgers University, where he held visiting professorships for several years. Dr. Adamo further progressed in his career at Monmouth University, where he taught for a brief time, and found additional success at Georgian Court University from 1990 to 2010, whereupon he fully retired from teaching.

Prior to beginning his career, Dr. Adamo attended New Jersey City University, where he obtained a Bachelor of Arts. Following this accomplishment, he went on to earn a Master of Science from Fairleigh Dickinson University and a Doctor of Philosophy from Rutgers University. Dr. Adamo also completed postgraduate work at the University of the Philippines in Los Baños. He launched his career in 1965 at Fairleigh Dickinson University, where he served as an instructor of botany before accepting a role as the assistant professor of biology at Jersey City State College in 1966. The focus of his research has involved genetically engineered microorganisms, DNA transfer in the environment, and nanotechnology.

As an acclaimed scientist and an educator, Dr. Adamo achieved recognition as a Fulbright-Hays fellow and was a recipient of the Hammond Science Award. His professional achievements and prominence have also earned him inclusion in numerous honors publications, including multiple editions of Who's Who in America, Who's Who in American Education, Who's Who in Medicine and Healthcare, Who's Who in Science and Engineering, Who's Who in the East and Who's Who in the World. Notably profiled in the 73rd edition of Who's Who in America, Dr. Adamo is also the recipient of the prestigious Albert Nelson Marquis Lifetime Achievement Award, presented to individuals who have made outstanding contributions to their industry and who have demonstrated exemplary leadership. As he reflects on his exciting livelihood, he considers the highlight of his career to be his work modeling nature in the laboratories. One of Dr. Adamo's greatest joys was building models and working with machines, and among his more memorable creations was a buzz bomb with a jet engine that flew more than 120 miles per hour.

To remain current with scientific developments, Dr. Adamo maintains membership with organizations including the American Society of Microbiology, the Society of Nematologists, Sigma Xi, Iota Mu Pi, Phi Theta Kappa and Phi Sigma. Widely recognized as a forerunner in his industry, he has previously shared his time and expertise as a high school mentor. Adjacent to his career in academia, Dr. Adamo served in the U.S. Air Force from 1955 to 1959 and strove out of college to support himself in flight school in an effort to earn a license to pilot as a civilian. He currently utilizes this knowledge as a lieutenant colonel and commander of aerospace education in the Civil Air Patrol. Dr. Adamo is the proud father of four children: Thomas Anthony, Jo Anne, Samantha and Connie, as well as grandfather to 11 grandchildren.

A Lifetime of Achievement in **Research & Science**

James A. Amick, PhD

Consultant
Department of Energy
PRINCETON, NJ UNITED STATES

With more than 65 years of professional experience, James A. Amick, PhD, has been a consultant with the Department of Energy in Washington, D.C., since 1988. Serving in the same capacity at his own eponymous firm, Amick Associates, from 1993 to 1995, he previously was a photovoltaics process group leader at Mobile Solar Energy Corp. from 1986 to 1993, as well as a photovoltaics area manager for Exxon Corp. from 1976 to 1986 and a materials and process manager with RCA Solid State from 1971 to 1976. Earlier in his career, he held a number of positions with RCA Laboratories, including group leader from 1965 to 1971, and research chemist and member of the technical staff from 1953 to 1965.

Outside of his primary endeavors, Dr. Amick has authored many creative works, including "Single Crystal Films" in 1964, "Photoelectronic Materials" in 1965, and two volumes of "Materials and Proceedings for Photovoltaics" in 1981 and 1983. An author and editor for RCA Review in 1963, 1968 and 1970, he has also contributed over 50 articles to professional journals. Moreover, he holds 10 patents in the field. He is very proud of his publications in the electronics area.

Prior to establishing himself as a trusted voice in the field, Dr. Amick sought to expand his knowledge through the pursuit of a formal education. He first attended Princeton University in Princeton, New Jersey, where he earned a Bachelor of Arts in chemistry in 1949. He continued his studies at the same esteemed academic institution and ultimately achieved a Master of Arts in chemistry in 1951 and a Doctor of Philosophy in physical chemistry in 1952. He subsequently served as a research associate at Princeton University from 1952 to 1953.

An active presence in the field, Dr. Amick maintains memberships with a number of prestigious organizations. A fellow of the American Institute of Chemists, he is involved with the American Chemical Society, Sigma Xi, and the New York professional chapter of Alpha Chi Sigma. A past member of the Masons, he was a member of the Princeton Independent Consultants in 1993. With The Electrochemical Society, he served on the board of directors as secretary from 1984 to 1988, vice president from 1991 to 1994 and president from 1994 to 1995.

Throughout his career, Dr. Amick has been recognized for his contributions, including having been named an Ethyl Corp. fellow of Princeton University from 1951 to 1952. He has received awards and accolades for his accomplishments and achievements. He has been featured in numerous honors publications, including multiple editions of Who's Who in Science and Engineering. He considers one of his most important achievements to be pioneering a new, low-cost technology for forming high-efficiency crystalline silicon solar cells at Mobile Solar Energy Corp. Reflecting on his career, he recognizes this to be one of the highlights.

Dr. Amick was born on February 18, 1928, in Lawrence, Massachusetts, to mother Marcella E. Hoover Amick and father Chester Albert Amick. He later married Nancy Jane Scott on September 9, 1961, and together, they had one child named D'Maris Ann Amick Dempsey. Nancy passed away in 2016. Currently, Dr. Amick is the proud grandfather to two grandchildren named Connor Dempsey and Bryan Dempsey. In his free time, he sings with the two choirs in the church. He also enjoys getting together with people, working with other people, gardening, and reading and working with kindergarteners because he feels it keeps him young.

A Lifetime of Achievement in **Research & Science**

Amiya Kumar Banerjee, PhD, DSc
Biochemist
CHAGRIN FALLS, OH UNITED STATES

With 44 years of academic experience to his credit, Amiya Kumar Banerjee, PhD, DSc, most recently served as section head of the department of virology at the Cleveland Clinic from 2003 to 2010. Previously, he chaired the foundation's department of molecular biology from 1987 to 2003 and served as vice chairman of its research institute from 1990 to 1996. He began his professional career as a postdoctoral fellow at the Albert Einstein College of Medicine at Yeshiva University in the Bronx, New York, in 1966, completing this position in three years before joining the Roche Institute of Molecular Biology in Nutley, New Jersey, as a staff associate from 1969 to 1971. He then moved up the ranks to assistant member from 1971 to 1974, associate member from 1974 to 1980, and full member from 1980 to 1987. In addition to these appointments, Dr. Banerjee has been a professor at the Case Western Reserve University in its department of micro and molecular biology since 2002, the department of molecular medicine since 2004 and the department of biochemistry.

Born in 1936 in Rangoon, Burma, Dr. Banerjee later prepared for his professional career by pursuing a formal education at the University of Calcutta in India, where he obtained a Master of Science in 1958 and a Doctor of Philosophy in 1965. He then immigrated to the United States in 1965 before returning to his alma mater to earn a Doctor of Science in 1970. He ultimately became a naturalized U.S. citizen in 1976. Following these achievements, Dr. Banerjee went on to provide major contributions to understanding the mechanism of gene expression of negative-strand animal RNA viruses. The mentors who motivated and inspired him were Dr. Aaron Shatain, Bernadine Geely, S.C. Roy, Debabrata Biswas, and his father, Dr. Phanindra Nath Banerjee.

Active in his local community, Dr. Banerjee served as president of the Tagore Society in New York from 1978 to 1982, which was originally formed in 1958 by a group who wished to present Bengali poet Rabindranath Tagore's ideals of international understanding and cooperation. He was also president of the Bengali Cultural Society in Cleveland in 1998, which promotes Bengali culture and literature in the United States and friendship and cultural exchange with other organizations and groups. Additionally, he has a life member of the Cultural Association of Bengal of New York. A prolific writer, Dr. Banerjee was an associate editor for Virology from 1983 to 2010 and served on the editorial board of the Journal of Virology from 1988 to 1996. He has also been an editor of Advances in Virus Research since 1998 and Gene Expression since 1992.

A fellow of the American Association for the Advancement of Science and the American Association of Microbiology, Dr. Banerjee has received numerous accolades for his accomplishment throughout his career. He received the Phoebe Weinstein Award from the National Institutes of Health in Washington in 1977 and the Professor S.C. Roy Commemoration Medal from the University of Calcutta in 1983. Years later, he was honored with the Scientific Achievement Award by the Cleveland Clinic in 2001. In 2008, the University of Calcutta awarded him with the Alumni Association Scientific Achievement Award and the Best Alumni Award of Applied Chemistry. Furthermore, Dr. Banerjee was selected for inclusion in the 24th edition of Who's Who in the Midwest and several editions of Who's Who in America and Who's Who in Science and Engineering.

A Lifetime of Achievement in **Research & Science**

James L. Blankenship Jr., PhD

Nuclear Physicist & Research Professor

POWELL, TN UNITED STATES

James L. Blankenship Jr., PhD, has enjoyed an illustrious career as a nuclear physicist and a research professor for more than five decades. His academic foundation was laid at Knoxville Central High School in Tennessee, where he excelled in his classes and achieved the role of valedictorian of his graduating class, which was made up of 400 students. Following this accomplishment, Dr. Blankenship attended The University of Tennessee, Knoxville, where he explored his love of physics and his fascination with electronics. He completed a Bachelor of Science in engineering physics in 1954 and a Master of Science in physics in 1955. Dr. Blankenship continued to further his education at The University of Tennessee, Knoxville, with a Doctor of Philosophy in physics in 1973.

Dr. Blankenship thrived as a developer and an engineer in the physics division for Union Carbide, now known as Lockheed Martin UT-Battell, in Oak Ridge, Tennessee, for more than 35 years. He concluded his career in 2012 at the Joint Institute for Heavy Ion Research, a collaborative endeavor between The University of Tennessee, Vanderbilt University and Oak Ridge National Laboratory. In addition to being a patentee in the field, Dr. Blankenship has written research papers centered on physics and contributed a number of articles to various professional journals. He has also shared his expertise in semiconductor nuclear radiation detectors and spectrometers as a speaker in the Institute of Electrical and Electronics Engineers' traveling lecture series.

Toward the end of his career, Dr. Blankenship was inducted into the Knoxville Central High School Alumni Association's Wall of Fame. Making this accomplishment even more poignant was that his eldest daughter was presented with the same honor several years later for her contributions to the community. For his many achievements in the field of physics, Dr. Blankenship has also been recognized in the fourth edition of Who's Who in Science and Engineering and the 73rd edition of Who's Who in America.

Dr. Blankenship was motivated to pursue his goals by a number of his college professors, particularly Dr. Harold Schweinler, the thesis chairman for his doctorate. Another influential mentor was his generous and inspirational grandfather, Samuel Franklin Toole. Education has played a vital role in Dr. Blankenship's success. He credits his professional growth to his strong academic background and his wide range of knowledge in the field of engineering, as well as his intellect and commitment to hard work. A former member of the American Physical Society and a senior member of the Institute of Electrical and Electronics Engineers, Dr. Blankenship is well-known among his peers for his sense of humor, diligence and competent nature, in addition to being a troubleshooter who is able to quickly and efficiently find solutions.

Outside of the world of physics, Dr. Blankenship has attained numerous certifications. He is a state-certified emergency medical technician, a state-certified fire department instructor and a certified CPR instructor as well as a certified first-class commercial radio technician. An active member of his local community, he enjoys contributing his time and talents as a volunteer fire department communications officer and as an elder at the Cumberland Presbyterian Church. Dr. Blankenship was born on March 26, 1931, to James Lynn Blankenship Sr. and Louise Franklin Toole in Knoxville, Tennessee. He and his wife, Jamie Marguerite Gillenwaters, have four children, Sylvia, Maria, Bruce and James III, as well as five grandchildren and six great-grandchildren. In his free time, Dr. Blankenship enjoys photography and carpentry.

A Lifetime of Achievement in **Research & Science**

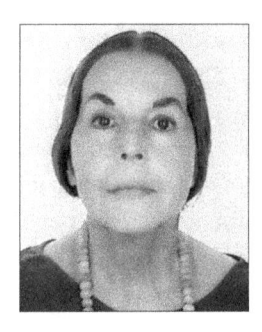

Fairfid Monsalvatge Caudle, PhD

Psychology Professor (Retired)

NEW YORK, NY UNITED STATES

Backed by 45 years of practiced experience, Fairfid Monsalvatge Caudle, PhD, has emerged as a notable leader in psychology and academia. With a wide range of knowledge to her credit, she possesses valuable expertise in the psychology of advertising, early childhood development and developmental psychology. Dr. Caudle began her career in the field of psychology as a research assistant with the Institute of Developmental Studies, where she went on to obtain the role of an assistant research scientist. Subsequently, she accrued valuable expertise with the Responsive Environments Corporation in Englewood Cliffs, New Jersey, as the director of educational services and the director of early childhood programs. In the mid-1970s, Dr. Caudle began teaching at the university level and has since worked in assistant, associate and full professorial positions with Richmond College and The City University of New York.

A fellow of the Institution of Engineering and Technology, Dr. Caudle's passion for education originates from a love of learning and sharing her knowledge with others. After retiring from teaching in 2011, she continues to remain engaged in her industry by serving on the executive committee of the Institution of Engineering and Technology for the New England Network, a post she has thrived in since 2003. An expert in her field, Dr. Caudle has also contributed chapters to books and articles to professional journals.

Prior to embarking on her professional career, Dr. Caudle pursued an education at Duke University in Durham, North Carolina, graduating with a Bachelor of Arts in 1963. She later earned a Master of Arts and a Doctor of Philosophy from The New School for Social Research in 1966, and 1975, respectively. She has been a licensed psychologist in the state of New York since 1979. Dr. Caudle credits her myriad achievements to the outstanding professors she met in her undergraduate program, as well as to Nathan Kogan, the PhD adviser at The New School for Social Research. In order to remain aware of changes in the field, she affiliates herself with the Royal Society of Arts, the American Psychological Association and the Institution of Engineering and Technology, from which she accepted a Companion Award in 1995.

Throughout her career, Dr. Caudle has been celebrated many times, having been presented with a Presidential Award for Excellence in Teaching and a Dolphin Award for Outstanding Service from The City University of New York. Additionally, she has been honored with features in the 62nd and 63rd editions of Who's Who in America and the 27th and 28th editions of Who's Who of American Women. She is also the recipient of the prestigious Albert Nelson Marquis Lifetime Achievement Award, presented to individuals who have demonstrated exceptional leadership and made outstanding contributions to their field.

Looking toward the future, Dr. Caudle intends to continue parlaying her impressive knowledge to the next generation of professionals in her industry. A New York City resident, she enjoys singing, art, traveling and the theater in her free time. Continually striving to learn more about her interests, Dr. Caudle is involved as a member of Phi Beta Kappa, an honor society focused on the liberal arts and the sciences. A talented vocalist, she has been actively engaged with The Cecilia Chorus of New York, a widely recognized mixed chorus that performs concerts at Carnegie Hall among other notable venues, since 1972.

A Lifetime of Achievement in **Research & Science**

Michael Chase Davis, ScD

Program Manager & Director (Retired)
Lockheed Martin Missiles and Space Co.

Captain (Retired)
U.S. Navy

TECUMSEH, MO UNITED STATES

P rior to retirement in 1996, Capt. Michael Chase Davis, ScD, was a program manager and director at the Lockheed Martin Missiles and Space Co. from 1979 to 1996. At Lockheed in Sunnyvale, California, he was responsible for the development of the stealth ship Sea Shadow, the DARPA Simulation Based Design program and other marine programs. He was a program manager for naval high energy laser weapons systems with Science Applications International Corp. from 1977 to 1979.

As a Navy captain, he was the commanding officer of the David W. Taylor Naval Ship Research and Development Center with over 3,000 employees from 1975 to 1977. From 1970 to 1975, he was a ship design director of Trident submarines and Aegis warships at the Naval Sea Systems Command, and from 1968 to 1970, he was a systems analyst with the Office of the Secretary of Defense, whose responsibilities included preparation of the annual Draft Presidential Memorandum on shipbuilding. Earlier in his career, Dr. Davis was the design superintendent at both the Mare Island and Hunters Point Naval Shipyards from 1966 to 1968.

Dr. Davis was the project coordinator for submarine preliminary design at the Bureau of Ships from 1963 to 1966. As a research analyst at the David Taylor Naval Ship R&D Center from 1961 to 1963, he won the prize for the top scientific work in any area among all the BuShips laboratories in 1963. His area of research dealt with the use of transient waves in ship model testing.

In preparation for his career, Dr. Davis joined the U.S. Naval Academy in Annapolis, Maryland, obtaining a Bachelor of Science in 1953 and standing second in his class. Following this accomplishment, he pursued destroyer and submarine assignments at sea, followed by further education at the Massachusetts Institute of Technology in Cambridge, where he completed a Master of Science in naval architecture and marine engineering and a Doctor of Science in electrical engineering, with a thesis on automatic control, in 1961. In order to keep abreast of developments in his field, Dr. Davis maintains professional affiliation with the U.S. Naval Institute.

After retirement from Lockheed in 1996, Dr. Davis developed a website on ovarian cancer treatment. This website, called Ovarian Cancer Research Notebook, can be viewed through the Internet Archive Wayback Machine at http://web.archive.org/web/19990430033200/www.slip.net/~mcdavis/ovarian.html. This was the largest single-cancer website on the internet in the 1990s, but development of it stopped after the death of his wife, Edna, from ovarian cancer in 1999. Subsequently, and up to the present, Dr. Davis has focused on website creation and study in the areas of afterlife and consciousness.

Throughout his career, Dr. Davis has been recognized for his contributions, including having received the Legion of Merit. He was also the recipient of the Daughters of the American Revolution Award for Seamanship, the DW Taylor Award for Scientific Achievement, the Award for Scientific Achievement from the Bureau of Ships and the Joint Service Commendation from the secretary of defense. In light of all his accomplishments, Dr. Davis been previously been featured in numerous honors publications, including multiple editions of Who's Who in Finance and Industry, Who's Who in America, Who's Who in Science and Engineering, Who's Who in the West and Who's Who in the World.

Janet E. Del Bene, PhD

Professor Emerita of Physical Chemistry
Youngstown State University
WARREN, OH UNITED STATES

J anet E. Del Bene, PhD, is a professor emerita of physical chemistry at Youngstown State University in Ohio. She was a faculty member for nearly 30 years, retiring from teaching in 1999. As a faculty member, she taught honors first-year chemistry to the students in the six-year Bachelor of Science/Medical Doctor program with the Northeastern Ohio Universities College of Medicine. In addition to her teaching responsibilities, Dr. Del Bene carried out quantum chemical studies of chemical systems. Her first paper, published in The Journal of Chemical Physics in 1968, was denoted a Science Citation Classic. Since then, Dr. Del Bene has published 300 scholarly papers in her field.

Dr. Del Bene served as a consultant in the basic medical sciences at the Northeast Ohio Medical University, and as a consultant to the newly formed computational chemistry group at the Goodyear Tire and Rubber Company. She was a BBVA visiting fellow at the University of Madrid in 2002 and a visiting professor of chemistry at the University of Sydney, Australia, in 1999, 2000 and 2004. She also spent the winters between 2000 and 2005 as a visitor at the Quantum Theory Project of the University of Florida. Dr. Del Bene delivered the Maria Goeppert-Mayer lecture at the University of California, San Diego, and the San Diego Supercomputer Center. An expert in her field, she was an invited speaker at many national and international meetings, including the 2017 Conference on Halogen Bonding in Supramolecular and Solid State Chemistry in Ottawa, Canada.

The recipient of research grants from the Dreyfus Foundation, the National Institutes of Health and the National Science Foundation throughout her career, Dr. Del Bene was awarded a two-year National Science Foundation Grant Extension for Special Creativity in 2002. She also received the first CERFnet Award for Excellence in Networked Applications in 1991. Dr. Del Bene later received the Heritage Award from Youngstown State University in 2003 and a Morley Medal presented by the Cleveland Section of the American Chemical Society in 2008. For her many accomplishments and contributions to the field, she received an honorary doctorate in science from Youngstown State University in 2009.

Dr. Del Bene is an elected fellow of the American Association for the Advancement of Science. A member of the American Chemical Society, she served on the organization's Irving Langmuir Award canvassing committee from 1978 to 1983, and the executive board of the newly created Division of Computers in Chemistry from 1974 to 1976. A longtime member of Iota Sigma Pi, she was the recipient of a 1972 Agnes Fay Morgan Research Award and a 2002 Honorary Life Member Award. Dr. Del Bene was also active as a member of the Statewide Users Group of the Ohio Supercomputer Center from 1986 to 2001, where she served as the chair for the 1988-1989 year. Locally, she is a member of the board of directors of Ursuline High School, the bishop's advisory council for the Roman Catholic Diocese of Youngstown, and parish council of St. Rose Church.

Originally planning to pursue a career as a mathematician, Dr. Del Bene instead went into chemistry, completing undergraduate research in computational chemistry and earning a Bachelor of Science and Bachelor of Arts from Youngstown State University in 1963 and 1965, respectively. She subsequently attended the University of Cincinnati, where she obtained a Doctor of Philosophy in chemistry in 1968. Upon graduating, Dr. Del Bene completed a postdoctoral fellowship at the University of Wisconsin-Madison Theoretical Chemistry Institute in 1969 and a postdoctoral fellowship at the Mellon Institute at Carnegie Mellon University in 1970. At the Mellon Institute, she studied with Sir John A. Pople, the 1998 Nobel laureate in chemistry. She also spent sabbatical leaves at the Mellon Institute in 1980-1981, The Ohio State University in 1988-1989, the University of Cambridge in 1996 and the University of Florida in 1997.

A Lifetime of Achievement in **Research & Science**

Stevens Heckscher, PhD

Naturalist & Conservation Biologist (Retired)
Natural Lands Trust
HAVERFORD, PA UNITED STATES

Interested in biology since his formative years, Stevens Heckscher, PhD, began his scientific endeavors in the field of meteorology. Prior to embarking upon his professional path, he pursued an education at Harvard University, earning a Bachelor of Arts in 1952, Master of Arts in 1954 and Doctor of Philosophy in 1960, all in mathematics. While studying toward a doctoral degree, he taught as an instructor at Rutgers, The State University of New Jersey, between 1959 and 1960. Following these appointments, he worked at Swarthmore College, rising from the post of an instructor to a professor of mathematics between 1960 and 1980. From 1980 until his retirement in 2007, he excelled as a naturalist and conservation biologist with the Natural Lands Trust in Media, Pennsylvania.

Alongside his primary endeavors, Dr. Heckscher served as a member of multiple committees with the U.S. Environmental Protection Agency, with the Partnership for the Delaware Estuary and on the science and technology advisory committee of the Habitat Task Force. He is additionally affiliated with the Church of the Good Shepherd in Rosemont, Pennsylvania, as a member of the parish staff as spiritual director and warden. A lecturer on cosmology and the interconnection between science and religion, he has authored a number of articles published in professional journals.

In an effort to remain aware of developments in his industry, Dr. Heckscher has been associated with the Delaware County Institute of

Science, where he serves as a referee, consultant and member of the editorial board. He is also a member of the Phi Beta Kappa Society and Sigma Xi, The Scientific Research Honor Society. Moreover, he has donated approximately 200 of his botanical photographs to PhytoImages through Southern Illinois University. His remaining 5,000 photographs will be placed in the public domain.

As a testament to his success, Dr. Heckscher was recognized as a Fulbright scholar from 1958 to 1959, having subsequently accepted a National Science Foundation fellowship from 1966 to 1967 and an Alfred P. Sloan Foundation grant from 1972 to 1973. He was also highlighted in the 25th edition of Who's Who in the East. However, he cites the highlight of his career to be the manuscript he has drafted regarding a church-going woman in England named Dorothy Kerin, who was a pioneer in the interface between religion and medicine. Dr. Heckscher also described and successfully advocated for the preservation in perpetuity of the 110-acre black gum, red maple, sweetbay magnolia virgin swamp forest known as Bear Swamp West in Cumberland County in southern New Jersey. This pristine tract of land is now owned jointly by Natural Lands of Media and the state of New Jersey.

From the beginning of his life, Dr. Heckscher has been dominated by the pursuit of two loves: religion and science. Neither is complete without the other, yet there must be no confusion caused by the attempt to use the methodology of one to settle questions that arise within the other. Scientific method, and scientific method only, is appropriate for scientific investigation, while theological method, and that only, is proper to the quest for truth in theology. Understanding that foundational fact has undergirded all of his intellectual pursuits. Now, at a late age, he is in awe of the results that he sees, as each discipline illuminates the deep insights of the other.

Dr. Heckscher was born on August 21, 1930, in Philadelphia, Pennsylvania, to mother Constance Antelo Butcher Heckscher and father Maurice Heckscher. He is the proud father of five children named Jurretta, Arianne, Lucretia, Christopher and Marguerite. Moreover, he has six grandchildren named Stevens, Chantal, Gregory, Brandon, Anna and Eliza. In his free time, he enjoys music, fly-fishing, aquarium culture and astronomy.

A Lifetime of Achievement in **Research & Science**

Gertrude Wilma Hinsch, PhD

Biology Professor (Retired)
University of South Florida
THONOTOSASSA, FL UNITED STATES

W ith more than 50 years of professional experience to her credit, Gertrude Wilma Hinsch, PhD, has emerged as a well-respected leader in the fields of embryology and reproductive biology. She most recently excelled as a professor at the University of South Florida in Tampa from 1980 until her retirement in 2002. Prior to this appointment, Dr. Hinsch began her tenure with the aforementioned institution in 1974 as an associate professor. From 1960 to 1974, she held the posts of an assistant professor and an associate professor with the University of Mount Union in Alliance, Ohio, as well as an associate professor with the University of Miami from 1966 to 1974. Earlier in her career, Dr. Hinsch was associated with Mount Holyoke College, located in South Hadley, Massachusetts, where she contributed her talents and expertise as an instructor from 1957 to 1960.

Before embarking on her professional journey, Dr. Hinsch became the first person in her family to attend college, pursuing a formal education at Northern Illinois University, located in DeKalb, Illinois, and earning a Bachelor of Science in education in 1953. Following this tremendous achievement, she attended Iowa State University in Ames, Iowa, and received a Master of Science in 1955, where she was the only female graduate student in the department. Subsequently, Dr. Hinsch concluded her education with a Doctor of Philosophy from Iowa State University in 1957. An expert in the field, she has contributed many articles to professional journals, including "Comparative Ultrastructure of Cnidarian Sperm" in 1974 and the "Ultrastructure of the Sperm and Spermatophores of the Golden Crab Geryon fenneri and a Closely Related Species, the Red Crab G. quinquedens, from the Eastern Gulf of Mexico" in 1988.

Dr. Hinsch's fascination with biology was sparked in childhood, with a particular interest in animals and insects. As a young child, she gained practical, hands-on experience by taking care of her family's chickens and ducks. After receiving encouragement to pursue biology from a doctor whom she knew since birth, she narrowed her focus to specific crustacean and cnidarian reproduction. In a career filled with countless highlights, Dr. Hinsch is proud to have pioneered research on the reproductive system of spider crabs and conducted work in the field of biochemistry. Over the years, many others have repeated her work with the same results and used her research as a launching pad. Guiding Dr. Hinsch along her professional journey were mentors Sidney Fox and Charles B. Metz.

As a testament to her success, Dr. Hinsch has been the recipient of the Accrued Development Award from the National Institutes of Health. An exceptionally distinguished Marquis listee, she has been selected for inclusion in multiple editions of Who's Who in America and Who's Who of American Women. Further, Dr. Hinsch is the recipient of the prestigious Albert Nelson Marquis Lifetime Achievement Award, presented to individuals who have demonstrated exceptional leadership and success in their field. A trailblazer in the field of biology, she credits her success to her perseverance and unwavering commitment to her work.

Dr. Hinsch was born on October 20, 1932, to Hans Rudolph Hinsch and Gertrude Kalb Hinsch in Chicago, Illinois. She has two nieces and one nephew as well as six grandnieces and nephews. An avid traveler, she holds the distinction of having been to all seven continents.

Barbara F. Howell, PhD

Materials Engineer (Retired)
Naval Surface Warfare Center
MELBOURNE VILLAGE, FL UNITED STATES

After accruing many years of practiced industry experience, Barbara F. Howell, PhD, retired from her position as a materials engineer with the Naval Surface Warfare Center in Annapolis, Maryland, a job she held from 1987 to 1996. She considers her time spent there to be one of the highlights of her career because they appreciated her and her work. The division chief hired her, and he would give her many prerogatives. Before accepting this post, she served as a research chemist with the National Institute of Standards and Technology in Gaithersburg, Maryland, from 1971 to 1987. In the two years prior, she was a postdoctoral fellow at the University of Missouri in Rolla, Missouri. There, she was proud of having worked on polywater and proving that making polywater was not possible. Her first professional role was as an assistant professor at the Kansas State College of Emporia, now Emporia State University, from 1964 to 1969.

As a high school student, Dr. Howell was fascinated by everything she read in her chemistry textbook. Outside of school, her father would talk to her often about chemistry when she was a little girl. Together, they would draw sugar molecule formulas. Prior to establishing herself as a trusted voice in the field, Dr. Howell sought to expand her knowledge through the pursuit of a formal education at a number of esteemed academic institutions. She first attended the University of Minnesota and earned a Bachelor of Arts in 1946. She continued her studies at Kansas State University, where she obtained a Master of

Science in 1949. Ultimately, she achieved a Doctor of Philosophy from the University of Missouri in 1964.

Wanting to remain an active presence in the field, she maintains memberships with such prestigious organizations as the American Chemical Society, where she contributed her time and knowledge to the post of councilor from 1983 to 1997. She is further associated with the Chemical Society of Washington, where she acted as president in 1983. Moreover, she held the post of president of Sigma Xi in 1980. She also spends her time dedicated to her community as a commissioner of the town of Melbourne Village from 2003 to 2017. Utilizing this knowledge as well as her experience in the industry, she has contributed numerous articles to professional journals. She also holds many patents.

In light of her professional accomplishments, Dr. Howell has gained recognition in the form of various awards. Notably, she was the recipient of the Gordon Award from the Chemical Society of Washington in 1987. She was previously selected for inclusion in multiple editions of such honors publications as the 47th through 53rd editions of Who's Who in America, which were published between 1992 and 1998. She has also been listed in the 24th edition of Who's Who in the East and the 17th edition of Who's Who of American Women. Reflecting on her successes, she is grateful for the mentorship of David Troutner, her research adviser at the University of Missouri. He motivated her and inspired her.

Dr. Howell was born on December 18, 1924, in Chicago, Illinois, to mother Fern Alma First Fennema and father Nick Fennema. She later married Wilbur Alexander Howell on June 29, 1946. He has since passed away. Dr. Howell is the proud mother of three children named Susan Barbara, Gary Wilbur and Michael Owen. Moreover, she has two grandchildren named Nora and Zachary. In her free time, she enjoys painting with oils and watercolor.

A Lifetime of Achievement in **Research & Science**

David Arthur Lienhart

Consultant
DAL Engineering Geologic & Petrographic Services
CINCINNATI, OH UNITED STATES

Inspired by a childhood love of rocks, minerals and fossils, David Arthur Lienhart is now a consultant with DAL Engineering Geologic & Petrographic Services regarding construction rock properties and the evaluation of rocks for erosion control, a role he has held since 2000. At the start of his career, he worked as a petrographer for the Ohio River Division Laboratories of the U.S. Army Corps of Engineers from 1964 until 1970. From there, Mr. Lienhart became a geologist for the Ohio River Division from 1970 to 1976 and subsequently served as a laboratory director from 1976 until 1990.

Prior to moving into a consulting role, Mr. Lienhart worked as a hydrologist in geotechnology for the HTRW division of the U.S. Army Corp of Engineers from 1990 until 1995. In a career filled with highlights, he is especially proud of being requested as a member of the 45-member U.S. delegation led by former Sen. Mary Landrieu to meet with Dutch engineers and scientists on coastal protection in the Netherlands in 2006 and serving as a consultant to the U.S. Department of Justice on the hydrogeology of the Fernald Feed Materials Production Center Superfund Site in Hamilton County, Ohio. Additionally, Mr. Lienhart designed a rock mechanics direct shear device, which was sold to an engineering firm in Lexington, Kentucky.

Outside of his primary endeavors, Mr. Lienhart has contributed articles to professional journals and authored and edited numerous technical publications. Notably, he is the co-author of "Rock quality, durability and service life prediction of armourstone" in 2006, "Evaluation of Potential Sources of Riprap and Armor Stone—Methods and Considerations" in 1981, "The Geographic Distribution of Intensity and Frequency of Freeze-Thaw Cycles" in 1988, "Rock Engineering Rating System for Assessing the Suitability of Armourstone Sources" in 1998 and "A Systems Approach to Evaluation of Riprap and Armor Stone Sources" in 2003. He won a Publication Award for his 2013 paper titled "Long-Term Geological Challenges of Dam Construction in Carbonate Terranes." This paper is now required reading in several civil engineering classes.

A certified professional geologist, Mr. Lienhart earned a Bachelor of Arts and a Master of Science from the University of Cincinnati in 1961 and 1964, respectively. Subsequently, he pursued coursework in nuclear radiology at the U.S. Army Chemical, Biological, Radiological and Nuclear School in Fort McClellan, Alabama, in 1969 and in advanced rock mechanics engineering at the Massachusetts Institute of Technology in Cambridge, Massachusetts, in 1978. Subsequently, he was certified as a professional geologist in Indiana, a registered geologist in Delaware, and a licensed professional geologist in North Carolina. In 1986, he won a full U.S. Department of the Army fellowship to return to the university for one year and continue studies in engineering and geology.

Profiled in the 73rd edition of Who's Who in America, Mr. Lienhart maintains professional affiliation with the Geological Society of America, the Geological Society of London, the American Society of Civil Engineers, the Association of Environmental & Engineering Geologists, the National Ground Water Association and the International Society for Engineering Geology and the Environment. He is further associated with the Geological Society of Kentucky and Sigma Xi. For his work with the American Society for Testing and Materials, now ASTM International, he was recognized for Excellence in Symposium and Publication Management in 1995. Furthermore, he also devotes his time to the department of geology at the University of Cincinnati as an adviser.

For his outstanding work in geology, Mr. Lienhart earned a Publication of the Year Award from the Association of Environmental & Engineering Geologists in 2013. Mr. Lienhart was born on September 28, 1939, in Cincinnati, Ohio, to mother Grace H.J. Burger Lienhart and father Arthur C. Lienhart. He later married Donna Klosterman Lienhart, and together, they are the proud parents of two children named Devin Scott Lienhart and Dana Ann Lienhart Boehmer. In his free time, he enjoys fishing and listening to music.

A Lifetime of Achievement in **Research & Science**

Gerard Rushton, PhD

Professor Emeritus
Department of Geographical and Sustainability Sciences
The University of Iowa

IOWA CITY, IA UNITED STATES

O ver the span of nearly six decades, Gerard Rushton, PhD, has emerged as a leader in geography, building a well-respected name for himself as an expert on geographic information science and medical geography both on the field and in the classroom. He thrived as a professor in the department of geographical and sustainability sciences at The University of Iowa in Iowa City from 1969 until his retirement in 2013. Prior to this position, Dr. Rushton was an assistant professor at Michigan State University in East Lansing from 1967 to 1969. His career in academia began at McMaster University in Hamilton, Ontario, Canada, where he contributed as an assistant professor from 1964 to 1967. His professional experience has also included a role as professor at the University of San Diego from 2005 to 2007, in addition to serving as a reviewer for the National Institutes of Health.

To prepare for his professional career, Dr. Rushton completed his academic foundation at the University College of Wales, Aberystwyth, where he obtained a Bachelor of Arts in 1959 and continued on to earn a Master of Arts in 1961. Following these accomplishments, he furthered his education at The University of Iowa, completing coursework to receive a Doctor of Philosophy in 1964. Dr. Rushton credits his professional success to the good teachers who led him along his educational journey. His respect for interdisciplinary work has also been a major benefit to his career.

Dr. Rushton was inspired to pursue a career in geography because of the tremendous potential it held for the future during the early 1960s.

He saw the influence the developments in the computerization of geography would have on the field and was introduced to a professor who was teaching the use of computers. Dr. Rushton's interest was piqued when he subsequently began attending classes in hydraulics computerization. He soon emerged as a front-runner in his discipline, becoming one of the early experts on how to use computer-based research to aid geographical analysis and its application on human health.

Dr. Rushton's specific interests center on the spatial analysis of disease burdens and in spatial decision support systems: interactive, computer-based systems that assist in providing data to planners and designers needing to solve spatial problems. Over the years, he has done considerable work in India, first as a Ford Foundation consultant on four occasions between 1971 and 1974, and through the National Science Foundation beginning in 1978. An industry leader, he has contributed to various professional journals over the years, including the American Journal of Preventive Medicine, the Journal of Biomedical Informatics and the Journal of Medical Systems. Dr. Rushton was also an editorial board member of the American Association of Geographers from 2000 to 2003.

For his many contributions to the field, Dr. Rushton was honored with an award from the American Association of Geographers, a recognition he considers the highlight of his career. Additionally, his accomplishments have been commemorated in several Who's Who publications, including multiple editions of Who's Who in America and Who's Who in the Midwest. Most notably, he was profiled in the 73rd edition of Who's Who in America. His groundbreaking research has also earned him more than $1 million in grants and funding from various agencies. Further commemorating his influence on the field is a book written to honor him, authored by students who received their doctoral degrees under his direction.

Dr. Rushton has been happily married to Carolyn Arnell Lucken since 1963 and is the proud father of two sons, Edward James and John Palmer. He is also the grandfather of two wonderful grandchildren.

A Lifetime of Achievement in **Research & Science**

Charles Ozwin Rutledge, PhD

Professor Emeritus of Pharmacology
Purdue University
WEST LAFAYETTE, IN UNITED STATES

A professor emeritus of pharmacology, vice president emeritus for research and dean emeritus of pharmacy nursing and health sciences, who spent the last few years of his career as the vice president of research at Purdue University, Charles Ozwin Rutledge, PhD, officially retired in 2008 after spending more than 40 years in his field. Prior to his 21 years at Purdue University, he spent 12 years as a professor and chairman of the pharmacology and toxicology department at the School of Pharmacy of the University of Kansas and eight years as an assistant and associate professor of pharmacology at the University of Colorado School of Medicine.

An active member with the American Association of Colleges and Pharmacy for many years, Dr. Rutledge was chairman of the Council of Faculties, chairman of the Council of Deans, and association president. He has also served on the Volwiler Award Committee, the Research and Graduate Affairs Committee, the Committee on the Present and Future Needs of the Council of Faculties, and the Academic Management System Organizing Committee, and he was a member of the Commission on Implementing Change in Pharmacy Education. Furthermore, he was the first chair of the Indiana Drug Utilization Review Board.

A registered pharmacist in Kansas and Indiana, Dr. Rutledge first earned a Bachelor of Science in pharmacy and a Master of Science in pharmacology at the University of Kansas, followed by a Doctor of Philosophy in pharmacology at the prestigious Harvard University. He then completed a one-year NATO postdoctoral fellowship at the University of Gothenburg in Sweden from 1966 to 1967. Since earning his degrees, his research has included the establishment of a model for studying the mechanism by which amphetamine releases biogenic amine neurotransmitters from nerve endings. He has also conducted studies on the biochemical-behavioral correlations in the use of levodopa for the treatment of Parkinson's disease, as well as studies that involve an examination of the lipid microenvironment of nerve endings as a determinant of the activity of proteins involved in neurotransmission.

Dr. Rutledge has been credited with authoring and co-authoring more than 150 peer-reviewed articles and abstracts in the areas of neuropharmacology and pharmacy education in such journals as the American Journal of Pharmaceutical Education. He has also contributed several chapters to books by other authors, was field editor for the Journal of Pharmacology and Experimental Therapeutics, and editor of Biogenic Amines. Dr. Rutledge has been a member of two National Institute of Mental Health review committees and the National Institute of General Medical Sciences pharmacological sciences review committee, which reviews training grants in the pharmacological sciences.

A 50-year member of the American Society for Pharmacology and Experimental Therapeutics, where he has served in a number of capacities, including president from 1996 to 1997, Dr. Rutledge was recently selected as a member of the inaugural class of fellows of the society. He has also lectured in his field on numerous occasions. The recipient of a National Institutes of Health grant from 1970 to 1987, he has been highlighted in every edition of Who's Who in America since 1989, as well as many more editions of Who's Who in American Education and Who's Who in Science and Engineering.

Attracted to the profession of pharmacy by his interest in chemistry and biology and a strong desire to help people, Dr. Rutledge was inspired by several mentors throughout his school years, including Otto Krayer, the chairman of the pharmacology department at Harvard University. He had the opportunity to participate in a laboratory rotation with Dr. Krayer, who taught him many of the techniques of the pharmacologists and physiologists in Germany during the

1920s and 1930s, which were used to explore the actions of drugs on various biological systems. Now fully enjoying his retirement years later, Dr. Rutledge, who has been married to his wife, Jane Ellen Crow, for over 50 years and is the proud father of four children and grandfather of 10 grandchildren, enjoys traveling, working in his garden and playing the ukulele.

A Lifetime of Achievement in **Research & Science**

John M. Snyder, PhD

President & Founder
Strategic Studies, Inc.
CENTENNIAL, CO UNITED STATES

With more than 50 years of experience to his credit, John M. Snyder, PhD, has excelled as the president and the founder of Strategic Studies, Inc., in Littleton, Colorado, since 1983. Prior to this appointment, he worked for the URS Corp. as the director of development analysis from 1980 to 1983, Abt Associates as a senior resource analyst from 1979 to 1980, and the Oblinger-Smith Corp. as the vice president from 1977 to 1979. Holding a position in economic development in the Department of City Planning and Development for Kansas City, Missouri, from 1976 to 1977, he previously served as an economic research associate in the Warner College of Natural Resources at Colorado State University in Fort Collins, Colorado, from 1972 to 1976. Dr. Snyder began his career in the U.S. Army, rising to the rank of a first lieutenant in military intelligence between 1968 and 1972.

Notably, Dr. Snyder dedicated an extensive part of his career to the preservation of Native American cultural and natural resources. He worked with more than 20 tribal governments, including in the Navajo Nation and the Ute Mountain Ute Tribe. Furthermore, he has spent much time involved with the conservation of wildlife and environmental and heritage resources. Dr. Snyder conducted this work across the globe in such areas as Egypt, India, Africa, Eastern Europe and the polar regions.

Before embarking on his professional path, Dr. Snyder pursued an education at Franklin & Marshall College, earning a Bachelor of Arts in 1968. He continued his academic efforts with a Master of Science at Colorado State University in 1974. Following these accomplishments, he obtained a Doctor of Philosophy in 1982, also at Colorado State University. Dr. Snyder concluded his studies at Harvard University, completing postdoctoral coursework in planning and design in 1981 and graduating with a certificate from the Harvard Graduate School of Design in 1987. Additionally, he is a registered sport fishing guide in the state of Alaska.

Beyond his responsibilities within the field, Dr. Snyder has participated in numerous endeavors outside of his professional circles. The senior adviser on the leisure and hospitality industry in the Leeds School of Business at the University of Colorado Boulder, he has contributed to the economic faculty at Regis University since 1984 and the faculty for environmental policy and management at the University of Denver since 1990, where he had been active as the director of environmental policy and management from 1997 to 2000. Flourishing as a benefactor for Le Bal de Ballet in Denver, Colorado, since 1989, Dr. Snyder further held such roles as the economic adviser for the treasurer and the governor of Colorado from 1979 to 1984, an officer for the YMCA Guides Program from 1984 to 1985, a senior adviser for special family recreation in Denver from 1985 to 1990, and the president of Glacier Bay Outfitters from 1990 to 2001.

Dr. Snyder found success with his written works as well, authoring poems for such publications as "A Far Off Place" and "Best Poems of 1995" in 1995. He also penned "Polar Tourism: The Sustainability Challenge," "Arctic Marine Shipping Assessment" and "Arctic Sea Ice Thickness: Past, Present, and Future." Providing his research to a number of articles featured in professional journals, Dr. Snyder co-authored "Prospects for Polar Tourism" alongside Bernard Stonehouse in 2007.

In addition to his primary vocation, Dr. Snyder remains affiliated with various organizations in relation to his areas of expertise. Since 1994, he has maintained his involvement as the co-founder of Ecotourism International. He was also associated with the National Geographic Society as a sustainable tourism adviser. Dr. Snyder was a member of The American Legion, the Colorado Woodworkers' Guild, the Denver Zoological Foundation, the Federation of Fly Fishers and Trout Unlimited.

In light of his exceptional undertakings, Dr. Snyder has accrued several accolades throughout his impressive career. He was notably recognized as a fellow of The Explorers Club. Likewise, he was selected for inclusion in the Critical Issues Honors Program at Yale University. Additionally, Dr. Snyder was inducted into multiple honor societies, including the Honor Society of Phi Kappa Phi, and Xi Sigma Pi, the National Forestry Honors Society.

Facing many obstacles throughout his career, Dr. Snyder credits his success to his creativity, tolerance for new ideas, his ability to listen and arbitrate sensitive issues, his wealth of knowledge, his persistence and his integrity. Proud of having attained tangible life experience, he was mentored by the likes of William Sloan Coffin, Maj. George Van Schelt, Bernard Stonehouse, William D. Van Dyke and Lawston Brigham. Looking toward the future, Dr. Snyder hopes to continue dedicating his time to his wife, Glenda, as well as woodworking and advocating for the environment while cementing his legacy as an explorer of truth.

A Lifetime of Achievement in **Research & Science**

Moon K. Song, PhD

Sponsor & Mentor
VA Greater Los Angeles Healthcare System

Research Professor
David Geffen School of Medicine
University of California, Los Angeles

NORTHRIDGE, CA UNITED STATES

With more than 55 years of experience to his credit, Moon K. Song, PhD, has worked for the VA Greater Los Angeles Healthcare System as a sponsor and a mentor since 1998 as well as the David Geffen School of Medicine at the University of California, Los Angeles, as a research professor since 1993. Previously, he served as the chief of the research laboratory for the Department of Veterans Affairs Medical Center in Sepulveda, California, from 1983 to 1998, and a research chemist at the Department of Veterans Affairs Medical Center in North Hills, California, from 1974 to 1983. During this time, he held a number of positions in the David Geffen School of Medicine at the University of California, Los Angeles, such as an associate research professor from 1987 to 1993 and an assistant research professor from 1980 to 1987. Dr. Song began his career at the University of Hawai'i in Honolulu, excelling as a research assistant from 1962 to 1965 and a junior researcher from 1965 to 1969.

Before embarking on his professional path, Dr. Song pursued an education at the University of Hawai'i, earning a Bachelor of Arts in 1964. He continued his academic efforts at the aforementioned university, obtaining a Master of Science in 1966. He concluded his studies at the University of Hawai'i in 1972, graduating from the John A. Burns School of Medicine with a Doctor of Philosophy. Following these accomplishments, Dr. Song completed a postdoctoral fellowship at the Indiana University School of Medicine in 1974.

Beyond his responsibilities within the field, Dr. Song has participated in numerous endeavors outside of his professional circles. Since 1980, he has held the role of a manuscript reviewer for 10 scientific journals. Furthermore, he contributed to the National Institutes of Health, the Department of Veterans Affairs Research Services, the American Diabetes Association, and the U.S. Department of Agriculture Research Services as an ad hoc research application reviewer. Holding the patent for new drug development with Pro-Z for the treatment and prevention of diabetes and cancer treatment and Cyclo-Z for the prevention and treatment of diabetes, obesity, Alzheimer's disease, immune disorder, atherosclerosis and cancer treatment, Dr. Song found success with his written works as well, authoring more than 80 peer-reviewed articles for academic journals.

In addition to his primary vocation, Dr. Song remains affiliated with various organizations in relation to his areas of expertise. A fellow and a board member of the American College of Nutrition, he has maintained his involvement on two committees for the Northridge United Methodist Church since 1988. He was also active with the American Diabetes Association as an invited international speaker, having provided speeches around the globe on five occasions in 2017. Moreover, Dr. Song was a member of the American Institute of Nutrition and the American Society of Clinical Nutrition.

In light of his exceptional undertakings, Dr. Song has accrued several accolades throughout his impressive career. In 1974, he accepted a cancer research grant from the Indiana University Melvin and Bren Simon Cancer Center. Garnering a medical research service grant from the Department of Veterans Affairs in 1982 and 1985, he was further presented a grant with the National Institutes of Health in 1998. Dr. Song was selected for inclusion in the first edition of Who's Who in Medicine and Healthcare, the fourth edition of Who's Who in Science and Engineering, the 12th edition of Who's Who in the World, the 23rd edition of Who's Who in the West, and the 50th and 73rd editions of Who's Who in America.

A native of Korea, Dr. Song was originally advised to seek a career in chemistry but found biological science to be a more fulfilling field. He most fondly recalls his development of new, patented drugs to treat diabetes and obesity with no side effects, which will soon be translated for human use, as well as relocating to the United States. Looking toward the future, Dr. Song hopes to continue cementing his legacy as a dedicated and selfless professional.

A Lifetime of Achievement in **Research & Science**

Larry E. Stevens

Founder & Principal Consultant
Pharma Analytic

FORT WORTH, TX UNITED STATES

With over 40 years of professional experience, Larry E. Stevens is an accomplished pharmaceutical consultant who holds significant expertise in his field. Since 2013, he has excelled as the founder and principal consultant for Pharma Analytic, a company that strives to promote and advance quality, state-of-the-art pharmaceutical product development and production. Prior to attaining his current role, he served as the director of research and development and quality control for Neos Therapeutics, Inc., from 2010 to 2013 and principal scientist with Alcon Laboratories from 1981 to 2009. He began his career as a chemist with McGraw Laboratories in 1978.

Having consulted extensively throughout his career, Mr. Stevens has worked for many companies, including PepsiCo, Alere, Epocal Inc., Evonik, Janssen Pharmaceuticals and Ei Pharmaceuticals, among others. Additionally, he also spent time as a U.S. compounding director with Teva Pharmaceutical Industries Ltd. Having conducted much research while with Alcon Laboratories, he was able to publish numerous papers with professional journals, and one of his papers was the feature for the Second Annual Research Consortium in the United States. He has also been a conference chair and speaker and has further conducted numerous webinars and conduct training programs.

Mr. Stevens is also responsible for the development of high-performance dissolution and hundreds of analytical methods as well as the creation of bioequivalent drug delivery products that have been approved and marketed by the U.S. Food and Drug Administration. His further work with the FDA includes the development of novel products from concept through to CMC submissions, and he has done much work toward the advancement of physical-chemical relationships of materials and their mechanisms for controlling drug release, especially for polymers. Also developing predictive in vitro models to study drug delivery devices, he has done significant research on analytical methods of development, bioequivalence and availability, and quality systems advancement and remediation.

Mr. Stevens has always felt that it is the people you work with who make a difference, while the companies you work for are quick to forget you. Because of this, he always strives to invest in the people around him as he goes and is actively involved in his neighborhood and community. A national delegate for his locality, he also once ran for city council in his hometown. Very early on in his career trajectory, he also served as an admiral in the Texas Navy.

Having always been interested in helping people through medicine and science, Mr. Stevens combined this with his early interest in chemistry to pursue a career in the pharmaceutical industry. Embarking on his education at Oral Roberts University in Tulsa, Oklahoma, he obtained a Bachelor of Science in chemistry in 1978. Following this accomplishment, he went on to earn a Master of Science in chemistry from the University of North Texas in Denton in 1995. In order to keep abreast of developments in his field, he maintains professional affiliation with the American Chemical Society and the American Association of Pharmaceutical Scientists.

Working in a number of cutting-edge areas throughout his career, Mr. Stevens has been widely recognized for his accomplishments. Notably, he was presented with the Alcon Laboratories Research Award for his research work with the company, which he considers to be a major highlight in his career. He is also incredibly proud of being recognized and invited to conferences. He currently speaks at international conferences around two-to-three times a year. In light of his exceptional achievements, he was previously featured in the fourth edition of Who's Who in Science and Engineering.

A Lifetime of Achievement | **Larry E. Stevens**

Born in Hollywood, California, to Wilbur and Doreen Stevens, Mr. Stevens has been happily married to his wife, Melissa, since 1979. He is also the proud father of two children, Jessica and Kristel. In his free time, he enjoys reading as well as community and church activities.

A Lifetime of Achievement in **Research & Science**

Paul J. Voss Jr.

Senior Physicist (Retired)
Applied Physics Laboratory
Johns Hopkins University

COLUMBIA, MD UNITED STATES

With 34 years of industry experience to his credit, Paul J. Voss Jr. worked his way up from an associate physicist to senior physicist in the Johns Hopkins University Applied Physics Laboratory (JHU/APL) in Laurel, Maryland, from 1969 to 2003. During this time, he also served JHU/APL as facility manager of the Guidance System Evaluation Laboratory from 1983 to 1995. In addition to these appointments, he served on the Standard Missile Simulation Accreditation Review Panel from 1984 to 1996 and chaired the AEGIS Scenario Certification Committee in Washington from 1987 to 1996. Among his many accomplishments, Mr. Voss conducted operational evaluation of the experimental vessel traffic system for the U.S. Coast Guard Sector San Francisco in 1974 and led the development of six-degree-of-freedom standard missile simulations at JHU/APL in 1976.

Prior to embarking on his professional path, Mr. Voss sought to expand his knowledge through the pursuit of a formal education at a number of esteemed academic institutions. He first attended Syracuse University, earning a Bachelor of Science in 1969. He continued his studies at Johns Hopkins University in Baltimore, Maryland, where he obtained a Master of Science in 1972. Mr. Voss became involved in his career because he liked science, specifically physics. The highlight of his career was receiving commendations from people for whom he completed work in the U.S. Navy, including Adm. Greene and Capt. Stark.

A Lifetime of Achievement | **Paul J. Voss Jr.**

Through the first quarter of 1995, Mr. Voss provided significant contributions to the AEGIS program as a member of its core doctrine development team. Due to the team's outstanding efforts, a new document provided the fleet with critical and definitive tactical guidance concerning the development and implementation of AEGIS Weapon System (AWS) doctrine necessary to effectively counter the threats faced by ships today. Team members designed and validated recommended tactics against six of today's most stringent threats, and then integrated this information into the document. The efforts of Mr. Voss' team resulted in increased operator awareness concerning the employment of the AWS and continues to be reflected in the improved warfighting capability of ships.

As a result of these efforts, Mr. Voss was bestowed with a special team award, the AEGIS Excellence Award for Outstanding Performance. Prior to this, he was awarded a certificate of recognition by the Naval Ship Weapon Systems Engineering Station for his expert assistance, support, and cooperation rendered during post-commissioning tests and trials aboard the USS Thomas S. Gates in 1988. He also received two letters of appreciation from AEGIS shipbuilding manager Rear Adm. John F. Shaw and the commanding officer of the Naval Weapon System Engineering Station in 1986, among other accolades.

Moreover, Mr. Voss was previously selected for inclusion in such honors publications as the second edition of Who's Who in Science and Engineering, the 12th edition of Who's Who in the World, and the 24th through 27th editions of Who's Who in the East. Reflecting on his career, he is grateful for the mentorship he received from I.J. Sheppard, Joe Luber, Woody Simone, Dennis Serpico and E.J. Himmons. Mr. Voss was born on March 10, 1943, in Chicago, Illinois, to mother Irene Esther Bergman Voss and father Paul Joseph Voss. He himself is now a father to two wonderful children named Lisa Voss and Laurel Voss. In his free time, he enjoys doing yoga and going swimming. Previously, he liked to go skiing.

Holland D. Warren, PhD

Physicist (Retired)

LYNCHBURG, VA UNITED STATES

Amassing more than three decades of professional experience, Holland D. Warren, PhD, is an esteemed physicist who has established himself in the industry as a prominent expert. Prior to retiring from his illustrious career in 1994, he worked as an advanced engineer with Framatome, known then as Areva, for more than five years. Dr. Warren formerly served the company B&W, known at the time as Babcock & Wilcox Company, in several capacities, including as a research specialist and a senior physicist beginning in 1964. Prior to these respected roles, he built his career as a development physicist at the Celanese Corporation from 1963 to 1964 and as a research associate at the University of Virginia from 1960 to 1962.

Following his retirement, Dr. Warren thrived as a consultant for Areva from 1994 to 2006 and B&W from 2009 to 2013. He has contributed myriad articles to professional journals in his area of expertise. A prolific author with a focused interest in genealogy, Dr. Warren has also written a book on his own family history, titled "Warrens and Related Families of North Carolina and Virginia," published in 1990.

Inspired by his high school science teacher, Dr. Warren knew he wanted to delve into the sciences from an early age. Upon graduation from high school, where he earned valedictorian distinction, he volunteered for service in the U.S. Navy for four years during the Korean War. Attending aviation schools while in the military, Dr. Warren became especially interested in physics and was afterward transferred to a blimp squadron and shore duty in North Carolina before his release to the Naval Reserve in 1955. He subsequently attended Wake Forest University in Winston-Salem, North Carolina, where he earned a Bachelor of Science in mathematics, summa cum laude, in 1959, as well as the University of Virginia, earning a Master of Science and Doctor of Philosophy in physics in 1961 and 1963, respectively.

Dr. Warren is renowned for his research in the theoretical and experimental development of self-powered neutron detectors for application inside the cores of nuclear power plants, expertise that he has shared around the world. A holder of multiple patents in the field, he was a member of the American Nuclear Society, the American Physical Society, Kappa Mu Epsilon and Phi Beta Kappa. As a testament to his professional success, Dr. Warren was honored with the IR-100 Award in 1984. A highlight of his career was the successful completion of a nine-year experiment at a nuclear power plant with self-powered neutron detectors he developed alongside his team.

In recognition of outstanding contributions to the field of physics, Dr. Warren has been recognized in multiple editions of Who's Who in the World. He is also the recipient of the prestigious Albert Nelson Marquis Lifetime Achievement Award. A North Carolina native, Dr. Warren has enjoyed building a life for himself and his family in Lynchburg, Virginia, and has given back to his community as an election official from 1997 to 2007, and a volunteer for Meals on Wheels beginning circa 2008, a role in which he continues to thrive. He enjoyed more than 55 years of marriage to Nancy Wall Warren before her unfortunate passing in 2011, subsequently marrying Mary Beasley Swan Warren in 2014. Dr. Warren is the father of Douglas, Jill and Karen, stepfather to Wilson, Phil and Don Swan, the grandfather of Nikolas Warren and Olivia Wade, and stepgrandfather to Lauren, Kaitlyn, Leah, Lydia and Laney Swan.

A Lifetime of Achievement in **Research & Science**

Oliver Wendell Welch

Pharmaceutical Executive (Retired)

LUBBOCK, TX UNITED STATES

With more than 50 years of experience to his credit, Oliver Wendell Welch has achieved major strides in the pharmaceutical industry. Prior to his retirement, he held the positions of the associate director of regulatory affairs and the deputy director of regulatory affairs at Sterling Winthrop Inc. in New York City from 1977 to 1994. During this tenure, Mr. Welch ensured company compliance, worked on product recalls and helped drugs get approved for market. He supervised a department of 30 people and took regular trips to Washington, D.C., to work with the Food and Drug Administration, in addition to collaborating with medical and legal departments to resolve 65 different court cases and serve as an expert witness.

Initially interested in becoming a teacher, Mr. Welch achieved a Bachelor of Arts in English from Texas Tech University in Lubbock, Texas, in 1952 before enrolling in Columbia University in the city of New York to obtain a Master of Arts in English. Four years after graduating, he was introduced to a district manager for Warner Lambert who offered him a position in the pharmaceutical industry. Mr. Welch's career began as a pharmaceutical representative covering territory in Missouri, Kentucky and Illinois. He quickly ascended to leadership roles, thriving as a supervisor in marketing research and in manpower development in the Warner Lambert office in Morris Plains, New Jersey. Mr. Welch has also found success as the vice president of

Biomedical Data Co. in New York City and the manager of corporate development at Boehringer Mannheim Corp.

Mr. Welch has enjoyed his entire career, particularly because of the companies for which he has worked and the people he has met along the way. He was well-known by his peers for his integrity and his ability to build relationships with the teams of people with whom he worked. Mr. Welch loved the social components of his job and interacting with everyone from doctors in hospitals to government employees in Washington, D.C., His five-decade career has also been very rewarding, as it has allowed Mr. Welch to be involved in discovering new drugs that have improved people's quality of life.

Mr. Welch's accomplishments have earned him inclusion in several editions of Who's Who in the World, Who's Who in the South and Southwest, Who's Who in the East, Who's Who in America, Who's Who in Medicine and Healthcare, Who's Who in Finance and Industry, and Who's Who in Finance and Business. For his impact on the community and the world, he was also recognized with the Marquis Who's Who Distinguished Humanitarian Award.

Mr. Welch was born in Jacksonville, Texas, on January 9, 1930, to Jackson Andrew Welch and Annie Laura Welch. He was married to Wanda Virginia Urrey for almost 70 years prior to her unfortunate passing in 2016. In his free time, he enjoys music, traveling and theater. Mr. Welch continues to remain up to date with advancements in his field as a member of the Regulatory Affairs Professionals Society and the Drug Information Association. Outside of his professional activities, he is also involved with the Order of Saint John of Jerusalem and served as the master of ceremonies for Saint Thomas Church in New York City for 20 years.

A Lifetime of Achievement in **Research & Science**

Fritz G. Will, PhD

Founder & Owner (Retired)
Battery Vision, Consulting and Innovative Research
SANTA BARBARA, CA UNITED STATES

With a career spanning over five decades, Fritz G. Will, PhD, is currently retired, having most recently been active as the founder and owner of Battery Vision, Consulting and Innovative Research, in Santa Barbara, California, from 1998 to 2011. Prior to this activity, he was a visiting professor at the National University of Singapore in 1998. From 1993 to 1998, he was a visiting scientist for two years and later appointed manager of electrochemical science and technology at the Electric Power Research Institute (EPRI) in Palo Alto, California. From 1990 to 1993, Dr. Will was a research professor at The University of Utah and director of the National Cold Fusion Institute in Salt Lake City from 1990 until its closure in 1991. His move to Utah followed a 30-year career, from 1960 to 1990, at the General Electric Research Laboratory — later called the GE Research and Development Center — in Schenectady, New York. During this time, he variously served as research scientist, unit manager and project manager. Immediately prior to joining GE, he worked at the U.S. Army Engineering Research and Development Center in Fort Belvoir, Virginia, for six months. From 1973 on, Dr. Will repeatedly went on sabbatical leaves, spending time teaching and doing academic research at the University of Bonn, Germany; The University of Western Australia; Murdoch University in Perth, Australia; The University of Utah; and National University of Singapore

(NUS). During his stay in Singapore, he was also appointed chair of the international advisory panel at the Institute of Materials Science and Engineering at NUS.

Dr. Will holds 24 patents in his field of electrochemistry. In 1975, he was granted the original patent (U.S. patent 3,874,928) on rechargeable nickel-metal hydride batteries employing AB5 compounds. For many years, this type of battery was used by Toyota in their Prius hybrid cars and continues to be the battery of choice for portable electric tools and personal appliances such as electric toothbrushes. Other notable inventions include an oxygen sensor for manned space craft, advanced positive electrodes for lead acid batteries and a long-life solid electrolyte battery for heart pacemakers. This battery received an Industrial Research Award, IR-100, as one of the 100 most significant inventions in the U.S. in 1975.

Dr. Will has published his research in over 60 articles in refereed journals. His most noteworthy contribution to electrochemical science was his development and application of a new technique (potential sweep voltammetry or surface coulometry) for the study of chemisorption layers on metallic catalyst surfaces. Specifically, this technique allowed him to study the chemisorption of hydrogen and oxygen atoms on platinum and other noble metal electrode surfaces with an accuracy of a fraction of an atomic monolayer. Optimal catalytic activity for the oxidation of fuels, such as hydrogen gas, depends upon the formation of a complete monolayer of hydrogen atoms. Impurities in the electrolyte or the hydrogen gas can interfere with monolayer formation and, hence, catalytic activity. Such factors can be studied readily with potential sweep voltammetry and established the method as an important tool for the evaluation of catalysts for use in hydrogen/oxygen fuel cells. The rapid increase in the number of industrial and academic laboratories involved in fuel cell research in the 1960s, 70s and 80s, both in the U.S. and abroad, led to the widespread use of the method. By 1984, researchers had cited the journal article describing the technique and its application (Z. Elektrochem, volume 64, pages 258-269, 1960) more than 300 times in the technical literature. It was named a "Citation Classic" by the Institute for Scientific Information.

Another widely recognized contribution to the field of electrochemistry is Dr. Will's elucidation of the working mechanism of gas diffusion electrodes, as employed in hydrogen/oxygen fuel cells. Such electrodes typically consist of a thin microporous composite of very small catalyst particles and a polymeric binder, pressed onto a metallic current collector screen. The electrode side facing the hydrogen (or oxygen) is provided with a thin hydrophobic, gas-permeable film, such as Teflon. The fine pores in the electrode have tortuous paths and a range of diameters, from microns to tens of microns. (One micron equals one millionth of a meter.) Dr. Will developed a scale-up model of a single, straight pore, comprised of the outside of a cylindrical platinum electrode, 1 cm long and 0.6 cm in diameter, partly immersed in an aqueous electrolyte. The model enabled microscopic observation and micrometer-controlled vertical movement of the electrode during the measurement of current-voltage curves. The formation of a liquid meniscus and an adjacent film above it were thus established: The reaction zone for the oxidation of hydrogen was shown to be a narrow band of millimeter width next to the junction of meniscus and film. The regions farther up in the film (increasing ohmic resistance) and farther down in the meniscus (increasing hydrogen gas diffusion distance) contributed negligibly to the reaction rate (current). Significantly, the shape of the current-voltage curves was found to be dramatically different from fully immersed electrodes, but similar to the curves observed on hydrogen gas electrodes in fuel cells. A mathematical analysis of the "meniscus/film model," performed by Dr. Will, resulted in complete agreement between predicted and actual experimental current-voltage curves. The similarity between the curves determined on the model and those measured on hydrogen diffusion electrodes, as used in fuel cells, sows that the meniscus/film model explains the working mechanism of hydrogen/oxygen fuel cells. This study was recognized by receiving The Electrochemical Society's Battery Division Award in 1964.

Before embarking on his career, Dr. Will pursued an education at the Technical University of Munich in Germany, where he earned a Bachelor of Science in physics in 1954 and a Master of Science in physics in 1956. He obtained a doctorate degree in physical chemistry in 1959 and emigrated to the U.S. the same year. He became a member of The Electrochemical Society in 1960 and later served as a division editor of the Society's Journal. He was elected chair of the society's physical electrochemistry division and later chaired the honors and awards committee. In 1979, he was elected president of The Electrochemical Society.

For excellence in his field, Dr. Will has been the recipient of a number of honors and accolades. First recognized with the Fourth Battery Division Research Award from The Electrochemical Society in 1964, he was also presented with an Industrial Research Award from the Industrial Research Institute in 1975 and a Citation Classic Award from the Institute for Scientific Information in 1984. In light of all his accomplishments, Dr. Will has previously been featured in Who's Who in America, Who's Who in Science and Engineering, and Who's Who in the World. He was notably profiled in the 73rd edition of Who's Who in America.

A Lifetime of Achievement in **Research & Science**

Laszlo Zaborszky, MD, PhD

Neuroscientist & Researcher

Editor-in-Chief

Brain Structure and Function

VERONA, NJ UNITED STATES

Supported for more than three decades by the National Institutes of Health in his neuroscience research, Laszlo Zaborszky, MD, PhD, has been serving as the editor-in-chief of "Brain Structure and Function" since 2007. Impressively, he has taught and completed research for 30 years. Having grown up and completed all of his studies in Hungary, he moved to the United States after being invited to work at many different schools, including the University of Virginia in Charlottesville, Mount Sinai Medical Center and Yale University.

Dr. Zaborszky decided on the University of Virginia in Charlottesville and served the school as an associate professor between 1981 and 1993. Upon his departure from this school, he began working at Rutgers, The State University of New Jersey, in multiple capacities, including as associate professor from 1993 to 2017, full professor from 2004 to 2017 and distinguished professor between 2014 and 2019. Likewise, he also served Rutgers, The State University of New Jersey, as a faculty chair between 2016 and 2017 as well as a neuroscientist.

In a career filled with highlights, Dr. Zaborszky is especially proud of conducting research on the basal forebrain. He has also contributed his knowledge through several creative works. Earlier, he authored the monograph "Afferent Connection of the Medial Basal Hypothalamus" in 1982. He also edited the textbooks Neuroanatomical Tract-Tracing Methods 2: Plenum, which was published in 1989, and Neuroanatomical Tract-Tracing 3: Molecules, Neurons and Systems, which was published in 2006. In his spare time, Dr. Zaborszky gave back to those in the scientific community as the president of the New York Hungarian Scientific Society between 2012 and 2016. Currently he is president of the Association of Hungarian American Academicians.

Prior to establishing himself as a trusted voice in the field, Dr. Zaborszky sought to expand his knowledge through the pursuit of a formal education. He first attended Semmelweis Medical School in Budapest, Hungary, where he earned a Doctor of Medicine in 1969. During this time, he was inspired by John Szentágothai, a famous neuroanatomist and chair of the anatomy department. He continued his studies at the same esteemed academic institution, and he achieved a Doctor of Philosophy in 1981. Ultimately, he obtained a Doctor of Science from the Hungarian Academy of Sciences in 1999.

In light of his professional successes, Dr. Zaborszky has gained recognition in the form of various awards and accolades. Since 1986, he has been a grantee of the National Institute of Neurological Disorders and Stroke of the National Institutes of Health. Moreover, he is the recipient of the Board of Trustees Award for Research Excellence from Rutgers, The State University of New Jersey, in 2016 and a Knight's Cross of the Order of Merit of Hungary in 2013. In 2009, he was named a foreign member of the Hungarian Academy of Sciences.

Dr. Zaborszky has previously been selected for inclusion in numerous honors publications, including the 24th edition of Who's Who in the World, the ninth edition of Who's Who in Science and Engineering, and the 61st through 63rd, 66th and 73rd editions of Who's Who in America. Dr. Zaborszky was born on October 9, 1944, in Budapest, Hungary, to mother Ilona Hegedus and father Geza Zaborszky. Now, he is the proud father to one child named Sarah. Looking to the future, he intends to continue excelling in his neuroscience research.

Gloria Christine Blair

Senior Instructional Assistant
Downey Unified School District

Pipefitter (Retired)
Union Local 250

DOWNEY, CA UNITED STATES

Through hard work, perseverance and patience, Gloria Christine Blair has enjoyed a satisfying career working skilled trades as well as helping young students achieve their dreams.

Backed by many years of professional experience, she currently serves as a senior instructional assistant for the behaviorally challenged at the Downey Unified School District, located in Downey, California. Ms. Blair's career in education follows a successful four decades of thriving in a variety of roles.

Ms. Blair embarked upon her professional path as a long-distance operator for Pacific Telephone in Huntington Park, California, from 1965 to 1966. A hardworking and dedicated professional, Ms. Blair further built her career as a phone operator for the Tel-Page Answering Service from 1966 to 1976 and a supervisor for the Rowe Service Company from 1972 to 1979. Subsequently, she served as a receptionist for the Hacker Clinic from 1980 to 1981, and a secretary for the Spring Anesthesia Group, Inc., from 1985 to 1991.

Ms. Blair is also a retired pipefitter with Union Local 250, of which she has been a member since 1991. She was accepted into the apprentice program and received a certificate of completion as a journeyman air conditioning and refrigeration pipefitter, which is now classified as building trades journeyman A/C and refrigeration, pipefitter and steamfitter. When she retired from Local 250, she began her career in

A Lifetime of Achievement | Gloria Christine Blair

education. Ms. Blair credits her father, a tradesman, as the greatest influence on her early vocation as a pipefitter, in addition to a scribe at Union Local 250 who helped her to realize she could continue working after retirement and pursue her dream of teaching.

In 1984, Ms. Blair obtained a Bachelor of Arts from Chaminade University of Honolulu in Hawaii, where she also served as a library assistant. Though her life has been filled with amazing moments, she is especially proud of graduating from college, an accomplishment many told her she would not be able to achieve. The experience was a labor of love, but due to her determination, Ms. Blair is now working in a fulfilling job helping students with behavioral challenges overcome their obstacles and follow their dreams.

Outside of Ms. Blair's professional endeavors, she has taught religion at several parishes for the past 25 years. It was her volunteer work at church that sparked Ms. Blair's initial interest in special education; when she had a special needs student in her class, she began researching the best ways to teach him, eventually designing the whole class for him. In addition, she further contributes to her community through the Coalition of Residents of Lynwood. For her commitment to excellence, Ms. Blair has been celebrated numerous times, having been featured in the 22nd edition of Who's Who in the West and the third and fourth editions of Who's Who of Emerging Leaders in America. In recognition of her achievements, leadership qualities and the successes she has accrued in her field, she has also been presented with the Albert Nelson Marquis Lifetime Achievement Award.

Ms. Blair was born on September 5, 1946, in South Gate, California, to Arthur Chester Blair and Gloria Magdalen Neilson Blair. She is the mother of Christopher Arthur and proud grandmother of three grandchildren. In her free time, Ms. Blair enjoys bicycling, sewing and crafts. Looking toward the future, Ms. Blair intends to experience the continued growth and success of her career.

A Lifetime of Achievement in **Technology**

Wes Coates, MBA

General Manager
Delaware & Ulster Railroad

RENSSELAER, NY UNITED STATES

With more than 20 years of experience in general management to his credit, Wes Coates, MBA, has become an authority in passenger train operations. Since 2017, he has thrived as the general manager of the Delaware & Ulster Railroad, a scenic tourist railroad based out of Arkville, New York, that travels through the Catskill Mountains. Prior to assuming this role, Mr. Coates excelled as the general manager of the Empire Corridor of Amtrak from 1995 to 2001, overseeing operations of the railroad's route between Niagara Falls, New York, and Manhattan, which includes stops in Buffalo, Rochester, Syracuse and Albany. His previous positions include serving as an employee for railroad planning and operations at URS Corporation, now known as AECOM, from 2002 to 2013 and a sector manager of operations analysis and planning at SYSTRA, a rail and public transport engineering and consulting group, from 2013 to 2014.

Mr. Coates' love of the railroad began at a young age, as he is the fourth member of his family to work for the railroad. He has had a lifelong love of trains and enjoys the feeling of accomplishment that comes with working in the office, on the route and with people. Prior to becoming an esteemed railroad management professional, Mr. Coates pursued higher education with a Bachelor of Science in managerial economics from Lycoming College in Williamsport, Pennsylvania, in 1976. He later continued his education at the Sage College of Albany, where he earned a Master of Business Administration in operations management and supervision in 2002. Throughout his career, Mr. Coates was mentored by Perry A. Shoemaker, the president of the Delaware, Lackawanna and Western Railroad.

A prolific author with a wide breadth of knowledge, Mr. Coates wrote "Electric Trains to Reading Terminal" in 1990. The paperback provides a detailed history of the electrification of the suburban lines leading to and from the Reading Terminal. Prior to that, he penned "50th Anniversary, 1931-1981: Suburban Electrification, Delaware, Lackawanna & Western R.R.," in 1981. Well-regarded as an expert in his industry, Mr. Coates has spoken and presented at various institutions in his field. He most recently shared his expertise by presenting at the New York State Society of Professional Engineers in 2019 and further worked with HBO for a miniseries on the historic Delaware & Ulster Railroad. An avid lover of trains, Mr. Coates has a notably large collection of books about railroads.

Outside of his professional responsibilities, Mr. Coates remains aware of the changes and advancements in his industry through relevant organizations. He is a member of the American Association of Railroad Superintendents, the Lexington Group in Transportation History, the National Railway Historical Society, and the Railway & Locomotive Historical Society. He is further affiliated with the HeritageRail Alliance, an organization that works to support rail preservation and outreach efforts throughout the world.

In light of his many achievements in the field, Mr. Coates has received a number of accolades throughout his career. He won the Tourism Achievement Award from the Delaware Chamber of Commerce in 2018, the Distinguished Service Award from the National Park Service in 2001, and the President's Achievement Award from the Empire State Passenger Association in 1997. For his many years of leadership and professional excellence, Mr. Coates has also been presented with the prestigious Albert Nelson Marquis Lifetime Achievement Award and featured in the 73rd edition of Who's Who in America.

A Lifetime of Achievement in **Technology**

Ronald Jack Crymes

Founder & President (Retired)
Accurate Detailing Associates
NORCROSS, GA UNITED STATES

Marquis Who's Who, the world's premier publisher of biographical profiles, is proud to present Ronald Jack Crymes with the Albert Nelson Marquis Lifetime Achievement Award. An accomplished listee, Mr. Crymes celebrates many years' experience in his professional network, and has been noted for achievements, leadership qualities, and the credentials and successes he has accrued in his field. As in all Marquis Who's Who biographical volumes, individuals profiled are selected on the basis of current reference value. Factors such as position, noteworthy accomplishments visibility, and prominence in a field are all taken into account during the selection process.

Now retired, Mr. Crymes has accrued nearly four decades of experience as a structural steel detailer and draftsman. A high school math teacher, Mrs. Witcher, inspired him to become a draftsman. When she repeatedly caught him sketching spaceships in math class, she recognized where his talents lay. She encouraged him to acquire some drafting tools and pursue that talent.

Prior to embarking on his professional journey, Mr. Crymes enlisted in the U.S. Air Force in 1954. During his service as an electronic counter measures operator on RB36 and RB47 bombers, he was asked to draw plans for some special ground support equipment. The equipment he designed won an award from SAC (Strategic Air Command). When he realized his knack for drafting design, he was inspired to seek a higher education. Subsequent to the conclusion of his service in 1957, he completed coursework in architectural history at the Georgia Institute of Technology between 1957 and 1961. He then attended the Atlanta Division of the University of Georgia for additional mathematics in 1961 and 1962.

At the beginning of his career, Mr. Crymes learned the detailing business working for Jack Zwecker and Associates in Atlanta. In 1961, beginning as a print boy and a trainee draftsman, he quickly rose to a position of a draftsman and then as a draftsman checker and a field checker. He continued his success at Jack Zwecker and Associates through 1984. His last position was the founder and the president of Accurate Detailing Associates in Atlanta from 1984 to 2015. After establishing Accurate Detailing Associates, he worked with Addison Steel to establish the Atlanta offices in the 1990s. He was also associated with L. N. Ross Engineering as a draftsman checker and a field checker in the 1990s.

Throughout his impressive career, Mr. Crymes worked on a multitude of diverse projects. The most extensive was all of the bridges on Interstate 10 between New Orleans, Louisiana, and Lake Charles, Louisiana. He is proud to have been the detailer of all the steel required for the creation of the Buckhead Library in Atlanta. The library was the recipient of the 1993 National AIA Honor Award of Excellence, the 1991 National AIA / ALA Award of Excellence, the 1990 Georgia AIA Award of Excellence and the 1990 Urban Design Commission Award of Excellence. The rolled steel canopy in front of the library required that Mr. Crymes write a special computer program to find all the points needed for drawing each individual component.

In addition to the Buckhead Library, Mr. Crymes worked on the Atlanta High Museum of Art, the 1988 Olympic Stadium in Seoul, South Korea, the Georgia World Congress Center in Atlanta, multiple power plants throughout the world, high-rise office buildings in Atlanta, New York and other cities, multiple Publix stores, Home Depot stores, and JCPenney warehouses, a garbage shredder, a separator and bailer for New York City, and many other projects. The files of the VA and FHA have over 100 house plans drawn by him, which allowed home loans to be made during the time of the Jimmy Carter presidency when interest rates rose to 26%.

Mr. Crymes is particularly proud of the contributions he made to various NASA space programs. He worked with different teams on the Huntsville, Alabama, facilities where the Redstone and Atlas rockets were built. He later worked on the gantry for the spaceflight to the moon as well as the gantry for the space shuttle. Mr. Crymes' military jobs included creating a special rail flatcar modification for transporting modified B52 wings, details for a B58 maintenance shed and modifications to the Lockheed Aircraft plant in Georgia.

Outside of work, Mr. Crymes enjoys collecting electric trains, watches, pistols, and almost anything mechanical or electrical. He is an active elder in the Presbyterian Church. He has been married to Josephine Boyd Crymes for 56 years and has one daughter and two sons.

A Lifetime of Achievement in **Technology**

Gus A. Galatianos, PhD

Founder & President
ACCI Properties

Professor Emeritus
State University of New York

WHITESTONE, NY UNITED STATES

Backed by more than 45 years of practiced industry experience, Gus A. Galatianos, PhD, is currently the founder and president of ACCI Properties, as well as a professor emeritus with the State University of New York. Earlier in his career, he was aligned with numerous computer firms, including Solomos Business Machines, as the operations manager; University Computer Centers, as a consultant; Computer Dynamics Corp., as the vice president and technical director; Computer Corporation of America, as a senior consultant; and as the founder and president of Advanced Computer Consulting Inc., which is the parent company of ACCI Properties. From 1979 to 2000, concurrently with the above computer industry positions, Dr. Galatianos was also a computer science professor at SUNY, as well as the department chair from 1988 to 2000, teaching courses such as software engineering, systems design and implementation, distributed databases, artificial intelligence and expert systems. Additionally, he has made many public presentations on the state-of-the-art computer matters in hotel auditoriums attended by hundreds of data processing and corporate executives.

An alumnus of the New York Institute of Technology; the Stevens Institute of Technology; the Polytechnic University, now the New York University Tandon School of Engineering; and the prestigious Columbia

University, Dr. Galatianos holds a Bachelor of Science in electrical engineering and a Master of Science in systems engineering, as well as a Master of Science and a Doctor of Philosophy in computer science. His doctoral thesis was titled "On the Concurrency Control in Distributed Database Systems," today's internet.

Throughout his career, Dr. Galatianos has contributed his knowledge to a number of works, including "Principles of Software Engineering" and "Principles of Database Systems," which were both published in 1986. A contributor to numerous articles on local and wide-area networks in professional journals in the United States and abroad, he has earned a number of awards for his work in the field. Since the late 1980s, Dr. Galatianos has been featured in many volumes of Who's Who of Emerging Leaders in America, Who's Who in the World, Who's Who in Science and Engineering, Who's Who in America and Who's Who in American Education. He was notably profiled in the 73rd edition of Who's Who in America.

A Lifetime of Achievement in **Technology**

Roy B. Woolsey, PhD

Vice President of Regulatory Affairs
TCI International Inc.
LOS ALTOS HILLS, CA UNITED STATES

With nearly 50 years of professional experience to his credit, Roy B. Woolsey, PhD, has excelled at TCI International Inc. as the vice president of regulatory affairs since 2001, having previously served as the vice president of programs beginning in 1992 and the vice president of engineering beginning in 1991. Prior to obtaining these posts, he worked for the aforementioned company, known as Technology for Communications International until 1988, as the director of research and development from 1988 to 1991, the director of strategic systems from 1983 to 1988, and a program manager from 1980 to 1983. Earlier in his career, Dr. Woolsey found success with TCI as a manager of radio direction finding systems from 1975 to 1980 and a senior physicist from 1970 to 1975.

Outside of his primary endeavors, Dr. Woolsey has co-authored a number of creative works, including Applications of Artificial Intelligence to Command and Control Systems in 1988 and Antenna Engineering Handbook in 1993. In addition, he has contributed articles to professional journals as well as papers to professional symposiums. He also contributes to International Telecommunication Union recommendations, reports and handbooks. He considers the highlight of his career to be having been in charge of several sophisticated communications-receiving and spectrum monitoring systems installed in various countries around the world.

Before entering the field, Dr. Woolsey pursued a formal education to prepare for his career. He first completed coursework at the California Institute of Technology from 1962 to 1964. During his time there, the Richard Feynman lectures on physics sparked his interest in the study of physics. He then attended Stanford University and earned a Bachelor of Science, with distinction, in 1966. Continuing his studies at the same esteemed academic institution, he obtained a Master of Science in 1967 and ultimately achieved a Doctor of Philosophy in 1970. He also held a fellowship with the National Science Foundation from 1966 to 1970. To acquire more management experience, in 1982, Dr. Woolsey attended the Stanford Executive Institute for Management of High-Technology Companies in Stanford, California.

An active presence in his field of interest, Dr. Woolsey has been an active leader in his community through memberships with myriad prestigious organizations. He was inducted into Sigma Xi and Phi Beta Kappa and is a member of the Sequoia Yacht Club and the Palo Alto Elks Lodge. He is further associated with the Liberty Forum of Silicon Valley, the Stanford Club of Palo Alto and the South Peninsula Area Republican Coalition, where he served as treasurer from 2005 to 2014. Moreover, he has been involved with the Los Altos Hills Community Relations Committee as a member from 1994 to 2012 and again beginning in 2016. He also dedicated his time to serving the committee as chairman from 1997 to 2009 and again from 2016 to 2018. Named a life master of the American Contract Bridge League in 2005, he notably accepted the Los Altos Hills Volunteer Service Award in 2003.

Throughout his career, Dr. Woolsey has been recognized for his contributions to his field. He has previously been selected for inclusion in such honors publications as the 54th edition of Who's Who in America, the 21st through 28th editions of Who's Who in the West, the 18th edition of Who's Who in the World, and the second and third editions of Who's Who of Emerging Leaders in America. Reflecting on his career, he is grateful for the mentorship he received from Drs. Robert Tanner and Eugene Sharp, both of whom worked with him at Technology for Communications International.

Dr. Woolsey was born on June 12, 1945, in Norfolk, Virginia, to mother Louise Stookey Jones Woolsey and father Roy B. Woolsey. He later married Patricia Bernadine Elkins on April 17, 1988. In his free time, he enjoys playing contract bridge, attending the theater and traveling. He also likes to stay active by playing racquetball and going sailing.

DISCLAIMER

The information submitted to Marquis Who's Who Ventures LLC ("the Company") is obtained primarily from those profiled themselves. Although every effort has been made to verify the information submitted, the Company makes no warranty or representation as to the accuracy, reliability, or currency of the data provided, and accepts no responsibility for errors, factual or otherwise. Furthermore, the Company will not be held responsible for any damage or loss suffered by any person or entity arising from the use of this information, including identity theft or any other misuse of identity or information, to the fullest extent permitted by law.

By using the information we provide in our publications, you agree to indemnify and hold harmless, and at the Company's request, defend, the Company, its parents, subsidiaries and affiliates, as well as the directors, officers, shareholders, employees, agents and owners from and against any and all claims, proceedings, damages, injuries, liabilities, losses, costs and expenses (including reasonable attorneys' fees) arising out of your acts or omissions.

CPSIA information can be obtained
at www.ICGtesting.com
Printed in the USA
BVHW031322170721
612013BV00001B/1

9 780837 978062